British Television Drama

A History

2nd Edition

Lez Cooke

palgrave

A BFI book published by Palgrave

First edition published by the British Film Institute 2003

This edition published in 2015 by
PALGRAVE

on behalf of the

BRITISH FILM INSTITUTE
21 Stephen Street, London W1T 1LN
www.bfi.org.uk

There's more to discover about film and television through the BFI. Our world-
renowned archive, cinemas, festivals, films, publications and learning resources are
here to inspire you.

PALGRAVE in the UK is an imprint of Macmillan Publishers Limited, registered in
England, company number 785998, of 4 Crinan Street, London N1 9XW. Palgrave
Macmillan in the US is a division of St Martin's Press LLC, 175 Fifth Avenue, New
York, NY 10010. Palgrave is a global imprint of the above companies and is
represented throughout the world. Palgrave® and Macmillan® are registered
trademarks in the United States, the United Kingdom, Europe and other countries.

Designed by couch
Cover image: *Coronation Street* (1960–), ITV

Set by Cambrian Typesetters, Camberley, Surrey
Printed in China

This book is printed on paper suitable for recycling and made from fully managed
and sustained forest sources. Logging, pulping and manufacturing processes are
expected to conform to the environmental regulations of the country of origin.

British Library Cataloguing-in-Publication Data
A catalogue record for this book is available from the British Library
A catalog record for this book is available from the Library of Congress

ISBN 978–1–84457–623–4 (pb)
ISBN 978–1–84457–624–1 (hb)

Contents

Acknowledgments

The original idea for this book came out of teaching a third-year undergraduate course at Staffordshire University from 1992–2002 and I am grateful to all my students who contributed to the development of the book. Since 2002 I have taught students at Manchester Metropolitan University and Royal Holloway, University of London, and used the first edition of the book with them, so my thanks also go to those students as their responses have undoubtedly influenced my thinking about this second edition.

Once again I am grateful to the staff at the BBC Written Archives Centre, especially Trish Hayes, and the staff of the BFI National Archive and the BFI Library. Thanks also to Robin Nelson, my colleague at Manchester Metropolitan University from 2003–10, whose ideas and writings about television drama have influenced my own writing, and to my colleagues at Royal Holloway, especially John Hill, who will be relieved that I have finally finished this second edition so that I can concentrate on the new project we are working on.

Of the new material in this edition, some of the section on *Talking to a Stranger* in Chapter 3 first appeared in the *Journal of British Cinema and Television*, vol. 2, no. 1 (2005), and the new section on *Clocking Off* in Chapter 6 is extracted from a chapter in Jonathan Bignell and Stephen Lacey's *Popular Television Drama: Critical Perspectives* (Manchester University Press, 2005).

Finally, I am grateful to Rebecca Barden, who commissioned this second edition when she was at BFI Publishing, and to Jenni Burnell, who inherited it when Rebecca left and who has been very considerate in letting me complete this edition at my own pace. This book is dedicated to little Benjamin, who is perhaps the main reason why it has taken me so long to finish it!

Introduction

When this book was first published, in 2003, there were relatively few books available on television drama and the academic study of the subject was in its infancy. Since 2003 there has been an explosion of interest in television drama, both within the academy and outside of it.[1] This has coincided with television drama, in the UK, USA and other parts of the world, becoming one of the most important forms of programming as television has entered a more competitive, multi-channel, digital age, where programmes are available on a variety of platforms and can be watched wherever and whenever the viewer chooses. While the increase in channels and modes of viewing has fragmented the audience, television drama is still central to the schedules and remains one of the most popular forms of television, with UK audiences exceeding 10 million for 'high-end' dramas[2] such as *Downton Abbey* and for special occasions such as anniversaries or the Christmas episodes of *Coronation Street*, *Doctor Who* and *EastEnders*, proving that television drama can still, on occasion, be an 'appointment to view' in the way that it regularly was in the 1960s–80s, when there were far fewer channels.

This second edition of the book considers some of the changes that have taken place in British television since the first edition was published and includes a new chapter on 'British Television Drama in the Digital Age, 2002–14' which discusses the dramas produced since 2002, when the first edition ended.[3] The addition of a new chapter is not the only new material, however, and I have taken the opportunity with this edition not only to correct some errors in the first edition but to revise and add material to all of the chapters.

Chapter 1, for example, now includes material on the 'pre-history' of British television drama, before the official launch of BBC Television in 1936, with reference to John Logie Baird's collaboration with the BBC on *The Man With the Flower in His Mouth* (1930), an experimental production which is often cited as the first television play (although, as I mention in a note, Baird made an experimental transmission of a play nearly two years before this). Some other additional material is included in Chapter 1 as a result of further research into what is still a relatively unexplored period of British television

drama history, the difficulty of researching the period being exacerbated by the complete lack of broadcast material available before 1953.[4]

Chapter 3 includes a new section on *Talking to a Stranger* (1966), a quartet of plays by
John Hopkins which was described by the *Observer* television critic, George Melly, as 'the
first authentic masterpiece written directly for television'. Whether one agrees with
Melly or not, *Talking to a Stranger* deserves a place in any history of British television
drama for its originality and innovation. When the quartet was repeated in 1968 Melly
wrote: 'On the evidence of this work alone the medium can be considered to have come
of age,' an assessment which is reflected in the title of this chapter.

Further research on the single play has resulted in some significant revisions to
Chapter 4, while Chapter 6 now contains new sections on *Clocking Off* and 'slow television' and incorporates, with amendments, some material that was in the conclusion
to the first edition. The major change to the book is the addition of a new chapter which
updates the first edition by considering the ways in which television drama has
changed, and is changing, in the 'digital age', which really began to take off with the
launch of new digital channels, offering outlets for new forms of television drama targeting younger viewers. Divided into sections on 'Historical drama and literary adaptations', 'Social-issue drama post 9/11', 'Authored drama', 'Generic hybridity', 'New
forms of TV drama' and 'Internet drama', this new chapter provides an extensive survey
of British television drama in the twenty-first century.

Like the first edition, the aim of this new edition is to summarise the main aesthetic,
technological, institutional, social, political and cultural developments which have characterised and influenced the development of television drama in Britain since the 1930s.
In doing so it is necessarily selective. This book does not provide a survey of every television
drama made in Britain, nor does it mention every writer, producer or director who has
worked in British television – such an ambition would be beyond the scope of one volume.[5]
Neither does it extend its remit to include situation comedy, a related but formally distinct
genre, or children's drama, both of which deserve their own written histories.[6]

Unlike many of the books on television drama published in the last thirty years, the
present volume embraces the complete spectrum of television drama, not just the tradition which John Caughie describes as 'serious' television drama,[7] that of the single
play and the authored serial, but also popular series drama and soap opera. Given the
chronological approach that the book takes, it has not been possible to fully represent
all of these different forms in equal measure in every chapter. Instead, the approach has
been to focus on important moments in the historical development of the single play
(*Armchair Theatre*, *The Wednesday Play*, *Play for Today*), serials (costume dramas and literary adaptations, plus landmark serials by Trevor Griffiths, Troy Kennedy Martin, Dennis
Potter, etc.), series (which became increasingly important with the arrival of ITV in the
mid-1950s) and soap operas (the beginnings of *Coronation Street*, the academic interest
in soap opera as popular culture in the 1970s and 80s, the ascendancy of soap opera to
dominate the ratings in the 1990s).

This selective approach inevitably prioritises some dramas over others and some
writers and directors over others. Given the extensive literature already available on

Dennis Potter I have chosen to acknowledge his importance at particular moments but not to devote excessive space to an analysis of his work. Similarly, while certain moments within the development of soap opera as a dramatic genre are acknowledged and discussed, there are no lengthy analyses here of *Coronation Street* or *EastEnders* as these are also available elsewhere. In all such cases reference is made to the relevant literature and readers of this volume are referred to the bibliography for further reading on each subject.

In seeking to provide an overview of the main tendencies and important moments in the history of British television drama some dramas have been selected for more detailed examination. In some cases the choice may be unsurprising. There is so little available for viewing from before 1955 that Rudolph Cartier's *Nineteen Eighty-Four* almost selects itself. Yet this is clearly a seminal drama of the period (even if not entirely representative) which it would be perverse not to discuss at some length. Readers may find the choice of some dramas contentious but, for me, they each represent an important moment, whether for aesthetic, technological, institutional, social, political or cultural reasons, in the historical development of British television drama.

Each chapter includes at least one such drama: in Chapter 2 it is *Lena, O My Lena* as an example of the *Armchair Theatre* single-play tradition; in Chapter 3, *Up the Junction* (rather than the more well-known *Cathy Come Home*) is an example of a key transitional drama from the mid-1960s and *Talking to a Stranger* is an original 'authored' series of four plays; in Chapter 4, *The Cheviot, the Stag and the Black, Black Oil* was a unique 1970s experiment representing a highpoint in the production of radical television drama; in Chapter 5, *Boys from the Blackstuff* and *Edge of Darkness* are examples of progressive drama from the 1980s, marking a shift from the single play to series and serial drama; in Chapter 6, *This Life*, from the 1990s, provides an example of an innovative drama serial, which, it is argued, offered a model for the production of low-cost 'quality' drama in a more competitive marketplace, and *Clocking Off*, from the early 2000s, provides an example of how television drama was reinventing itself, in this case by offering a new form of social realism for the twenty-first century. With several of these dramas I have drawn on original interview material to illuminate the discussion and to provide a perspective on them which is not available elsewhere.

These more detailed studies are counter-balanced by sections focusing on a range of other forms of television drama, from costume to crime drama, from soap opera to science fiction, from drama documentary to experimental drama, from realist drama to telefantasy. The interview material is not confined to the special studies, but is also used in other sections of the book, supplementing information drawn from a range of sources including reviews and articles in newspapers and magazines, the trade press, specialist magazines, academic books and journals. This history, which is inevitably to some extent a personal history reflecting my own interests and preferences, draws from all of these sources, as well as from official documents, from scripts and from unpublished research. In all cases the analysis of individual dramas is based on extensive viewing of archive material.

There is an unavoidable problem in trying to write a 'history' of British television drama, or of anything for that matter. If organised chronologically there is the danger of giving the impression that history unfolds teleologically, with a linear trajectory which develops from 'primitive' beginnings towards a state of complexity and 'sophistication'. Traditional histories have also tended to subscribe to the 'great man' theory of history in which individual men (rarely women) are identified as being responsible for historical landmarks which are, apparently, achieved solely through their own individual genius. In television drama this role has been associated primarily with writers, such as David Mercer, Dennis Potter, Troy Kennedy Martin, Trevor Griffiths, Alan Bleasdale and Stephen Poliakoff, with some credit being given to the occasional creative producer or director, such as Rudolph Cartier, James MacTaggart, Philip Saville and Tony Garnett. This approach clearly informed George Brandt's 1981 collection of essays on writers, including Griffiths, Mercer and Potter, which was modified in the 1993 sequel when individual dramas became the object of study (but with the 'author' still identified in brackets, as if the editor was reluctant to relinquish this approach completely).[8]

In contrast, this book, while adopting a chronological approach, tries to avoid being teleological, noting instead how technological, institutional and cultural changes have affected the form, aesthetics and content of television drama at particular historical moments, without wanting to see this as part of an increasing 'sophistication' in the medium. While the book considers the contributions made by creative personnel – especially writers, producers and directors – it is within the context of aesthetic, technological, institutional, social, political and cultural developments generally. One of the themes of the book is the question which has exercised many critics in recent years: whether there has been a decline in the quality of television drama since the so-called 'golden age' of the 1960s and 70s. Addressing this issue has involved considering the relative creative freedom enjoyed by television dramatists in the 1960s and 70s, compared to the more subservient role performed by their counterparts today. It is through examining such questions that the historical approach adopted in the book will hopefully prove its worth.

There is a particular problem in writing a history of television drama in that very few programmes exist from before 1955 and there is a very incomplete archive of material right up to the mid-1970s. As other writers have noted, this makes the study of early television drama very difficult. In his book The Intimate Screen (2000), for example, Jason Jacobs was required to construct a history of British television drama before 1955 largely from scripts, set designs and production records, and to hypothesise as to what many of those early live dramas actually looked like when they were transmitted.

Early British television drama might well be compared to an iceberg, with a small extant amount viewable, while the vast majority of it will never see the light of day, surviving only in production records and in the minds of those old enough to have witnessed the original live transmission. This makes the need to record oral histories of the first twenty to thirty years of television drama in Britain an urgent priority, while those involved in its production, as well as those who can remember seeing the programmes, are still alive. It also makes the task of preserving material from that period an essential one and archives such as the BBC Written Archives Centre, the BBC Film and Video Library, the BFI National Archive and the Kaleidoscope Archive must be commended for their part in preserving what remains of this history.

In a paper given at the 1980 Edinburgh International Television Festival, Carl Gardner and John Wyver identified three phases in the development of the single play on British television: 'the post-war Reithian phase which lasted roughly until the late '50s; the transitional phase ... from the late '50s until the beginning of the '70s; and the present phase ... which one could dub the era of cost-effectiveness'.[9] More than thirty years later it is possible to extend and modify their periodisation and suggest that the history of British television drama in its entirety can be divided into three distinct periods. The first is the period of the BBC's monopoly, from 1936–55, when nearly all television was transmitted live and very little was recorded for posterity. The second period begins with the arrival in 1955 of a commercial competitor for the BBC and ends with the 1990 Broadcasting Act, a piece of legislation which did much to usher in a new deregulated era of multiple channels and new working practices, a 'third age' of British television which continues to the present.

This tripartite periodisation is unique to British television. Other writers, while also dividing television history into three periods, differ in their assessment of when each period begins and ends, according to their own criteria. In his book *Seeing Things: Television in the Age of Uncertainty* (2000), John Ellis identifies three eras, beginning with an 'era of scarcity', which lasted for most countries until the late 1970s or early 1980s', followed by 'an era of availability, where several channels broadcasting continuously jostled for attention, often with more competition in the shape of cable or satellite services' and a third 'era of plenty ... in which television programmes (or, as they will be known, 'content' or 'product') will be accessible through a variety of technologies'.[10] In America, the terms 'TVI', 'TVII' and 'TVIII' have been used to describe, respectively, the network era of US television (roughly 1948–75), the post-network era (roughly 1975–95) and the post-1995, digital-global era.[11]

While there is some logic, especially in the American context, to periodisations such as TVI, II and III, which overlap to some extent with Ellis's eras of scarcity, availability and plenty, in the British context there seems a greater logic in identifying 1936–55 as the 'first age' of British television, when television was not only scarce but remains largely invisible to us today as a consequence of the almost complete absence of recorded programmes. While television was more 'available' in Britain from 1955–90, despite there being only two channels until 1964, when BBC Two was introduced, and only three until 1982, when Channel 4 began broadcasting, the logic behind identifying this as a 'second age' of British television resides in it being a period governed by the principles of 'public service' broadcasting, which began to be eroded when satellite television arrived in 1989, signalling a shift to a deregulated, multi-channel age which the 1990 Broadcasting Act (introduced by a Conservative government advocating 'free-market' principles) did much to encourage. The 'third age' of British television, therefore, really begins in 1990 and is marked by similar attributes to those of TVIII and Ellis's 'era of plenty', with particular consequences for the concept of public service broadcasting and the production of television drama, consequences which are still transforming British television today.

Periodisations such as this are only useful in tracing general shifts in the socio-economic infrastructure. There are no clear-cut dates when one period ends and another begins, but such a periodisation does enable us to identify certain broad tendencies in the historical development of British television drama. The first period is represented in this book by Chapter 1. There is undoubtedly more work to be done on this era, although Jason Jacobs has laid a firm foundation for such work in *The Intimate Screen*. Much more work has been done on the second period, during which television emerged as the dominant mass medium. With far more material available for study from this period, which encompasses not only the 'golden age' of single-play production but also the emergence of series drama, serial drama and soap opera as important and hugely popular forms, the bulk of this book is devoted to it, with Chapter 2 covering the impact of ITV on the BBC, Chapter 3 covering most of the 1960s, during which television drama can be said to have 'come of age', Chapter 4 covering the 1970s, a particularly rich period for television drama which deserves a book to itself, and Chapter 5 examining the last phase of the post-Reithian, public service broadcasting era, a transitional period during which Channel 4 ended the BBC/ITV duopoly, acting as a publisher rather than a producer of programmes, while Margaret Thatcher's Conservative government sought to introduce greater competition into broadcasting by initiating a shift from a regulated public service broadcasting system to a deregulated, commercial free market. The extent to which this ideological objective was successful is discussed in Chapter 6, while Chapter 7 assesses the changes in British television drama in the new, deregulated, multi-channel, multi-platform digital age. The third period in this tripartite history of British television drama, therefore, is addressed in Chapters 6 and 7.

The first edition of this book highlighted the need for books on a number of television writers, directors and producers, for studies of individual dramas, anthology series and genres. Since then several of the writers, directors and producers mentioned, including Alan Clarke, Tony Garnett, Troy Kennedy Martin, Lynda La Plante and Jimmy McGovern, have been the subject of book-length studies in the Manchester University Press *Television Series*,[12] and books have been published in the BFI TV Classics series on *Bleak House*, *Cathy Come Home*, *Cracker*, *Doctor Who*, *Edge of Darkness*, *Law and Order*, *Our Friends in the North*, *Prime Suspect*, *Queer as Folk* and *The Singing Detective*.[13]

While it is as true now as it was in 2003 that this book has 'barely scratched the surface of the long and fascinating history of British television drama, only beginning to explore the tip of the iceberg', it is now one volume among a large and ever-increasing body of work on a subject which is attracting attention from a new generation of academics, enthusiasts, fans, scholars and viewers, enough to ensure that British television drama will continue to be discussed, researched, watched, argued over and written about for many years to come.

1

The Early Development of Television Drama, 1930–54

Until recently, television drama in Britain before 1955 was largely unexplored territory. Apart from John Caughie's pioneering 'Before the Golden Age: Early Television Drama', published in 1991, and Charles Barr's 1997 essay on live television, there had been no substantial study of the first twenty years of television drama in Britain until the publication of Jason Jacobs' *The Intimate Screen: Early British Television Drama*.[1] Jacobs' book illustrated one of the reasons why it had taken so long. Prior to 1955, at which point his book ends, nearly all television drama was transmitted live, as indeed much of it continued to be until well into the 1960s. With little of it being preserved through recording, even when recording became technically possible, early television drama is now largely a lost history, traces of which remain in surviving scripts, studio plans, production records and contemporary reviews.

This chapter will sketch in that lost history, describing the beginnings of television drama in the UK, the nature of the drama broadcast by the BBC during the period of its monopoly, the relationship between television, radio, theatre and the cinema, the importance of 'liveness' and 'immediacy' as defining characteristics of early television drama, the gradual expansion – in audience size, transmission area and aesthetic scope – of television drama after the war, the appearance of *The Grove Family* as a popular serial and the significance of Rudolph Cartier's 1954 production of George Orwell's *Nineteen Eighty-Four*, a landmark television drama which marked the culmination of the experiments of the previous two decades and the beginnings of a new phase in the development of television drama in Britain.

In fact, there was only a little over twelve years of regular television between the formal launch of the BBC's fledgling television service on 2 November 1936 and the first transmission of the new commercial television network on 22 September 1955, television in Britain having closed down for the duration of the Second World War, from 1 September 1939 to the restoration of the service on 7 June 1946. Furthermore, the BBC's pre-war service was restricted to those households which could afford to buy the first television sets, located within a twenty-five mile radius of Alexandra Palace in north

London from where the first programmes were transmitted. When the first broadcast was made in 1936 there were fewer than 300 television sets in use.[2] By the time the service closed down in 1939 the number was estimated to be between 20,000 and 25,000.[3]

Compared to radio, with over 9 million licences sold in 1939, television was a minority-interest medium, limited to a relatively small number of mainly middle-class viewers, and this continued to be the case until well into the 1950s. This may help to explain the nature of the programming in this early period, for BBC television, before the arrival of ITV, has been characterised as a class-bound service where: 'The programmes offered were largely based on the middle-class concept of a night out in the West End.'[4] This has led to the dismissal of early British television drama as 'photographed stage plays', electronic reproductions, if not actual live transmissions, of the middle-class theatre playing in London's West End.[5]

It is this notion that early television drama reproduced the conventions of the middle-class theatre, broadcasting 'photographed stage plays', that Jacobs takes issue with in *The Intimate Screen*. Because of the almost total absence of recordings of the live broadcasts, Jacobs' account of the early history of British television drama was largely based on an examination of scripts, studio floor plans, production notes and official correspondence and it is from this material that he makes an assessment of what those early dramas might have looked like when they were transmitted.

The key to early television drama was its 'liveness' and much of the significance of those early dramas resides in the unique combination of vision and immediacy, the fact that the television audience was seeing a programme that they knew was happening at the same time they were watching it, and which was subject to all the possible pitfalls and unknown outcomes of a live performance. While live television drama was usually well rehearsed, with every camera position plotted and every shot planned in fine detail, what was broadcast on the day of transmission was a live performance, and a performance not only of the actors in front of the cameras, but one which was choreographed by the producer in the control room and in which the camera and boom operators in the studio also played their part.

An analysis of a camera script, production notes and reviews, where they are available, can tell us a certain amount about what appeared on screen, but, ultimately, they are no substitute for an actual recording of the programme, which we have in only a few instances before 1955. Early television drama, therefore, was very much an ephemeral product, existing only for the duration of the performance, until it became possible, in the early 1950s, to film from a television monitor and make a 'telerecording', thus preserving the performance for posterity. Even when this became technically feasible, it was done very selectively, and even then there was no guarantee that a telerecording would be kept.[6] The ephemerality of live television drama highlights one of the difficulties in assessing early television drama and helps to explain the relative paucity of serious attention afforded it. What is undoubtedly needed are more oral histories, from participants and viewers, to supplement the academic research of Barr, Caughie and Jacobs.[7]

Television drama before the war

The development of television in Britain, before the official launch of the service in 1936, has been well documented by Mark Aldridge in *The Birth of British Television*.[8] The pre-history of television goes back well before 1930, the year in which the TV pioneer John Logie Baird collaborated with the BBC on the experimental transmission of a short television play, *The Man With the Flower in His Mouth* (14 July 1930), which is usually cited as the first drama to be shown on British television.[9] Baird had been working on a mechanical television system since the early 1920s, giving the first public demonstration of his system at Selfridges department store in London on 25 March 1925, followed by the first successful transmission of a television picture on 2 October 1925. Baird was an enthusiastic pioneer, more interested in the technology than the content or social purpose of television, and was undoubtedly a leading figure in the development of television as a technological apparatus. In 1927 he transmitted the first long-distance television signal, by telephone from London to Glasgow, and in the following year made the first transatlantic television transmission. He was also responsible for the world's first colour television transmission, in 1928, and experimented with stereoscopic transmission in the same year.

Baird made several test transmissions from his studio in the late 1920s but was forced to end these when they interfered with other broadcasts.[10] In 1929 he reached agreement with the BBC to make experimental broadcasts using a BBC transmitter and this led to the 1930 broadcast of Luigi Pirandello's *The Man With the Flower in His Mouth*, a one-act play written in 1923. The play was chosen for the experimental broadcast because it was short, featured just three characters and was limited in its setting. It was directed by Val Gielgud, who had been appointed Head of Productions at the BBC in 1929, working on radio drama, and was one of the first television drama directors when regular television transmissions began in 1936. Transmitted in Baird's low-resolution thirty-line system, the quality of *The Man With the Flower in His Mouth* would have been relatively poor, but it was generally regarded as a successful experiment; the play was watched by Prime Minister Ramsey MacDonald when it was transmitted in the afternoon of 14 July 1930, Baird having installed one of his prototype television sets at 10 Downing Street so that the Prime Minister could view the Baird/BBC test transmissions.[11]

Higher resolution television services than Baird's were developed in the early 1930s but Baird's thirty-line system was more economical because the BBC could use their existing audio transmitters for the low-bandwidth signal. Experimental transmissions continued on the BBC until 1935, by which time Baird had developed a 240-line system and Marconi-EMI had developed a 405-line electronic system. On 2 November 1936, the world's first regular high-resolution television service was launched by the BBC, with the two competing television systems operating in tandem: Baird's mechanical system and EMI/Marconi's more versatile electronic system. After four months of trial and error, the EMI/Marconi system proved its superiority and the BBC rejected the Baird system in February 1937. As Jacobs notes:

If the BBC had adopted the Baird system, then the description of early television drama as 'photographed stage plays' would be accurate. For drama productions Baird's team used the Intermediate Film (IF) technique, whereby the studio scene was filmed using non-standard 17.5mm film, the film developed in under a minute and then scanned electronically to convert it into a television signal. Its single camera was fixed in concrete, there was no camera mobility, no tracking, and only twenty minutes' worth of film capacity; to change to a close-up view the turret with four lenses had to be swung over, and this could not be done during recording without stopping the camera, halting transmission.[12]

In contrast the EMI/Marconi system was 'more mobile and more flexible' and it is significant that the electronic system won out over a system which was a mechanical hybrid of film and television, enabling television to pursue its own aesthetic instead of replicating some of the conventions of early cinema. From this moment, the sense of novelty and amateurism which had marked the first few months of television began to fade away and the schedules became more standardised.

Drama was central to the schedules from the very beginning. John Caughie notes that, in Christmas week 1938, fourteen of the twenty-two hours transmitted during the week were taken up with drama.[13] The weekly total of twenty-two hours, even at the end of 1938 when the television service had been in operation for two years, indicates how far the fledgling service offered by the BBC was a part-time one, transmitting for a limited number of hours each day. Initially, this was in three blocks, with a sixty-minute *Television Demonstration Film* being shown in the morning, and two periods of live television in the afternoon and evening, with the afternoon schedule sometimes consisting of a live repeat of a play which had been transmitted on a previous evening. With no facility for recording a broadcast at this time, a 'repeat' meant the cast and production team returning to the studio to do the show all over again.

This tradition of live repeats was already standard practice on BBC radio and its replication on television illustrates how far television drama modelled itself on radio, in terms of scheduling, and on the theatre, where the live repeated performance was the norm. Evening repeats on television were not always possible, because the actors would most likely be performing on stage at a West End theatre in the evening. Given television drama's reliance on theatre personnel, it is easy to see how Sunday evening, when theatres were closed, became established as the main night of the week for the transmission of a television play, which would then usually be repeated, live, on a Thursday. With each evening's viewing being organised around a main event, the Sunday night play became the centrepiece of the Sunday evening schedule, just as a variety show may have been the main event on a Friday or Saturday night. This tradition, once established, was to remain in place for many years and was adopted by ITV in the late 1950s, when the regular announcement before ABC's *Armchair Theatre* play was 'And now for your Sunday night dramatic entertainment'.

Like any new medium, television was initially considered inferior to its more established counterparts of radio, cinema and the theatre, and its ephemerality and low-resolution image may have contributed to this. Cinema and radio were already established: cinema had emerged as the pre-eminent medium of mass entertainment by the 1930s, and radio was to consolidate its position during the war, both for the 'immediacy' of its news reporting and for its light entertainment programmes.

In contrast, television seemed like a poor relation, incapable of conveying the visual spectacle of cinema, restricted by technological limitations and confined to a small audience because of the limited range of the transmitter and the huge cost of the first television sets. However, television had advantages as a new medium which, once it became available to a larger proportion of the population, would eventually see it triumph over cinema, radio and the theatre, to emerge as the most popular medium of them all by the end of the 1950s.

The distinctive features of television in these early years can be summarised in two words: 'intimacy' and 'immediacy'. Jason Jacobs sees television's 'intimacy' as its most important quality at this time (hence the title of his book, *The Intimate Screen*). The intimacy derives from television's place as a *domestic* medium, to be consumed within the home, unlike cinema or the theatre, and Jacobs expounds at length on the nature of television's 'intimate' form of address with its viewers, citing numerous commentators at the time who identified this as part of television's appeal, which established its difference from both cinema and the theatre.[14]

Television shared this domesticity, of course, with radio, with which it also had in common the second quality of 'immediacy' – the ability to communicate directly and simultaneously with its audience, in a way that cinema was unable to do. For news reporting this was an obvious advantage, but it also added excitement and expectancy to other programming, including drama. However, where radio involved listening to a disembodied voice, television had the extra dimension of the visual.

It is difficult now to imagine the first effect of seeing images, and 'live' images at that, in one's own home. The smallness of the early television screens, about eight inches by ten on average,[15] required viewers to sit close and encouraged an emphasis in programme production on medium shots, rather than long shots with lots of detail. This technological constraint led to an emphasis on 'talking heads' in early television which, together with a reliance on the spoken word inherited from radio and the theatre, set the agenda and determined the aesthetic for television drama for years to come.

Early television drama, theatre and public service broadcasting

As a new and subordinate medium, television sought ways of establishing itself in the early years. While it had the potential advantages of intimacy and immediacy over cinema and theatre, and the advantage of vision over radio, it still needed to prove its worth through its programming. That television drama turned to the theatre for inspiration was a consequence of the perceived cultural value of Britain's literary and theatrical heritage, combined with the Reithian ideology of public service broadcasting within the BBC.

John Reith, the first Director General of the BBC, was no great advocate of television and he left the BBC in 1938 before the new medium had really become established. But,

by the time of his departure, an ethos of public service broadcasting had been established within the BBC which was to prevail, in television and in radio, long after the
arrival of a commercial competitor in the mid-1950s. When the television service began,
this ideology was in its relative infancy, but it informed the early development of television in Britain, from the mid-1930s to the mid-50s, the years of the BBC's monopoly.

From the beginning, Reith was concerned that the BBC should fulfil its designated
responsibility as a national broadcasting organisation and set a high moral tone for the
whole of the nation. The BBC, according to its Royal Charter, had a duty to 'inform, educate and entertain' and in his policy statements Reith left little doubt that the first two
of this famous trinity were paramount and that the entertainment should be of an
'improving' kind. This ideology of public service broadcasting was established from the
early days of radio broadcasting at the BBC and carried over into the new television
service.

So pervasive and influential has this ideology been that it was still being cited and
argued over in debates about the future of the BBC in the 1980s and 90s, at a time when
the notion of public service broadcasting was coming increasingly under threat. In their
1980 Edinburgh International Television Festival paper on the decline of the television
play, Carl Gardner and John Wyver identified the first phase of the history of the single
play as a period of 'Reithian reverence', lasting 'roughly until the late '50s':

> The first phase, primarily under the aegis of the BBC, was one of the last
> sustained gasps of a paternalistic Reithian project to bring 'the best of British
> culture' to a grateful and eager audience – a mission of middle-class
> enlightenment. Thus in its early days TV drama picked up the predominant
> patterns, concerns and style of both repertory theatre and radio drama (as well as
> their personnel, with their distinct training and working practices) and consisted
> of televised stage plays, 'faithfully' and tediously broadcast from the theatre, or
> reconstructed in the studio, even down to intervals, prosceniums and curtains.
> Such an approach, which takes the television process itself as transparent, almost
> by definition precluded any innovation of TV style or any attempt to develop a
> specifically televisual form for small-screen drama. On the other hand the
> uniqueness of each production was recognised and valued, but any merit such
> production had was derived from elsewhere, rather than from TV.[16]

The 'elsewhere', for the most part, was the theatre. There was a pragmatic reason for
this. Early television had to get its material from somewhere and the fact that it was a
visual medium which, because of the smallness of the television screen, was dependent
on the 'intimacy' of the spoken word, rather than visual spectacle, almost inevitably led
it towards the literary tradition of the English theatre. But there was another, cultural,
reason why the theatre was the natural ally of early television drama. This was because
television, as a new, but subordinate, branch of public service broadcasting, needed the
prestige of the theatre to raise its cultural profile, to help establish itself as a legitimate
part of a British Broadcasting Corporation which still had John Reith as its Director

General, and which still adhered to his 'mission of middle-class enlightenment' long after he had departed. The consequences of this were to be seen in the different types of television drama that were produced in the early years.

Types of pre-war drama

According to Jacobs, television drama took three main forms before the war: extracts from plays, broadcast from the television studios at Alexandra Palace; full-length adaptations of novels and plays, also transmitted live from the TV studios; and live 'outside broadcasts' from London theatres. Initially, extracts from current or recent theatre plays was the dominant form and these were transmitted under the banner of *Theatre Parade*, a clear signifier, like the titles of many subsequent drama series, of the origins and affiliation of television drama from the beginning. Tise Vahimagi includes the following examples in his guide to British television programmes: scenes from the Little Theatre production of *Alice Through the Looking Glass*, transmitted on 22 January 1937 and lasting twenty-five minutes; Act Two of Eugene O'Neill's *Anna Christie*, from the Westminster Theatre production, with Flora Robson in the title role, transmitted on 7 May 1937 and lasting twenty minutes; and a twenty-five-minute adaptation of a previously unperformed Agatha Christie mystery called *The Wasp's Nest*, transmitted on 28 June 1937.[17]

After these hesitant beginnings, there was a gradual move towards presenting longer productions and full-length adaptations. Jacobs cites the transmission of George More O'Ferrall's sixty-minute production of *Journey's End*, in November 1937, and Eric Crozier's ninety-minute production of *Once in a Lifetime*, in December 1937, as marking 'an increase in ambition and technical proficiency'.[18] This was the beginning of a shift towards plays as 'special events' in the schedule, acquiring a status over other programmes which was to lead to the enshrinement of the single play as a prestigious form of television, a status which it was to enjoy right up to the late 1970s.

Outside broadcasts from the theatre had a different status, however, to the production of a drama in the studio. Indeed, outside broadcasts were under the control not of TV drama producers but of Outside Broadcast personnel and had a similar institutional status to the televising of a Test Match or any other outside broadcast event. They were also restricted in terms of aesthetic possibilities, as a result of the more limited camera positions available in the theatre. While they might capture the excitement of a live production, garnishing the programme with backstage interviews with the stars, it is here that the denigration of early television drama as 'photographed stage plays' is probably entirely apt.[19] Writing in *The Listener*, following the first live transmission of a complete play from a West End theatre (rather than just the first act or individual scenes), Peter Purbeck reflected on the main disadvantage of an outside broadcast of a theatre play, compared to the advantages of restaging a play in the television studios:

> Where the studio production scores over last Wednesday's performance is in the movement of the actors … the television screen, owing to its size, cannot show more than two or three players in detail at one time. In the studio this trouble is overcome by grouping the actors accordingly. On the stage they could not be so

neatly grouped; and so the camera had to chase from one speaker to another with rather bewildering effect.[20]

Jacobs does not include serials in his categories of pre-war drama, but the first example of this new form, which was to become one of the staples of television, was *Ann and Harold*, transmitted in five short episodes from 12 July to 9 August 1938.[21] The story of a London society couple's romance, ending in a big society wedding, the serial was written by Louis Goodrich and produced by Lanham Titchener, with Ann Todd and William Hutchison in the title roles.

Style in early TV drama

The dependence on theatre plays inevitably located early television drama closer to theatre than cinema and the restaging of plays in the TV studio was largely naturalistic, with three or four cameras (depending on the size of the production) positioned to cover the action from a limited number of angles and the cutting from one camera to another usually motivated by the need to follow the conversation. In fact, before the war, 'cutting' was not technically possible. The only transitions between shots that the early technology would allow were mixes or fades. This inevitably slowed the narrative tempo, which was already sluggish as a result of the tendency towards long takes on each camera.

It was the producer, sitting in the studio control room, who orchestrated the transmission of a drama from the television studio, directing the cameras, via their operators, and instructing the vision mixer when to mix from one camera to another. Of course, each production was rehearsed and a camera script produced with the camera positions and transitions between cameras worked out in advance. This provided the blueprint to which the actors and production team worked. Nevertheless, there remained the possibility of adjustments having to be made, even during a transmission, and it was the producer who was the main decision-maker on the day, dictating the tempo of the production in the same way as a conductor would lead an orchestra. In this sense, it was the producer who was the 'auteur' in early TV drama, and different producers had different styles, just as film directors did in the cinema:

> The planned organization of studio space in terms of set and performers and the structured segmentation of that space by the cameras in real time was further inflected by the stylistic preferences of individual producers, some of them well-known – such as Fred O'Donovan's 'one camera technique' or George More O'Ferrall's 'close up technique'. Different producers ascribed different levels of agency to the technology itself: some situated the performance as that which took place beyond the television cameras and was relayed by it; others conceived of television drama as an art form constructed live in the Control Room.[22]

Fred O'Donovan's 'one camera technique' epitomised the most conservative form of early television drama, with only one camera being used for each scene. While this did not necessarily mean each scene was covered in one long take, as there may have been captions, telecine inserts (the inserting into the transmission of scenes previously shot on film) and fades, this style was closest to that which sought to simply photograph a stage play, without the technology intruding and segmenting the theatrical space.

Other producers were more ambitious. Jacobs includes a description of a complicated montage sequence which George More O'Ferrall included in his 1938 production of *Clive of India*, which involved a lot of fast cutting between four studio cameras and two telecine cameras, and which was very ambitious for its time, lasting for several minutes of screen time.[23] Yet, despite this attempt to innovate, the rest of *Clive of India*, to judge from Jacobs' analysis of the script, sounds fairly conventionally theatrical, with an average shot length (ASL) (not including the montage sequence) of two minutes, suggesting a fairly slow narrative tempo in the remainder of the sixty-minute play.

Another innovative pre-war drama was *Condemned to be Shot* (4 March 1939), written by R. E. J. Brooke and produced by Jan Bussell, who wrote one of the first books on television production, *The Art of Television*.[24] One of the first plays to be specially written for television, *Condemned to be Shot* was the first television play to use the subjective point-of-view shot:

> For the first time the television camera will be one of the characters, the central figure of the play. You will hear a 'voice off', but the owner of the voice is invisible from the opening scene to the end, where he faces the raised rifles of a firing squad. You will, in fact, see the television camera courtmartialled and riddled with bullets. Thus you as a viewer, looking at the screen of your set, will have the horrific experience of being condemned to be shot.[25]

Only twenty minutes long – its brevity perhaps a consequence of its experimental nature – *Condemned to be Shot* was one of the first television dramas to highlight the stylistic possibilities of the new medium.

While clearly dependent on theatre and the novel for its source material, and working with obvious limitations in the technology available at the time, television drama producers before the war nevertheless laid the foundations on which the new form could develop. The close relationship with theatre undoubtedly led to the transmission of many static and unambitious 'photographed stage plays', but there was also the beginning of the development of a new aesthetic, one which, through its combination of 'liveness', immediacy and intimacy, announced television drama as an important new form, sufficiently distinct from radio, theatre and cinema to guarantee it a promising future.

Post-war television drama

Many of the same personnel who had pioneered the development of television drama before the war picked up where they had left off when the television service resumed on 7 June 1946. Initially, the pre-war policy of adapting material from literature and the theatre was continued, but the need for TV drama to produce its own original work if it was to develop as an important medium in its own right was increasingly recognised after the war. While some moves were made towards this – for example J. B. Priestley wrote a one-act play for television called *The Rose and Crown* (27 August 1946), which attempted to escape from the ubiquitous middle-class drawing room by setting the action in the bar of a public house in north-east London – the development of TV drama in the immediate post-war period was overshadowed by arguments within the BBC about the development of the television service as a whole, in relation to the already well-established radio service.

In the absence of television during wartime, BBC radio had flourished, providing a combination of morale-boosting entertainment programmes and information about the progress of the war. After the war, the radio service was reorganised into three different strands, to reflect the three elements of the public service ethos: the Light Programme for entertainment, the Home Service for information and the Third Programme for serious music and experimental drama – although the division was never this clear-cut, all services carrying a mix of entertainment and information but with a distinct differ-ence in tone between the three strands.

As John Caughie notes, within the BBC more attention was paid to this reorganisa-tion of radio than was paid to television, and there was a suspicion within the higher echelons of the BBC about the new medium which bordered on cultural snobbery:

> The cultural mission in the postwar years had a slightly edgy relationship to
> television, preferring the known territory of radio and its place within a homely
> domesticity to the *terra incognita* of television with its slightly heady potential for
> entertainment. Asa Briggs points out that 'key figures in the BBC were more
> interested in 1946 in the starting of the Third Programme than in the resumption
> of television', and it was not until 1950 that television was promoted to the status
> of a Department as opposed to that of a Service: the same status, that is, that the
> Third Programme had enjoyed since it was opened.[26]

While these internal struggles went on, those working in television continued to explore the possibilities for drama production in the new medium. In addition to adaptations, like George More O'Ferrall's production of George Bernard Shaw's *The Dark Lady of the Sonnets*, transmitted on the afternoon that the television service resumed, and Fred O'Donovan's production of J. M. Synge's *The Playboy of the Western World* (9 August 1946), there was the emergence of more contemporary material after the war, reflecting some of the concerns and anxieties thrown up by the war. One such drama was Harold Clayton's production of *Frieda* (7 July 1946), about the reception given to the German wife of an RAF officer when he brings her to the small English town where he lives towards the end of the war. Although this had already been staged in the theatre, its television dramatisation took place prior to it being made into a film for Rank by Basil Dearden in 1947; it was sub-sequently restaged as a television drama, with a new cast, in October 1948.[27]

It should be noted that cinema and television had an antagonistic relationship in the late 1940s and 50s. The film industry was concerned about the impact of television on its box office and mounted an embargo on the transmission of films on television, except for some European art films, which were occasionally used by television to fill a gap in the schedules. Consequently, television would often produce more than one version of a production, like *Frieda*, in 1946 and 1948, or *Rope*, the Patrick Hamilton play, in 1947 and 1950, despite the fact that cinema films of the same subject were released around the same time – in the case of both *Frieda* and *Rope* the cinema film was released in the period between the transmission of the two television versions. It seems likely that this worked to the advantage of both television and the film industry: cinema benefiting from the interest aroused by those who had seen the television play and the second television production benefiting from the interest generated by the release of the film in cinemas.

Television's relationship with theatre also grew more antagonistic after the war, with West End theatres refusing to allow the live transmission of plays from their theatres.[28] The Outside Broadcast Department was forced to turn to repertory theatres instead, but the demise of this aspect of television's relationship with theatre was not disadvantageous as far as the future of television drama was concerned, forcing it to develop its own aesthetic, rather than pursuing its more parasitical dependence on the theatre with the live transmission of 'photographed stage plays'.

Developments in genre, form and style

In keeping with the desire to express contemporary concerns and anxieties, a genre of 'horror plays', as they were referred to in the BBC, emerged after the war: crime thrillers, macabre murder mysteries, supernatural and Gothic horror stories, echoing a similar trend in the cinema with the release of films like *Dead of Night* (1945), *Brighton Rock* (1947) and Hitchcock's American production of *Rope* (1948). In fact a pre-war television production of *Rope* had been transmitted in March 1939 and billed at the time as 'A TV Horror Play'.[29] The two subsequent post-war television productions of Hamilton's play – in which two Oxford undergraduates strangle a fellow student and deposit his body in a trunk, from which they then proceed to serve supper to their invited guests, who include the victim's parents – seems to confirm an appetite for this more macabre kind of story.[30]

While there was inevitably a 'theatrical' aspect to the two television versions of *Rope*, a legacy of its origins as a theatre play in which all the action takes place in one room, in real time, during the course of an evening, Jacobs' analysis of the studio floor plans and scripts of the 1947 and 1950 productions illustrates how television drama was evolving at the end of the 1940s. By 1946 it was possible to make straight cuts between cameras, rather than having to mix, which facilitated a faster narrative tempo. While the ASL of forty-two seconds in the 1950 version of *Rope* is still long by present-day standards, it marked a significant advance on the two-minute ASL of the pre-war *Clive of India*. Furthermore, as Jacobs notes, ASLs do not reveal the extent of camera movement *within* a shot, which may significantly affect the viewer's relationship to a drama by departing from the more static, frontal perspectives to be found in more conventional early television drama:

The apparent 'theatricality' of the script for the 1950 version of *Rope* conceals another, very different, approach to the staging of narrative space. This version contains 114 separate shots, typically alternating between medium two-shots and close-shots, giving an average shot length of around 42 seconds. This arithmetic suggests long takes, but it does not account for the variation of shot-scale afforded by a style that favoured frequent camera movement and reframing to follow actors or emphasize dialogue and reaction.[31]

Rope was a fairly typical example of a naturalistic drama of the period, unfolding in real time and confined to a drawing-room set, but there were some attempts to depart from this model. While writers like J. B. Priestley moved out of the middle-class drawing room with dramas such as *The Rose and Crown*, other post-war productions attempted to escape from the naturalistic straightjacket of telling a story in a linear narrative. *I Killed the Count* (14 March 1948) was a comedy-thriller which departed from the more conventional narrative structure by using flashbacks. But where flashbacks were a standard convention in films noirs, they were far more difficult to achieve in live television drama, without resorting to telecine flashback sequences, previously shot on film, which could be inserted into the live transmission. As Tise Vahimagi explains: 'instead of using pre-shot film to effect the flashback sequences, producer Ian Atkins continued the play live, so the cast had to get around from set to set with only split seconds to spare'.[32]

It may seem perverse to choose to mount a production in such a way, although there may well have been financial reasons why it was done in this manner rather than going out and filming a number of expensive film sequences in advance of the production. Telecine sequences might have made life easier for the actors and the production team but the number of sequences that would have been needed for this production, apart from being financially prohibitive, would have turned it into more of a pre-recorded, filmed drama, and would have detracted from the 'intimacy' and 'immediacy' that were the distinctive features of live television drama. As producer George More O'Ferrall wrote in a co-authored article on 'Television's Challenge to the Cinema', published in 1950:

> having to use film at all is a confession of failure … Television with its small screen and intimate presentation does not lend itself – and I will question whether it ever will – to the same vastness of approach that the film can achieve. You could not put, say, *The Covered Wagon* on television because those long wonderful shots of the wagons winding across the plain just wouldn't mean a thing …
>
> … You have to come back every time to the benefits and limitations of intimate presentation, the small canvas, the limited field.[33]

Intimacy and immediacy were part of the aesthetic of early television drama which separated it from the cinema, so the objective was to use these to advantage, rather than see them simply as limitations. This meant, however, that any attempt to be more ambitious, for example by using flashbacks, posed considerable production difficulties. But as writers and producers grew more confident with the new medium and as new technology – such as the variable lens cameras which were introduced in 1952 – allowed more freedom in production techniques, there was an increased appetite for experimentation and innovation in television drama.

The move towards producing 'horror plays' in the post-war period can be seen as part of this desire to develop a new aesthetic. Working with new material encouraged producers and writers to experiment with the form of television drama in a way that the restaging of classics from literature and the theatre generally did not. The Head of BBC Television Drama in the late 1940s, Robert MacDermot, certainly saw the possibility for innovation in the dramatisation of ghost stories, as he wrote in a memo to the Head of Television, Cecil McGivern, in 1948:

> as far as I know this hasn't been done before, either in sound or television, and would make a good contrast to our dramatic output of drama, comedy and straightforward mystery thrillers. I believe that television could create a very effective eerie atmosphere in this way and suggest that, if you agree, the plays are placed at the end of the evening transmission only and are advertised as being unsuitable for children.[34]

One such production, although it was not transmitted until four years after MacDermot wrote this, may have been *Markheim* (28 December 1952), a thirty-minute play described by Tise Vahimagi as 'a visually eerie television adaptation'[35] of the Robert Louis Stevenson short story, co-produced by Christian Simpson, one of the producers interested in experimenting with television drama in the 1950s, and Tony Richardson, who became one of the leading British 'new wave' film directors in the late 1950s. Unfortunately, due to the absence of a telerecording of this and other dramas from the period, we will probably never know how successful such productions were in departing from the naturalistic norm.

The concern expressed by MacDermot about the possible effect of such dramatisations on the audience, especially children, is indicative of an awareness that the television audience was steadily growing in the late 1940s, with the number of combined radio and television licences increasing from 45,564 in March 1948 to 126,567 in March 1949 and to 343,882 in March 1950.[36] The larger increase in 1950 can be explained partly by the opening of a new transmitter at Sutton Coldfield in December 1949, enabling the television service to reach the Midlands for the first time. This expansion reinforced the need to extend the boundaries of television drama as well, by targeting a wider audience than the predominantly middle-class London one. The need to offer dramas for different audiences, with different settings, was stated by the *Radio Times* TV drama critic Lionel Hale in 1949:

> What people are some ninety per cent of plays about? The upper-middle class. And what is the scene of ninety per cent of plays? Why, the drawing room – or

that curious habitation, the 'lounge hall'. Television seems to be doing its best to get away from this convention. It was excellent to be taken in *The Director* to the street of an Irish village and the back rooms of a pub. New writers for television may seize every chance of showing us scenes unfamiliar to a theatre – a corner of a street market, the jetty of a seaport, the bell tower of a church.[37]

As British television moved into the 1950s, the variety and ambition of television drama increased and, with the arrival of Rudolph Cartier at the BBC in 1952, TV drama entered a new period of innovation and stylistic development.

Into the 1950s

The expansion of the service, and the need for more programmes, put increasing strain on the original studios at Alexandra Palace after the war. Consequently, the BBC acquired the Rank Film Studios at Lime Grove in 1949, which they moved into the following year, giving an additional five studios in which to work.

In recognition of the need to produce more original work, a Script Unit was set up in 1951 and writers like Nigel Kneale and Philip Mackie were hired as staff scriptwriters to generate new material. This was partly to circumvent the copyright problems which ensued from using other material, but it also marked the beginnings of a concerted effort within the BBC to see television drama more firmly established by nurturing and developing new talent and new plays.

In 1952 Michael Barry was appointed Head of Television Drama, succeeding Val Gielgud who had held the position for seventeen months from January 1950, but whose 'aesthetic standards were really those of radio drama'.[38] That this was so was not surprising, given that Gielgud had been Head of Radio Drama at the BBC since 1929. Michael Barry, however, had firmly held beliefs about the visual power and potential of television drama. It was Barry who appointed Rudolph Cartier as a new producer at the BBC in 1952 and who commissioned *The Quatermass Experiment* (1953) and *Nineteen Eighty-Four*, the two productions which were to mark television drama's decisive break with 'filmed theatre'. Jacobs sees Michael Barry as an important and unfairly maligned figure in the history of British television drama:

> When Barry succeeded Val Gielgud as Head of Television Drama, he believed the potential of television that was more than 'illustrated radio', arguing that television drama had to rely less on dialogue, more on the 'power of the image': that television had to be visibly 'televisual'. It is one of the injustices of television history that Barry's achievements in this respect have been denigrated by comparison with the self-aggrandisement of Sydney Newman.[39]

Series and serials

Up to the 1950s the vast majority of television drama had been single plays, or extracts from plays, but in the early 1950s there was a move towards producing drama series and serials. *Little Women* (December 1950–January 1951), adapted in six thirty-minute episodes by Winifred Oughton and Brenda R. Thompson from Louisa May Alcott's novel, was the first of a number of drama serials to be shown at 5.30 pm, as part of the BBC's new *Children's Television* slot. The first adaptation to be presented as a 'classic serial' which, as Ellen Baskin notes, was to become 'a banner heading used by the BBC for decades to come',[40] was *The Warden* (May–June 1951), adapted by Cedric Wallis from the Anthony Trollope novel and screened on Saturday evenings at 8 pm in six thirty-minute episodes. The first of many subsequent Jane Austen adaptations was broadcast in February–March 1952 when *Pride and Prejudice* was screened, again at 8 pm on Saturday in six thirty-minute episodes, with Peter Cushing playing Mr Darcy.

While literary adaptations comprised a large number of the serials transmitted during the 1950s, there was also a significant number of original drama serials. The first of these was Francis Durbridge's thriller, *The Broken Horseshoe* (March–April 1952), broadcast once again in six thirty-minute episodes (the standard format for most of the 1950s), on Saturday evening at 8 pm. Durbridge was to become one of the most prolific television dramatists in the 1950s and he followed *The Broken Horseshoe* with other thrillers, such as *Operation Diplomat* (October–November 1952) and *The Teckman Biography* (December 1953–January 1954).

In 1952 the first long-running drama serial on British television began, as a programme for children. *The Appleyards*, described by Vahimagi as a 'lightweight, domestic series about the trivial ups and downs of the rosy Appleyard family',[41] was shown fortnightly in the late-afternoon *Children's Television* slot and ran for five years, until 1957. It was joined in 1954 by a version for adults, *The Grove Family*, which ran for three years and was immensely popular. Centred upon a lower middle-class suburban family living in Hendon, north London, *The Grove Family* is often described as British television's first soap opera, yet it did not utilise the continuous storylines that were to become a feature of later soaps and was really a series rather than a serial. In fact, it was more of a generic hybrid, fifty years before generic hybridity became a feature of British television drama (see Chapter 7), incorporating elements of comedy, crime, documentary and melodrama in its 146 episodes, many of which included a strong injection of public service information amid the domestic light entertainment. In this respect, *The Grove Family* followed in the footsteps of the BBC's radio soaps, ensuring that this venture into popular culture territory would not depart too far from Reith's 'morally improving' public service ethos. As Jeff Evans describes it in his *Guinness Television Encyclopedia* entry, *The Grove Family* was:

> Reassuringly British (with no intruding US culture), its action focused instead on petty squabbles and occasional domestic strife, but a 'public service' element was also built in. Viewers were made acutely aware of the need to purchase a TV licence, for example, or to protect themselves from burglaries.[42]

The formula proved very successful. According to a BBC Audience Research Report after the transmission of the first twenty-minute episode on Friday, 9 April 1954, 7.50–8.10 pm,

Happy families: British television's first soap opera, *The Grove Family*

11.8 per cent of the adult population watched the programme, equivalent to 50 per cent of the adult television audience.[43] *The Grove Family* proved to be one of the BBC's most popular programmes in the mid-1950s, with audiences exceeding 8 million, but it is symptomatic of the lack of a competitive ethos at the BBC, even after ITV started, that it would not commit to the continuation of the serial, much to the disappointment of its large and dedicated audience. This institutional aversion towards the lowbrow form of the soap opera lingered for a long while within the BBC. It was another thirty years before the corporation fully embraced the form when *EastEnders* began in the mid-1980s.[44]

Television was well on the way to becoming the dominant mass medium by the time that *The Grove Family* started. By 1952 the service had been extended to Scotland and the north of England and the number of combined sound and television licences had grown to 1.5 million. The following year, the televising of the Coronation of Queen Elizabeth, on 2 June 1953, was a significant moment in the development of television as a mass medium in Britain. While the number of TV licences held at the time of the Coronation was little more than 2 million, it was estimated that about 20 million people watched the BBC's transmission on television sets in the homes of friends and relatives, and on screens erected in public venues for the occasion. This shared national event proved to be an excellent marketing exercise for the new medium and within two years the number of licences had more than doubled to 4.5 million.

The Quatermass Experiment (1953)

Shortly after the televising of the Coronation came the screening of one of the land-marks of early British television drama, *The Quatermass Experiment*. The critical and public response to the six-part serial, transmitted between 18 July and 22 August 1953, may be seen to mark the moment at which television drama in Britain finally broke free from the shadows of cinema, radio and the theatre to offer its first truly original production.

It is significant that *The Quatermass Experiment* took the form of a six-part serial, rather than a single play, and that it was an original script for television, written by Nigel Kneale. It was also significant that the genre was science fiction, immediately signalling a departure from the prevailing naturalist orthodoxy; further, that it was produced by Rudolph Cartier, an Austrian émigré who had worked in European cinema before join-ing the BBC in 1952. Between them, Kneale and Cartier were responsible for introducing a completely new dimension to television drama in the early to mid-1950s. As Cartier later reflected in a 1990 television interview, 'the BBC – they needed me like water in the desert',[45] and it is to the credit of Michael Barry that Cartier was given the opportunity and the freedom to shake up BBC television drama to the extent that he did, first with *The Quatermass Experiment* and then, the following year, with his production of George Orwell's *Nineteen Eighty-Four*.

The Quatermass Experiment was an extension of the 'horror plays' that had been popular in the post-war period and, like them, it tapped into the concerns and anxieties of the contemporary audience, in this case reflecting anxieties thrown up by the Cold War about the atomic bomb and the possibility of invasion and 'infection' by unknown forces. As such, it proved to be very potent and is renowned for terrifying the early 1950s television audience, which was nevertheless gripped by the serial during the course of its six-week run. *The Quatermass Experiment*, which was followed by two sequels on the BBC in 1955 and 1958–9, and by another on ITV in 1979, told the story of the lone sur-vivor of a three-man rocket crew who, after contracting an infection from an alien organism during an experimental rocket flight, gradually mutates into an enormous vegetable-like creature after returning to Earth, and is eventually destroyed in Westminster Abbey.

All three serials were transmitted live, but, unlike *Quatermass II*, which was broad-cast from Lime Grove, *The Quatermass Experiment* was transmitted from the old Alexandra Palace studios and had to make use of the more primitive cameras and equipment installed there, some of which dated back to before the war. Given the limi-tations of the available technology, and the difficulties of achieving sophisticated special effects in live television drama, Kneale concentrated on characterisation, while Cartier did his best to create and maintain tension.

In the opening episode, 'Contact Has Been Established', after a short opening sequence on telecine, in which we see a rocket taking off and shots of a planet, the drama cuts to a studio set of the mission control room where Professor Quatermass and his assistants are trying to determine what has happened to the missing rocket, which they have lost track of on its experimental flight. Although there is a mobile, tracking camera in the first shot, most of the shots in this first scene are static, framing the characters and cutting to follow the conversation in conventional manner. The ASL in the first scene is fifteen seconds, with one shot of Quatermass talking to his assistant held for forty seconds. Transitions between scenes are accomplished by fades, some of them quite long to enable the actors to get in position for the next scene, accompanied by dramatic music. By today's standards the exposition seems very slow, but the serial is effective in building and maintaining tension. When the rocket crashes back to Earth the narrative tempo increases and the transitions between scenes are accomplished more quickly as the episode moves towards its cliff-hanging climax, in which Quatermass demands of the sole surviving crew member, as he staggers from the rocket: 'Victor, what happened?'[46]

While the restrictions of live television drama may seem inhibiting for a serial like *Quatermass*, the nervous tension that live TV inevitably built up among the cast and crew was later cited by Kneale as one of the positive aspects of live television which contributed to the success of the production:

> One of the few enjoyable things about working live at Alexandra Palace was that you knew you were doing a performance to people, rather like being on stage; you'd stagger out into the daylight afterwards and you'd look down the hill at the aerials below and you knew that a large proportion of those people down there had been watching what you'd just been doing. There was a real feeling of audience contact. The other good thing was that going out live engendered an extraordinary nervous excitement and tension among the cast, which added enormously to the on-screen drama.[47]

These aspects of live television, the excitement and nervous energy generated by doing a live performance which both the cast and production team knew was being watched live by millions of people, are easy to overlook in discussing, and viewing, early television drama, but they are central to gaining an understanding of the nature and impact of television drama before pre-recorded programmes became the norm.

Telerecording

The significance of *The Quatermass Experiment* as a ground-breaking production is helped enormously by the fact that the first two episodes of the serial have survived and are now available on DVD. They are among the earliest surviving examples of live television drama in Britain and they exist because they were telerecorded at the time of transmission by filming from a television monitor.[48]

The first demonstration of a process for telerecording had taken place in 1947. Although it simply involved setting up a 35mm film camera in front of a television monitor and filming the live transmission from the screen, there were problems in sychronising the film camera with the television signal which meant that the early experiments with telerecording were not very sophisticated, although they improved during the 1950s. Several potential benefits of telerecording were anticipated, but the main motivation was that programmes could be repeated, without having to do the whole thing over again. It is symptomatic of the low cultural status afforded television at the time that it was this, rather than the advantage of being able to preserve the products of such an ephemeral medium for posterity, that was seen to be the main benefit of telerecording. Even when the technical problems had been overcome, only selected programmes were telerecorded, and even then there was no guarantee that the resulting film recording would be kept.

One of the obstacles was that telerecording threatened the fees that artists received from a repeat performance of a drama and it was not until an agreement was reached with Equity, the actors' union, that it became possible to telerecord the second performance of a *Sunday Night Theatre* play such as *It Is Midnight, Dr Schweitzer*, on Thursday, 26 February 1953, rather than the first performance, which was broadcast on Sunday, 22 February 1953. There was also a copyright problem with material that was not written originally for television, which sometimes prevented a telerecording being made or required such a recording to be destroyed after transmission.

All of which explains why the history of early television drama in Britain is largely a lost history. Of the hundreds of dramas transmitted before 1955 only a few have survived. The claim, therefore, that *Quatermass* is ground-breaking may be spurious because, without further research, we do not know whether other original, innovative productions preceded it, only to disappear, without trace, into the ether.

In the light of this it is worth reiterating that the immediacy of continuous, live television drama, and the visual aesthetic which it encouraged, sets early TV drama apart from the subsequent history of television drama in Britain, making it, in its ephemerality and invisibility, something of an archeological mystery, constituting effectively a 'prehistory' of television drama. 'Liveness' determined the aesthetic of British television drama for more than twenty years, even after telerecording had become more prevalent, and when the shift towards pre-recorded drama began, in the late 1950s and early 60s, the nature of television drama began to change irrevocably.

Shooting on film

While 35mm film was used in telerecording to achieve a visual record of a live transmission, there was also a move towards pre-recording television drama on film in the mid-1950s. In 1954 the BBC used film to shoot its first police series, *Fabian of the Yard*, instead of transmitting it live from the studio. *Fabian of the Yard* was a police detective series based around the investigative skills of Detective Inspector Robert Fabian, a real-life Scotland Yard detective, played in the series by Bruce Seton. Transmission of the series began in November 1954, but in July of that year the BBC had already screened their first, bought-in, filmed serial: the American police drama, *I Am the Law*.

Shooting television drama on film had been taking place in the USA for some time in order to enable programmes to be repeated in different parts of the country that were in different time zones, and the possibility of selling programmes to English-speaking territories, such as America, Canada and Australia, was one of the prime reasons for the BBC shooting *Fabian of the Yard*, and other subsequent dramas, on film. In other words,

Location filming in Britain's first police series: *Fabian of the Yard*

there was an economic incentive, even for the BBC, before commercial television started in Britain, for shooting on film.

The financial incentive was also a factor in the telerecording of live programmes, but the visual quality of a live telerecording, compared to a drama shot originally on film, made the latter by far the better option as far as overseas sales were concerned. Another advantage of pre-recording drama on film, and telerecording live transmissions, was that it allowed greater flexibility in scheduling:

> Using made-for-television filmed material meant that programmes such as *Fabian* could be moved with relative ease from Saturday to Wednesday; an episode of *I Am the Law* could be replaced or delayed without cancelling actors' bookings or having to reorganize studio time and storage space. Serial drama on film allowed a greater flexibility with schedule organization.[49]

Shooting on film brought television drama closer to the aesthetics of cinema films by enabling reverse-angle shooting, extreme close-ups and a much faster narrative tempo to be achieved, more easily than in live TV drama. This is clearly evident in *Fabian of the Yard*, where there is a greater freedom in the organisation of space within each scene, with a greater variety of camera angles, more close-ups and more use of location filming. There is also a faster narrative tempo than in most live TV drama as a result of a shorter ASL and faster transitions between scenes. In the episode of *Fabian* entitled 'The Executioner' (6 April 1955), for example, the ASL is twelve seconds, considerably shorter than most live TV drama, and in line with ASLs in cinema films at the time.[50] In keeping with the conventions of investigative detective drama, there is also an increased use of voiceover, which, like the use of location filming and a more 'realistic' (i.e., less 'frontal') organisation of space, marks a significant departure from the conventions of naturalism which prevailed in live studio drama.

Fabian of the Yard, therefore, marks a significant moment in British television drama, not just for being the first police series on British TV, but for being the first series to adopt a more cinematic aesthetic as a result of being shot on film. However, not only was shooting television drama on film more expensive than producing live TV drama, it also meant a move away from the dominant aesthetic of 'intimacy' and 'immediacy' in live TV drama, and was, therefore, viewed with some suspicion by those who believed that live television drama was a unique form, with its own virtues.

Nineteen Eighty-Four (1954)

December 1954 saw the screening of what has become a major landmark in the history of British television drama. The adaptation of George Orwell's 1948 novel, *Nineteen Eighty-Four*, about a post-apocalyptic totalitarian society where the population lives in fear of Big Brother, tapped into contemporary Cold War anxieties about the atomic bomb and oppressive totalitarian regimes. Following their success with *The Quatermass Experiment*, writer Nigel Kneale and producer Rudolph Cartier collaborated once again to bring Orwell's bleak vision to the television screen as a two-hour live drama.

The play was transmitted on 12 December 1954, 8.35–10.35 pm, and was repeated the following Thursday, when the cast and crew returned to the studio to do the production for a second time. This second broadcast of the play was telerecorded, giving us a visual record of one of the most important early television dramas, which has enabled its ground-breaking reputation to be established.[51]

Following on from the generic precedent set by *The Quatermass Experiment*, and coming shortly after the transmission of the first episodes of *Fabian of the Yard* as a drama series shot on film, *Nineteen Eighty-Four* was a landmark in television drama production not only because it was the most expensive TV drama to date, and because of the controversy that it generated, but also because of the way in which Cartier attempted to combine the intimate virtues of live TV drama with the ability of film to open out the production, clearly important in a drama which sought to make a statement about big themes like atomic destruction, totalitarianism and the future of humankind.

Nineteen Eighty-Four uses fourteen filmed sequences to supplement its twenty-three studio scenes. While the film sequences, which were telecined seamlessly into the live transmission, may not have been as long as the studio scenes, they serve to open out the drama and give it a presence in the real world, albeit a fictional future world, as well as being used in some cases to provide continuity within studio scenes – for example, the close-up shot of the note handed to Winston Smith (Peter Cushing) by Julia (Yvonne

A landmark in live studio drama: *Nineteen Eighty-Four*

Mitchell) in the Ministry of Truth, declaring her love for him. While film inserts were being used in television drama from the early 1950s, *Nineteen Eighty-Four* represented the most extensive use of them in a TV play up to that time, and signalled Cartier's determination to extend the boundaries of television drama. They also serve to increase the narrative tempo, by reducing the ASL to around fifteen seconds:

> for the film sequences alone the ASL works out at 6 seconds; for studio/film composite scenes the ASL is around 13 seconds; counting the studio scenes alone, the ASL works out at 17 seconds. It is no surprise, therefore, that film inserts reduce the overall ASL significantly, although this is partly as a result of a fast montage scene.[52]

The success of *Nineteen Eighty-Four* in realising Orwell's dystopian vision owed much to the way in which Cartier combined the intimate qualities of live television drama with an expansiveness made possible by the use of film inserts and location sequences. As a live drama in which, as previously noted, the nervous excitement and tension generated by a live production contributed enormously to the successful generation of tension in the audience, the ability of live television to bring the audience close to the action and involve it in the nervous immediacy of the live performance was crucial to the success of *Nineteen Eighty-Four*.

The generation of a tense and claustrophobic atmosphere in the drama was achieved through a combination of the immediacy of live drama, powerful performances from the cast and a televisual style which foregrounded intimacy and interiority, especially in relation to the main character, Winston Smith. Jason Jacobs offers a fascinating analysis of how this is achieved in a scene early on in the drama, when Winston is eating in the canteen and a newsflash from Big Brother is broadcast on the telescreen. In a drama which is largely concerned with the paranoia ensuing from constant surveillance, part of the challenge in the television production was to communicate this to the audience, and to make the viewers experience the paranoia felt by the central characters. Cartier achieves this by giving us access to Winston Smith's inner thoughts and this is brilliantly realised in the canteen scene when Winston is trying to conceal his hatred of Big Brother and the Party, without revealing his 'thoughtcrime' to the omniscient telescreen. This could only be achieved through the use of a voiceover, providing an example of a voiceover being used to break with the mode of naturalism which, in its emphasis on surface detail, cannot accommodate any attempt to get beneath the surface. But to achieve this in a live production was a technical feat, demonstrating Cartier's mastery of the form and Peter Cushing's skill in 'close-up' acting for the camera.

As has already been noted, the key to live television's 'intimate' style was its ability to bring the viewer close to the drama, hence the obsession with 'talking heads' in early television drama. Cartier takes this to an extreme in the canteen scene by cutting to a big close-up of Cushing in which his face fills the frame, enabling us to register the subtleties of Cushing's acting as he communicates the character's inner feelings of revulsion towards Big Brother. This could have been achieved in the studio by cutting to a close-up of Winston and playing his pre-recorded voiceover during the live transmission, but it seems more likely, given the subtleties of Winston's changing expression as he thinks his secret thoughts, that this short twenty-second shot was a film insert, pre-recorded so that Cushing could act to his own recorded voiceover, and then telecined into the live broadcast.[53] The canteen scene in *Nineteen Eighty-Four* shows how live television drama was able to combine elements of theatre (the expressiveness of Cushing's acting, tailored for the television camera), cinema (the movement of the camera into an extreme close-up to register emotion) and radio (the disembodied voice giving us access to Winston's inner thoughts) in a unique and intimate manner.

There are other extraordinary moments in the production – such as the scene in the room that Winston and Julia rent in the Prole Sector, so that they can be together, where Cushing, speaking to Julia who has gone behind a screen to change into a dress, turns to the camera to deliver a key speech:

If there's any hope for the future it lies in the Proles. Eighty-five per cent of the population – if only they became conscious of their own strength, all they'd need is to rise up and shake themselves like a horse shaking off flies, they'd throw off the Party.

It is a powerful anti-authoritarian statement that is doubly effective in being addressed to the camera. The implicit socialist message may still have had resonance for many in the television audience who had experienced the collective struggle against fascism in recent memory, followed by the overthrow of the old order with the election of a radical Labour government in 1945. While some of the controversy provoked by *Nineteen Eighty-Four* concerned its sexual morality and torture scenes, it was also attacked from certain quarters for being 'anti-capitalist', an accusation which suggests that scenes such as this one, in which Winston Smith posits a belief in the ability of the proletariat to overcome oppression, had hit their mark. The BBC, in fact, received a number of threatening telephone calls following transmission, which it took seriously enough to hire bodyguards to protect Rudolph Cartier, as he later recollected:

> I had two tough guys hired by the BBC who said 'You stick to Mr Cartier and don't let anyone come near him,' because there were very threatening 'phone calls to the BBC, because everybody thought that this was pro-communist, anti-fascist subject.[54]

The formal and stylistic innovations of *Nineteen Eighty-Four*, together with its powerful portrayal of individuals crushed by a ruthless totalitarian state, places it in a tradition of radical, progressive television drama, a tradition for which the BBC was to become renowned in the 1960s and 70s. In this respect, as well as in its frightening vision of Britain thirty years in the future, it was especially prescient. As a television play which combined the intimate aesthetic of live drama with the expansive ambitions brought to it by Rudolph Cartier and Nigel Kneale, it is transitional, utilising the unique virtues of live TV drama but adapting them for a new purpose.

While some of its studio scenes are still slow and frontal in their spatial organisation, there is an undeniable visual and emotional power in many scenes, not least the torture scenes towards the end of the play, which caused much of the controversy and brought forth criticism from viewers about their suitability for television. Nearly fifty years later, when we have become both more sophisticated and more sceptical in our reading of television fictions, these scenes, such as the final one in which Winston and Julia meet again, broken in body and spirit, their dream of happiness evaporated, carry a powerful emotional charge. It is not difficult to see why viewers at the time found *Nineteen Eighty-Four* both shocking and disturbing. As John Caughie notes:

> The interest in 1984 is not simply as a relic of style, or as a monument of early television; it lies also in the social history of its transmission. Like the other 'terrifying' Cartier productions of the time, *The Quatermass Experiment* and *Quatermass II* (also scripted by Nigel Kneale), it points to a history of a subjectivity in which the conventions which we now find slow and distancing produced then an intense involvement, evoking terror and pity in an audience which was not yet schooled in home entertainment, and had not yet become immune to undomesticated television.[55]

In the history of British television drama, *Nineteen Eighty-Four* is seminal. Progressive in both its form and subject matter, while retaining many of the 'primitive' features of live television drama, it can now be seen as marking a transitional moment between the more conservative 'filmed theatre' of early TV drama and the new era which was about to dawn, heralded by the appearance on the broadcasting scene of a commercial competitor for the BBC.

2

Popular Drama and Social Realism, 1955–61

There is a tendency to see the arrival of commercial television in Britain as representing a complete break with what had gone before, a departure from the paternalistic moralising of the BBC and the embracing of a less elitist, more populist form of broadcasting based on the American model. While the introduction of Independent Television (ITV) undoubtedly transformed the broadcasting map in Britain, the long and heated debate which led to the setting up of an Independent Television Authority in 1954 to oversee the introduction of commercial television ensured that ITV would not go completely down the American road of sponsored television, but would incorporate elements of the public service tradition, even if not to the same extent as the BBC.

In practice, also, the new Independent Television companies poached many of the BBC's trained personnel, with the lure of more money, with the result that there was some continuity in production practices, rather than a radical break, in the same way that there had been when BBC Television resumed broadcasting after the six-year hiatus of the Second World War.

The major change that ITV brought was a promise to cater for the rapidly growing television audience in ways that the BBC had not, to be unashamedly populist in its programming and to turn around John Reith's famous, patronising assertion that 'few people know what they want and even fewer what they need' by giving the public what they wanted rather than what it was felt they needed. In fact, even at the BBC this superior, paternalist attitude had been relaxing in the 1950s with the introduction of programmes like *The Grove Family*, as a popular soap opera, and *Fabian of the Yard*, as an American-style crime drama which, being shot on film, could be commercially exploited by being sold to foreign markets. It is not coincidental that both these programmes started in 1954, the year in which the Television Act finally gave the go-ahead to commercial television, after several years of discussion. The BBC knew by the early 1950s that commercial TV was on its way and had started to review its programming in anticipation of the arrival of the new channel.

Nevertheless, the impact of ITV should not be underestimated. When Associated Rediffusion began broadcasting in the London area on 22 September 1955, with a separate company, ATV, taking over from it at weekends, it really did represent the beginning of a new era in broadcasting which, over the next six years, was to completely transform television in the UK and see it become established as the dominant mass medium, surpassing both radio and the cinema.[1]

The impact of ITV

In its first year ITV struggled financially as it tried to increase audiences in order to attract enough advertising revenue to survive. The limited availability of the new commercial channel, which was made up of a network of regional companies, meant that, as in the early days of the BBC, the service was restricted to certain parts of the country. For example, ITV did not become available in the Midlands and the north of England until February and May 1956, respectively, while other parts of England, Scotland, Wales and Northern Ireland had to wait between one and four years for it.[2] It was not until 1960 that three-quarters of the population had access to both BBC and ITV, by which time the success of ITV was assured and it had considerably surpassed the BBC in audience share.

Initially, the BBC had anticipated a drop in its share of the audience to around 40 per cent, but such was the success of ITV, after it had overcome its early difficulties, that by 1958 it had gained three-quarters of the television audience that had access to both channels. By the following year the profits that the ITV companies were making had proved the wisdom of Roy Thomson's famous quote, made at the launch of Scottish Television in August 1957, that owning an ITV company was 'like having a licence to print your own money'.[3]

While the biggest successes with the audience were the new game shows, quizzes and variety programmes, ITV went much further than the BBC had done hitherto in targeting new audiences – that is, working-class audiences – with its popular drama programming. It did this in four ways: by buying in American drama series like *Dragnet* (1951–9), *Highway Patrol* (1955–9) and *Gunsmoke* (1955–75); by producing its own fast-moving American-style drama series, shot on film; by targeting working-class audiences with its own home-grown soap operas; and by recruiting new writers to inject a dose of working-class realism into the single play.

Popular drama series and serials

Along with the imported American drama series, one of the most popular early dramas on ITV was *The Adventures of Robin Hood* (ABC, 1955–9). Initially targeted at children, it was scheduled before the 'toddlers' truce', a one-hour gap in transmission from 6–7 pm which was designed to allow younger children to be put to bed and older children to get on with their homework – the addictive and distracting qualities of television being a genuine concern. Commercial imperatives soon overode these concerns, however, and *The Adventures of Robin Hood* was moved into this slot when the 'truce' was abandoned in February 1957.

An early ITV export: *The Adventures of Robin Hood*

Featuring Richard Greene as the eponymous hero, *Robin Hood* was a fast-moving, action-packed adventure which championed Robin and his band of outlaws living in Sherwood Forest, whose selfless attempts to redistribute wealth brought them into weekly confrontation with the dastardly Sheriff of Nottingham (Alan Wheatley). Using some location filming to link the studio scenes, the series was shot mainly in the small Nettlefold Studios at Walton-on-Thames, where Sherwood Forest was recreated using minimal scenery. There was plenty of opportunity for action sequences and the story was considered to be sufficiently universal in interest to be pre-sold to American television before transmission had even begun in the UK.[4]

The success of *The Adventures of Robin Hood* spawned a number of similar swash-buckling dramas, such as *The Adventures of Sir Lancelot* (1956–7), *The Buccaneers* (1956–7) and *The Adventures of William Tell* (1958–9). However, it should be noted that the genre was not without precedent on the BBC: *The Three Musketeers* had been screened in late 1954 as a six-part serial, while an earlier version of *Robin Hood*, featuring Patrick Troughton as Robin, had been transmitted in 1953, as a six-part serial for children.

In 1957, the same year that the BBC terminated *The Grove Family*, ITV began its own soap opera, *Emergency – Ward 10* (ATV, 1957–67), as a twice-weekly continuous serial. Departing from the family-centred milieu of *The Grove Family*, *Emergency – Ward 10* was the first hospital-based drama, a genre destined to become one of the most popular on

British television. Originally developed as a six-part serial entitled *Calling Nurse Roberts*, written by Tessa Diamond, *Emergency – Ward 10* began in February 1957 and immediately established itself as one of ITV's most popular programmes, which it continued to be for the next ten years.

Transmitted live, as a thirty-minute drama on Tuesdays and Fridays, *Emergency – Ward 10* privileged characterisation, and the relations between staff and between staff and patients, rather than dramatic action. Compared to dramas shot on film, like *Robin Hood*, the narrative pace was fairly slow and the organisation of space more limited, as befitting a more conventional, live studio drama. Production values were not as high as in other dramas and the

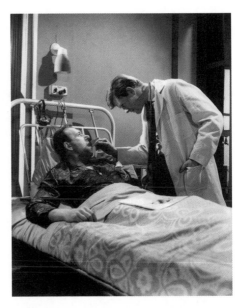

ITV's first twice-weekly serial: *Emergency – Ward 10*

quality of acting was variable, but this was no more than might be expected from a long-running, twice-weekly drama serial, where there was less time for rehearsal or for elaborate dramatisation.

Interestingly, *Emergency – Ward 10* was referred to as a 'documentary drama' in the ITA's 1959/60 Annual Report, suggesting that it was perceived as having claims to a degree of realism in its depiction of the daily workings of a hospital, despite the artificial studio sets. There were limits, however, to how far the series was prepared to go in striving for social realism. A 1964 storyline had an inter-racial relationship developing between two doctors, but the plan to televise British television's first inter-racial kiss proved controversial. Joan Hooley, who played the black doctor involved in the relationship, relates the story:

> I played the part of Louise Mahler, an African doctor from a wealthy family who has come to England to train and to work as a house-doctor. She has a love affair with one of the doctors, Giles Farmer, and they had the two of us walking out together for weeks. Then there was a scene where we were supposed to kiss in a bedroom. The papers got hold of it and all the objections started to be raised. It was suggested that the kiss would be unfit for viewing at 7.30 in the evening, because there might be young people watching! The ITV authorities bandied about for several weeks. ... Well, we never did get our kiss in the bedroom, instead we ended up kissing in the garden quite sedately. And then Giles' family objects to him having a black fiancee, so the romance had to be broken off, much to my disgust, I hasten to add, because I was really

looking forward to the character developing further and me actually getting married to Giles. But it never happened. Shortly after that, I was written out of the series.[5]

While this example may indicate the limitations of series drama, the inclusion of the storyline at all was perhaps a progressive development in popular television at the time, especially for commercial TV. The popularity of *Emergency – Ward 10* proved its success, and its ten-year lifespan indicated that ITV was aware of what was required in sustaining a long-running serial, unlike the BBC with *The Grove Family*. It was one of many blows which the new commercial network was to deliver to the BBC as it gained viewers and grew in confidence in the late 1950s.

Having succeeded with a hospital-based soap opera, ITV then went on to show that it could also succeed with a police series. *No Hiding Place* (Associated Rediffusion, 1959–67) was first transmitted in 1959 and featured Raymond Francis as Chief Detective Superintendent Lockhart, who had previously been seen in *Murder Bag* (Associated Rediffusion, 1957–9) and *Crime Sheet* (Associated Rediffusion, 1959), before being transferred to Scotland Yard for *No Hiding Place*. Although the main competitor for the series was the BBC's *Dixon of Dock Green*, which had started in 1955, the focus on the analytical detective skills of Chief Superintendent Lockhart in *No Hiding Place* placed it more in the mould of *Fabian of the Yard*, which also featured the use of forensics to solve crimes, than a routine police series. The superior skills of Lockhart in unravelling the crime and apprehending the villain was implicit in the series title, and the ideological function of the series was to ensure that there would be 'no hiding place' for those who contravened the law. Like *Fabian* and *Dixon*, *No Hiding Place* portrayed the police as heroes, the infallible upholders of law and order, and presented a rosy and reassuring image of the police, which was to be challenged in later representations.

Coronation Street and social realism

While *Robin Hood*, *Emergency – Ward 10* and *No Hiding Place* represented three different elements in ITV's successful popular drama output in the late 1950s, it took a regional ITV company, Granada, which had the weekday franchise for the north-west of England, to offer a different representation of the working class to the southern metropolitan one that had previously been dominant. Originally entitled *Florizel Street* and with a projected run of just thirteen weeks, *Coronation Street* (Granada, 1960–) was set in an industrial working-class district in the north-west of England, recognisable not just for the row of terraced houses which provided the main setting for the drama, but for the distinctive Lancashire accents of its working-class characters.

Where the BBC's *The Grove Family* had portrayed a lower-middle-class southern suburban household, it took Granada's new serial to break ranks and suggest that not everyone 'out there' was like the Groves in social class and speech patterns, or even aspired to be like them. In its iconography, character types and storylines, *Coronation Street* tapped into the new mode of social realism, or 'kitchen sink' drama, that had been popularised in the theatre, and in literature, since the mid-1950s, and which was also emerging in the 'new wave' of British cinema, and in *Armchair Theatre* plays (also produced by a regional ITV company), at the end of the 1950s.

Marion Jordan has identified some of the main features of social realism and it is worth quoting her definition at length in order to measure the extent to which these characteristics can be applied to *Coronation Street*:

> the genre of Social Realism demands that life should be presented in the form of a narrative of personal events, each with a beginning, a middle and an end, important to the central characters concerned but affecting others only in minor ways; that though these events are ostensibly about *social* problems they should have as one of their central concerns the settling of people in life; that the resolution of these events should always be in terms of the effect of social interventions; that characters should be either working-class or of the classes immediately visible to the working classes (shopkeepers, say, or the two-man business) and should be credibly accounted for in terms of the 'ordinariness' of their homes, families, friends; that the locale should be urban and provincial (preferably in the industrial north); that the settings should be commonplace and recognisable (the pub, the street, the factory, the home and more particularly the kitchen); that the time should be 'the present'; that the style should be such as to suggest an unmediated, unprejudiced and complete view of reality; to give, in summary, the impression that the reader, or viewer, has spent some time at the expense of the characters depicted.[6]

An analysis of any episode of *Coronation Street* would find most, if not all, of these features to be present. Take the very first episode, for example, transmitted on 9 December 1960. The title sequence establishes the world in which the drama is set with its opening shot of the roofs of terraced houses, accompanied by a melancholy signature tune, itself redolent with nostalgia, before taking us down into the world of *Coronation Street* and depositing us outside the local shop, where children are singing while playing a game with a skipping rope. Florrie Lindley is taking over the shop, by which dramatic device we are given initial character information by Elsie Lappin, the current shopkeeper, about the Street's inhabitants, before being introduced to the daughter of Elsie Tanner, one of the Street's key characters in the early days, when Linda Cheveski ('Linda Tanner as was') comes into the shop.

The first scene immediately establishes the ordinariness of the situation, with the shop as a focal place in the heart of the community where chance encounters can take place. The plainness of its decor, together with the naturalism of the acting and ordinariness of the dialogue, announces this as a drama of the everyday, a drama of social realism. It also establishes this as a drama in which women will play a central role and where gossip will feature as a key ingredient, underlining its ordinariness. Some emphasis is put on Linda's unusual married name – she has married a foreigner, an outsider – and this provides a link to the next scene, when we cut to the Tanner's house to find Linda's mother and brother engaged in a heated argument.

Not only does this transition enable Elsie Tanner (Pat Phoenix), one of the strong female characters in the serial, to be introduced, it also provides us with our first glimpse of an ordinary working-class family home, in which a typical family argument is taking place. Dennis, Elsie's son, cannot find work, through having been in prison, and his situation serves as a contrast to that of Ken Barlow, the scholarship lad to whom we are introduced in the next scene when we cut to the Barlow household, where we find them eating dinner in the living room.

The cutting and camera positions in these early scenes may remind us that this is a live drama – the staging of the living-room scene in the Barlow's house, for example, is very 'frontal' – but this could be said to add realism to the drama through the codes of 'immediacy' associated with live television drama.[7] Even when *Coronation Street* moved over to pre-recording for subsequent transmission, this element of 'immediacy' was still seen to be an important signifier of realism to be strived for, and the serial continued to be recorded as a live performance for many years:

> In the early days, Friday's episode was transmitted live and was immediately followed by a tele-recording of the Monday episode – that is the two episodes were recorded in one session. Even after the introduction of VTR the two programmes were recorded as a continuous performance until 1974.[8]

The first episode continues in this vein, introducing us to characters, taking us into homes, to the local pub, establishing relationships. In doing so it provides us with an example of the interweaving of narratives, and of the personal lives of the characters, in a manner that has become a distinctive feature of soap opera. The fusion here of the conventions of soap opera with those of social realism results in what Marion Jordan describes as 'soap-opera realism', 'a specific televisual form'.[9]

Television soap opera provides 'a narrative of personal events', but not necessarily starting at the beginning with an expectation that we will be led through to a resolution, in the manner of series drama or the self-contained single play. Following on from *The Grove Family* and *Emergency – Ward 10*, *Coronation Street* was to be a continuous serial, with two thirty-minute episodes per week, presenting 'an unmediated, unprejudiced and complete view of reality', a world which the viewer could look in on and spend 'some time at the expense of the characters depicted'.

For working-class audiences, especially in the Midlands and the North, who were watching television in huge numbers by the early 1960s, a programme like *Coronation Street* offered a shock of recognition, of ordinary lives in ordinary circumstances, such as television had never really offered before. But while *Coronation Street* may have introduced a new dimension to popular television drama at the beginning of the 1960s, it was not without precedent. In fact, it was part of a broad movement in the arts which reflected changes that were taking place in society generally. As Richard Dyer wrote in 1981:

> It is important to remind ourselves that *Coronation Street* came out of a particular moment in British cultural history, a moment most strikingly and decisively

A drama of the ordinary and the everyday: working-class realism in early *Coronation Street*

marked by Richard Hoggart's book, *The Uses of Literacy* (1957). This book, together with other sociological works and novels, as well as films and theatre, was concerned to 'discover' and legitimate a tradition of culture that could authentically be termed 'working-class'.[10]

Coronation Street can be seen, at the beginning of the 1960s, to be part of this project, and its success in attracting audiences in excess of 20 million, in less than a year, can be attributed to its convincing portrayal of a 'whole way of life', to use the phrase made famous by Raymond Williams in one of the other 'sociological works' published in the late 1950s, a way of life that had previously been largely absent from the television screen.[11] Like Hoggart, Williams was concerned with redefining 'culture' and rescuing it from its previous elitist connotations, enabling it to be used to describe a whole range of popular cultural activities, including television and soap opera.

Richard Dyer identifies four elements of Hoggart's book that became key ingredients of *Coronation Street*: 'the emphasis on common sense, the absence of work and politics, the stress on women and the strength of women, and the perspective of nostalgia'.[12] These elements indicate both the strengths and weaknesses of the serial, highlighting the role of women as one of its central positive features, while also identifying its tendency to look back fondly through rose-tinted spectacles at a self-contained community which was, in reality, in the process of disappearing even as it was being established as a fictional TV community. The huge success of *Coronation Street*, however, was such that it became more and more difficult to disrupt the cosy insularity of the community the longer the serial continued. As a drama of social realism, *Coronation Street* became a victim of its own success.

Armchair Theatre

The success of ITV in winning audiences with its dramas was not restricted to series and serials. From the very beginnings of the commercial network the single play featured in its scheduling. If the first programme on ITV's opening night was a variety programme, 'featuring some of the stars who will be regularly featured in Independent Television's variety programmes',[13] the second was a half-hour programme of extracts from classic plays: Oscar Wilde's *The Importance of Being Earnest*, Saki's *Baker's Dozen* and Noel Coward's *Private Lives*. Like the BBC, ITV turned to the theatre for prestige and it was clearly thought that extracts from classic theatre plays would add an element of 'high culture' to its opening gala.

The scheduling of 'serious' drama after a variety programme was also indicative of ITV's astuteness in the art of scheduling, providing a public service mix of the 'high' and the 'low' in classic BBC fashion. In fact, the opening night programme offered a genuine cultural mix, with a programme of professional boxing following the drama extracts, to be followed in turn by the news, at ten o'clock.

Among the drama strands introduced by the new ITV companies, *Television Playhouse* (1956–63) was an important part of Associated Rediffusion's schedule from the beginning and featured regularly in the national top ten programmes. This showcase for the single play did not just screen classics from the theatre, however. An early original play, and an example of the new 'kitchen sink' drama, was Ted Willis's *Woman in a Dressing Gown* (Associated Rediffusion, 28 June 1956). This was one of the first British television plays to focus on 'ordinary people' and, in doing so, it formed part of that movement which, seen retrospectively, was launched with the May 1956 premiere of John Osborne's vitriolic *Look Back in Anger* at the Royal Court Theatre. In fact, given that *Woman in a Dressing Gown* was already written when *Look Back in Anger* was staged, a greater influence on Willis is likely to have been the American writer Paddy Chayefsky, whose 1953 play *Marty*, for the American channel NBC, was a product of what has come to be described as the 'golden age' of American television drama, naturalistic dramas focusing on ordinary people, like Marty (Rod Steiger), 'an "ordinary man", a New York butcher, who defies the collective opinion of friends and family in sticking to the unattractive girl he loves'.[14]

Willis was one of a group of new writers in the mid-1950s interested in writing original contemporary dramas. Stimulated by the example of Chayefsky in America, and by the emergence of a new social realism in literature and theatre at home, these writers jumped at the opportunity offered by the ITV companies, who were in desperate need of writers to help fill the schedules. In this way ITV made a major contribution to the growth of television drama in the late 1950s, not just in developing new drama series and serials, but also in commissioning new writers for the more prestigious single play.

The counterpart of Associated Rediffusion's *Television Playhouse*, and the most famous showcase for the single play in the 1950s, was ABC's *Armchair Theatre*. Nowhere was ITV's astuteness in scheduling better illustrated than with *Armchair Theatre*, which began with a preview on 8 July 1956, an adaptation of a stage play by Dorothy Brandon called *The Outsider*, and which was launched as a weekly programme on 16 September 1956, with *Tears in the Wind*, an adaptation of Andre Gide's *Symphonie Pastorale*.[15]

Continuing the by now well-established BBC tradition of the Sunday night play, *Armchair Theatre* followed ATV's *Sunday Night at the London Palladium*, replicating the opening night tactic of following a light entertainment programme with 'serious' drama. *Sunday Night at the London Palladium* was one of the most popular programmes on ITV, regularly topping the ratings, and *Armchair Theatre* benefited enormously from being scheduled immediately after it, inheriting a large proportion of the audience that had watched the variety programme and thus achieving exceptional viewing figures for many of its plays. It should be remembered that, with only two channels and considerable channel loyalty, especially towards ITV in the late 1950s, the inheritance factor was very significant at this time, far more so than it is today with the increased choice of multi-channel television and a more fragmented audience.

Armchair Theatre scheduled a wide range of drama in its early days: genre plays, theatre classics, literary adaptations, as well as plays from America and Canada. It was after seeing Arthur Hailey's *Flight into Danger* (originally a Canadian Broadcasting Corporation production) on the BBC (25 September 1956) that Howard Thomas, Managing Director of ABC Television, invited the play's Canadian producer, Sydney Newman, to come to Britain to produce a series of plays for ABC. Shortly after his arrival Newman was appointed Drama Supervisor for *Armchair Theatre*, with a brief 'to continue the development of a programme having its roots in the North and Midlands, but conceived as family entertainment for a Sunday night viewing circle in homes throughout the British Isles'.[16]

Following his appointment in April 1958, Newman set about transforming drama production for *Armchair Theatre*, just as he was later to do at the BBC. Although *Armchair Theatre* continued to screen a wide range of plays, Newman wanted there to be more original, contemporary work and he was particularly keen to tap into the recent developments in the theatre, having been taken (ironically by Michael Barry, Head of Drama at the BBC) to see *Look Back in Anger* at the Royal Court Theatre when he was in London. As one of his innovations at ABC, Newman introduced the role of story editor, whose job was to find new writers who could provide *Armchair Theatre* with contemporary dramas. Peter Luke was appointed to this position early on and among the new writers he found were Alun Owen and Harold Pinter, two of the new generation of dramatists who were to help revolutionise the single play on British television. In a 1961 survey of British television drama, television critic Philip Purser summarised Newman's aims and achievements with *Armchair Theatre*:

> When Sydney Newman came from Canada to take over ABC's *Armchair Theatre* he eventually produced the first recognisable house style in British television drama, though it took him nearly two years to do it. He knew what he wanted: a school of

realism dramatising the social revolution he felt had taken place in Britain after the war; the specific example shuttled round the department like a battered Holy Grail was a story-line about a small shopkeeper facing competition from a supermarket (it eventually turned up for someone else altogether); unfortunately Newman lacked an understanding of the country, and at first he didn't have the writers to help him. His first production was *The Pillars of Midnight*, a glossy fiction which subordinated a smallpox outbreak to the adulteries of the doctors supposed to be fighting it. An emphasis on plays of action followed, then a phase of realism over-dependent on delinquency and violence. But almost from the beginning there was a three-dimensional quality to *Armchair Theatre* productions which was ahead of rival efforts. Sets were adventurous and elaborate and the geography was convincing – the camera followed people through doors and along corridors and into the next location instead of switching arbitrarily from scene to scene. The use of music and teaser openings was explored. With the script machine finally beginning to bear fruit a period of supremacy began which was unchallenged from early 1959 to late in 1960.[17]

The innovations in set design and style in *Armchair Theatre* productions were not entirely due to Sydney Newman. Purser's reference to there being a three-dimensional quality to *Armchair Theatre* productions 'almost from the beginning' suggests that the attempts to break with fourth-wall naturalism were evident in *Armchair Theatre* plays before Newman's arrival.

Indeed, one of Newman's young protégés at CBC, the director Ted Kotcheff, had gone to ABC in November 1957, several months before Newman was appointed Drama Supervisor. One of Kotcheff's early directorial assignments, *Emperor Jones* (ABC, 30 March 1958), an adaptation of the Eugene O'Neill play, updated for television by Terry Southern, was extremely adventurous in its use of studio space and in the mobility of its camera-work. In Acts 2 and 3, for example, Brutus Jones (Kenneth Spencer) wanders through a jungle, recreated in ABC's Didsbury Studios in Manchester, followed by a constantly moving camera. Much of the action is set at night and shadowy lighting and mist are used to disguise the fact that this was a studio production as the full extent of the studio space is utilised. In one astonishingly bold camera movement in Act 2, the camera tracks rapidly backwards away from Jones, who has just fired a gun in the direction of the camera, from one side of the studio to the other, leaving Jones as a tiny figure in the distance. So dramatic and ambitious was this camera movement that one of the technicians gets caught in shot as the camera sweeps back – not the only occasion in this production when a technician gets caught in the camera's field of view! In fact, studio staff were camouflaged with black clothing and black body paint in the play's jungle scenes in an attempt to conceal them from the cameras. Such were the problems in live TV drama of trying to achieve elaborate spatial movements with bulky cameras and lots of technicians in a confined studio space.

Emperor Jones also uses several stylised fantasy sequences, which are achieved by a change in the lighting design and by the actors moving in slow motion, or freezing their movement for the duration of the sequence. In the days of live television drama, non-naturalistic fantasy sequences like these were difficult to achieve, but dramatically they are quite effective here, given the technological constraints, and testify to the ambitions of *Armchair Theatre* to be stylistically adventurous in lighting, set design and camera-work.[18] Talking in 1987 about his early work on *Armchair Theatre*, Kotcheff stressed the interest that he and his *Armchair Theatre* colleagues had in experimenting with the form of television drama, an interest which Sydney Newman nurtured:

> At the time that we came and started at *Armchair Theatre*, Philip Saville and myself and other directors wanted really to push against the limitations of the media, the way it was presently conceived. We continually wanted to approach, I guess, the freedom of film, and not enslave it to the almost theatrical tradition in which we found it when we arrived here in '57.[19]

Unlike in early television drama where there was no 'director' and it was the producer who was the main decision-maker, developing a play from the writer's script and orchestrating the production from the control room during the live transmission, by the time of *Armchair Theatre* the director had taken over this function and the roles of the producer and the director had become more distinct. This was partly a result of the development of television drama into series and serial form during the 1950s, as well as into single-play series like *Armchair Theatre* and *Television Playhouse*, where the role of the producer became more of an executive position, approving plays and writers who, on *Armchair Theatre* at least, would initially be commissioned by the story editor, who would then act as an intermediary between writer and producer. It was the responsibility of the producer then to appoint a director for each production (or episode) according to their availability and suitability for the drama. Once this had happened, the director would then have a certain degree of freedom to develop the production as they saw fit. John Russell Taylor describes how the process worked on *Armchair Theatre*:

> Since *Armchair Theatre*'s producer is also the drama supervisor, his duties as executive and impressario to his department make it necessary for him to delegate more of his creative work than is usual with the producer of a drama series. He discusses the play with the director at the start of production, but this is only a preliminary briefing, and he may withhold any ideas which he himself has about the play if he feels it best not to influence the director's as yet unformed impressions of the subject. He remains available from the outset for consultation on all matters from interpretation to budgets and casting, but he does not attend the first reading nor go to rehearsals unless there is some special problem attached to the production.
>
> In fact, his presence only really manifests itself during the last week, when the play is run through for his benefit and he gives notes to the director. By this time, of course, the general conception of the play is determined, and all the producer can reasonably do is to make suggestions on points of detail. His final

opportunity to intervene comes on the day of recording, when he sits alongside
the director in the control room for the two dress rehearsals, and joins the author
and story editor in giving notes to the director after each run-through. Here again,
these notes are only suggestions: the director can argue or explain if he feels the
producer has misunderstood, and finally disregard the advice if he thinks it
mistaken.[20]

Despite the canonisation of the writer as the 'author' in television drama, especially in
the realm of the single play, the role of the director was always important, and when
plays went out 'live' the director's role was crucial. Directors like Philip Saville saw the
relationship between the writer and director as a collaborative one but with the director by no means subordinate, having an important creative role to play in any production: 'The collaboration must be two-way but – as long as he is to *create* television – the
director must be more than simply a servant to the playwright.'[21] Not only was it the
director's responsibility to ensure that the play went out as planned, but he (and the
rigid gender divisions in TV production in the 1950s and 60s meant that directors invari-
ably were male) would be the person to sort out any problems that arose during the
course of the transmission, and in live television anything could happen. As Philip
Saville reflected in 1987: 'The director's chair in the control room was not called the hot
seat for nothing!'[22]

Ted Kotcheff provides an example of the ultimate test that any television drama
director may have had to face, when a leading actor collapsed and died during the live
transmission of an *Armchair Theatre* play called *Underground*, on 30 November 1958:

> The worst experience I had, in this respect, one that I rarely talk about, because
> it's so morbid, is that I had an actor die on me, have a heart attack, right in the
> middle of a live television play, up at Didsbury. This play was about an H-bomb
> hitting London … and the only people who survive are those people in the tubes,
> and slowly they're moving towards Piccadilly Station and eating raisins and
> chocolate out of machines, and we follow five or six of them, scrambling over the
> rubble and going down these long tubes … and Gareth Jones suddenly passed out,
> died right in the middle … towards the end of Act 2. So I went out at the end of
> Act 2, during the commercial break, Verity Lambert was in the control room, and I
> said to her as I went out of the control room: 'Listen, get master control room and
> tell them to have a Charlie Chaplin two-reeler standing by in case we grind to a
> halt,' because we could easily have ground to a halt, totally. He was the antagonist
> – it's like having 'The Last Supper' without Judas.[23]

Kotcheff had to use the two and a half minutes of the commercial break to reorganise the
production, giving Gareth Jones' lines to different actors, in order to compensate for the
absence of a leading member of the cast. Then, during Act 3, he went into the studio, leaving Verity Lambert to run the production from the control room, while he tried to anticipate and deal with the problems that might arise as a result of the hasty adjustments he

had made to the script. Through a process of improvisation, they got through Act 3, but this extreme example illustrates the unforseen problems inherent in live television production, problems which made directing television drama in the 1930s, 40s and 50s such a nerve-wracking task.

Through a variety of innovations in set design, lighting and camerawork, *Armchair Theatre* extended the frontiers of television drama production in the late 1950s and early 60s. While some of this may have been happening before Newman arrived at *Armchair Theatre*, the major innovation for which he was justifiably credited was the commissioning of new writers to write contemporary plays about the everyday lives of ordinary people. Ted Willis, who had already shown an interest in this with *Woman in a Dressing Gown* for *Television Playhouse*, was one of the new writers recruited by Newman:

> A group of writers had begun, very slowly, to develop. I was one of the first – there were others, like Alun Owen … Eric Paice, Clive Exton. This group was just beginning to develop and along came this man with this dream of putting the story of ordinary people and of our times, contemporary times, on the screen, and doing them with quality and giving writers freedom to write, and we jumped at it, we thought this was marvellous, and this natural force blew through the corridors of television and blew a lot of the cobwebs out and made a space for us.[24]

With his 1959 *Armchair Theatre* play *Hot Summer Night* (ABC, 1 February 1959, directed by Ted Kotcheff), Willis wrote about the social and emotional consequences of an interracial relationship (five years before *Emergency – Ward 10* tackled the subject), exploring an issue that was very topical at the time, following the 'race riots' in several British cities in 1958, by looking at how 'ordinary people' might adapt to a relationship between a black man and a white woman. Other writers also took up the challenge to produce new plays about contemporary life and ordinary people, including Alun Owen, who had three plays transmitted by *Armchair Theatre* within the space of a year: *No Tram to Lime Street* (ABC, 18 October 1959), *After The Funeral* (ABC, 3 April 1960) and *Lena, O My Lena* (ABC, 25 September 1960), which led to him winning the award of 'TV Playwright of 1959–60'. According to Billie Whitelaw, who featured in two of the plays, *No Tram to Lime Street* was

> an absolute watershed in drama, I don't think they realised what they'd started. Because of that, things like *Softly, Softly, Z Cars* and *Coronation Street* [followed] … because it became okay to have ordinary people going through ordinary emotions – but all the others were imitations.[25]

Another playwright who made his television debut with *Armchair Theatre* was Harold Pinter, whose *A Night Out* (ABC, 24 April 1960) achieved one of the biggest audiences for an *Armchair Theatre* play, topping the ratings for that particular week. This despite (or perhaps because of) the fact that the play went out with a warning that it was only suitable for adults, presumably because of the inclusion of a scene with a prostitute in Act 3, although by today's standards the scene is fairly innocuous. A *Night Out* is undeniably powerful drama, demonstrating not only how effective live studio drama could be, but also that *Armchair Theatre* plays were hugely popular, and that well-written, well-acted, serious drama could appeal to all sections of the television audience. After discovering the viewing figures for *A Night Out* Pinter calculated that his stage play, *The Caretaker*, would have to play for thirty years at the Duchess Theatre to match the audience of 6,380,000 viewers who watched *A Night Out* on the evening of 24 April 1960.[26]

Lena, O My Lena (1960)

Although Sydney Newman was keen to stress that *Armchair Theatre* plays were not all 'kitchen sink' dramas, the genre with which the programme is most associated is that of northern working-class realism. This is partly because it is this genre which most clearly fulfilled the brief that Newman was set when he was appointed Drama Supervisor at ABC, to produce plays for a programme that had its roots in the North and the Midlands. Of these plays, *Lena, O My Lena* (ABC, 25 September 1960), is perhaps the best example, dealing with themes that were common to other dramas of social realism being produced in the theatre and the cinema during this period.

Alun Owen's play is set in Salford, with most of the action taking place in the yard of a warehouse, employing male packers, which backs onto a factory, Salford Press Tool Ltd, employing a large number of women machine workers. The action moves freely in, around and between the two workplaces, focusing in particular on the relationship that develops between Lena (Billie Whitelaw), one of the women working in the factory, and Tom (Peter McEnery), a student who takes a summer job at the warehouse in order to be near 'real people'. Through their relationship, the play explores class difference, with Tom having a romanticised notion of the working class, from which he is removed as a result of his upbringing and education. Tom tells Ted (Colin Blakely), the warehouse foreman, that he is working class but that he has been 'separated from his class origins' by his father, who Ted correctly guesses is a foreman, rather than a manual worker. On many occasions in the play attention is drawn to Tom's middle-class 'educated' accent and his often verbose manner of speaking.

Lena takes an interest in Tom, who is described by her friend Peggy (Jeanne Hepple) as looking 'like Anthony Perkins, only younger'. Tom tells Lena that he did not want to join his fellow students pea-picking up the road and gets annoyed when Lena refers to the students as 'his sort'. When Lena asks him what he is studying, he is embarrassed to tell her it is 'English Literature'. 'Oh well,' she replies chirpily, 'san farian!' in mock French. The class difference between Tom and Lena is clearly established. It also becomes clear that Lena is using Tom to make her boyfriend Glyn (Scott Forbes), a lorry driver, jealous.

The action takes place over two days. Act 1 (eighteen minutes of screen time) takes place on the morning that Tom arrives at the factory, while Act 2 (lasting twenty-six minutes) covers the remainder of the day and the evening, when Lena and Tom meet at a pub 'up the road' where the student pea-pickers go (enabling some amusement to be had at the students' expense, with one stereotypical bearded student, wearing dark glasses, sitting reading *Finnegan's Wake*). It is after the pub scene that Tom professes his love for Lena and she kisses him, though it is clear that her action is prompted more by hearing Glyn, who has annoyed her by turning up at the pub and flirting with the female students, singing in his strong Welsh voice. The play builds to a climax in the short Final Act (lasting nine minutes) when Glyn lays claim to Lena. As he leads her away, Tom runs after them and tries to hit Glyn, only to be pushed to the ground. Tom is bewildered when Lena tells him that their fling was 'just a bit of fun' and she echoes Glyn's suggestion that Tom should go back up the road, where he belongs. Humiliated, Tom takes their advice and leaves.

The theme of the scholarship boy (although Tom is not actually identified as such) from a working-class background having to negotiate his changed social status was a common one at the time, to be found in Richard Hoggart's *The Uses of Literacy* (and feeding into *Coronation Street* in the shape of Ken Barlow), and also in the early work of Dennis Potter, who explored the issue autobiographically in the 1960 BBC documentary, *Between Two Rivers*, as well as in his 1965 *Wednesday Play, Stand Up, Nigel Barton*. More generally, class difference was a prominent theme in many films and plays in the late 1950s and early 60s, from *Look Back in Anger* to *Room at the Top* to *A Hard Day's Night* (the latter also scripted by Alun Owen). As Philip Purser wrote in 1961, the subject and the gritty northern setting completely fulfilled Sydney Newman's objective to put on the screen contemporary plays about 'ordinary people':

> Every flat endearment and giggle and uncomprehending stare in *Lena, O My Lena* emphasized the ditch that separates someone who came originally from a working background and someone who has never left it. It's hardly a problem but it's a social phenomenon, and one which has become common only since the war. Though the final run-through is said to have been better than the actual take, the rhythm of Ted Kotcheff's production, the careless sexuality of Billie Whitelaw's Lena and the tension of the climax in Assheton Gorton's dusty, sun-drenched factory yard must have seemed to Newman to add up to everything he had ever hoped for.[27]

As befitting a play in a series entitled *Armchair Theatre*, there is a strong sense of the 'theatrical' about *Lena, O My Lena*. While much is done to break down the frontality of early television drama and create a more three-dimensional space in which the actors, and the camera, can move around freely (if a little bumpily where the camera is concerned), the play still conveys a strong sense of the actors giving a performance. This was perhaps an inevitable consequence of live television drama, where the whole production schedule was organised so as to build up to 'the big night', with two or three weeks of rehearsals for the cast leading up to two days of camera rehearsals in the studio and then a final dress rehearsal in the studio on the afternoon before the evening transmission, or recording.[28] This replicates how a cast might prepare for a play in the theatre, without, of course, the camera rehearsals, and puts an emphasis on growing

into a part, as the actors become more familiar with their roles, with the material and
with each other.

Most significantly, this way of working is geared towards preparing for a continuous
live performance of the play, rather than the discontinuous recording of film, and in this
respect it has more in common with theatre than it does with cinema. This continued
to be the case even after plays started to be recorded for subsequent transmission. Due
to the initial difficulties, and cost, of editing videotape, television drama was still being
recorded as a continuous 'live' performance until well into the 1960s. Speaking in 1987,
Billie Whitelaw reflected on the experience of acting in live television drama, compared
to theatre and film:

> I used to think that live television had the worst of theatre and the worst of film,
> because a film is very small and you had to bring the performances down, and
> the theatre you could expand, even though it was all in sequence, but I found
> actually, looking back, that it had the best of theatre and the best of film, because
> you could, in fact, do it all from A to B, and as an actor to me that's very
> important, because one scene to me grows out of another.[29]

While the continuous performance of live television drama may have made it similar to
the theatre, the presence of the television cameras brought an extra dimension which
required the actors to give a performance to the cameras, rather than to the theatre
audience beyond the invisible 'fourth wall'. With Sydney Newman's insistence that the
cameras move on set, and with sets being designed to be more three-dimensional, this
made for a complex organisation of the *mise en scène* in *Armchair Theatre* plays.

It also brought a new meaning to camera mobility in television drama. As Jason
Jacobs has shown, cameras were rarely completely static in early television drama,
but where they moved it was usually to follow the movement of an actor. In this
sense, camera mobility was subordinate to performance in early TV drama. One of
the innovations of *Armchair Theatre*, however, was to make camera movement an integral part of the performance. Jacobs describes this as 'exhibitionistic camera movement, a mobility on display as mobility, and not motivated by performance, but is the
performance'.[30]

This can perhaps best be illustrated through a detailed analysis of the first scene in
Lena, O My Lena. From the very first shot of the play the camera is mobile. The play begins
with a camera moving forward[31] towards the gates of the factory as the workers arrive
for work, two workers conveniently pushing the gate open as they enter, enabling the
camera to continue moving forward into the yard. Over this opening shot are superimposed the title of the play, the name of the writer and the leading members of the cast.
We also hear the melancholy musical motif, played on a single flute, which establishes a
slightly mysterious, wistful mood, reprised at the beginning and end of each act and
again at the end of the play. The camera continues moving forward, in one continuous
movement, into the factory yard, past the lorry (a real lorry, adding realism to the setting)
which is parked outside the warehouse. As the music ends the camera comes to a halt

Social realism and class difference in the *Armchair Theatre* play *Lena, O My Lena*

beside the lorry and the action of the play starts with the warehousemen loading boxes onto the lorry. This is still the first shot, a long take lasting one minute and eight seconds. It is an exhibitionistic camera movement, not motivated by performance, but where the camera is *part* of the performance.

As Glyn, the lorry driver, stops one of the warehousemen getting onto his lorry, we get the first cut to a slightly closer camera position, presumably so that we can see the faces of the characters more clearly as they speak. This is a much shorter shot, followed by a cut to a third camera position, looking back across the space of the factory yard towards the gates, framing Glyn and three warehousemen in the foreground. Shot four takes us back to where the first camera had ended up, beside the lorry, the camera clearly being positioned just outside of the field of view of the previous camera shot. Shot five takes us to the second camera position, as Glyn is called back by Ted, the foreman, to sign a requisition sheet. The camera then pans around with Glyn (a camera movement motivated by, and subordinate to, the movement of an actor) as he moves towards the driver's door, but instead of staying with Glyn the camera continues moving towards the factory gates. This seems like a superfluous camera movement, camera movement as performance. The camera does not *need* to continue moving forward here, as the women factory workers arrive for work, but by doing so it enables the first studio camera to move in behind it to frame Glyn in a medium close-up (MCU), which becomes the next shot as he says to the women: 'I'll see you later ladies,' as he prepares to drive away.

The next shot is a continuation of shot five, from the same position, as the women continue to enter the factory yard, with Lena and Peggy bringing up the rear. Tom can be seen in the background, outside the factory gates, where he is looking at the sign that we saw on entering: 'Help Wanted'. This shot continues, with the camera following Lena (camera movement subordinate to performance) as she parks the bicycle which she has wheeled into the yard, pretending to take no notice of Glyn despite Peggy referring to him, until she walks across in front of his lorry and he revs up, causing her to come to an annoyed halt. Meanwhile, two of the other cameras have taken up positions to give us MCUs of Lena and Glyn as they exchange looks, before Lena continues walking towards the factory door.

As she does so the camera tracks in slightly to give us a closer view of Glyn as he drives the lorry past the camera out of the factory gate. The camera pans round to follow the movement of the lorry, watching it disappear from view as it turns the corner (well almost – the very end of the lorry just remaining in view – presumably studio space did not allow the lorry to be driven any further!), leaving us looking at Tom, in long shot, standing outside the factory gates. As a reminder that this is 'live' drama (or at least a 'live' recording), the bottom of a camera plinth just sneaks into view at the end of the shot, outside the gates, as it gets into position to give us the next shot, which is a big close-up of Tom's face as he thinks about entering the factory.

The next shot (shot thirteen in this opening sequence) returns us to the same position as shot three, giving us a long shot from inside the warehouse, framing Ted, the foreman, sitting in the foreground, on the other side of the factory yard to Tom who is still standing outside the gates, an excellent example of the use of deep space in an *Armchair Theatre* production. It takes Tom thirteen seconds to walk across this space, the shot continuing as they begin to talk. The next eleven shots are alternating shots (not shot/reverse shot, because this is not possible in live TV drama without getting the cameras in view) of Ted in close-up and Tom in medium close-up, with two shots from the camera position inside the warehouse, as Tom asks Ted about casual work, the scene ending with Ted agreeing to take him on as casual labour.

This first scene lasts three minutes and fifty-two seconds with an ASL of 9.6 seconds, considerably faster than the ASL of seventeen seconds for *Nineteen Eighty-Four*, despite the fact that the long mobile camera shots in the opening sequence of *Lena* tend to increase the ASL. The complexity of some of these shots, with the camera moving to take up different positions in the same shot and with a lot of movement within shots, results in a fluid and busy *mise en scène* and a fairly brisk narrative tempo. The conversation between Tom and Ted, with its faster cutting, is probably largely responsible for the shorter ASL in the opening scene. Over the entire play the ASL works out at twelve and a half seconds.[32] As Jacobs notes, a later *Armchair Theatre* play, *Afternoon of a Nymph* (ABC, 30 September 1962), has a longer ASL of eighteen seconds, 'And yet the pace of the play is very rapid. The intense sensation of visual mobility is largely the result of continual – often very complex – camera movements.'[33]

Armchair Theatre, in these ground-breaking plays, introduced a new realism into television drama in the late 1950s and early 60s as a result of rising to the challenge of dealing with issues and concerns of interest to ordinary people. In order to express this new subject matter it was necessary to find a new form and this was achieved by opening up the set and liberating the actors, allowing them to move freely within an enlarged studio space. The viewer, also, was liberated by the mobility of the cameras and allowed to enter into the space of the drama in a manner comparable to the way in which films 'sutured' spectators into the diegesis through the rhetoric of continuity editing. The difference, with Armchair Theatre, was that the diegetic space into which viewers were transported was not so much a 'narrative space' but a 'performative space', as described by John Caughie:

> Crucially for notions of realism in television, what is created in plays like Lena, O
> My Lena is a performative space – a space for acting – rather than a narrative
> space – a space for action. The studio remains a studio, but the actors invest it
> with meaning. It is the actors who create a kind of reality: a reality which is
> watched rather than inhabited, a performed reality rather than the absorption
> into a narrative space driven by the logic of cause and effect and the fantasy of
> identification. Armchair Theatre's significance is not only that it introduced a new
> social space to television drama – the social space of class and region which it
> drew thematically from the New Wave in theatre and literature – but that it
> created a new televisual space in which the dramas of social relationship and
> social situations could be acted out.[34]

The importance of Armchair Theatre plays like Lena, O My Lena in the history of British television drama resides in the way in which they reinvigorated naturalism, as the dominant form of television drama, by introducing a new social realism into television, a realism which was not constricted by the confined sets of earlier studio drama, but which attempted to open the drama out, to embrace settings, issues and emotions that ordinary people were experiencing in the real world.

Technological development: video recording

Of the three Alun Owen plays transmitted in 1959–60 only After the Funeral and Lena, O My Lena survive, and this is because they were recorded on Ampex videotape. The possibility of recording on magnetic videotape, as opposed to telerecording on film, was officially unveiled in an episode of Panorama in April 1958, when the process was demonstrated by the presenter Richard Dimbleby, live on air.[35] Initially, the system was inferior to telerecording, but it was not long before video recording had replaced telerecording – a system only useful for recording a live transmission – by offering the possibility of pre-recording programmes for subsequent transmission. This had clear advantages in terms of greater flexibility in scheduling, as well as offering the possibility

of eradicating mistakes and problems which might occur during the course of a live production. However, the cost of videotape (£100 per tape) made it prohibitive to cut tape
for the purpose of editing, even when technicians had worked out how to do this successfully, and until the electronic editing of videotapes became possible programmes
continued to be recorded as continuous live productions.

This did not prevent sequences being inserted during the course of transmission, as
telecine sequences had been for a number of years, or the recording being halted to
allow for set or costume changes, as Howard Thomas, Managing Director of ABC
Television describes:

> key scenes or 'flashbacks' could be pre-recorded and fed into the final recording.
> Recording also provided breathing time between acts and also time for an artiste
> to change clothes or be 'aged' with make-up. Re-takes were also possible,
> although this was regarded as a last resort in television, because it could lead to
> the time-consuming system of numerous 'takes' which is common practice in the
> film industry.[36]

Consequently, programmes were still transmitted with 'mistakes' left in (such as a
camera lead or microphone boom coming into view) simply because it would prove too
expensive to retake the scene, which, in a continuous production, might mean redoing
the whole play. Once electronic editing became technologically possible retakes became
feasible, although the cost of doing so was still a financial deterrent.

It is significant, however, that the more experimental, and therefore more complicated, Armchair Theatre productions, like The Rose Affair (8 October 1961) and Afternoon of
a Nymph, were pre-recorded. To have transmitted these plays live would have put even
greater pressure on both actors and technicians. With the move to pre-recording, the
high-octane pressure of live television production that Ted Kotcheff and Philip Saville
refer to was eased somewhat.[37]

BBC Drama

BBC drama in this period was inevitably overshadowed by the appearance onto the
scene of ITV, with its new popular drama series, continuous serials and topical single
plays. Certainly, in terms of ratings, BBC television drama was eclipsed by ITV, with
very few of its dramas managing to compete with programmes like The Adventures of
Robin Hood, Emergency – Ward 10, Coronation Street, or even Armchair Theatre, for the mass
audience.

One of the few successes for the BBC, in this respect, was Dixon of Dock Green, which
began in July 1955 and was attracting audiences in the region of 10 million by the
middle of 1957, by which time both The Grove Family and Fabian of the Yard had come to
an end. Dixon of Dock Green was, in many respects, a hybrid of these two programmes,
as a police drama about ordinary people, written by Ted Willis who, as we have seen,
went on to write further plays about ordinary people and contemporary issues for ITV.
Willis had originally written the character of George Dixon for the Ealing Studios film,

Dixon of Dock Green: a comforting, reassuring image of the police

The Blue Lamp (1949), where he was shot and killed by Dirk Bogarde's juvenile delinquent. In 1955, seeking a police drama to replace *Fabian of the Yard*, Willis was persuaded by the BBC to resurrect Dixon for a television series, where he was again played by Jack Warner.

Dixon of Dock Green was transmitted live as a half-hour drama series, moving to forty-five minutes in 1960, and has gained a reputation as a 'cosy' representation of the police and their relationship with the public in the mid- to late 1950s. Certainly by the 1960s and, even more so, the 70s, *Dixon* had been superseded by more hard-hitting and up-to-date representations of both the police and the criminal underworld, but in 1955 *Dixon of Dock Green* was considered to be a realistic portrayal of the police, largely because it focused on an ordinary, working-class policeman on the beat, rather than the more idealised detectives of other crime dramas. This was a representation that viewers could relate to and accounts no doubt for them tuning in to the programme in huge numbers. Ideologically, *Dixon* offered a comforting, reassuring image of the police, and George Dixon's personal address to camera at the beginning and end of each episode was designed to reinforce this.

Writing in 1964, when PC George Dixon was about to become a sergeant in the series – a promotion which was resisted for nearly ten years, perhaps because of the risk of it damaging Dixon's popular appeal as an 'ordinary bobby' – Ted Willis admitted that the decision to focus on the ordinary and the everyday was a conscious one, right from the beginning, and that this may have resulted in *Dixon* becoming a more cosy programme:

We began with the idea that we would never put in violence for its own sake, that we would concentrate on the smaller everyday type of crime, and put the emphasis on people rather than problems.

We have often been assailed for this policy and accused of presenting a rather cosy picture of police work. Of course, there is some truth to this criticism, just as it is true that other programmes on the police emphasise the tougher and more violent aspects of crime prevention ... We set out to show a part of police work and I think we were right to stick to an approach which, within its self-imposed limits, is a true one.[38]

Like *Coronation Street*, *Dixon of Dock Green* proved to be an enduring success, lasting for twenty-one years. However, it is an indication of the ephemerality of popular television programmes that nearly 400 (out of 430) episodes of *Dixon* have been lost, and only five of the 1950s episodes exist today – all from the 1956 season. The BBC did not consider that series such as *Dixon* would be of any lasting cultural significance.[39]

While the BBC may have anticipated the arrival of ITV with popular drama series like *The Grove Family*, *Fabian of the Yard* and *Dixon of Dock Green*, by broadcasting innovative and less 'cosy' drama serials like *The Quatermass Experiment* and its sequels, *Quatermass II* (October–November 1955) and *Quatermass and the Pit* (December 1958–January 1959), as well as more expensive, prestigious plays like *Nineteen Eighty-Four*, the BBC was declaring itself to be at the forefront of original drama production in the mid-1950s, and was setting ITV a challenge to live up to. While ITV did schedule single plays from the beginning, it had neither the resources nor the ambition to mount expensive and innovative drama productions like *Nineteen Eighty-Four*, and its need to attract large audiences led it down the *Armchair Theatre* road towards social realism, rather than into murkier waters.

The dystopian worlds of Nigel Kneale and Rudolph Cartier were the remit of the BBC, which saw the potential, with drama serials such as *Quatermass*, to attract audiences which were perhaps not being catered for by the more populist programming on ITV. As Joy Leman has argued, in an essay on the *Quatermass* serials and the 1961 *A for Andromeda*, science fiction offered possibilities for progressive, even political statements to be made, and these drama serials became important initiatives in the BBC's attempt 'to capture and address a wider audience following the start of ITV'.[40]

Another important initiative was the dramatised documentary, or the 'story documentary' as it was generally referred to within the BBC at the time. This was not, in fact, a new initiative. A Dramatised Documentary Group had been formed at the BBC in 1946 in order to reconstruct, in the studio, stories, events and situations which were difficult or impossible to achieve in the real world because of the limitations of the cumbersome technology in use at the time:

week by week, dramatized documentaries on the courts, marriage, old age, delinquency, prostitution, industrial relations, and immigration were transmitted from the BBC studios. Robert Barr, who was responsible for the first programmes in this strand, started out by simply dramatizing 'How to' guides to the professions with titles like *I Want To Be An Actor* (1946) and *I Want To Be A Doctor*, but storylines soon became increasingly complex. The narrativization of public service – the placing of educational or informational content into entertaining form – was the origin of the so-called 'story documentary'.[41]

By the late 1950s the genre saw some interesting programmes being produced, especially through the creative partnership of writer Colin Morris and producer/director Gilchrist Calder, whose play *Who, Me?* (BBC, 15 October 1959) dramatised the interrogation of three robbery suspects by a Liverpool CID sergeant. The significance of drama documentaries like *Who, Me?* was the influence they had on drama series like *Z Cars*, a new, more realistic police series which began in 1962, and on other dramas, such as the influential *Cathy Come Home* (1966), which mixed the conventions of drama and documentary in an attempt to achieve a greater degree of realism. By the 1970s, the drama documentary form was proving to be increasingly controversial, but its lineage can be traced back to the studio dramas of the 1940s and 50s.

Of interest here is a 1958 BBC play called *Incident at Echo Six* (9 December 1958). Produced by Gilchrist Calder, *Incident at Echo Six* marked the television debut of writer Troy Kennedy Martin, who went on to develop *Z Cars*, with writer/director John McGrath, and who was a key figure in the history of British television drama, both for the many dramas he wrote over a period of nearly fifty years and also for his influential 1964 polemic against naturalism in TV drama (see Chapter 3). *Incident at Echo Six* also saw the acting debut of Tony Garnett, another key figure in British television drama who switched from acting to story editing and then to producing in the 1960s, in which capacity he was responsible for some of the most innovative and radical dramas produced on British television.

For *Incident at Echo Six*, Kennedy Martin drew on his National Service experience in Cyprus, basing the story around a small army unit in the Cypriot mountains. That the play had a documentary impulse was highlighted in the *Radio Times* a few days before it was transmitted:

> Documentary in its authenticity, it is a powerful play, written without sentiment and without any false glamour. For Martin has caught exactly the sense of inadequacy and the feeling of nerve-racking anxiety that must come to these young officers as they consider not only their own defensive actions against savage and unheralded attacks but the retaliatory measures that in a declared war would be straightforward and acceptable. For one false move, one ill-considered act of reprisal could become headline news throughout the world, and the subject of bitter argument for many months.[42]

At a time when Cyprus was a source of world news – 'an island upon which the eyes of the whole world are nervously focused, an island which has already become the critical centre of a political hurricane'[43] – *Incident at Echo Six* had a documentary significance, to which Kennedy Martin added drama: 'It was an attempt to recreate what was going on out there, so there are fights and they end up being marooned in a police building with barbed wire around, with people firing and that sort of stuff.'[44] The play was transmitted live from the BBC's Lime Grove studios, and was not recorded, but with Gilchrist Calder producing, and with the objective of recreating, or dramatising, the events of a long winter's night at a police station in the Cypriot mountains, *Incident at Echo Six* can be located in the tradition of drama documentary, seeking to achieve the kind of documentary realism that Colin Morris and Gilchrist Calder were also striving for in plays like *Who, Me?*[45]

The BBC continued with its *Sunday Night Theatre* plays in the late 1950s, but, although the series included further productions by Rudolph Cartier, such as *The White Falcon* (5 February 1956), *The Cold Light* (29 July 1956) and *A Midsummer Night's Dream* (29 November 1958), the *Sunday Night Theatre* series was overshadowed by *Armchair Theatre* during this period, especially after the arrival of Sydney Newman with his more contemporary, socially conscious agenda. Such was the dominance of ITV drama at the turn of the decade that 'Between the autumn of 1959 and the summer of 1960 *Armchair Theatre* plays were in the top ten programmes for thirty-two weeks out of thirty-seven.'[46] Against this, the BBC could not compete.

One of the last *Sunday Night Theatre* plays to be transmitted, in December 1959, led to a successful BBC drama series in the early 1960s. *Maigret and the Lost Life* (6 December 1959) was adapted from a 1954 novel by the Belgian novelist, Georges Simenon. Securing the worldwide rights to Simenon's novels, which revolved around the exploits of the pipe-smoking French detective Chief Inspector Maigret, the BBC embarked on one of its most ambitious drama series, with a total of fifty-one episodes of *Maigret* being screened from 1960–3 and with audiences exceeding 15 million by the third series. Though largely studio-based, the series made use of location filming (frequently in France) to open the drama out and the production values were of a standard that was designed to ensure overseas sales.

From 1957–9 the BBC transmitted a series of plays under the title of *Television World Theatre*. These were adaptations of stage classics such as *The Cherry Orchard* (5 January 1958), *The Government Inspector* (9 February 1958) and *Mother Courage and her Children* (30 June 1959), the latter produced by Rudolph Cartier. Of these plays, *The Government Inspector* attracted an audience of nearly 10 million, a phenomenal audience for a nineteenth-century Russian play. Yet the key to its popular success was the presence of Tony Hancock, whose comedy series *Hancock's Half Hour* had been showing on the BBC since July 1956. Hancock's presence in a 'serious' drama production, playing the eponymous government inspector, was an inspired piece of casting, highlighting the popular appeal of television personalities, even in classic drama, and *The Government Inspector* provided an object lesson in how a nineteenth-century Russian classic could be popularised for mass consumption.

In 1960, *Sunday Night Theatre* was replaced by *The Sunday Night Play*. The change of name suggested a shift away from the BBC's previous allegiance to the theatre and dependence on literary adaptations, for *The Sunday Night Play* was to provide a showcase for new plays written especially for television. Among the productions screened under this series title were plays by Alun Owen – *The Ruffians* (9 October 1960) – and John Osborne – *A Subject of Scandal and Concern* (6 November 1960) – established playwrights who had already made their name elsewhere. Outflanked by Sydney Newman's drama policy at ABC, the BBC was clearly intent on trying, in the early 1960s, to develop its own original play strand and by doing so regain some of the ground it had lost to ITV. With ABC and Granada pioneering new drama and commissioning new playwrights the BBC had been left behind, but at the beginning of the 1960s there were signs that the BBC was preparing to fight back.

First, new blood was being recruited. Following *Incident at Echo Six*, Troy Kennedy Martin was taken on as a scriptwriter/adapter and, over the next two to three years, he was joined by others, such as John McGrath and Roger Smith, who were to form the nucleus of a new young drama group at the BBC, a group that was interested in experimenting with the form of television drama. They were not the first to be interested in this. Early in 1956 a proposal had been made to set up a group to 'chew over the problem of experimental Television programmes'.[47] In December 1958 a 'Drama Experimental Unit' was officially formed, becoming known subsequently as the Langham Group, due to it being based in the BBC's Langham House. The unit's remit was to consider the potential for experimentation in television and in its short existence (it was wound up in 1960) there was much discussion about technology and the possibilities for an avant-garde or 'art' television, and a few productions, including *Torrents of Spring* (21 May 1959) and *Mario* (15 December 1959). While the achievements of the group may have been limited, it did have some influence. As Anthony Pelissier, the central figure in the group, wrote in a letter to Head of Drama Michael Barry in 1960:

> The Langham Group's real contribution has been, it seems to me, to question …
> the validity of present-day story and drama construction, the soundness of old-
> fashioned theatrical design, acting as 'projected' for proscenium presentation,
> cutting for cutting's sake … the possibility that there are [sic] more than one level
> of consciousness at which a programme may be appreciated and found
> stimulating and, finally, the intellectual 'West End' attitude of mind – a parochial
> and 'conditioned' point of view.[48]

One of those influenced by the work of the Langham Group was James MacTaggart, a producer/director working at BBC Scotland whose *Three Ring Circus* (BBC, 2 February 1961) led to him being invited to join the Drama Department in London.[49] MacTaggart became the catalyst around whom writers, directors and actors like Kennedy Martin, John McGrath, Roger Smith, Tony Garnett and others gathered and he was central to the new developments in drama at the BBC in the early 1960s. One of the first series with which MacTaggart was involved was *Storyboard* (BBC, July–September 1961), six experimental plays written and adapted by Kennedy Martin:

> They were all exercises in telling stories for television and they were all confined
> to the studio. They all used video, but we did manage to use cuts and narration

and try and objectify, also to cut things to music. I remember on one we used 'Fantasy for a Gentleman' [a Spanish guitar piece by Rodrigo] and we cut all the shots – and it was live too – to the actual music – so we got this cinematic effect.[50]

The play was *The Magic Barrel* (4 August 1961), adapted from a story by Bernard Malamud. Kennedy Martin referred to it again in his 1986 MacTaggart Lecture at the Edinburgh International Television Festival:

… how pleased we were when the bride-to-be slowly walked across the studio towards her lover, with the music sweeping around her, its modalities altering with every hesitation in her eyes. It was so on target that we might have been excused for thinking that Rodrigo himself had been commissioned to score it. Of course, it could be argued that in our looney way we were trying to anticipate film, trying to insert into our Heath Robinson pre-production process the kind of items which would have been at the tips of our fingers in any facility-house today. This is true, but we were also trying to work out specific ways of dealing with and exploiting the limitations of the medium.[51]

The significance of the *Storyboard* series was that it was the first step towards the development of a new form of television drama in the 1960s. It was also done live, making some of the innovations that MacTaggart and Kennedy Martin were trying to achieve a real challenge. On *The Middle Men* (11 August 1961), which was an original script by Kennedy Martin, six cameras were used on the half-hour drama, which had 130 scenes and a cast of twenty-one characters. Towards the end there was a rapid montage sequence comprising twenty shots, cutting between five different studio sets, with big close-ups on several characters and a clock, and no dialogue. This may have been one of the first attempts to incorporate a form of Eisensteinian montage into television drama, and to attempt to do so in a live studio drama illustrates the aesthetic ambition of the series.

   In contrast to the formal experimentation of Troy Kennedy Martin and James MacTaggart, 1961 also saw the television debut of a playwright who was to become one of the leading television dramatists of the 1960s. David Mercer's first TV play, *Where the Difference Begins* (BBC, 15 December 1961) was not particularly radical in form, being recorded almost entirely in a single studio set, but it introduced a new, socialist politics into television drama, paving the way for subsequent socialist playwrights, such as Jim Allen and Trevor Griffiths. Where Troy Kennedy Martin was pioneering experiments in dramatic form, David Mercer was the first of a new generation of TV playwrights who were, over the next two decades, to establish the BBC's reputation for the production of radical television drama.

The Pilkington Committee

In 1960, five years after the commencement of ITV, and ten years after the Beveridge Committee had met to consider the development of broadcasting in Britain at the turn of the previous decade, the Conservative government set up another broadcasting committee, this time under the chairmanship of industrialist Sir Harry Pilkington. The remit this time was to consider the impact of ITV on broadcasting and to make recommendations for a third television channel.

The agenda and, some would say, the conclusions of the committee were largely predetermined. As John Caughie notes in his discussion of the Pilkington Committee Report, which was made public in June 1962, the inquiry focused on the question of cultural values, and in the eyes of the members of the committee (which included Richard Hoggart, who had already written disparagingly of the commercialisation of culture in his book *The Uses of Literacy*) ITV was responsible for what would today be described as a 'dumbing down' of culture with its plethora of quizzes, game shows and other 'light entertainment' programmes.[52]

When the report was delivered, the committee was scathing in its criticisms of ITV, accusing it of trivialisation, of sacrificing quality and variety in its quest for ratings and revenue. These criticisms were mainly aimed at the 'Americanisation' of British TV through the abundance of bought-in programmes, as well as the home-produced quizzes and game shows, rather than being aimed at the network's domestically produced television drama. In fact, programmes such as *Armchair Theatre*, which the committee might have acknowledged as an exception to the general tenor of their argument, were largely ignored in the report. Consequently, virtually all ITV programming tended to be damned by implication in the sweeping criticisms made by the committee.

The ITV companies did not really help their own cause. Reaping in the profits by 1960, they tended to ignore Pilkington, wallowing in their financial success and taking advantage of the failure of the ITA to rein in their excesses. The BBC, on the other hand, chastened by the extent to which ITV had eroded its audience, had, under the leadership of a new Director General, Hugh Carleton Greene, actively courted Pilkington, presenting a renewed case for itself as the responsible curator of public service television and the organisation most fitted to running a third television channel. Furthermore, while there were some innovative ITV dramas produced while the Pilkington Committee was active, including some of the best *Armchair Theatre* productions under Sydney Newman, ITV could not match the range of original drama being produced by the BBC: drama documentaries such as *Who, Me?*, popular series such as *Maigret*, experimental dramas like the *Storyboard* series, David Mercer's early television work and *Z Cars*.

While not all of the Pilkington Committee's recommendations were met by the Conservative government, the BBC was rewarded for maintaining public service values in the face of commercial 'excess' by being given the third channel, enabling an expansion of public service broadcasting and the beginnings of a period of equanimity between the BBC and ITV in terms of audience share. In fact, such had been the success of Carleton Greene's leadership of the BBC since his appointment in 1960 that the BBC had won back an equal share of the audience by the time Pilkington reported and had already gained an edge on ITV in the recruitment of a new generation of writers, producers and directors who were to help forge the BBC's reputation for quality, originality and innovation in its programming over the next two decades.

3

British Television Drama Comes of Age, 1962–9

Where 1955, and the arrival of ITV, marked a new stage in the development of television in Britain, 1962 marks the end of that stage, with the publication of the Pilkington Committee Report and its fierce denunciation of ITV's 'low standards'. In July 1962 a government White Paper was published, approving a number of Pilkington's rec-ommendations, including the recommendation that the third channel be given to the BBC. As we have seen, a new era for the BBC was already being ushered in following the appointment of Hugh Carleton Greene as Director General in 1960 and the recruitment of a new generation of television practitioners, not least in the field of television drama. Some consequences of this new era were already in evidence in 1961, but it was in 1962, and the years that followed, that the real impact of the structural changes at the BBC began to be seen on the screen, with a host of new programmes making their first appearance, including *Compact* (1962–5), *Dr Finlay's Casebook* (1962–71), *Steptoe and Son* (1962–5), *That Was The Week That Was* (1962–3) and *Z Cars* (1962–78). While the late 1950s had belonged to ITV, in terms of audience share and new drama initiatives, in 1962 the pendulum swung back in the direction of the BBC.

Z *Cars* and series drama

If the dawning of the new era was to be given a precise date, it might be 2 January 1962, when the first episode of *Z Cars* was transmitted. If any one programme was to be sin-gled out as marking a break with 1950s conservatism and the beginnings of 1960s modernity, it would surely be *Z Cars*. Not that the series was without precedents. It followed a four-part series, focusing on Liverpool policemen, called *Jacks and Knaves* (BBC, November–December 1961), written by Colin Morris and produced by Gilchrist Calder, the team responsible for *Who, Me?*, the 1959 drama documentary about police interrog-ation methods. *Z Cars* was, in some ways, an amalgam of *Who, Me?* and *Jacks and Knaves*: a documentary drama set in Liverpool, populated with believable, realistic characters and enlivened by the kind of masculine humour that was characteristic of the series creator, Troy Kennedy Martin.

Kennedy Martin took the idea for Z *Cars* to Elwyn Jones, then responsible for the Drama Documentary section within BBC Drama, in early 1961. Jones secured the cooperation of the Lancashire County Police and sent Kennedy Martin off to research the series, to be joined later by director John McGrath and writer Allan Prior, who shared the writing of most of the early episodes with Kennedy Martin. Extensive research was done into policing in and around Liverpool, an area with which McGrath was familiar, having lived there, but which was unfamiliar to Kennedy Martin. The intention was to set the series in a new town area in the north of England as a way of tapping into social changes taking place in Britain in the early 1960s, and Newtown

A way of 'finding out about people's lives': the new realism of Z *Cars*

was, in fact, the name given by Kennedy Martin to one of the fictional areas where the drama was set.

The concern to get the details of modern policing methods right, and to accurately reproduce the local dialect, was part of the documentary attention to detail in the series, and the extent of the field research was comparable to that undertaken by Colin Morris for his drama documentaries in the 1950s. This documentary research, as well as the decision to show violence as a routine fact of life, contributed to Z *Cars*' reputation for being more realistic than other police dramas, especially *Dixon of Dock Green*, which had settled down to become one of the most popular programmes on the BBC by the early 1960s, but at the cost of becoming cosy and inoffensive.

Not that the intention of Kennedy Martin and McGrath was to focus exclusively on the police. As McGrath said, they wanted

> to use a Highway Patrol format, but to use the cops as a key or way of getting into a whole society … And it was very cleverly worked out … the two kinds of communities these cops were going to work in. The first was called Newtown, which was roughly based on Kirkby. The other was Seaport, which was based on the sort of Crosby-Waterloo water front. The series was going to be a kind of documentary about people's lives in these areas, and the cops were incidental – they were the means of finding out about people's lives.[1]

Transmitted live, the early episodes used an unusually large number of filmed inserts in order to give the drama a presence in the real world, thus increasing its documentary veracity. In this respect *Z Cars* marked a real departure from previous series, like *Dixon*, and helped pave the way for the breakthrough into filmed drama that Tony Garnett and Ken Loach were to achieve on *The Wednesday Play* in the mid-1960s.[2] The narrative pace of some of the early episodes was very fast, and Kennedy Martin, in particular, special-ised in interweaving a number of different stories in each episode, thereby increasing the complexity of the narrative and maximising audience interest and involvement with a range of different characters and stories. To a large extent episodes were character-driven, rather than plot-driven, all part of the objective of 'finding out about people's lives'.

In an article on the series published in the summer of 1962, Peter Lewis highlighted the significance of *Z Cars*, for its working methods, realism and technical innovation:

> It is done live. Only the scenes showing open streets are filmed. The Z car, suitably soiled, stands on wooden rollers for easy manoeuvring in front of back projection screens that produce the 60 mph illusions. The studio is littered with 14 or 15 different sets each week. Five cameras travel the floor ceaselessly. There are something like 250 changes of shot in each episode – an average of five a minute. The actor's worst problem is to remember which scene he is in. All this is rehearsed in two days of studio time. Each week they shoot the equivalent of a fast-moving feature film in fifty minutes flat with no retakes. In the control room every Tuesday night they do what might take a film studio cutting room at least a week. That is a measure of the technical advance that *Z Cars* represents.[3]

This suggests an ASL of about twelve seconds, but the number of scene changes, as a consequence of the interweaving of different stories, the amount of action involved within scenes and the fast talking of the many characters involved, all contrive to give the impression of a *Z Cars* episode being action-packed and fast moving. This would have been especially evident when compared to an episode of *Dixon* or *Maigret* at the time.

It was not just in form that *Z Cars* was ground-breaking, however. The series pulled no punches as far as a more realistic representation of the police was concerned, and it was this which signalled its immediate departure from the reassuring *Dixon*. Peter Lewis quotes the reaction of the Chairman of the Police Federation to the first episode:

> The programme showed the police in a pretty poor light – one officer a wife-beater, another gambling madly on horses. We know policemen are human but this was ridiculous. At a time when we are trying to raise the status of the police in the public eye this nonsense could do harm.[4]

Following the screening of the first episode, the Chief Constable of Lancashire paid a visit to Stuart Hood, the Controller of BBC Television, demanding that the series be taken off, but all that was taken off was the credit thanking the Lancashire County Police for their cooperation. The era in which the BBC was to gain a reputation for controversial, anti-establishment, socially conscious drama could thus be said to have begun on 2 January 1962, with that first episode of Z Cars.

Originally conceived as a thirteen-part series, Z Cars proved an immediate success, with audiences increasing from 9 million to 14 million in eight weeks. Consequently, the series was extended to thirty-one episodes, and a second series commissioned for the autumn of 1962. The extension and continuation of the series was a commercial decision, an acknowledgment of its success and of the importance of popular series like Z Cars in the ratings war. But commercial success often has an artistic price and the price for Z Cars was, as Peter Lewis described it, 'to blur the sharp outlines with which the series began. In spite of the efforts of the actors, the police have become less inter-esting as people, not more, as the series has worn on.'[5]

Troy Kennedy Martin and John McGrath, recognising the inevitability of the series becoming more formulaic as it became more successful, decided to leave. That Z Cars continued to be an interesting and influential police series for some time was largely due to the quality of its scripts, with Allan Prior and John Hopkins, in particular, pro-ducing some excellent material for the series, and to the steady hand of producer David Rose. As John McGrath later reflected: 'the series was very lucky, in that it got John Hopkins, who actually managed to write about policemen in a way that was interesting – but we didn't want to write about policemen'.[6]

This is the perennial problem with drama series. As we have already seen with Dixon of Dock Green and Coronation Street, dramas become successful when audiences become familiar with the characters, but then it becomes difficult to change the char-acters, because of the risk of losing the audience. Robert Barr, who was one of the executive producers on Z Cars and wrote two of the early episodes, summed up the dilemma: 'As soon as a series becomes successful you're on the tail of a comet. You can't start destroying the characters you have created – because now they belong to the public.'[7]

Peter Lewis referred to this dilemma as 'Sharples' Disease' in his 1962 article on Z Cars, having seen the same thing happen with Coronation Street, which had been running for over a year when he wrote the following:

> People like what they know, they like their expectations to be fulfilled, they get cross and feel let down if characters don't behave predictably; life doesn't perform to a formula, and the more you insist on a formula in fiction, the less you reflect life.[8]

It is a dilemma which recurs again and again in long-running drama series: how to keep a series fresh and innovative and avoid becoming stale and formulaic. As we shall see, the dilemma was still preoccupying drama producers over thirty years later.

Sydney Newman and the reorganisation of BBC Drama

The shift towards series drama in 1962, not just with Z Cars, but also with Compact and Dr Finlay's Casebook, was a commercial decision on behalf of the BBC, an acknowledgment of the fact that audiences can be built and maintained through series in a way that is not possible with single plays. This policy decision was a consequence of the new regime at the BBC under Carleton Greene and it led to the resignation of Michael Barry, who had been Head of Drama since 1952 and whose ideas about drama had been formed in the late 1940s, when he was a producer. His resignation was an acknowledgment that times were changing in television at the beginning of the 1960s and that the direction in which TV drama was heading was not where Barry wanted to go.

Following the departure of Barry, Norman Rutherford became Acting Head of Drama and Elwyn Jones Assistant Head of Drama, while a replacement for Barry was sought. The man that Carleton Greene wanted was Sydney Newman, who had proved with *Armchair Theatre* his ability to deliver both quality drama and audiences. Carleton Greene's priority on his appointment was to win back audiences from ITV, while still fulfilling the BBC's public service remit. What better way to do this, in drama, than by poaching the very man who had contributed to ITV's success at the end of the 1950s? Not only would it be a blow to ITV, it would install a more commercially minded figure at the helm of BBC Drama. It took some while for the BBC to complete the coup. Newman still had a year to run on his contract at ABC and it was not until January 1963 that he officially became Head of Drama at the BBC.

Newman's appointment was met with suspicion and apprehension by some of those working in BBC Drama at the time, as John Cook, who interviewed Newman in 1990, points out:

> For many in British television of the period, Newman's arrival was nothing short of a political earthquake. While ITV had been regularly luring BBC staff over to 'the other side' since the mid 1950s with the promise of greater riches, Newman's defection was the BBC's first major counter-strike in the new ratings war; a decisive signal it was now going head to head with ITV, challenging it on its own populist ground. Many could barely conceal their own dismay that the Corporation had appointed an 'outsider' – a product of the commercial system and a North American to boot – in order to run its TV drama output.[9]

The suspicion of Newman was not shared by everyone, however, and even those who had been apprehensive about his arrival could admire the professional way in which Newman set about reorganising BBC Drama, dividing what had become an unwieldy department into separate sections for the production of series, serials and plays and introducing the story editor system that had proved so successful on *Armchair Theatre*. As Philip Purser wrote in the autumn of 1962, anticipating Newman's appointment:

> All in all, it looks as if BBC TV is acquiring someone very much in the image it has lately been fashioning for itself: professional, good-humoured, competitive, self-reliant, in touch with the times and at heart on the side of the System.[10]

Doctor Who and 1960s science fiction

One of Newman's early programming initiatives at the BBC was the development of *Doctor Who* as a new science fiction series. Newman already had some experience of the genre, having produced *Pathfinders* as a science fiction series for children at ABC Television in 1960–1, which was itself preceded by a six-part children's series, *Target Luna*, in 1960. Then, in June 1962, John Wyndham's *Dumb Martian* was produced for *Armchair Theatre*, essentially serving as a preview for a thirteen-part science fiction anthology series on ABC called *Out of This World*. Irene Shubik, who had been working as a story editor on *Armchair Theatre*, had a particular interest in science fiction and she had persuaded Newman to let her put together the series. Apart from *Quatermass*, and the adaptation of *Nineteen Eighty-Four*, science fiction was not generally taken seriously on television, being seen primarily as a children's genre, but with a growing interest in technology and space travel in the 1960s *Out of This World* proved to be both a popular and critical success, and Shubik had little trouble finding good writers for the series:

> Much to my delight, after I had found the stories for the ABC series and started looking for adapters, I discovered that many first-rate writers like Clive Exton (and, as I discovered too late, David Mercer) were science fiction aficionados. It was, therefore, not difficult to find good adapters for the stories.[11]

Leon Griffiths and Terry Nation also wrote for the series, the latter contributing an original story, 'Botany Bay', and both Griffiths and Nation were subsequently to contribute, along with writers of the calibre of Troy Kennedy Martin, to another science fiction series that Shubik produced for BBC Two, *Out of the Unknown* (1965–71). Shubik had followed Newman to the BBC in November 1963, as part of the expansion in staff needed to make programmes for the third channel, BBC Two, which was launched on 20 April 1964. She worked as story editor on one of the first drama series produced for the new channel, *Story Parade* (BBC Two, April 1964–May 1965), following which she went on to produce the first two seasons of *Out of the Unknown*, from October 1965–January 1967, before becoming a producer on *The Wednesday Play* and *Play for Today*. *Out of the Unknown* went off the air for two years after her departure, but returned in January 1969, in colour, with Alan Bromley as producer.

It was *Doctor Who*, however, that really put 1960s TV science fiction on the map. Looking for a programme to fill the early evening slot on the BBC, Sydney Newman drafted the idea for *Doctor Who* in a two-page memo sent to Donald Wilson, Head of Drama Series in Newman's new tripartite Drama Department. As John Cook explains:

> The problem was that between 5.15 pm on Saturday evenings when the popular sports programme *Grandstand* ended and 5.45 pm when the equally popular teenage music show, *Juke Box Jury* began, there was a huge ratings dip as BBC 1 screened children's serial drama which consisted of adaptations of classic novels. Newman's brief from the programme controllers was to come up with a 'sexier' serial idea for a younger audience which would help build ratings as well as keep

The beginnings of a cult: William Hartnell as the original Doctor in *Doctor Who*

viewers tuned for *Juke Box Jury*. It was in this way that Newman, after considering various ideas, reached for science fiction as one 'catch-all' genre which might appeal to children and also bridge the gap between sports fans and the teenage pop music audience.[12]

Doctor Who, therefore, was never designed to be just a children's programme but was intended to cater for a broad audience. While its place in the schedules as a ratings winner was important, the programme was also to fulfil the BBC's public service remit, providing education, information and entertainment in one programme and thus confounding the concerns of some people at the BBC about Sydney Newman's commercial instincts. In fact, *Doctor Who* was to prove an exemplary form of popular drama, striving to educate its audience about historical events, about technology and about space travel, at the same time as entertaining them with its fantastic stories. So intent was Newman that *Doctor Who* should be seen as educational rather than escapist that he banned storylines featuring 'bug-eyed monsters', although it was not long before the monsters started making an appearance.

The first episode, 'An Unearthly Child', transmitted on 23 November 1963, was deliberately earthbound and lacking in the iconography of science fiction. Even the spacecraft was an ordinary police telephone box, which magically turned out to be larger inside than it appeared from the outside. The transformation required no elaborate special effects and the settings of a London scrapyard and a local school in the first episode were resolutely down to earth. While the first Doctor, played by William Hartnell, was an irascible, unconventional figure, his grand-daughter and her two teachers, who feature in the first story, were all seemingly ordinary characters, although the grand-daughter's extraordinary knowledge is the enigma which causes her teachers to follow her to her home, which turns out to be the police box – otherwise known as the TARDIS (Time And Relative Dimensions In Space). Gaining access to the TARDIS, the teachers are then whisked away to another dimension with the Doctor and his grand-daughter, initiating the first of countless adventures which were to entertain generations of children and adults alike over the next twenty-six years.

The first four-part story was a historical one, taking the Doctor and his companions back in time to the Stone Age, and these stories were seen as a way of educating the audience about different historical periods and events. Verity Lambert, the first producer on *Doctor Who*, and another of Sydney Newman's protégés who had worked as a production assistant on *Armchair Theatre*, explained how Newman wanted not only to modernise children's television drama with *Doctor Who*, but also to combine the educational and the informational in a manner that was not 'teacherly' or patronising:

> He was trying to find something which took into account the new things that fascinated kids, like space and other planets, and certainly he felt that he wanted a programme which, while not necessarily educational as such, was one which children could look at and learn something from. In the futuristic stories they could learn something about science and in the past stories they could learn something about history in an entertainment format.[13]

But it was the futuristic stories that were to prove more popular than the historical ones. The second story, written by Terry Nation, introduced the 'Daleks', who were to become the most famous of all of the Doctors' adversaries, becoming a popular cultural phenomenon over the next three decades. For this second story the viewing figures jumped from 6 million to 9 million and the success of the series was assured.

Doctor Who proved to be a highly successful attempt by Sydney Newman to break with the rather conservative tradition of previous BBC children's television. Its broad appeal was the result of a number of factors, not least of which was the casting of an, often 'childish', adult as the central character, with a teenage assistant as an additional identification figure for the younger audience. The emphasis on technology and space travel undoubtedly gave the series contemporary relevance. It was in 1963 that Harold Wilson, who was to lead the Labour Party to victory in the 1964 General Election, after thirteen years of Conservative government, delivered the speech in which he equated 1960s modernity with the 'white heat of technology', a modernity which *Doctor Who* had already anticipated.

With Patrick Troughton replacing William Hartnell as the Doctor in 1966, when Hartnell became ill, through the clever ruse of having the Doctor 'regenerate' (a plot device which has helped to ensure the longevity of the series), the 1960s Doctors appeared as anti-establishment figures, outsiders who had an 'alternative' appeal as the mid-1960s pop culture transformed into the late 1960s counter-culture. When Jon Pertwee replaced Troughton in 1970, the year in which the series went from black and white to colour, this changed somewhat, Pertwee's Doctor often working with establishment forces against external threats, and *Doctor Who* seemed to lose some of its alternative edge, although this did not diminish its popular appeal and it went on to become the longest-running science fiction programme on British television.

Towards a new drama

> Television drama at the moment is going nowhere fast. Informed management believe it is so bad it can't get worse. They are wrong. It can and will destroy itself

unless a breakthrough in form is made, substantiated and phased into the general run of drama programmes.[14]

So began an article by Troy Kennedy Martin, subtitled the 'First Statement of a New Drama for Television', which opened a hornet's nest in TV drama circles in March 1964, when it was published in the pages of *Encore*, the theatre magazine. Entitled 'Nats Go Home', the article was an attack on naturalism in television drama, especially the theatrical naturalism which had been the dominant form in TV drama since its beginnings. There were good reasons why television drama had leant so heavily on the form: the need to draw from the theatre for its source material; the cultural prestige which theatre could lend to television in its early days; the limitations of live TV drama, confined to the studio, where there was a tendency to privilege the spoken word, with the consequent emphasis upon 'talking heads' rather than narrative action; the dependence on the literary tradition, in theatre and the novel; and the work of authors who would lend respectability and credibility to drama on the new 'ephemeral' medium of television.

While Sydney Newman's *Armchair Theatre* brought new writers into television, the innovations which *Armchair Theatre* introduced served largely to revitalise naturalism, rather than replace it. Even *Z Cars*, which Kennedy Martin devised, and which reinvigorated the police series in 1962, was still working within the realms of naturalism, although Kennedy Martin and McGrath tried to shake the form up with a faster narrative pace and more location filming. Reflecting on the series in 1986, Kennedy Martin suggested that he was aware of the limitations of *Z Cars* and, rather than seeing the series as a new departure, he saw it as the last gasp of a dying form:

> I thought it was absolutely in line with naturalism. So one of the reasons why I didn't go overboard about *Z Cars* ... was that I felt all I was doing was contributing to what I thought then was the death-throes of naturalism.[15]

After resigning from *Z Cars* in the summer of 1962, Kennedy Martin started developing ideas and writing scripts for a new kind of non-naturalistic drama, and the 'Nats Go Home' article was an attempt to theorise the problem, as he saw it, of contemporary television drama, and to suggest a way out of the naturalist impasse. The essential problems of naturalistic drama were identified as (i) an overdependence on dialogue (a legacy of TV drama's theatrical origins), with the consequence that 'the director is forced into photographing faces talking and faces reacting', and (ii) the unfolding of the drama in natural time, where 'studio-time equals drama-time equals Greenwich Mean Time'.[16] Given these limitations, the main concern of the New Drama was, 'to free the camera from photographing dialogue, to free the structure from natural time and to exploit the total and absolute objectivity of the television camera'.[17]

Kennedy Martin proceeded to illustrate this with reference to an extract from what was, at the time, an unrealised script, written by himself and John McGrath, which was to be televised by the BBC later that year. The six-part series, *Diary of a Young Man* (BBC One,

Victor Henry, Nerys Hughes and Richard Moore in the ground-breaking *Diary of a Young Man*

August–September 1964), became a practical illustration of the New Drama, a further development of experiments begun with the *Storyboard* series in 1961, and with two subsequent 'experimental' drama series: *Studio 4* (BBC, January–September 1962) and *Teletale* (BBC, November 1963–March 1964). According to Kennedy Martin, *Studio 4* was 'a failure. Its aims were confused and made more so by the introduction of "nat" plays within the format.' Whereas *Teletale* was more successful in trying to develop a new narrative drama: 'one could see the faint emergence of a form, despite the fact that it was handled by novice directors in pocket-sized provincial studios'.[18]

Diary of a Young Man, of which only three episodes have survived, took the experiments of the previous three series much further, making extensive use of narration, as one means of freeing the camera from photographing dialogue, and of still images and montage sequences, as a way of freeing the structure from natural time. The montage sequences were also designed to involve the viewer in the drama, in a way that the more pedantic naturalist drama could not: 'Real montage demands total viewer interest and if it is good enough obtains total involvement of an emotional kind.'[19] In the first episode of *Diary of a Young Man*, 'Survival or They Came to a City', directed by Ken Loach, the degree of experiment and innovation is immediately evident in the juxtaposition of location sequences, shot on film and usually accompanied by a voiceover, with studio scenes, recorded on video, and the montage sequences of still images, accompanied by music and/or voiceover. The resulting collage of forms gives the drama an almost Brechtian feel, far removed from naturalism, and the goal of achieving a new kind of narrative storytelling through the juxtaposition of different forms is accomplished with tremendous vitality, in marked contrast to the vast majority of television drama at the time.

'Nats Go Home' provoked a considerable response among writers, directors and producers. The next issue of *Encore* devoted several pages to responses from Sydney Newman, Michael Barry, Dennis Potter, Tony Garnett and others, and there was further discussion when the article was reprinted in an issue of *Screenwriter* in spring 1964. It was not difficult to see why writers were inflamed by the article, for the New Drama that Kennedy Martin was advocating seemed to give more responsibility to the director, with its emphasis on a new form of 'visual storytelling', and was clearly influenced by modernist film theory: on the one hand Eisensteinian montage and on the other the more elliptical editing style of French New Wave cinema. This seemed to relegate the writer in television drama to a more subservient role, yet as *Diary of a Young Man* showed, it was possible for Troy Kennedy Martin and John McGrath to work creatively together with the two directors on the series, Ken Loach and Peter Duguid, and with producer James MacTaggart, in a way that was quite new in television drama production. Certainly the drama that resulted from the collaboration was a milestone in the development of a non-naturalistic television drama and, while it did not supplant naturalism, both 'Nats Go Home' and *Diary of a Young Man* paved the way for important new developments in television drama in the next two years, developments with which James MacTaggart, Tony Garnett, Ken Loach and Dennis Potter would be centrally involved.

The Wednesday Play

In the history of television drama, the BBC's *Wednesday Play* (1964–70) has taken on an iconic status. It is often seen as synonymous with a 'golden age' in British television drama, an age when playwrights had the freedom to experiment and regularly produced innovative drama, when there were not the commercial pressures to capture and retain audiences that were later to become such important factors in television, and when it was possible to engage with the pressing social issues of the day and provoke argument and discussion, even social change, through the medium of the single play. 'Golden ages' are always partly illusory, seen through the nostalgic rose-tinted spectacles of hindsight. Yet they are often not without some degree of truth – otherwise the myth of a 'golden age' would not arise in the first place. As Irene Shubik remarked at a conference on television drama in 1998, the 1960s were a 'golden age' because of the autonomy given to writers, directors and producers, an autonomy which was eroded as television became increasingly 'cost-conscious' during the 1970s.[20]

Developing his reorganisation of drama at the BBC, Sydney Newman did not stop at dividing the department into series, serials and plays; he wanted to apply the thinking behind series and serials – that audiences would keep coming back to something they liked and recognised – to the single play, which he felt did not have the identity on the BBC that *Armchair Theatre* had achieved on the commercial network. As Irene Shubik explains:

... although good plays were going out, audiences did not know what to expect; modern and classical were mixed and there was little evidence of a specific continuing taste of style behind the material. Also there was little sense of occasion attached to these transmissions.

Sydney's idea was to divide the type of plays into groups. 'Festival', under Peter Luke, who went with him to the BBC as a producer, was to do the more classical pieces, ancient and modern: plays by Noel Coward, Cocteau, James Joyce, Ionesco etc. were included in the first 1963–64 season. 'First Night', produced by John Elliot, was to concentrate on the new writers and was to go out on Sunday night in opposition to 'Armchair Theatre'. The first season included plays by Terence Frisby (later best known for *There's A Girl In My Soup*), Arnold Wesker and Alun Owen. Specific producers and editors would give the different slots their distinct character.[21]

Both *Festival* and *First Night* ran for only one season, from the autumn of 1963 to the summer of 1964. When BBC Two started, in April 1964, two single-play anthology series were introduced on the new channel: *Story Parade*, which ran until May 1965, and *Theatre 625* (named after the higher definition 625 line transmission system adopted for BBC Two), which ran from May 1964–August 1968.

Meanwhile, on BBC One, *The Wednesday Play* began in October 1964 with 'some orphaned productions left over from Peter Luke's "Festival"',[22] which included *In Camera*, an adaptation of the Jean-Paul Sartre play, directed by Philip Saville, and featuring Harold Pinter, Jane Arden and Catherine Woodville, recorded in a claustrophobic, 'modernist' studio set, with some telecine sequences inserted into what is otherwise an interior, dialogue-led, psychological drama. These first six plays, transmitted in the last four months of 1964, while going out under the banner of *The Wednesday Play*, are quite clearly leftovers from *Festival*. Newman wanted *The Wednesday Play* to be more in the *First Night* mould, commissioning new writers to produce contemporary plays, along the lines of the best of *Armchair Theatre*. He appointed James MacTaggart, fresh from producing the experimental *Teletale* series, to produce the first season, which opened with *Tap on the Shoulder* (BBC One, 6 January 1965), an original play by James O'Connor, directed by Ken Loach.

It was under the guidance of MacTaggart that *The Wednesday Play*, in its first two seasons, from January–December 1965, changed the face of television drama in Britain, introducing contemporary, social-issue drama, and initiating a technological breakthrough by moving over to film and location shooting with *Up the Junction* (BBC One, 3 November 1965), the play which took television drama out of the studio and into the real world. Central to the breakthrough made at this time was story editor Roger Smith who, like John McGrath, was an Oxford graduate who went to work at the BBC as a scriptwriter/adapter at the beginning of the 1960s, an early recruit to the group of progressive dramatists which formed around James MacTaggart. Along with MacTaggart, Smith guided the early development of *The Wednesday Play*, bringing in Tony Garnett and Ken Trodd as assistant story editors (Garnett deciding to forsake the acting career which he had been pursuing for five years and move behind the scenes) and commissioning the first plays from Dennis Potter and other new writers. This group formed the nucleus of a loose collection of people who pioneered a new form of television drama for *The Wednesday Play*, building on the foundations laid by Troy Kennedy Martin and John McGrath in the early 1960s, which set the standard for innovative and challenging television drama for the next two decades. Ken Trodd, who went on to produce some of the most radical plays over the next thirty years, describes the freedom they were given to experiment and the creative atmosphere which prevailed when *The Wednesday Play* first started:

> The quantity of plays we were making was amazing, and this meant that you could risk some failures – try out new talent, give it a chance. Tony Garnett used to say that, with a new writer, you should regard the first commission as an investment in the second – you weren't very likely to find the first one winning through. And the commissioning ratio was prodigally generous. You could commission ten and make one.[23]

Twenty-seven writers contributed thirty-three new plays, all but one written especially for television, to *The Wednesday Play* from January–December 1965.[24] Dennis Potter was responsible for four of them, a phenomenal output in one year, illustrating the opportunity the series offered to enterprising new writers. At the beginning of 1966 Peter Luke took over from James MacTaggart for a season and thereafter a number of different producers were given an opportunity to make their mark, with Lionel Harris producing most of the third season, from October 1966–May 1967, and Graeme MacDonald and Irene Shubik being two of the main producers from October 1967–May 1970, when the series came to an end, to be replaced, in October 1970, by *Play for Today*.

It was in the third season that Tony Garnett moved over from script editing to producing, with the ground-breaking *Cathy Come Home* (BBC One, 16 November 1966), perhaps the most famous *Wednesday Play* of all because of the public response it elicited, both from viewers and the authorities, as a result of the play's success in highlighting one of the social problems of the day: homelessness and its attendant side-effect of family breakdown. The impact of *Cathy Come Home* was reinforced by the adoption of a drama documentary approach and the filming of 90 per cent of the drama on location, in real streets and houses, with ordinary people appearing in the drama alongside professional actors. This gave the play, which no longer looked like a 'play' in the traditional sense, an authenticity and a veracity which heightened its emotional effect, undoubtedly contributing to its social impact. As Madeleine Macmurraugh-Kavanagh has argued, this was 'drama' turned into 'news', a deliberate strategy on behalf of Tony Garnett, director Ken Loach and writer Jeremy Sandford to try to make an intervention that would influence social policy.[25]

While *Cathy Come Home* and the earlier *Up the Junction* (see below) have become almost synonymous with *The Wednesday Play*, as a radical and progressive showcase for the single play on British television, these interventionist drama documentaries represented only a tiny part of *The Wednesday Play*'s total output, as Madeleine Macmurraugh-Kavanagh, who has conducted a research project on *The Wednesday Play* for the University of Reading, illustrates:

> The use of radical new representational techniques such as 'drama-doc' pioneered by Loach and Garnett may be what *The Wednesday Play* is best remembered for, but it by no means expresses the full range of the strand's output. Filmed comedies such as Peter Nichols's *The Gorge* (4 September 1968) jostled with traditional thrillers such as Marc Brandel's *Ashes To Ashes* (10 February 1965); literate, crafted scripts such as John Mortimer's *Infidelity Took Place* (8 May 1968) nestled alongside plays such as Paul Ableman's *Barlowe Of The Car Park* (23 May 1966) which was generally held to be a disaster in all its aspects; science fiction was placed beside broad farce; a three-part adaptation of Evelyn Waugh's *Sword Of Honour* trilogy found itself transmitted in the same season as a 'domestic' drama about the Vatican's Encyclical forbidding the use of birth control to Catholics (Julia Jones's *A Bit Of A Crucifixion, Father*; 30 October 1968). Diversity was the key and was itself an element of *The Wednesday Play*'s innovatory reformulation of television drama in the field of the single play.[26]

The role of producers and story editors in commissioning scripts from writers was crucial in determining the ideological and aesthetic nature of any particular *Wednesday Play*. Indeed, the question of 'authorship' on *The Wednesday Play*, and other single-play anthologies, would make an interesting study, with the producer, story editor and director all helping to shape and influence the work of a writer. The role of the producer on *The Wednesday Play* was certainly decisive in determining which plays appeared on screen, through the commissioning process, and the composition of a *Wednesday Play* season varied considerably according to the producer in charge:

> Where Peter Luke with his theatrical background and traditional tastes orientated the series towards adaptations from the classical repertoire, James MacTaggart with his political awareness and clear ideological agenda steered the strand towards contemporary, interventionist pieces. Tony Garnett followed in his footsteps, where Lionel Harris can be more closely aligned with Luke's ethos. As a result, to regard The Wednesday Play as a unified body of work, complete with a single, readily-definable identity, is to make a serious error.[27]

However, it is mainly for the 'interventionist' dramas, those produced by James MacTaggart and Tony Garnett, that *The Wednesday Play* is remembered. Of these, the one that really placed *The Wednesday Play* on the socio-cultural map, establishing its reputation for controversy, while at the same time wrenching it free from the confines of the television studio, was *Up the Junction*.

Up the Junction (1965)

Based on the novel by Nell Dunn, *Up the Junction* was a seminal 1960s television drama, capturing the zeitgeist of the mid-1960s at a moment when Britain was experiencing profound social and cultural change, with a new kind of popular music filling the airwaves, new fashions in the shops and on the streets, and a more liberal attitude towards sexual relationships, all bound up with an optimism for the future that followed in the wake of a Labour government being returned to power in the 1964 General Election, after thirteen years of Conservative rule. As a television play *Up the Junction* bore as much, or as little, resemblance to the television plays that had preceded it as *Lena, O My Lena* did to *Nineteen Eighty-Four*, such were the advances that TV drama was making during this period in form, style and content. In fact, the difference in style between *Up the Junction* and *Lena* was even more marked than that between *Lena* and *Nineteen Eighty-Four*, because with *Up the Junction* the single play on British television breached the walls of the television studio, venturing out into the real world and establishing a precedent which was to change the nature of TV drama and the public's attitude to it.

In her novel, Nell Dunn had written an impressionistic account of life in and around Clapham Junction, at that time a mainly working-class area in south London, focusing in particular upon the lives of young working-class women. Script editor Tony Garnett and director Ken Loach then took this source material and used it as the basis for a drama that broke most of the unwritten rules of what a television play should be. Ken Loach describes the intentions behind the drama:

> ... it was meant as a kaleidoscope of fragmented images. The idea of a story that is complete and resolved and too well worked never feels right to me because it doesn't have any loose ends. It's just phony; life is full of loose ends. And when you put together incidents and anecdotes and images from people's lives, they do add up to a set of experiences that indicate the way they live and why they live that way, and that raises all sorts of questions. So that fragmentation was deliberate ...
>
> I had read Nell Dunn's book *Up the Junction*. It was made up of little vignettes, like newspaper pieces or descriptions, and there are these three young women characters who run through them. The script was pieced together more or less directly from the book, which is very visual and quite cinematic.[28]

This meant, however, that the script bore very little resemblance to what was normally expected of a script for a television play, and this caused some consternation in the Drama Department at the BBC. Interviewed in February 2000, thirty-five years after the event, Tony Garnett recalled the background to the drama and the battle he had with producer James MacTaggart, who was not happy with the kind of project that Loach and Garnett were developing:

TG: *Up the Junction* arose because Jeremy Sandford, who wrote *Cathy Come Home*, and Nell Dunn, who wrote *Up the Junction*, were married at the time and living in south London, near Clapham Junction, and *Up the Junction* got made first and it got done when Jim MacTaggart, who was the producer of *The Wednesday Play*, was on holiday, and so when the cat was away we decided to play!

LC: Do you think he might not have approved then?

TG: No, he wouldn't have allowed it, and neither would the BBC management, but by the time he came back the plans for the show were so advanced that it would have been extremely difficult to cancel them. I showed him the script, which was really a series of scenes taken straight from Nell's book and not a conventional screenplay at all. I mean there were narrative threads going through the film, if you remember, like Ruby's abortion and so on ...

LC: But it's a loose narrative ...

TG: Very loose narrative, and allusive as well as loose, and not, certainly in those days, what anybody would call a television script, and there was a huge row with Jim when he came back from his holidays. In fact, there was a screaming match in his office – although he was a very good and nice and generous man – he was absolutely shocked and affronted that we would consider making this and calling it television drama. And I said it's a mass resignation if you don't allow it, and he then said he didn't want anything to do with it.

LC: Was it the content that he objected to?

TG: The content and the style, and the fact that it wasn't a proper script and so on. He then, in his generous way, said that he didn't want anything to do with it and he didn't want to take credit for it and he said you can be the producer. I said I wasn't going to take his credit away from him – he'd been enormously good to me. So this row has got to be in the context of a very protective man. This was one step too far for him. But he was a man who had been, and was, trusted by the BBC. He was a BBC man through and through and the fact that he was completely trusted allowed us to get away with a whole lot of stuff, but this was just too much for him.[29]

While MacTaggart retained a producing credit on *Up the Junction* his antipathy towards the project meant that Garnett was more centrally involved than his credit of story editor might suggest. He and Loach worked closely together on developing *Up the Junction* as a radically new kind of television drama and this was the beginning of what was to prove a very productive working relationship between the two, extending over the next fourteen years. The disagreement that Garnett had with MacTaggart over *Up the Junction* was just the first battle that had to be fought in order to get the drama on to the screen in the form that they wished. Like Troy Kennedy Martin and John McGrath before them, Garnett and Loach wanted to get away from the confines of the television studio and from the theatrical influence on television drama that resulted in the kind of enclosed, naturalistic drama that Kennedy Martin was attacking in 'Nats Go Home'. Both Garnett and Loach had worked with Kennedy Martin and McGrath, and both the theory expressed in 'Nats Go Home' and the practical experiment of *Diary of a Young Man*, on which Loach had worked as a director, were to be influential on the development and realisation of *Up the Junction.*

In spite of the shift towards pre-recording, and an increase in location filming, *Diary of a Young Man* was really pushing against the technological limitations of the medium as they existed in 1964. The introduction of videotape had freed television drama from the shackles of having to be broadcast live, marking an advance towards achieving the kind of 'visual storytelling' that Kennedy Martin was calling for. Yet it was still difficult, and expensive, to edit videotape in 1964–5 and the montages of *Diary of a Young Man* could only be achieved through the use of film, which did not present the technical difficulties that editing videotape did. The montage sequences in *Diary*, with their non-synchronised voiceovers and music tracks, were to be a direct influence on *Up the Junction*, which made extensive use of voiceovers and layers of non-synchronous sound over the top of its 'kaleidoscope of fragmented images'.

In an enthusiastic article on *Up the Junction* following its transmission, Kennedy Martin extolled the virtue of editing on film which enabled *Up the Junction* to achieve more extensively what *Diary* had only been able to achieve in part, due to the limitations of the electronic editing (vision mixing) in *Diary*'s studio scenes. Such complexity, in the editing of sound and visuals, could not possibly be achieved in live studio drama and it illustrated why the New Drama had to embrace new technology and move away from the confines and constraints of the electronic studio:

> With conceptions as complex as Ken Loach is trying to realise, a director cannot cue in and out three sound tracks and the cameras and run in telecine with dead accuracy over the period of an hour or so. Such orchestration requires physical facilities – superhuman responses, as well as studio time – which he has not got. The only solution is the possibility of subsequent editing as afforded by telerecording.
>
> This kind of complex creation cannot be done live; nor is VTR by any means an ideal solution. There is only one right moment to cut to anything and to cut away again, whether it is sound or image that is involved. With live television and the present system of tape recording only a very clumsy approximation to editing is possible. (This is the reason why interpolations of telecine into a live or taped programme usually appear so chunky and obvious; the contrast of film and television editing, and the juncture of the two techniques cannot be disguised.) The answer, at present, lies in post-recording editing.[30]

This was the technological breakthrough that *Up the Junction* achieved. In order to make a drama about contemporary life among ordinary working-class people in south London, Garnett and Loach wanted to get out onto the streets, into the real world, as much as possible. After the battle with James MacTaggart over the script and the whole conception of the drama, Garnett then fought another battle with BBC management, and with the BBC Film Department, to be allowed to use 16mm cameras to go out and shoot the drama on the streets. After first denying permission, because the BBC had invested a lot of money in new studios at Television Centre and the last thing they wanted was for people to start abandoning them and filming on location, Michael Peacock, who was Controller of BBC One at the time, eventually relented. According to Garnett, Peacock's initial concern was that they would simply produce substandard 'B movie' material, because they were budgeting to shoot the drama for the same cost of producing it in the studio, whereas exterior filming is usually much more expensive. This was the same argument that Garnett encountered with the BBC Film Department, based at Ealing, whose attitude was '16mm is for news, not drama, and drama is 35mm, and we're not going to allow this substandard stuff to go out'.[31]

As far as Garnett and Loach were concerned this was precisely why they wanted to use 16mm. They wanted to achieve the look of 'immediacy' to be found in news footage, in order to reinforce the veracity of the drama that they wanted to put on screen. They wanted to turn 'drama' into 'news' and the use of 16mm hand-held cameras was an important part of the strategy of convincing viewers that what they were seeing was authentic. As Ken Loach said:

> We were very anxious for our plays not to be considered dramas but as continuations of the news. The big investigative documentary programme at the time was *World In Action* … and we tried to copy its techniques and cut with a rough, raw, edgy quality, which enabled us to deal with issues head on.[32]

Having won the concession from BBC management to make one filmed drama, as an experiment, and having fought another battle with the Film Department over using 16mm film, Garnett and Loach then faced yet another obstacle, which was that the Equity agreement did not allow them to go out and make films with actors. Garnett takes up the story:

> We looked very carefully at the agreement and the agreement said that at least a minimum of 10 per cent of the drama had to be shot in the studio. So, stupidly, with *Junction*, with *The Lump*, with *Cathy Come Home*, and maybe others I can't remember, we had to, against our wishes, go into the bloody studio, Riverside Studios somewhere, and shoot 10 per cent of the show.[33]

Thwarted in their ambition to shoot the drama entirely on location, Loach decided to shoot the studio scenes in the same style as the location scenes, in order to avoid the disjuncture referred to by Kennedy Martin, when material recorded in the studio clashes with the freer, liberated location footage, shot on film. Loach recounts the breakthrough that was made, not only in shooting the studio scenes differently, but in shooting them to be edited in post-production, rather than vision mixing them straight onto tape at the time of recording:

> … when the day of the studio shoot came, I didn't plan the shots like you'd normally plan them. The technicians were in an uproar, because they didn't know

what was going to happen. But we got the cameramen all together and said: 'Look, this isn't a normal TV drama; sometimes you're going to be on your own, you've got to find the shots. The action will happen, and I'll tell you roughly where it is, but you've got to find it, and that's how it will be.' We did record it like that, and we ended up with all these random studio shots to play with.

You were meant to vision mix on the spot, in the studio, to eliminate editing, but we shot it more like a film so that it would have to be cut. In those days, you were only allowed about two or three edits, because cutting tape in 1965 was like building Stonehenge, it was a very cumbersome, slow business, and in this case it would take a much longer time than we'd been allocated. At that point there was a crisis meeting. The people above said: 'You can't work like this. We can't cut the tape. You wasted two whole days in the studio. What are you going to do?'

The only solution was to cut it on the 16mm back-up print that the BBC used at that point as a safety measure. This was greeted with absolute horror because they said it wasn't up to broadcast quality – it was very grey and misty – except in an emergency. But they let us cut on 16mm in the end because it was the only way they could salvage the material. Now, we'd known of this possibility beforehand, which meant we could, in effect, make a film. But it was totally breaking the rules.

Up the Junction is a bit chaotic in many ways. But it showed there was a way of subverting the conventional, solid, 'man-walks-through-door, cut-into-centre-of-room, cut-to-close-up' style of TV drama at the time. Our whole intention, at that stage, was to make films – not studio-based theatre.[34]

By this roundabout, surreptitious route, *Up the Junction* came to be made as a filmed drama. While it is evident which are studio scenes and which scenes are shot on location, by adopting an elliptical editing style, which, as Kennedy Martin points out, would have been impossible using conventional methods, and by laying a patchwork of synchronous and non-synchronous sound over Loach's 'kaleidoscope of fragmented images', *Up the Junction* pioneered a new style of television drama, one which used modernist techniques to portray the modernity of mid-1960s London. This was a new drama for a new age and it marked a quantum leap in the development of British television drama.

It also did much to establish *The Wednesday Play*'s reputation for controversy, especially in the scene featuring the backstreet abortion. The acting, camerawork and editing combine to powerful effect in this scene, to be counterpoised by an objective, documentary-style voiceover of a doctor (Garnett's own GP) giving factual information about abortions. The intention of the voiceover, however, was not just to give the scene a documentary realism, according to Garnett:

It wasn't because we were thinking of documentaries. Ken and I were very influenced by Brecht at the time and we were interested in a sort of alienation effect on film, where what was going on on the screen would get the feelings of

The abortion scene from the BBC's controversial and innovative *Up the Junction*

the audience, and what was coming on the soundtrack would get the mind of the audience, it was trying to do that.[35]

The inclusion of the subject of abortion in the drama was an interventionist strategy, anticipating the more wholesale intervention of *Cathy Come Home*, a year later. It was a contribution to the campaign to get abortion legalised – David Steele's Abortion Law Reform Bill was being debated in parliament at the time the drama was screened – and as such it proved controversial, raising questions about balance and partiality in BBC drama which was to be a recurrent response to the work of Loach and Garnett.[36]

While the abortion scene in *Up the Junction* generated considerable controversy, it was by no means the main focus of the drama, comprising only a small part of the overall montage of scenes depicting working-class life around Clapham Junction. The political controversy it engendered marks an important moment in the history of social-issue drama on British television, but the radicalism of *Up the Junction* derives more from its formal and stylistic innovations and its successful breaching of the walls of the television studio, than it does from its politics. While studio drama continued to be made, for many years, *Up the Junction* pioneered the move away from recording in the electronic studio towards shooting in real locations, on film. Within a few years this had become the norm for the single play on British television, with series and serial drama following close behind.

Aesthetically, however, *Up the Junction* was transitional. While it closely conforms to the New Drama that Troy Kennedy Martin was calling for in 'Nats Go Home', it was an experiment which was not followed up, apart from in *Cathy Come Home* and, to some extent, the David Mercer-scripted *In Two Minds* (1967), which both share some of *Junction's* elliptical, impressionistic style.[37] Subsequently, Loach and Garnett's quest for veracity in television drama led away from the avant-garde modernism of *Up the Junction* and towards, ironically, a new form of naturalism, that of the observational documentary style adopted by Loach in dramas like *The Big Flame* (1969), *The Rank and File* (1971) and the four-part *Days of Hope* (1975).[38]

Drama documentary

Much of the controversy surrounding *Up the Junction*, *Cathy Come Home* and subsequent Loach/Garnett work revolved around a blurring of the line between the 'factual' and the 'fictional' in television drama. The move out of the studio to shooting on film, in real locations, contributed to an erosion of the division between what was obviously 'drama-tised' (as most studio drama obviously was) and what appeared 'real' when it was filmed in real locations using cinéma vérité techniques.

As the previous chapter indicated, the genre of drama documentary was not a new one, but the Loach/Garnett innovation of taking television drama out onto the streets and making it look like news footage saw a new development in the form, placing it at the forefront of debates about the extent to which television, and television drama in particular, should involve itself in social and political issues. This debate was particularly acute as far as the BBC was concerned as a result of its traditional public service ethos and the statutory requirement that it should be 'impartial' and 'balanced' in its programming.

Up the Junction was not the only programme to provoke controversy in this respect. Also in 1965, *The War Game*, written and directed by Peter Watkins, was so successful in mixing the conventions of drama and documentary that it was considered too hot to handle by the BBC at the time and was banned from transmission, ostensibly on the grounds that its graphic depiction of the aftermath of a nuclear strike on south-east England was 'too horrifying for the medium of broadcasting'.[39]

Peter Watkins had, the previous year, made a film in similar style, also, like *The War Game*, for the BBC Talks Division. *Culloden* (BBC One, 15 December 1964) was a dramati-sation of the Jacobite rebellion of 1745, shot in a cinéma vérité style with interviews to camera, voiceovers and captions. It was a fresh and ingenious approach to a subject which would normally have been dealt with in a more conventional documentary manner. Watkins' use of 16mm film was acceptable because he was making a docu-mentary film, not a drama, but his dramatisation of the events leading up to and during the battle, in which over a thousand Scottish peasants were slaughtered by the English army, blurred the previously unproblematic distinction between drama and documen-tary, confusing notions of the 'factual' and the 'fictional' in such programmes.

When, the following year, Watkins repeated the formula in *The War Game*, he found himself in the middle of a political controversy. While *Culloden*, on the one hand, was con-troversial, its eighteenth-century subject was sufficiently removed from the present day to be considered permissible, even if the form which it took was contentious. *The War Game*, on the other hand, was highly topical, tapping into, and irrefutably supporting, the arguments of the Campaign for Nuclear Disarmament (CND) against the manufacture of nuclear weapons. Not that CND was mentioned in the programme, but the horrific depiction of the consequences of a nuclear attack on Britain was so effective that there was little possibility of the film being seen as anything other than an attack on the whole notion of nuclear deterrence, the policy which successive governments had advocated. Therefore, while the ostensible reason for the withdrawal of the film by the BBC was that it was 'too horrifying' to be shown, the banning of the film raised the question of whether the government had put pressure on the BBC to withdraw the film because of its 'propaganda value' for CND.

There is little doubt that Watkins sought to make an intervention into the debate about nuclear weapons, just as Loach and Garnett did with the abortion scene in *Up the Junction* and the discourse on homelessness in *Cathy Come Home*. The move out of the studio and into the real world, the use of 16mm film cameras and cinéma vérité newsreel techniques, were an important part of this interventionist strategy. This new kind of 'dramatised documentary' or 'documentary drama' was a logical development of the 1950s 'story documentary' which, via the social realism of early 1960s drama series like *Coronation Street* and *Z Cars*, evolved in the mid-1960s into a powerful and controversial new form which would continue to trouble television companies and politicians alike for the next twenty years.

The television playwright

Troy Kennedy Martin's call for a new drama based on 'visual storytelling', and the subsequent adoption of cinéma vérité techniques by Peter Watkins and Ken Loach in their drama documentaries, seemed to mark an important shift in television drama, away from the electronic studio, with its historical dependence on the spoken word and a more theatrical form of naturalism, towards a new realism that was closer to cinema than theatre and which elevated the director to a position of greater importance in the creation of meaning.

Yet the idea of the 1960s as a 'golden age' for television drama rests largely on the reputation of a handful of playwrights who took advantage of the opportunity that television offered to produce original and challenging work for a mass audience. Foremost among this new generation of television playwrights was David Mercer, who had twelve television plays produced during the course of the 1960s. Even more prolific was Dennis Potter, whose reputation has since surpassed that of all others during the course of a thirty-year career and around whom a publishing industry has developed since his death in 1994. Potter also had twelve television plays produced in the 1960s, but in his case they came in just five years, from 1965–9, an indication not only of the demand for television plays at the time, but also of the opportunity television offered writers, to produce work for a medium that could attract a mass audience in the way that the theatre never could and in which there were fewer commercial constraints, and consequently fewer compromises that needed to be made, than might be encountered in writing screenplays for the cinema.

Apart from Mercer and Potter, other important writers to emerge during the 1960s included Jim Allen, John Finch, John Hopkins, Julia Jones, Alan Plater, Allan Prior, Jack

Rosenthal and Fay Weldon, some of whom started out writing for drama series like *Coronation Street* (Allen, Finch and Rosenthal) and *Z Cars* (Hopkins, Plater and Prior) before going on to make their name with single plays and serials. Writing episodes for popular drama series was (and to some extent still is) a training ground where a writer could learn the mechanics of writing for television, before progressing to write 'authored' drama in the form of a single play, or perhaps a multi-part serial, where ideas could be developed and social or political statements made. The difference between the 1960s and the situation in television drama today is that the possibility now of progressing from writing episodes for drama series to producing 'authored' single dramas or serials is much reduced, not least because of the decline of the single play, which has seen the very term 'playwright' (with its theatrical connotations) virtually disappear from television vocabulary.

Not that this should let us subscribe to the theory that everything was 'golden' for writers in the 1960s. In a 1963 article on the early television plays of David Mercer, Alan Lovell commented on the financial pressure on writers like Mercer to keep producing work, suggesting a more pragmatic economic reason as to why writers at this time were so prolific:

> The pressures of the medium are enormous. Mercer has received somewhere around £300 for each of his plays for the BBC. This means that he has to write at least three plays a year to make anywhere near a reasonable living – an impossibly large output (the pressure on television directors is even worse). Apart from the financial pressures such is the shortage of talent in television drama, that successful writers are worked to death.[40]

Lovell sees this pressure as having had a detrimental effect on Mercer's early 'Generations' trilogy of plays for the BBC: *Where the Difference Begins* (15 December 1961), *A Climate of Fear* (22 February 1962) and *The Birth of a Private Man* (18 March 1963). However, the 'failure' of these plays, as Lovell sees it, was a consequence of their naturalistic form. Apart from some exterior telecine sequences which frame the drama, most of the action of the plays is interior, recorded 'live' in the studio, and the emphasis is very much on 'talking out' the issues, of class and politics, that are the subject matter of the plays. While director Don Taylor makes some attempt to depart from a theatrical naturalism in the style of the dramas, this is essentially a 'theatre of dialogue', albeit one in which a new socialist politics is injected into what might otherwise have been seen as 'kitchen sink' drama.

Mercer had two more plays produced between the second and third plays of the trilogy. One of these was *A Suitable Case for Treatment* (BBC One, 21 October 1962) and Lovell sees this as far more successful than the other plays because of its departure from naturalism:

> From the first shot of the gorilla's face, one was aware of something new and exciting happening on the television screen. It was as if Mercer had suddenly

found his focus as a writer. The blurred themes of the trilogy were suddenly made sharp. There was a shape and coherence. Naturalism went by the board.[41]

A Suitable Case for Treatment saw the emergence of a different theme in Mercer's work – madness – and it also saw Mercer departing from the naturalism of the other plays to adopt a more non-naturalistic, surrealist-influenced style, which he was to develop further in subsequent work. In a 1975 interview, Mercer acknowledged that there were two quite different aspects to his plays, which can clearly be seen in the contrasting styles of early plays like Where the Difference Begins and A Suitable Case for Treatment:

> It was said that A Suitable Case for Treatment was a breakthrough, to use that hackneyed phrase ... it then seemed to me that really there were two strands in my imagination: one was naturalistic, anecdotal, politically orientated, emotionally, to some extent, tormented and trapped in class problems, and the other side of me was a kind of surrealist, free-wheeling, slightly happy-go-lucky, let's-see-what-we-can-do-chaps attitude, and I think in And Did Those Feet? I was trying to pull these two strands together.[42]

And Did Those Feet? (BBC One, 2 June 1965) was made as a Wednesday Play, as were Mercer's next four plays, although The Parachute (BBC One, 21 January 1968) was first shown as a Play of the Month, before being screened as a Wednesday Play in August 1969. In between those two plays came In Two Minds (BBC One, 1 March 1967), a drama based on the radical psychiatric theories of R. D. Laing, which again enabled Mercer to explore the theme of madness. In Two Minds was directed by Ken Loach and produced by Tony Garnett and Loach's drama documentary approach to the material provides a good illustration of how 'authorship' in television drama is not unproblematic but results from the combined contributions of writer, director and producer (and other members of the production team). This was increasingly the case once television drama moved out of the studio and into the real world. In the hands of Loach In Two Minds became a piece of cinéma vérité, the first Wednesday Play to be filmed entirely outside of the studio – the Equity agreement requiring 10 per cent of studio recording having, by this time, been relaxed – and it is arguable as to where the 'authorship' of the drama really resides.

The Parachute, produced by Tony Garnett and directed by Anthony Page, saw another departure, formally, with a mixture of studio scenes and location filming, and a complex narrative structure incorporating stylised flashback sequences, while the themes of class and politics in Germany during the Weimar Republic and under National Socialism are dealt with by Mercer in a 'free-wheeling', occasionally surrealist manner. Once again, the complexities of authorship would take some unravelling here, although stylistically and thematically The Parachute seems more clearly a Mercer play than In Two Minds, where the cinéma vérité approach to a contemporary social issue, schizophrenia, suggests a Loach/Garnett drama, even if the theme of madness is one that Mercer explored elsewhere.

There are certain similarities between the early work of Dennis Potter and Mercer's early television plays. Both Potter and Mercer were primarily television playwrights, although Mercer also wrote for the stage and, like Potter, subsequently for the cinema as well. Both believed in the democratising potential of television as a new mass medium, and this led them both to explore themes of class and politics in their early plays, subject matter which they felt a working-class audience could relate to. But both playwrights were also interested in experimenting with the form of television drama and this experimentation produces an interesting tension in their work, between a drama dealing with themes of class and politics which might engage the viewer, and plays which, increasingly, embrace non-naturalist or modernist techniques, tradition-ally the province of the avant-garde rather than that of mainstream drama.

Potter's interest in issues of class and politics are clearly evident in early plays like *Stand Up, Nigel Barton* (BBC One, 8 December 1965) and *Vote, Vote, Vote for Nigel Barton* (BBC One, 15 December 1965), while the asides to camera in these dramas are early examples of a desire to break the 'fourth wall' of naturalistic drama by directly addressing the viewer, a technique intended to shatter the illusionism of conventional television drama. As we shall see in subsequent chapters, non-naturalistic techniques became an increasingly important part of Potter's work, but the resolve to depart from naturalism was there from the beginning, and was being used quite extensively by his sixth play, *Where the Buffalo Roam* (BBC One, 2 November 1966), a study of mental disorientation which could have sprung from the pen of Mercer, were it not for Potter's characteristic use of popular music and the iconography of popular culture, in this case the Western.

Like many of the new breed of television playwright, Potter was aware of, and interested in, the Epic Theatre of Bertolt Brecht and some elements of Brecht's theories are clearly evident in Potter's work. But, as Glen Creeber points out, Potter was also influenced by Troy Kennedy Martin's 'Nats Go Home' article, published just a few months before Potter's first television play was screened:

> Above all, it was Martin's call to construct 'interior thought' and 'interior characterisation' which would be crucial to Potter's conception of television drama as a whole. Indeed, he responded to Martin's article in 'Reaction' in the following edition. Like Martin, he argued that TV naturalism had to be subverted and replaced by 'a mosaic of objects, details, moods, memories and conversations. Pictures in a real fire. Pictures ablaze.' Later he would pay tribute to Martin's article in his introduction to *The Nigel Barton Plays* (1967), restating his call that '[a]ll drama which owes its form or substance to theatre plays is OUT'.[43]

It seems significant that both Mercer and Potter began writing essentially naturalistic dramas, exploring themes of class and politics, and then began to stretch the bound-aries of television drama by introducing modernist or non-naturalistic techniques. Their uniqueness, perhaps, resides in their separate endeavours to experiment with the form of television drama in order to find the best means of expressing the themes and ideas they wished to explore. Yet this experimentation was not at the expense of popular understanding. While a play like Mercer's *The Parachute* may have been difficult, even perplexing, to the ordinary viewer, and while some of Potter's work may have been equally disorienting, their achievement was to use the medium of television drama to explore personal and political themes in new and different ways. As John Caughie puts it:

> Mercer and Potter seem to me to offer a consistent level of investment in some of the great modernist themes – sexuality, the individual in history, the irrepressible unconscious, class and power, the role of the creative artist, god and godlessness – which make their work exemplary. Within television drama, they also seem to pose quite different contexts and strategies of negotiation between modernism and the popular.[44]

While Mercer's playwriting career was shorter than Potter's (Mercer died in 1980), both writers accumulated a body of work which bears testimony to their enduring importance as television playwrights, even if some of the early plays, such as Mercer's *A Suitable Case for Treatment*, sadly no longer exist. That both Mercer and Potter were able to develop their craft, mainly at the BBC, in such a productive and prolific manner, along with countless others who were commissioned to write television plays for the first time during the 1960s, is testimony to the opportunity, and the creative freedom, that television offered writers at this time. In this respect, the 1960s were indeed a golden age for the television playwright.

Talking to a Stranger (1966)

One of the highlights of 1960s 'authored' drama, described by the *Observer* TV critic George Melly as 'the first authentic masterpiece written directly for television',[45] was *Talking to a Stranger* (BBC Two, 2–23 October 1966), four ninety-minute plays written by John Hopkins and directed by Christopher Morahan. The plays were transmitted over four weeks as part of BBC Two's *Theatre 625* (1964–8), an anthology series that often included three plays by the same writer on a similar theme, but here Hopkins went one step further and developed the drama as a quartet of plays.[46] Each of the four plays focused on the events of one Sunday from the perspective of a different member of the lower middle-class Stephens family. The first play, *Anytime You're Ready I'll Sparkle* (2 October 1966) was told from the point of view of the daughter, Terry (Judi Dench); *No Skill or Special Knowledge is Required* (9 October 1966) focused on the father (Maurice Denham); *Gladly, My Cross-Eyed Bear* (16 October 1966) featured the son, Alan (Michael Bryant); and *The Innocent Must Suffer* (23 October 1966) concentrated on the mother (Margery Mason) whose suicide at the end of the second play is the dramatic highpoint of the series. This was a new form of dramatic storytelling, not a serial in which the story develops as a linear narrative from episode one to the final episode, but a series of four related plays, each dealing with the same subject and featuring the same central characters, but where the story is told in a fragmented, non-linear structure.

While mostly set in the present, the narrative incorporates flashbacks as characters recall moments from their lives which have significance for how they are in the present.

Talking to a Stranger: a new form of dramatic storytelling

This strategy is established right from the beginning of the first play, when we are introduced to Terry as she lies on a bed in the flat she shares with her friend, Jess (Pinkie
Johnstone). Terry is staring at a bare wall but, having established where she is and what
she is looking at, the action immediately cuts to an exterior shot of the countryside,
accompanied by the laughter of children. This is followed by a cut back to Terry, still
staring at the wall in her room, while we hear a child's voice saying: 'I'll swing so high,
I'll kick the sky,' suggesting that the exterior shot was a flashback to Terry's childhood
and that the voice may be her own, as a child. Shots of a children's playground follow
and the child's voice continues: 'I'll kick the sky and make it cry.' The laughter of children bridges a cut to a high-angle shot of Terry, still lying in the same position on the
bed. The quality of the lighting here suggests the interior shots are recorded in a studio
– the lower-quality resolution of these images contrasting with the high-quality resolution of the exterior shots on film. Terry's flashback reverie is broken when her friend
Jess enters her room, causing Terry to shut her eyes as Jess calls out Terry's name, asking
if she is awake. Terry answers and sits up, reaching for her transistor radio on the bed-
side table, uttering 'Oh damn' when she finds it is not there. Sitting up, she holds her
position for a few seconds and the title of the episode is superimposed, accompanied by
a few notes of music.

We are one minute into the drama when the title appears. There have been fifteen
shots, an ASL of four seconds, with eight interior (studio) shots and seven exterior (film)
shots. The very short ASL in this opening sequence is explained partly by the use of film
inserts. The ASL in the next five minutes is nine seconds, more typical perhaps of the

production as a whole but still much shorter than the ASL in other studio dramas such as *Nineteen Eighty-Four* and *Lena, O My Lena*. Although most of *Talking to a Stranger* is recorded in the studio, film is used throughout for the flashbacks and occasionally for linking scenes, such as the short sequence in *Anytime You're Ready I'll Sparkle* when Terry walks past the playground which features in the earlier flashback, as she makes her way to her parents' house for Sunday dinner.

The mother's suicide lies at the dramatic heart of the plays. Revealed to us at the end of the second play, the other family members react to it in the third play, but then the fourth play goes back in time to tell the mother's story, ending with her suicide being shown again. Interviewed in 1976, John Hopkins explained the concept and organisation of the plays:

> When I was planning the quartet, I thought there was an opportunity to present not a narrative that begins at A and goes through to Z, but a narrative of depth perception, so that the plays, as it were, are piled on top of each other. They cover something more than 24 hours, which are examined over and over again.
>
> The first plays falls into three sections: the first section is away from the family in Terry's flat; the second section is the basic unit of the whole quartet, the hours of Sunday when they are all together; the third section is again away from the family with Terry and her flatmate. The second play – the father's play – restates the basic unit of the play, and I suppose is most responsible for feeling that the four plays are all exactly the same but seen from different points of view, but a large part of the second play is new material in that it is father's memory of his life coming through to this point. The third play, the son's play, is a complete break from the basic unit. It's the next morning, after mother has died, no material from the first two plays is explicitly repeated, although the same themes are explored. The fourth play again restates the basic unit and includes much material from the first two plays. It explores more fully the relationship between the mother and the son. The problem was that I had more material [for the fourth play] than I could honestly deal with in the same 90-minute segment. Christopher Morahan and I decided on 'Luc Godard' jump cuts through the scenes that had already been presented – the Sunday tea-party, the scenes before – leaving the maximum available time for Alan and his mother, and the latter part of the play, the concluding, almost silent resolution of the drama.
>
> By the time we reach the last play, the climax of the whole work, the audience is aware of all the facts – they have an opportunity to concentrate wholly on why what happens has happened.[47]

Clearly the narrative structure of *Talking to a Stranger* is innovative, eschewing the linear narrative of the conventional television drama serial, and opting for a multifaceted structure with multiple viewpoints on the events of the same day. But *Talking to a Stranger* is also stylistically innovative, not only in its use of film for the flashback scenes but also because of innovations made by director Christopher Morahan during the course of its production.

While the majority of the drama takes place in various studio interiors – mainly the suburban home of the Stephens family – Morahan used both single camera and multi-camera shooting for these studio scenes. But because of the complexity of the production, with frequent cutaways to different temporal and spatial locations, he chose to edit on a 35mm telerecording of the studio scenes, rather than on videotape, as he later explained:

> Though video editing had reached some sophistication, one had to use two vast tape machines and dub across from one machine to another to make the edited version. However sound editing for video was in its infancy, and the sound track as written by John Hopkins was very complex, so I decided on a completely different technique. It was made towards the end of the Black and White era, and as a back up all videos were simultaneously telerecorded on 35mm … So I decided to shoot in a conventional studio style but not record on tape, it went straight onto 35mm telerecording, the quality of telerecording being very high by that time. Instead of video editing, the final cut was on a Steenbeck editing table normally used for film and we were able to lay all the complex sound tracks as if we were making a film, culminating in a mix and dub just like a movie. I was also able to finesse the editing more successfully, taking more time, tightening sequences and so forth.[48]

The availability of a 35mm telerecording of the studio scenes meant that Morahan was able to achieve a more sophisticated and stylistically innovative final cut than if he had been editing on videotape, or producing a continuous studio recording of the production. While single-camera shooting was essential for the opening scene – both in the studio and for the flashbacks – the multi-camera scenes elsewhere achieved their complexity in part through this ability to edit on film. In this way, Talking to a Stranger is a hybrid: a studio recording, with some location filming, where it was necessary to edit on film in order to achieve a stylistic complexity which would not have been attainable using conventional methods of recording on tape.

Talking to a Stranger was a landmark in television drama, not only for its innovative narrative structure and radical approach to the theme of family crisis, with filmed flash-backs providing insights into the psyche of the characters, but also for the elaborate visual rhetoric made possible by the use of some single-camera shooting and the decision to edit on film. For a drama which is about interior, psychological states and the constricted, neurotic relationships within the Stephens family, the enclosed studio sets help to create an atmosphere of claustrophobia and psychological intensity, while the film inserts provide glimpses of escape, as well as flashes of memory, within what is otherwise an interior physical and emotional landscape. Highly acclaimed by the critics for its originality and psychological depth, Talking to a Stranger was repeated twice within the space of eighteen months, first on BBC Two and then on BBC One, an unprecedented occurrence for a television drama. On the occasion of the second repeat, on BBC One, George Melly wrote of the plays:

> For me the convincing proof of their importance is that each viewing reveals new dimensions, new layers of perception. Quite often a repeat of something which, first time round, appeared pretty impressive, shows up unexpected fissures and cracks, fake perspectives and inflated detail. But *Talking to a Stranger*, for all its deceptive looseness of structure and the liberties it takes with time, place and language, is as solid as a rock. Nothing in it has dated except the length of Judi Dench's dress. On the evidence of this work alone the medium can be considered to have come of age.[49]

Soap opera

The term 'soap opera' was not in common usage in Britain in the 1960s, but it was during this decade that the form became established on British television. Following the BBC's early flirtation with the genre in the mid-1950s, with *The Grove Family*, ITV, with its more commercial instincts, proved how successful a regular, half-hour, twice-weekly drama series could be with *Emergency – Ward 10* and *Coronation Street*. Although these programmes may have been described at the time as drama series, or even drama documentaries because of their 'realism', their continuous, episodic serial narratives led to their designation as 'continuous serials' when they began to attract academic attention in the late 1970s and 80s. This was to differentiate them from drama series like *Z Cars* and *Dr Finlay's Casebook* which, although they featured a regular cast of central characters, were usually longer (fifty minutes) weekly episodes with one main storyline that was resolved by the end of the episode, rather than a number of different storylines which continued from episode to episode, as in the continuous narratives of soap opera.

One of the intentions behind the academic revaluation of soap operas was to rescue the genre from its tarnished reputation as one of the cheapest and most denigrated of television forms, its low cultural status deriving from the genre's origins as American daytime radio serials, sponsored by soap manufacturers, for the housewife. These programmes were made quickly and cheaply and the use of the term 'soap opera' to describe them was both patronising and dismissive in its ironic conflation of the genre's early commercial origins (advertising soap products) with the high-culture associations of the classical opera. But the term stuck when the daytime serial transferred to American television in the 1950s, where it again took the form of a daily programme revolving around the emotional dramas and relationships of a small group of people. Needless to say, little was seen of the actual towns or communities in which these people lived as the early TV soap operas were broadcast live from the studio, where the scenarios were played out amid a restricted number of fairly rudimentary studio sets.

Unlike their American counterparts, British soaps were not sponsored by soap companies or shown daily (apart from *Crossroads* [ATV/Granada 1964–88], which was shown five days a week for its first three years). They have also mainly been shown in primetime, in the evening, rather than during the day. British soaps that originated in the 1960s, like *Coronation Street*, *Compact* (BBC One, 1962–5), *Crossroads*, *United!* (BBC One, 1965–7) and *The Newcomers* (BBC One, 1965–9), shared many of the characteristics of their American counterparts – the everyday problems and personal relationships of insular, small-town communities – being based in environments such as the offices of a women's magazine (*Compact*), a midlands motel (*Crossroads*), a second-division football club (*United!*) or a country village (*The Newcomers*). Apart from the daily *Crossroads*, the early British soaps were transmitted twice weekly from the studio, with some location material to add 'realism', although the production constraints resulting from having to produce two episodes per week on limited budgets meant that the amount of location material was very limited. Rehearsal time was also limited – a factor often cited to explain the 'poor acting' in some soaps, scripts had to be delivered on a never-ending conveyor-belt basis – necessitating the employment of a team of writers to keep the serial supplied with material, and directors were challenged, and constrained, by having to record again and again on a limited number of fairly basic studio sets.

Yet soap operas have consistently proved to be among the most popular programmes on television. *Coronation Street* soon became established as the market leader in the 1960s, overtaking *Emergency – Ward 10* in 1961 and frequently topping the ratings during that decade. *Compact* was the first of the BBC's attempts to challenge the supremacy of *Coronation Street*, but came no nearer to doing so than subsequent serials, like *United!* and *The Newcomers* – none of which lasted more than five years, barely long enough to merit the status of long-running serials. As with *The Grove Family*, which the BBC terminated after three years despite its popularity, the BBC always seemed ambivalent about competing with its commercial counterpart in the realm of such 'downmarket' popular programming, preferring to put more energy and resources into expensive, 'quality' drama like *The Wednesday Play* and *The Forsyte Saga* (BBC Two, 1967).

ITV had no such qualms and in 1964 *Coronation Street* was joined by *Crossroads*, produced in the Midlands by ATV and devised, ironically, by the team that had brought *Compact* to the BBC: Hazel Adair and Peter Ling. Initially going out on five nights a week, which was reduced to four nights in 1967 (and to three in 1979 following criticism by the Independent Broadcasting Authority regarding the poor quality of the programme), *Crossroads* gradually gained a huge following, as well as a reputation for low production values for which it would later become infamous.

The subsequent generic labelling of these long-running, continuous serials as 'soap opera', with the pejorative connotations implied by the term, has had the effect of relegating such programmes to an inferior form of television drama, operating at the opposite end of the spectrum to the elevated heights of the single play. Critically, soap operas have been dismissed as 'low culture', as ephemeral as the soap products they were originally designed to sell. This mattered little in the 1960s, however, when no one in British television considered that they were making 'soap operas', or even that they were making long-running, continuous serials. It was only as a result of the huge popularity of *Emergency – Ward 10*, *Coronation Street* and *Crossroads* that these programmes evolved into long-running drama serials, with *Coronation Street* now in its sixth decade, having produced over 8,000 episodes. In this respect, soap operas are a phenomenon which exists apart from the rest of television drama, and which needs to be considered on its own terms and not as a debased form of television drama. As such, we shall return to them in subsequent chapters.

Costume drama

While soap operas are resolutely contemporary, the BBC discovered a successful hybrid in 1967 with *The Forsyte Saga*, a long-running, historical drama based on the personal relationships and everyday problems of an upper-class family in the late nineteenth and early twentieth century. Derived from the novels by John Galsworthy, *The Forsyte Saga* realised a long-held ambition of producer Donald Wilson to bring Galsworthy's late Victorian/Edwardian saga to the screen, winning him an award from the Royal Television Society in the process.

It was significant that *The Forsyte Saga* should be screened on BBC Two, where it was peak-time viewing on Sunday evenings. Although BBC Two had been broadcasting for over two years, the channel was still trying to establish itself. In order to receive BBC Two, viewers needed to have their television sets adjusted to receive the ultra-high-frequency 625 signal, which was not immediately available in all parts of the country, and it was felt that the channel needed a prestigious programme, an 'event', in order to raise its profile and attract new viewers. The Galsworthy saga, more middlebrow than highbrow, was thought to fit the bill, having 'quality' overtones (as a literary, costume drama) yet also having sufficient popular appeal (its 'soap opera' qualities) to attract a broad audience. Part of the marketing of *The Forsyte Saga*, therefore, stressed that it would only be available on BBC Two (in fact, it was repeated on BBC One a year later) and this tactic succeeded in attracting an average audience of 6 million when the serial was transmitted from January–July 1967 (the audience tripled to 18 million for the BBC One repeat, from September 1968).

The Forsyte Saga was a studio drama, with some telecine sequences, and was made in black and white, but essentially it can be seen as the forerunner of the many histori-cal sagas that followed in its footsteps, from *Upstairs Downstairs* (1971–5) in the 1970s to *Downton Abbey* (2010–) in the 2010s. While it was by no means the first costume drama on British television, it was the first long-running serial, a hugely ambitious undertaking by the BBC, and it was the most expensive television drama up to that time, costing £250,000 to make.

The Forsyte Saga was also important in establishing BBC's reputation for 'quality' drama, where the quality is derived from a combination of (i) the literary source material, (ii) the best of British acting (the series featured Kenneth More, Nyree Dawn Porter, Eric Porter and Susan Hampshire – all actors with stage or screen pedigree), (iii) high production values, as a result of the money spent on it and (iv) 'heritage export': 'a certain image of England and Englishness (with little reference to the rest of Britain), in which national identity is expressed through class and imperial identity'.[50] Charlotte Brunsdon was referring specifically to *Brideshead Revisited* (Granada, 1981) and *Jewel in the Crown* (Granada, 1984) in elaborating these four 'quality components', but they apply

An Edwardian soap opera: *The Forsyte Saga* was the BBC's first 'heritage export'

equally well to *The Forsyte Saga*. Like the costume dramas that it spawned, *The Forsyte Saga* also proved its worth to the BBC as a 'heritage export', selling to forty-five countries and reaching a worldwide audience in excess of 165 million.

Pop culture and fantasy in 1960s TV drama

This chapter began in 1962, with the appearance of *Z Cars* and the emergence of a new realism in television drama, a development which fed into *The Wednesday Play*, perhaps the most celebrated of 1960s television programmes. Yet there has always been a tradition of fantasy in British television drama, co-existing alongside the dominant naturalistic tradition, and in the 1960s telefantasy was as important a part of the TV schedules as any of the dramas we have been considering, especially on ITV.

That 1962 was a key year is as much the case for telefantasy, or what might be described as 'pop television', as it was to social realism. Not only was it the year of the Pilkington Committee Report, new BBC programmes like *Compact*, *Steptoe and Son* and *That Was The Week That Was*, as well as *Z Cars*, it was also the year in which pop culture was launched with the release of the first Beatles record and the first James Bond film, *Dr No*. While Troy Kennedy Martin and John McGrath were revitalising social realism with a new kind of narrative storytelling in the early *Z Cars*, ITV was preparing to cash in on the popular success of the first Bond film with *The Saint* (ATV, 1962–9), a stylish action adventure series based on the Leslie Charteris novels, starring Roger Moore. A product of Lew Grade's ITC, a wholly owned subsidiary of ATV, *The Saint* was a popular success and just one of a number of stylish drama series from ITC, which specialised in the production of telefantasy and adventure series in the 1960s.

The other significant development in television drama in 1962 was the replacement of Ian Hendry by Honor Blackman in *The Avengers* (ABC, 1961–9). Originally a crime drama devised by Sydney Newman at ABC, *The Avengers* became a stylish espionage thriller with the arrival of Blackman as Cathy Gale, the strong female counterpart to Patrick Macnee's suave and sophisticated John Steed. Together they formed a partnership fighting against a variety of fiendish plots to subvert the established order. For whom they were working was never really made clear and it did not really matter. What mattered was that they overcame the threat with style, intelligence, physical prowess and plenty of humorous repartee.

Honor Blackman was in the series for two seasons, from 1962–4. At this time *The Avengers* was recorded on videotape in the studio. For the fourth season, however, from November 1965–March 1966, the series switched to film, giving far more scope for settings and action sequences, as well as increasing the narrative tempo. Also in the fourth season, Honor Blackman was replaced by Diana Rigg, as Emma Peel, an equally stylish, fashion-conscious, yet strong and liberated heroine. That Rigg was to continue Blackman's role as the strong but sexy female foil for Steed was embodied in the character's name: Emma Peel = M (Man) Appeal. Yet the relationship between Steed and Peel was purely platonic. This was a working partnership where the two characters were on an equal footing and Emma Peel, like Cathy Gale, was as likely to overcome the villains in physical combat as was Steed.

Following the shift to film in season four, the fifth *Avengers* season (January–November 1967) was shot in colour, although in Britain the series could only be seen in monochrome until it was repeated in 1970, after the switch from black and white to colour transmission by ITV and BBC One in November 1969 (BBC Two was available in colour from December 1967). Even then, not many people had colour television sets until well into the 1970s, so most people did not actually get to see *The Avengers* in colour until 1982, when Channel 4 re-ran the series. It seems ironic now that the ultimate 1960s pop series could not, at the time, truly reflect the colourful mood of the 'swinging 60s'.

The term 'swinging 60s' had come into popular currency in 1966, following an article in *Time* magazine. As a descriptive term which attempted to sum up a cultural phenomenon it applied mainly to the peak years of 1965–7, when London was the cultural capital of the world and Britain was the world leader in various branches of popular culture: fashion, music, art, design, photography and football. If any television programme captured the mood of the 'swinging 60s' it was undoubtedly *The Avengers* and the decision to film season five in colour was largely in recognition of its marketability abroad, especially in America, where the networks had so far resisted buying the series, partly because it was in black and white:

The colour series proved to be a big money earner worldwide. Foreign sales were in excess of £5,000,000 and the show was being screened in more than 70

Trend-setting: style and pop culture comes to television drama in *The Avengers*

countries. In May 1967, the show was put forward as a candidate for the best foreign dramatic series of the year by ABC in America. Diana Rigg was nominated for an American Emmy (television's equivalent of the Oscar) ... and voted Actress of the Year by the 16 European countries screening *The Avengers*.[51]

Diana Rigg left the series at the end of the fifth season, to be replaced by Linda Thorsen for a final season which was transmitted in 1969. Thus, *The Avengers* spanned the 1960s, the principal example of 'pop' television reflecting, and in turn contributing to, the profound social and cultural changes that were taking place in the decade in fashion, design, technology and sexuality. As far as television drama is concerned the series experienced all of the significant technological changes that took place during the 1960s, starting life as a live studio drama, then being recorded on videotape in the studio, before switching to film in 1965 and colour in 1967. In Britain, as Toby Miller notes, the success of the series saw it rivalling even the soaps in the ratings: 'The Avengers grew in popularity on the British market over the 1960s, spending 103 weeks in the Top Twenty series between 1961 and 1969. In 1967, it was the third most-watched programme and on the chart for 23 weeks.'[52]

The Avengers spawned many imitators, including *Adam Adamant Lives!* (BBC One, 1966–7), the BBC's ingenious variation on the theme, with Gerald Harper playing the dashing Edwardian adventurer Adam Adamant, frozen alive in 1902 and thawed in

The Prisoner: tapping into the 1960s anti-establishment zeitgeist

'swinging' London in 1966. Lew Grade's ITC contributed to the cycle with *Department S* (ATV, 1969–70) at the end of the decade, with one of the cast, Patrick Wyngarde, going on to feature in his own spin-off series, *Jason King* (ATV, 1971–2), and in 1976 Patrick Macnee returned in a sequel to *The Avengers*, playing Steed once more in *The New Avengers* (Thames TV, 1976–7), this time with Gareth Hunt and Joanna Lumley as his associates.

When *The Avengers* was at its peak, in 1966–7, ITC produced a series which quickly became a cult as a result of its enigmatic scenario and surreal visual style. *The Prisoner* (ATV, 1967–8) now ranks alongside *The Avengers* as the apotheosis of 'pop' television drama, or telefantasy, in the 1960s. Over seventeen episodes the series unfurled a surreal drama in which Patrick McGoohan played 'Number Six', a secret agent who has been abducted and is being held prisoner in a mysterious 'Village' (actually Portmeirion in North Wales), from which he repeatedly, but unsuccessfully, tries to escape. Number Six's adversaries are a succession of different characters called 'Number Two', who run the Village, and who Number Six repeatedly gets the better of in each episode, hence their regular replacement by a new Number Two. But Number Six is as unsuccessful in his attempts to escape from the Village, which is controlled by an array of futuristic technology behind its Victorian façade, as he is in his attempt to discover 'Who is Number One?', the question posed at the end of the title sequence of each episode.

The Prisoner, perhaps even more so than *The Avengers*, has acquired an enduring reputation as 'cult television', with successive generations succumbing to its alluring and enigmatic storyline. Why this should be so is suggested in the introduction to one of several books about the series which have been published in recent years:

> An ode to liberty, total nonsense, a defence of the individual threatened by a totalitarian society, a psychedelic trip, a voyage of initiation, a metaphysical parable or religious allegory, The Prisoner – and herein lies its profound originality – gives rise to as many interpretations as there are individual viewers, the oldest of whom recognise that their own vision of the series has changed with successive screenings.[53]

Whatever the reading, The Prisoner was undoubtedly making a statement against conformity and it is this which helps to explain its cult following, especially among the young, in the 1960s and since. By pitting a rebellious individual against an anonymous authoritarian regime, The Prisoner was tapping into the 1960s anti-establishment zeitgeist at a moment when the hedonism of the 'swinging 60s' was transforming into the counter-cultural rebellion of the late 1960s, anticipating the student demonstrations against the war in Vietnam which were an expression of a growing disenchantment with capitalism and the state. David Buxton gives a political inflection to the reading of the series as a contemporary parable:

> It is plausible to see The Prisoner as a parable of the modern world, an updated, Kafkaesque micro-society in which leisure on a mass scale has brought with it a sheep-like conformity, a 'soft' repression in which 'clean' techniques of mind manipulation are used to discipline troublemakers who assert their individuality.[54]

In one of the best analyses of the ideological significance of pop television, a genre usually dismissed as trivial and unworthy of serious consideration by cultural theorists, Buxton develops a persuasive argument about the pop series, and suggests that one of its defining features is its rejection of psychological depth in favour of an exciting, glamorous surface:

> Pop rejects 'depth', the idea that the true meaning is hidden behind the surface appearance, a fundamental axiom of the television play constructed around the 'in-depth' exploration of character. For pop, 'psychological depth' (or 'deep problems') can only detract from the display of designed surfaces which are themselves rich in meaning.[55]

This seems to support the case against pop TV as trivial and ephemeral, in relation to the 'serious' television drama of The Wednesday Play, for example. Yet to suggest that 'meaningful surface display' is a feature of the pop series is to make an important point about the cultural significance of series like The Avengers, The Saint, The Prisoner, Department S et al., within the history of British television drama. Their appearance in the

1960s, alongside the 'serious drama' mainly appearing on the BBC, marks a new development, for a younger generation, at a significant cultural moment.

It is significant, for example, that nearly all of these series, with the exception of *Adam Adamant Lives!*, appeared on the commercial network. New developments in design, fashion and technology were an important part of the scenarios of these programmes which made them very attractive to advertisers. Moreover, the inclusion of pop iconography and the display of new technology in these series meant that they contributed to the modernity of 1960s culture in a way that 'serious' television drama rarely did. In this category of drama programming ITV managed to steal the initiative from the BBC, whose Reithian public service ethos, even in the more liberal Carleton Greene era, made it wary of venturing too far down the road towards the commercialism and consumerism associated with pop culture.

The pop drama series, therefore, marks a shift in British television away from social realism towards fantasy, away from the notion of 'public service' in television towards a greater commercialism, from black and white to colour and from an emphasis on social issues and social problems towards a new hedonism in television drama, a hedonism which, in *The Prisoner*, took on the subversive slant of a symbolic rebellion against authority.

4

History, Realism and Ideology, 1970–9

If the 1960s was a decade of optimism, experiment and innovation in television drama, a period of creative endeavour in which writers and programme-makers echoed, and contributed to, the exciting cultural developments of the time, the 1970s were a more troubled time during which the social consensus and economic stability of the post-war period began to break down, leading to increasing instability and social unrest as the decade wore on. Historical change cannot conveniently be contained within discrete decades, yet the 1970s was, in many respects, a decade with a distinct identity, a period of escalating economic crises and industrial turmoil sandwiched between the permissive 1960s and the reactionary 80s.

After the exuberance and optimism of the 1960s, 1970 was a watershed year, marking a turning point with the election of a Conservative government under the leadership of Ted Heath, bringing to an end the enlightened period of social democracy of Harold Wilson's 1960s Labour governments which had presided over the cultural revolutions of the mid- to late 1960s, a period of liberalisation during which significant social advances were made. By 1979, however, those social advances were under threat as the mood of the country shifted to the Right, culminating in the election of Margaret Thatcher's reactionary Conservative government, a government whose political philosophy was entirely opposed to the liberalising ideologies of the 1960s.

Given the social and economic turmoil of the 1970s, television in Britain enjoyed a period of relative stability, with no major structural changes to upset the comfortable duopoly which had been established by the end of the 1960s. However, industrial unrest did affect the operation of the television companies in 1973–4 when the Conservative government ordered an early (10.30 pm) shutdown of television, ostensibly to conserve electricity during a period when major industrial unrest led to the imposition of a three-day working week. The miners' strikes of 1972 and 1974 were among many industrial disputes that took place during the decade, marking a return to class politics with a vengeance, and the 1974 strike was one of the most significant, leading ultimately to the downfall of the Heath government.

When Wilson's Labour government returned to power in October 1974 it set up a broadcasting committee, under Lord Annan, which it had been preparing to do in 1970 before losing the election to the Tories. When the Annan Committee reported, in 1977, it was much less critical of ITV than Pilkington had been in 1962. In fact, ITV had been increasing its 'serious' programming, at the same time as the BBC was trying to compete more with ITV on its own populist terms, so the two had come closer together, reducing the cultural gap which existed between them in the late 1950s and 60s. Consequently, for much of the 1970s, the BBC and ITV enjoyed a fairly equal share of the audience.

The breakdown in social and economic consensus in the 1970s did, however, have an important impact on the TV drama output of both the BBC and ITV. The consequences can be seen across the whole spectrum of 1970s TV drama, from the single play to the popular series; in the changing nature of police and crime drama; in the increase in historical drama – providing escapism but also opportunities to draw historical parallels between past and present; in the increased number of contentious drama documentaries – both contemporary and historical; and in the number of dramas subject to censorship as the social consensus fragmented and a more coercive state apparatus came into force.

The single play

The single, authored play continued to maintain its prominent position within the television schedules, despite the increasing importance of series and serials in the competition for ratings between the BBC and ITV. In fact, as George Brandt notes, the preoccupation with ratings 'made it possible at other times to take a chance on the not-so-popular single play'.[1] The single play, being a privileged and prestigious form of drama, was not yet subject to the commercial pressures to attract mass audiences that series and serial drama were subject to. Instead, the single play was important to the television companies as a sign that they were fulfilling a public service remit and providing 'quality' programming. For the BBC this was more important than for ITV, where there was greater commercial pressure to deliver audiences to advertisers. Given this situation, playwrights, directors and producers found they had more room to manoeuvre, artistically and politically, with the single play than with other forms of drama.

Shaun Sutton, who was Head of BBC Drama throughout the 1970s, from 1969 when he succeeded Sydney Newman to 1981, firmly believes that the period was a 'golden age' for television drama, and not only because of the artistic freedom afforded to dramatists:

> It was not only the quality of drama of those years that was remarkable, it was the quantity, the actual amount that was transmitted annually. In the early 1970s, I totted up the number of items we had presented during the year, and was amazed to find that it was 757. This, of course, included the episodes of all the soaps and series: it also contained over 100 single plays; plays in round-the-year series like 'Play for Today', 'Theatre Six Two Five' (on BBC 2), 'Play Of The Month',

'Thirty Minute Theatre', and all sorts of extra strands. The money was there, and the BBC was willing to spend it on drama.[2]

The BBC continued to forge ahead of ITV in single-play production and of its many anthology play series *Play for Today* is the one on which the BBC's reputation for radical, challenging drama undoubtedly rests. The fifth and final season of *The Wednesday Play* ended in May 1970, with a total of 176 plays having been transmitted in the space of nearly six years. When the series resumed in the autumn of 1970 it was moved to a Thursday evening, necessitating a change of title. *Play for Today* continued where *The Wednesday Play* left off. Irene Shubik, a producer on both *The Wednesday Play* and *Play for Today*, named her 1975 book *Play for Today* but it was not a history of the 1970s *Play for Today* series, with which she was only involved until 1973. Instead, she used the title generically as a description of the contemporary socially relevant plays being produced in both series. From the first MacTaggart season in 1965 *The Wednesday Play* had deliberately set out to produce plays with contemporary subject matter, and the change of title to *Play for Today* in 1970 was both an acknowledgment of this and a proclamation that the policy would continue.

While *Play for Today* may not have been under pressure to attract mass audiences in the same way as series and serials, it was not uncommon for a *Play for Today* to attract an audience in excess of 5 million, with some plays, such as Jeremy Sandford's *Edna, the Inebriate Woman* (BBC One, 21 October 1971), attracting nearly 10 million, while Robert Holman's *Chance of a Lifetime* (BBC One, 3 January 1980) – now almost completely forgotten – attracted one of the biggest audiences for a *Play for Today* with nearly 15 million viewers. To describe the single play, as George Brandt does, as 'less popular', therefore, is merely to acknowledge that the most popular series and serials were regularly attracting audiences in excess of 15 million. 'Popularity', in this respect, is relative.

A total of 298 *Play for Today*s were transmitted between October 1970 and August 1984, when the series ended, an average of nearly twenty plays each season.[3] Of these, ninety-four were shot on film, while 204 plays were recorded electronically in the studio. Although shooting on film was more expensive, the number of *Play for Today*s being made on film increased as the 1970s wore on. Only six of the twenty-one plays in the first (1970–1) season were shot on film,[4] but by the time of the tenth (1979–80) season more than half of the twenty-seven plays transmitted were made on film.[5]

The reputation which *Play for Today* has acquired as a vehicle for radical and original television drama is largely based on a relatively small number of plays – such as Jim Allen's *The Rank and File* (1971), *The Spongers* (1978) and *United Kingdom* (1981); David Edgar's *Destiny* (1978); Trevor Griffiths' *Through the Night* (1975), *Comedians* (1979) and *Country* (1981); David Hare's *Licking Hitler* (1978); Mike Leigh's *Hard Labour* (1973), *Nuts in May* (1976) and *Abigail's Party* (1977); Philip Martin's *Gangsters* (1975); John McGrath's *The Cheviot, the Stag and the Black, Black Oil* (1974); Alan Plater's *Land of Green Ginger* (1973); Dennis Potter's *Blue Remembered Hills* (1979); Jack Rosenthal's *Bar Mitzvah Boy* (1976); David Rudkin's *Penda's Fen* (1974); Jeremy Sandford's *Edna, the Inebriate Woman*; Peter Terson's *The Fishing Party* (1972); and Colin Welland's *Leeds – United!* (1974). Of these twenty plays only four (*Destiny*, *Through the Night*, *Comedians* and *Abigail's Party*) were recorded in the studio; the rest were shot on film, on location.[6]

There are good reasons why it is mainly the filmed *Play for Todays* which are cited when the series is championed as the 'golden age' of British television drama. First, shooting on film enabled the producers of the plays to locate them in the real world and to achieve an aesthetic of realism which has always been critically valued in British culture. Second, there is the practical reason that it is the filmed *Play for Todays* which are more likely to have survived, or been available for subsequent viewing, than plays that were recorded on videotape.

The cost of storing programmes on videotape reached a crisis point in the early 1970s. This was partly because of increased costs but also a result of the transition to colour which brought to an end the process of telerecording, which was technically unsuitable for recording colour programmes. With the rising cost of videotape, and the lack of a policy for preserving television programmes, the television companies wiped hundreds of tapes in the early 1970s. While light entertainment programmes and series drama were more vulnerable to wiping than the single play, many *Play for Todays* made before 1974, the year in which the BBC Film Library gained control of programmes recorded on videotape, were also wiped.[7] Those studio recordings which were kept have rarely received repeat screenings, so the reputation of *Play for Today* tends to rest on a relatively small percentage of the 298 plays transmitted between 1970 and 1984.

The difference between film and video, location shooting and electronic studio recording, can clearly be seen when comparing any of Mike Leigh's filmed *Play for Todays* with the one that was recorded in the studio, *Abigail's Party* (1 November 1977). Leigh made his television debut with *Hard Labour* (12 March 1973), a play commissioned and produced by Tony Garnett and one which is clearly in the social realist *Play for Today* tradition with which Garnett was firmly associated. *Hard Labour* was filmed in Salford, Leigh's home town, and is naturalistic in style, observing both its characters and the environs in which they move with studied curiosity. Leigh followed this with two more filmed *Play for Todays*: *Nuts in May* (13 January 1976) and *The Kiss of Death* (11 January 1977), plays which established his reputation for acute social observation of the working and lower middle classes – satirical dramas with a sharply comic edge.

Abigail's Party, however, was originally a stage play which had been running for several months at Hampstead Theatre in London before it was recorded as a *Play for Today*. When a slot became available in the series, the play was 'wheeled into the studio and, paradoxically, became the most successful of these things, although it wasn't actually generically a piece of television at all'.[8] Of all Leigh's work, *Abigail's Party* clearly looks like a stage play which has been transposed to the television studio without any attempt to open it out. Aesthetically, it harks back to the days of live studio drama, but its success on television was largely due to the fact that it was already a very polished play after many weeks of being performed by the same cast in the theatre:

> When we wheeled it into the studio in November 1977 the actors had just done
> 104 performances of it and it was fantastically solid and that shows ... stage plays

have to be thorough in a way that you don't have to be when you can go out and shoot any old thing in the street and then piece it together in the cutting room … *Abigail's Party*, for all the awfulness of its rushed studio quality, and I swore I would never go into a studio again, at the time when I swore that I didn't know that it was going to go out of fashion and it wasn't going to be a problem. At the time it was a major ideological crisis about whether one would go into studios. I never have done again, but, in fact, it ceased to be an issue, but I swore I wouldn't. But despite its technical sloppiness the play itself was solid and I think that accounts for its success. Also the other thing that accounts for its success, without any shadow of a doubt, is the fact that the second time it was repeated it went out during an ITV strike, on a very wet night, before Channel 4 was invented and when something very highbrow was on BBC Two. It was a stormy night throughout the UK and so we did score 16 million viewers and I think that contributed considerably to its fame and fortune.[9]

Aesthetically, the contrast between Leigh's filmed television plays and *Abigail's Party* is stark and it is ironic that it is *Abigail's Party* that is the best known of all his television work.

An earlier *Play for Today*, Colin Welland's *Kisses at Fifty* (22 January 1973), transmitted in the same season as Leigh's *Hard Labour*, provides an interesting example of a *Play for Today* which used film and studio recording in roughly equal measure, moving easily between the two, although the difference in visual quality is clearly evident. Unlike earlier TV drama, where film inserts had been used to provide brief linking sequences between studio scenes, the film sequences in *Kisses at Fifty* are more extensive and are as important to the story as the studio scenes.

The story revolves around the consequences of the decision by Harry (Bill Maynard), a working-class miner, to leave his wife of thirty years and his grown-up children for a younger woman, whom he meets on his fiftieth birthday. A dramatic highpoint of the play is the (studio) scene in which Harry tells his wife he is leaving, that there is no point in them trying to carry on. It is significant that this scene is played out in the marital home, in the bedroom in fact, and the oppressiveness of the situation, enhanced by the claustrophobia of the studio set, helps to emphasise Harry's need to get away.

This is followed by a scene in which the consequences of Harry's decision are forcefully illustrated when, having spent an uncomfortable night sleeping on a bench at a railway station, he is woken by a policeman, who tells him where he might find accommodation. Shooting this scene on film, on location, gives it a gritty documentary quality, emphasising the stark reality of Harry's decision to give up his comfortable life. In the cold light of day, on the station platform, the significance of his decision is brought home, to him and to us. Needless to say, the scene would have been less effective in the studio – the play needed location shooting at this point to reinforce the dramatic significance of the scene.

At other times in *Kisses at Fifty* the mixture of studio recording and location shooting contrasts strikingly, as in the sequence following a confrontation in the local pub between Rene (Rosemarie Dunham), Harry's wife, and Audrey (Marjorie Yates), the barmaid with whom he is having an affair. In the subsequent scene, shot on location, Harry is seen arriving at work, where he angrily starts shovelling coal. This filmed footage is interspersed with studio footage of Rene sitting despondently at home, intercut with another domestic studio scene of Audrey at home with her husband. A series of quick cutting between the three locations highlights the differences in visual quality: the rough, grainy quality of film for the workplace, helping to express Harry's anger, contrasted with the cold, bright studio light of the domestic scenes, showing the two women trapped in unhappy households. The contrast in quality between film and video, workplace and home, is stark, yet dramatically the scene is very effective. While the juxtaposition of film and video may appear slightly odd by the standards of thirty or more years later, an early 1970s audience is likely to have been sufficiently enthralled by the drama not to be distracted by its aesthetics.

Kisses at Fifty is a good example of an unpretentious, social realist *Play for Today*. Its strength, and its success as drama, resides in the writing and the acting. The filmed sequences 'open the play out' successfully, whereas the more confined interior (studio) scenes are often used to emphasise the sense of claustrophobia and entrapment from which the husband seeks to break away. In some ways, *Kisses at Fifty* seems caught at a transitional moment in the development of the single play, caught between the past and the future, between the electronic studio and the 'real world' captured on film, but the play succeeds, nevertheless, in presenting an intimate portrait of working-class relationships, capturing the reality of a social situation without moralising or didacticism.

Play for Today is synonymous with 'authored drama'. The early institutionalisation of the playwright as the 'author' of the single play enabled radical playwrights in the 1970s – writers like Jim Allen, Dennis Potter and Trevor Griffiths – to continue to produce progressive drama at a time when the opportunities for doing so were increasingly coming under threat as a result of economic constraints and political pressures. The list of seminal *Play for Todays* cited above foregrounds the writer as author, yet with the increasing use of film on *Play for Today* directors were gradually taking a more creative role. Another list could be produced naming Alan Clarke, Richard Eyre, Stephen Frears, Jack Gold, Roland Joffe, Ken Loach and John Mackenzie as auteurs. All of these directors came to prominence working on filmed television plays and all of them subsequently went on to work in the film industry.

Conversely the studio *Play for Todays* are more unequivocally authored by the writer: David Edgar's *Destiny*; Trevor Griffiths' *All Good Men* (1974), *Through the Night* and *Comedians*; Dennis Potter's *Angels Are So Few* (1970), *Traitor* (1971), *Only Make Believe* (1973), *Joe's Ark* (1974), *Schmoedipus* (1974) and *Brimstone and Treacle* (1976, not transmitted until 1987) – all studio plays. At the time of the non-transmission of *Brimstone and Treacle*, due to be broadcast on 6 April 1976 but replaced at the last minute by Potter's *Double Dare* (a rare example of a filmed *Play for Today* shot in the studio, rather than on location), Dennis Potter was already lamenting the shift from studio recording to shooting on film and the likely consequences of this for the television playwright: 'It will soon all be done on film and it'll be a director's medium like the cinema. It only remains an author's medium at the moment because of British anachronisms.'[10]

With a few notable exceptions most *Play for Todays* were naturalistic in form, although with the increasing tendency towards filming on location the dominant aesthetic of *Play for Today* is perceived to be social realism, rather than the studio naturalism against which Troy Kennedy Martin directed his 'Nats Go Home' polemic in 1964. It is these filmed plays, plays like *Edna, the Inebriate Woman, The Spongers* and *United Kingdom*, which maintained the progressive, social realist tradition initiated by *Up the Junction* and *Cathy Come Home* in the 1960s. Yet some of the naturalist *Play for Todays*, recorded in the studio, proved that naturalism could also be used as a vehicle for radical drama in, for example, Trevor Griffiths' critique of the National Health Service, *Through the Night*, in David Edgar's powerful anti-National Front drama *Destiny* and in Caryl Churchill's dramatisation of the trial of two men accused of a bombing in Northern Ireland, *The Legion Hall Bombing* (1978).[11]

Play for Today is looked back on as the 'golden age' of the single play on British television, a time when writers, directors and producers enjoyed unprecedented freedom. Yet as early as 1980, at the Edinburgh International Television Festival, Carl Gardner and John Wyver were bemoaning a decline in the single play and noting a shift towards 'cost-effective television' in the 1970s.[12] Identifying three phases of the single play, the 'post-war Reithian' phase, the 'Sydney Newman' phase from the late 1950s to the beginning of the 1970s, and the 1970s 'era of cost-effectiveness',[13] Gardner and Wyver explored the economic and ideological reasons for a perceived decline in the single play during the 1970s:

> … the wind of change was felt most sharply at the BBC. Inflation began slowly to outstrip the Corporation's fixed revenue and the licence fee fell more and more out of phase with costs – from being an other-worldly institution where vulgar things like money were somehow slightly sordid considerations compared with the fondly-paraded 'enrichment' of the cultural life of the nation, we slipped inexorably into the era of 'cost-effective' television. Slowly accountancy, rather than 'creativity', became the most important talent. Nowhere was this more important than in the single play.[14]

However, it was not only the BBC which became subject to economic constraints in the 1970s. While the ITV companies did not experience quite the same financial pressures as the BBC, they were increasingly conscious of the need to attract advertising revenue at a time when the economy was going into recession. This, Gardner and Wyver argue, was the reason behind the prioritising of series and serial drama over the single play during the 1970s, a tendency which was already becoming apparent in the 1960s. Series and serial drama were more 'cost-effective' for two reasons. First, the costs of a drama series could be spread over a number of episodes: sets and costumes could be used again and again and less rehearsal time was needed because the actors were not starting from scratch as they were with the single play. Second, series and serial drama was a more attractive proposition for overseas buyers than was the one-off play and in the harsher economic circumstances of the 1970s co-production money was becoming increasingly important.

An early casualty was ITV's *Saturday Night Theatre*, which began in 1969 with Alun Owen's *Park People* (Yorkshire, 11 January 1969) and ended two years later with an adaptation of James Joyce's *The Dead* (Granada, 2 January 1971). Later the same year there was an indication of how the single play was vulnerable to being sacrificed in favour of the more cost-effective series when *Sunday Night Theatre* made way in the ITV schedules for *Upstairs Downstairs*, a historical drama made by LWT, modelled on the BBC's highly successful *The Forsyte Saga*. While *Sunday Night Theatre* returned after the first six episodes of *Upstairs Downstairs*, it was eventually terminated in April 1974, three months before ITV's long-running anthology series *Armchair Theatre* ended with Dominic Behan's *According to the Rules* (Thames, 9 July 1974). ITV's *Playhouse* series, which began in 1967 with an adaptation of Oscar Wilde's *Lady Windermere's Fan* (Rediffusion, 25 September 1967), also ended in 1974, although it was revived in 1980 for a final series of nine plays, which included one of David Mercer's last plays, *A Rod of Iron* (Yorkshire, 29 April 1980).

Two more ITV anthology series also ended in 1974: *Late Night Theatre* (ITV, 1972–4) and *Late Night Drama* (ITV, 1974) were both anthologies of short plays (25–35 minutes), by writers including David Edgar, John Osborne and N. F. Simpson. A short-lived ITV anthology series called *The Wednesday Special* (1975–6) also included a short play by John Osborne – *Almost a Vision* (Yorkshire, 1 September 1976), but this series of four plays was probably more notable for its first play, *The Naked Civil Servant* (Thames, 17 December 1975), about the renowned homosexual Quentin Crisp, played flamboyantly by John Hurt. The play was distinguished by a witty, elliptical script written by Philip Mackie which never allowed the pace to slacken, effortlessly conveying Crisp's remarkable life story in a breezy seventy-five minutes. Before being picked up by Thames TV *The Naked Civil Servant* had been turned down by the BBC, who were concerned about its risqué subject matter – a sign of the changing climate at the BBC which led to the banning of two *Play for Todays* in the next two years (see below). The BBC's loss was Thames Television's gain and *The Naked Civil Servant*, despite the Independent Broadcasting Authority's qualms about some scenes, proved to be a huge critical success, winning the 1976 Prix Italia.

Thames originally commissioned *The Naked Civil Servant* for *Armchair Theatre*, which the company had inherited from ABC Television in 1968, when Thames TV was formed out of the merger of ABC and Rediffusion. But whereas *Armchair Theatre* plays were recorded electronically in the studio, *The Naked Civil Servant* was shot on 16mm colour film, enabling director Jack Gold to film in real locations and achieve a mixture of gritty realism and stylised fantasy that was perfectly suited to the realisation of Quentin Crisp's often difficult but also very colourful life. The film described Crisp's life as an extrovert homosexual from the 1920s through to the post-war period – a period when most gay men remained firmly in the closet, concluding in the 1970s, by which time he had become 'one of the stately homos of England', as he proudly told a group of queer-baiting boys. Ultimately, the film was life-affirming, a celebration of queer sexuality which encouraged many gay men to come out in the 1970s. The film made Quentin Crisp a celebrity in his late sixties and John Hurt's magnetic performance won him a British Academy of Film and Television Arts (BAFTA) award for Best Actor.

The Naked Civil Servant was part of the transition towards filmed drama at ITV in the mid-1970s, along with Thames TV's *Armchair Cinema* (1974–5), a short series of six films which succeeded *Armchair Theatre* in 1974, but both *The Wednesday Special* and *Armchair Cinema* were short-lived. The producer of *The Naked Civil Servant*, Barry Hanson, also produced *Plays for Britain* for Thames in 1976, a short anthology series which included the first television play by Stephen Poliakoff, *Hitting Town* (27 April 1976), alongside plays by Howard Brenton, Brian Glover, Henry Livings, Roger McGough and Roy Minton. ITV's *Playhouse* was revived in 1977 as *ITV Playhouse*, lasting until 1982, and there were two seasons of *The Sunday Drama* on ITV from 1977–8, plus a short season (four plays) of *Saturday Drama* in 1978, but the attenuated form of many of these anthology series was a sign of ITV's reduced commitment to the single play in the 1970s.

With the scaling back of ITV's anthology series in the 1970s the onus was placed much more on the BBC to continue to support the single play – another reason why the continued existence of *Play for Today* throughout the 1970s was so important. Yet the pressures on the BBC were beginning to show by the mid-1970s. The radical *Play for Today*, *The Cheviot, the Stag and the Black, Black Oil*, had stirred things up in 1974, as did the Loach/Garnett/Allen four-part series *Days of Hope* in 1975, but these highly political dramas were transmitted. After turning down *The Naked Civil Servant* because of its subject matter, the first victim of internal censorship at the BBC was Dennis Potter's *Brimstone and Treacle*, originally intended to be shown as part of a trilogy of Potter plays in April 1976, but withdrawn by Alasdair Milne, Director of Television Programmes, because of concerns that the story of a mentally handicapped young woman who is raped by a 'demonic visitor',[15] as a result of which she is liberated from her vegetable state, would cause 'real outrage'.[16]

In his book on Potter, John Cook outlines the political background to the banning of *Brimstone and Treacle* and the increasing political pressure on the BBC as a public institution which had been harbouring 'left-wing radicals' within its Drama Department since the 1960s, people like Jim Allen, Tony Garnett, Ken Loach, Roger Smith and Ken Trodd:

> The *Brimstone and Treacle* affair was only part of a much wider backlash in the mid-seventies against the so-called 'radicals' within BBC drama. Moreover, like allegations of 'dirty tricks' campaigns against the Labout Government of the time under Harold Wilson, that reaction was ultimately instigated by the Security Services in the shape of MI5.[17]

The BBC Drama Department, through *The Wednesday Play* and *Play for Today* in particular, had built up a reputation for radical drama to such an extent that by the mid-1970s, at a time of political turmoil, BBC Drama became the target of a right-wing backlash and left-wingers within the BBC were subject to the scrutiny of an MI5 'mole' at the BBC. It was not just political pressure, however, but accusations of increasing sex and violence in BBC drama that were a factor in Milne's decision to ban *Brimstone and Treacle*. The right-wing pressure group, the National Viewers and Listeners Association, led by Mary Whitehouse, kept up its pressure on the BBC and, as a reaction to the 'permissive' 1960s set in, other right-wing organisations and newspapers contributed to the growing pressure on the BBC during the 1970s.

Following the *Brimstone and Treacle* debacle, where the explosive mix of sex and religion was the catalyst for the controversy, it was the degree of violence in Alan Clarke's *Scum*, written by Roy Minton, which was the ostensible reason for it becoming the second *Play for Today* to be banned, in 1977. The film portrayed life in a boys' borstal in graphic detail and was clearly a savage indictment of the whole borstal system. Again, it was Alasdair Milne who took the decision not to show it, but David Hare, whose first television play *Man Above Men* was directed by Alan Clarke in 1974, saw the decision as a political one, illustrating the extent to which the BBC had become subject to governmental pressure:

> The decision about *Scum* was particularly craven, it was a pure political decision dressed up as an artistic decision. And there wasn't any real justification for it, except sheer fear of government. And once you had the simple equation – the Home Office licenses the BBC, therefore you cannot make films which are critical of Home Office institutions – then the BBC's credibility was destroyed. The government looked Alasdair Milne in the eye, and he blinked, he simply said, 'I'll destroy my own work.' To not back your own creative people when they haven't done anything wrong was a very grim moment in the history of the BBC.[18]

Yet, despite the increasing political pressure on the BBC, *Play for Today* continued to be a showcase for radical work. Jim Allen's *The Spongers* and *United Kingdom*, Alan Bleasdale's *The Muscle Market* (1981), Caryl Churchill's *The Legion Hall Bombing*, David Edgar's *Destiny*, Trevor Griffiths' *Comedians* and *Country*, Ian McEwan's *The Imitation Game* (1980), Horace Ove's *A Hole in Babylon* (1979) and Dennis Potter's *Blue Remembered Hills* all bear witness to the possibility of getting progressive drama onto BBC One, in primetime, in the late 1970s and early 80s.

Form and politics in television drama

With the growth in importance of series and serials and the increasing pressures, both economic and ideological, on the single play, some radical dramatists began to look to the possibility of utilising series and serial drama for political purposes in the 1970s. One of the most important examples is Trevor Griffiths' eleven-episode series for Thames Television, *Bill Brand* (June–August 1976), about a Labour politician, played by Jack Shepherd. While Griffiths has incorporated non-naturalistic techniques into some of his theatre and television plays, *Bill Brand* was resolutely naturalistic, expressing his concern to engage with the popular audience on familiar terrain:

> I have to work with the popular imagination which has been shaped by naturalism. I am not interested in talking to 38 university graduates in a cellar in

Soho. It's my guess that we still have to handle realism. One of the things about realistic modes is still that you can offer through them demystifying, undistorted, more accurate, counter descriptions of political processes and social reality than people get through other uses of naturalism. So that if for every *Sweeney* that went out, a *Bill Brand* went out, there would be a real struggle for the popular imagination.[19]

Bill Brand came out of the political turmoil of the early to mid-1970s and was an attempt to intervene within the popular medium of television at a time when political struggle, through industrial disputes and demonstrations as well as at the ballot box, was very much a part of everyday life. Even so, it was a brave move by a commercial television company, Thames, to commission a multi-episode series dealing with the bureaucratic machinations of party politics and schedule it at peak-time (9 pm) on a Monday evening.

With Jeremy Isaacs as Director of Programmes and Verity Lambert as Controller of Drama at Thames, this was an adventurous period for the company, demonstrating that it was not only the BBC that was capable of producing progressive television drama during the 1970s. Lambert wanted Thames to produce drama series 'which were attempting in one way or another to tackle modern problems and life',[20] an ambition which echoed the philosophy of her mentor Sydney Newman, with whom she had worked at ABC in the late 1950s and again at the BBC in the 1960s. For a socialist playwright like Trevor Griffiths this was an opportunity not to be missed; indeed, he believed that it was essential for socialist playwrights to make this kind of 'strategic penetration' within the mass medium of television:

The essence of strategic penetration is to pick your ground and to know it fairly well ... I simply cannot understand socialist playwrights who do not devote most of their time to television ... it's just thunderingly exciting to be able to talk to large numbers of people in the working class, and I just can't understand why everybody doesn't want to do it.[21]

Being one of the first drama series to use video cameras for its location scenes, *Bill Brand* had a distinctly different look to other television dramas of the time, different to *Play for Today*, which was either recorded in the studio on videotape or shot on location on film, and different to other Thames series like *The Sweeney*, which used film in order to achieve a more gritty, realistic quality. *Bill Brand*, however, was not seeking to emulate the gritty realism of *The Sweeney* but wanted to achieve the naturalistic feel of popular drama series, like *Coronation Street* and *Crossroads*, in order to compete with mainstream drama on its own terrain, to be indistinguishable in form, but radically different in subject matter.

A year before *Bill Brand* was transmitted Jim Allen, Tony Garnett and Ken Loach had attempted to make a similar political intervention on BBC One, with the four-part series *Days of Hope* (BBC One, 11 September–2 October 1975). After the radical analysis of contemporary industrial conflicts in *The Big Flame* (BBC One, 19 February 1969) and *The Rank and File* (BBC One, 20 May 1971), Allen/Garnett/Loach went back to an earlier period of class and industrial conflict with *Days of Hope*, following the growing political awareness and involvement of a working-class family from the First World War to the General Strike of 1926. While the subject matter was historical, the political objectives of its makers were as contemporary as those of Trevor Griffiths, as producer Tony Garnett emphasised in the *Radio Times* at the time of its transmission: 'Our motive for going into the past is not to escape the present: we go into the past to draw lessons from it. History is contemporary.'[22]

Stylistically, however, *Days of Hope* was quite removed from *Bill Brand*. After the modernist experimentation of *Up the Junction* and *Cathy Come Home*, with their jump-cuts, rapid editing and asynchronous sound jubilantly celebrating the liberation from the constraints of the studio, Ken Loach began to develop a more naturalistic style in the late 1960s. Both *In Two Minds* (BBC One, 1 March 1967) and his first feature film *Poor Cow* (1967) were transitional, showing some of the modernist experimentation of the mid-1960s plays but also a greater degree of observational documentary realism which was to become Loach's trademark style. By 1969 the aesthetic experimentation of the earlier works had been superseded by the documentary realism of *The Big Flame* and the cinematic naturalism of *Kes* (1969).

The Big Flame was the first collaboration between Ken Loach and Jim Allen. Allen had worked as a labourer and manual worker in a variety of jobs before turning to writing, learning the craft of television dramatisation on episodes of *Coronation Street* from 1965–6. In his first television play, *The Lump*, produced by Tony Garnett and directed by Jack Gold as a filmed *Wednesday Play* in 1967, Allen drew upon his experience as a labourer in what was to be the first of several scripts dealing with industrial conflict. The formidable Loach/Garnett/Allen partnership was formed in 1968, when they collaborated on *The Big Flame*, a play about a strike at the Liverpool docks. This was followed by another play about industrial conflict, *The Rank and File*, which recreated (in Stoke-on-Trent) a strike which had taken place at the Pilkington Glassworks in St Helens in 1970.

The Loach/Garnett partnership, already part of the radical Left at the BBC in the 1960s, now took on a more overtly political dimension in the collaborations with Jim Allen, whose Marxist-Trotskyist politics are clearly evident in his work. There is not a lot of 'action' in these plays, considering that they were filmed on location, but an emphasis instead on exploring the political issues at the heart of the dramas through argument and debate, often in smoke-filled rooms and bars. Loach's use of naturalistic lighting and unobtrusive camerawork contributes to the documentary look of the dramas, establishing their realism, which is further emphasised by the use of black-and-white film and the employment of a documentary-style voiceover. The political and industrial struggles depicted in *The Big Flame* and *The Rank and File* are shown to be part of an ongoing struggle, illustrated at the end of *The Rank and File* when, over photographs of working-class children, the voiceover of one of the workers is heard: 'I go along with Trotsky, that life is beautiful, that the future generation cleanses of all the oppression, violence and evil, and enjoy life to the full.' For all the didacticism of these political dramas, Allen's optimistic humanism is given the final word.

Four years after *The Rank and File* the Allen/Garnett/Loach partnership delivered one of the outstanding examples of radical BBC drama in the four-part series *Days of Hope*. This series of four feature-length plays, filmed in colour, entirely on location, described the lives and changing political experiences of three working-class characters between the years 1916 and 1924. Each of the four episodes focused on one significant historical moment in that period: the First World War, the miners' strike of 1921, the first Labour government of 1924 and the General Strike of 1926. The concentration on crucial moments of labour history and the emphasis on the miners in two episodes was of particular significance given the miners' strikes of 1972 and 1973–4, underlining the reason for returning to the past – not to escape from the present but 'to draw lessons from it'.

Employing, once again, a distinctive naturalistic style, and clearly favouring a revolutionary analysis of the political events of the period, *Days of Hope* provoked considerable controversy when it was transmitted, with various representatives of the political Right accusing the BBC of left-wing bias. The drama documentary form of the series was seen as particularly contentious because of the way in which it 'naturalised' the historical events depicted, giving them a veneer of authenticity which was highly persuasive. This authenticity was reinforced by the epic scale of the series, covering ten turbulent years in over six hours of screen time, during which the lives and political beliefs of the three central characters undergo radical changes.

Sarah and her younger brother Ben emerge as the key characters in the series whose revolutionary political positions at the end are privileged over the Labourist social democracy of Philip, Sarah's husband. The epic scale of the drama enabled Allen/Garnett/Loach to show the growing political awareness of the characters in a realistic manner as their experiences are shaped by a series of significant political events: the fate of conscientious objectors in the First World War, the role of the British Army in Ireland, the miners' strikes of 1921 and 1926, the election of the first Labour government in 1924 and its role in the 1926 General Strike. During this ten-year period Ben (Paul Copley) undergoes a radical political education as he moves from being a naive army recruit to become an active member of the Communist Party, developing a revolutionary Trotskyist perspective – clearly that of Allen himself – which is fully articulated in the fourth episode, where the historical conclusion is drawn that the working class was betrayed in the General Strike by the Labour Party and the TUC leadership.

The historical accuracy of the series was criticised by those who objected to its political message, but the accusations that the drama documentary style distorted the truth was a smokescreen – what clearly worried the right-wing critics who made the accusations was that a forthright socialist perspective on these historical events could be presented on the main BBC channel at peak viewing time. What was really at issue in the public debate sparked off by *Days of Hope* was the radical socialist politics, so effectively communicated in the form of a naturalistic costume drama, hitherto primarily a 'bourgeois' genre.

A different kind of historical drama: working-class politics in *Days of Hope*

That *Days of Hope* came so soon after the 1973–4 miners' strike, which had led to the downfall of Ted Heath's Conservative government, was clearly a significant factor, helping to explain the vehemence of the right-wing attacks upon the series. In its radical analysis of an earlier near-revolutionary moment in working-class history, *Days of Hope* served, in the mid-1970s, to emphasise the ideological role that radical TV drama could play at a time when the political consensus was breaking down and industrial and class conflict were once more back on the social agenda. It also reaffirmed the effectivity of television, and BBC TV drama in particular, as a forum for political debate and oppositional voices, providing one instance in a growing number of political controversies involving television programmes in the 1970s.

In addition to the public controversy sparked off by *Days of Hope*, the series also stimulated an academic debate, mainly in the pages of *Screen*, the theoretical journal of film and television, about the relationship between dramatic form and politics in television drama and the ability of TV drama to have a significant political effect on the viewer. The debate hinged upon the question of realism and the effectivity of the naturalistic style adopted in the series. Essentially, the case for *Days of Hope* as radical TV drama was put by Colin McArthur when he argued against the dominant theoretical position of *Screen* in the mid-1970s which was critical of forms of representation (including films and TV dramas) that utilised the 'bourgeois' form of the classic realist text. This position had been articulated by Colin MacCabe in a 1974 *Screen* article on 'Realism and the Cinema', which highlighted the limitations, as MacCabe saw them, of the classic realist text, the dominant form in literature and cinema, and argued for a revolutionary practice based on the theories of the Marxist playwright Bertolt Brecht.[23]

MacCabe's polemic focused on the reactionary form of the classic realist text and its 'hierarchy of discourses' which tended to privilege a dominant ideological point of view, and he made no allowance for the possibility that the classic realist text might be used for the purpose of communicating progressive political content. It was against MacCabe's formalist position that Colin McArthur made his case for *Days of Hope* as a progressive realist text. McArthur argued that the style adopted by the makers of *Days of Hope* was effective and appropriate for communicating its revolutionary argument and that, rather than the naturalistic form being reactionary, the retention of certain 'classical features' rendered the series accessible to a popular television audience in a way that the more avant-garde anti-realist text that *Screen* was advocating in the mid-1970s would not have been.[24]

Colin MacCabe responded to McArthur by arguing that the problem with *Days of Hope* was not just that it adopted the 'bourgeois' form of the BBC costume drama but that, in doing so, it adopted the 'closed' form of the classic realist text. Because of this, MacCabe questioned the limited nature of the knowledge which the viewer acquires about the events depicted, arguing that by apportioning the blame for the defeat suffered by the working class in the General Strike to the Labour leadership the series offered no vision of social change which could be acted upon by contemporary viewers. An anti-realist or 'Brechtian' strategy might have interrupted the naturalistic flow of the drama, drawing direct political parallels between 'then' and 'now' and suggesting ways in which lessons might be learned from past experience.[25]

An important footnote to this theoretical debate was added by John Caughie in a 1980 *Screen* article on 'Progressive Television and Documentary Drama'. Moving on from the argument about the relative merits of different formal strategies, Caughie argued for the necessity of taking the conditions of production and reception of television programmes into consideration, not just the political and institutional contexts in which a drama is produced but also the circumstances under which it is consumed by the audience. Consideration of this conjuncture of circumstances, Caughie argued, was crucial in trying to assess the political effectivity and 'progressiveness' of any television programme:

> Under certain conditions, of which the present may be one, I want to be able to say that, *for television*, in its specific conditions, it may be politically progressive to confirm an identity (of sexuality or class), to recover repressed experience or history, to contest the dominant image with an alternative identity. Documentary drama seems to me to have occupied a progressive role within television insofar as it has introduced into the discourses of television a repressed political, social discourse which may contribute to an audience's political formation, and may increase its scepticism of the other representations which television offers [original emphasis].[26]

Caughie's contribution was to argue for the possibility that television programmes might have political effects upon the viewer that cannot be measured by focusing on the formal operations of the text alone. In doing so he signalled a shift in the academic study of television towards the role of the television institutions and the political and economic context of production, as well as giving greater emphasis to the social and political context of reception and the ability of the viewer to make 'progressive' readings of television programmes.

The Cheviot, the Stag and the Black, Black Oil (1974)

As a footnote to the *Days of Hope* debate Colin McArthur, in his 1978 BFI monograph *Television and History*, cited the example of a 1974 *Play for Today* that had, until then, been overlooked in the arguments about form and politics in television drama. Not only was this particular *Play for Today* politically progressive, McArthur argued, but it was also presented in a populist style, thus avoiding the danger of obscurity which a more austere vanguard text, such as that which McArthur believed MacCabe was advocating, might have engendered:

> Among the substantial issues raised by MacCabe about *Days of Hope*, the concession appears to be made that the kind of text MacCabe is canvassing in his critique of the classic realist text, the kind of text which provides the necessary space for the operation of a conceptual apparatus, must of necessity attract a smaller audience than works such as *Days of Hope*. That conclusion is premature on the evidence of what is, in many respects, the most interesting attempt thus far to unite television and radical historiography in a dramatic mode which promotes both pleasure and analysis – the television adaptation of the 7:84 Theatre Company's play *The Cheviot, the Stag and the Black, Black Oil* (BBC).[27]

The Cheviot, the Stag and the Black, Black Oil (BBC One, 6 June 1974) epitomises the progressive nature of the *Play for Today* series, providing arguably its most radical manifestation. As an adaptation of the stage play by the 7:84 Theatre Company this ninety-minute single play is a unique amalgam of theatre performance, historical reconstruction and documentary footage, brought together in a dialectical montage to create a drama documentary which is qualitatively different to those drama documentaries, like *Cathy Come Home* and *Days of Hope*, which used documentary techniques to imbue the drama with a greater realism. One of the founding members of the 7:84 Theatre Company was John McGrath, an alumnus of the radical Left at the BBC in the early 1960s who, like his colleague Troy Kennedy Martin, had grown disenchanted with television in the late 1960s and turned to writing scripts for the cinema. In the early 1970s McGrath briefly returned to television with two more *Play for Todays* before turning to agit-prop theatre, co-founding the 7:84 Theatre Company in 1971. McGrath explained the reason for the name of the company in programme notes written for the 1974 tour of the play:

Deconstructing history in the radical *Play for Today: The Cheviot, the Stag and the Black, Black Oil*

7:84 was chosen as the name of the group as a means of drawing attention to a statistic published in *The Economist* in 1966 which asserted that 7% of the population of Great Britain owned 84% of the capital wealth. Although this proportion may have fluctuated marginally over the years, we continue to use it because it points to the basic economic structure of the society we live in, from which all the political, social and cultural structures grow. The company opposes this set-up, and tries to present in its work a socialist perspective on our society, and to indicate socialist alternatives to the capitalist system that dominates all our lives today.[28]

In 1973 McGrath and two other members of the company formed a Scottish branch of 7:84 and their first production was *The Cheviot, the Stag and the Black, Black Oil*, a play 'conceived in the form of the traditional Highland ceilidh. To tell the story of the people of the Highlands to the people of the Highlands.'[29] The play toured extensively throughout the Scottish Highlands from April–June 1973 and again from September–December that year. In between the two tours a film version was made for the BBC, directed by John Mackenzie, another BBC graduate who had worked as a floor manager on *Diary of a Young Man* in 1964.

Mackenzie had seen the touring show and asked McGrath if he would write a screenplay based on the stage production. In agreeing to do so McGrath was concerned that a television version should retain the interactive agit-prop spirit of the theatre play. He proposed using the stage play as a Brechtian alienation device, cutting backwards and forwards between the stage play and the documentary and drama footage that would be filmed for the television version:

I didn't want to try to make television naturalistic soup out of what was a very determinedly anti-naturalistic piece and I said it would have to be done in front of an audience, because it was about the interaction between the stage and the audience, and that would give us the liberty then to cut away and shoot scenes on film which would help it along.[30]

In many respects the television version of *The Cheviot, the Stag and the Black, Black Oil* was a continuation of the non-naturalistic tradition with which McGrath was involved at the BBC in the early 1960s, the difference being that *The Cheviot* was produced at a time when the opportunities for experimentation in television drama were becoming more limited. The other difference was that *The Cheviot* had a more radical political agenda than some of the modernist experiments of the early 1960s. In view of its political agenda McGrath was convinced that naturalism was not the mode in which to tell the story of the exploitation of the Scottish Highlands. The theatre play had adopted a variety of methods – including actors directly addressing the audience, the use of jokes, songs and dancing, and the involvement of the audience through their being invited to participate in the singing and dancing – which were designed to shatter the invisible fourth wall of naturalist drama by eroding the division between the cast and the audience. The challenge was to find a means of doing this with the television production of the play:

The actual writing and shooting of the thing, which was the important bit, was a very conscious attempt to try to use television over a timespan – it covers 200 years of history – and that is really difficult because television naturalism can't do that, it just cannot cope with more than two or three years. So the idea of using the stage show as a rather entertaining, almost light entertainment, way of linking historical episodes, which were shot on film, seemed to me to work, to be the only way to do it.[31]

That the television production of *The Cheviot* was to be a very different kind of *Play for Today* was signalled by the opening title sequence, a montage of images drawing together the three periods of Scottish history with which the play is concerned. The opening shot uses NASA footage filmed from an American spacecraft looking down on Scotland – a caption informs us that this is 'Scotland from 270 miles' – and we hear the voices of American astronauts as they comment on the beauty of seeing the Earth from space, an ironic opening statement given the American oil companies' exploitation of Scotland during the 1970s. This is followed by a shot of a Scottish castle, filmed from a helicopter, as we come down to Earth. A different angle on the same castle follows in a shot which pans across the loch to pick up two transit vans, the touring 7:84 Theatre Company as they travel to their next gig. In the background we hear music playing, a fiddle and drumming, and we cut to a shot of the fiddler, a member of 7:84, as he plays for the audience arriving for the evening performance, which the poster in the next shot tells us is of *The Cheviot*, 'Tonight' at Dornie Hall.

Cut back to a close-up of the fiddler before a dramatic contrast – a shot of a huge JCB truck bouncing over rough ground, the small figure of the driver dwarfed by the size of the truck. Cut to another sharply contrasting image – an eighteenth-century Highlander being chased by soldiers – and then another contrast with a cut to some equipment attached to a buoy being pushed into the sea from a helicopter, followed by an explosion in the sea. The explosion is followed by swirling, inky colours which fill the screen, heralding the title of the drama, *The Cheviot, the Stag and the Black, Black Oil*, the sound of the fiddle and drumming continuing. Next a shot of an oil rig taken from a helicopter flying around it, followed by a return of the swirling colours and another title, 'by John McGrath'.

In the next shot sheep fill the screen – the music now just drumming as the title sequence builds to its climax. Cut to a brief close-up of a man wearing a deerstalker firing a rifle, followed by a long shot of a stag falling to the ground as it is shot – the drumming stops. Then a cut to an oil worker firing a Verey pistol, which ignites a gas jet on an oil rig. The title sequence ends with the camera zooming in to the flame from the jet of gas.

In two minutes and twenty seconds the title sequence has embraced the three periods of Scottish history referred to in the title of the play: the period of the Highland Clearances when the crofters were moved out to make way for Cheviot sheep, the subsequent transformation of the Highlands into a deer-hunting playground for the rich, and the 1970s oil boom which heralded a new era of exploitation with American companies moving in to drill for the black, black oil. This opening montage sequence, starting slowly and building to a dramatic climax as the cutting gets quicker and the shots more sharply contrasted in subject matter, culminating with the present-day image of the burning gas jet on an oil rig, provides a digest of the subject matter of the rest of the film. A brief analysis of the ten minutes following the title sequence will give some indication of the strategy adopted for the television version of the play by McGrath and Mackenzie.

After the rapid montage of the title sequence, a dramatic attention-grabber for the television audience, the pace slows as we are given a wide shot of a Scottish landscape, a loch surrounded by mountains. The camera zooms in towards a community hall by the side of the loch, the lights from its windows glowing brightly in the surrounding darkness, and we hear the sound of community singing. Cutting inside the hall we are presented with the opening of the 7:84 Theatre Company performance of *The Cheviot, the Stag and the Black, Black Oil*, the singing led by Bill Paterson, a member of the company when the play first toured. Cutaways to the audience singing confirms for us, the television audience, that the theatre audience are involved and enjoying themselves. A large sheet, on which are printed the words of the song, is held up by members of the company so that the audience can join in. The lyrics, 'These are my mountains and this is my glen ...', creating a sense of communal solidarity.

The song ends with applause and a drum roll and Bill Paterson introduces the play, with the promise of 'more songs like that ... and afterwards we're going to have a dance'. He continues:

... in between we're going to be telling a story of what's been happening here, in the Highlands. It's a story which has a beginning, a middle, but as yet no end. It begins, I suppose, in 1746, with Culloden and all that. The Highlands are in a bit of a mess. Speaking or singing the Gaelic language is forbidden. The wearing of the plaid is forbidden.

As he speaks the camera zooms in towards a member of the cast who has been quietly singing in Gaelic but who falls silent and has a shawl ripped from her head, an action which is followed by a cut to the location footage of the period reconstruction and the Highlander, seen in the title sequence, being pursued by soldiers. Paterson's voiceover continues over the historical footage, narrating the story which he is telling to the theatre audience, but which, in the television version, becomes the narration for the film. Shortly, another voice continues the narration as two gentlemen, dressed in period costume, are seen riding in the Highlands. Through a combination of their discussion, which we hear, and what we are told in the narration, we learn that these two men are the Edinburgh lawyers, James Loch and Patrick Sellar, who proposed to the landowner, the Marquis of Stafford, later Duke of Sutherland, that the estate which he had acquired in the Highlands could be made more profitable by moving the Highland people out to the coast and replacing them with Cheviot sheep.

The TV production cuts to a sketch from the stage play in which the two lawyers are caricatured and the audience is encouraged to view the deal that they strike as the beginnings of the exploitation of the Highlands by the English. The song which the lawyers sing in the theatre show, in which they teach the audience 'the secrets of high industry', reinforces the message. The theatre sketch is intercut with filmed footage of a Highland family at its cottage. As the song ends we cut to a conversation that the father has with his wife when he tells her of the threat of eviction by English soldiers. In the next scene the threat is carried out and their cottage is burned down. The scene is accompanied by the haunting rendition of a song, sung in Gaelic, from the stage play, with the theatre audience joining in the chorus, and the ominous words of the narrator: 'Strathnaver, June 1814. The clearance of the people begins.'

This strategy, of juxtaposing the stage play (with its mixture of songs, dance, narration, argument, jokes and audience involvement) with the scenes of historical reconstruction filmed on location, is continued throughout the television version of the play. The structural organisation of the TV play is complex, with filmed footage of the stage play and the audience reaction to it being combined with the two kinds of material filmed on location: the historical drama footage and, later on in the play, the documentary material featuring oil workers and their bosses. Throughout, the narration, songs and music from the stage show are used over the historical footage, with the narration, in particular, being used to bind the whole together and create a seamless flow, guiding the viewer through what might otherwise be a bewildering mixture of forms and material.

It is in the juxtaposition of different forms that *The Cheviot* most clearly differs from the dominant naturalist ethic in television drama. In this it also adopts a different strategy for dealing with political subject matter to the one adopted by Ken Loach in the filming of *Days of Hope* and his other social realist dramas. The approach was a self-consciously Brechtian one, as John McGrath admitted, designed not only to politicise the audience but to involve them as active participants in the production of meaning, rather than passive consumers of a predetermined, closed narrative: 'Oh yes, that was consciously Brechtian that was. Brechtianised television – it wasn't a Brechtian stage play but it was a Brechtian way of approaching television, fairly consciously.'[32]

Among the variety of discourses used in this 'Brechtianised' television play the role of the theatre audience was crucial, as Chris Pawling and Tessa Perkins point out:

> The Audience takes the place of the central character in a more conventional drama. These people are the heirs and the descendants of those whose history we are seeing re-enacted. We have witnessed their 'recognition' of the validity of this version of history. They are used throughout to give authenticity and validity to the actors. They act as guarantors of McGrath's history; there are no dissenting voices; we are shown no shots of members of the Audience looking bored rather than amused or shocked or sad or interested. The Audience is a collective subject with whom we identify as strongly as with any individual.[33]

This collectivity is emphasised at the end of the play, when members of the audience are shown listening intently, first of all to a Gaelic lament as we see contrasting shots of oil refineries and unspoiled Scottish lochs, then, in a summing-up of the lessons to be learned from the history of exploitation that has just been recounted, to a speech which is delivered by all the cast members, the camera moving from one person to another as they make their individual contribution:

> The people do not own the land.
> The people do not control the land.
> Any more than they did before the arrival of the Great Sheep.
> In 1800 it was obvious that a change was coming to the Highlands.
> It is obvious now that another change is coming to the Highlands.
> Then as now, the economy was lagging behind the development of the rest of the country.
> Then as now, there was capital elsewhere looking for something to develop.
> In those days the capital belonged to southern industrialists.
> Now it belongs to multi-national corporations with even less feeling for the people than Patrick Sellar.
> In other parts of the world – Bolivia, Panama, Guatemala, Venezuela, Brazil, Angola, Mozambique, Nigeria, Biafra, Muscat and Oman and many other countries – the same corporations have torn out the mineral wealth from the land. The same people always suffer.
> Then it was the Great Sheep.
> Now it is the black, black oil.

> Then it was done by outside capital, with the connivance of the local ruling class
>   and central government –
> And the people had no control over what was happening to them.
> Now it is being done by outside capital, with the connivance of the local ruling
>   class and central government.
> Have we learned anything from the clearances?[34]

Following this sequence, made more powerful by the direct address to the audience/camera, another song is sung in Gaelic and a simultaneous spoken translation is given by one of the cast members, accompanied by shots of the theatre audience, male and female, young and old:

> Remember that you are a people and fight for your rights –
> There are riches under the hills where you grew up.
> There is iron and coal there, grey lead and gold there –
> There is richness in the land under your feet.
> Remember your hardships and keep up your struggle
> The wheel will turn for you
> By the strength of your hands and hardness of your fists.
> Your cattle will be on the plains
> Everyone in the land will have a place
> And the exploiter will be driven out.[35]

The song and its spoken translation is followed by a montage of still images from the play, showing the different moments in the history of exploitation of the Highlands that the play has analysed, intercut once more with shots of the audience. The effect is to make an explicit connection, for the television audience, between then and now, between the generations of Scots that have been exploited for over 200 years and the current and future generations, with the finger of blame clearly pointed at the ruling class and the multi-national corporations.

It was this explicit political message that concerned the BBC, rather than the radical style in which the play was presented. According to McGrath, Alasdair Milne, then Controller of BBC One, demanded that a number of changes were made before the play could be transmitted:

> So a meeting was set up with Alasdair and he invited a guy who was Controller of
> BBC Two to sit in and I said: 'Could we just go through these point by point
> because I have got evidence to back up everything that I've said, a lot of
> evidence?' and I went very quietly and not histrionically and rather academically
> through. Alasdair was sort of slowly beginning to get worn down and then, finally,
> he said, 'Look this piece sounds as if you don't want the oil to be dug out of the
> sea,' and I said, 'Well, if it sounds like that then I'll change it.' That was one line –
> so I changed one line, a little bit. Then at the end of this process he turned to the

other guy from BBC Two and said, 'Well what do you think? It's very extreme,' and the other guy said, 'Well, you know Alasdair, the more extreme the point of view expressed in this play, the less likely the audience will be to think it's the BBC's point of view. So I think we're quite safe to put it out.' And that was how it got put out.[36]

The Cheviot, the Stag and the Black, Black Oil remains unique within the history of British television drama. Stylistically, with its montage of different forms, and politically, with its radical socialist agenda, it is a product of its time, a period when such an 'extreme' play could not only get made within the BBC but could also get screened on BBC One at primetime. Aesthetically, it is an experiment that has not been followed up, remaining a rare example of 'Brechtianised television' amid the naturalistic and social realist drama that, in the 1970s, formed the vast majority of drama broadcast on British television.

Historical drama and literary adaptations

In a paper on the representation of history on television, delivered at the Edinburgh International Television Festival in 1980, Taylor Downing argued that 'history on television should be doing more to help create an understanding of the issues of the present by putting them in the context of the past'.[37] This is clearly what *The Cheviot, the Stag and the Black, Black Oil* was trying to do, to give its audience an understanding of the exploitation of Scotland by multi-national corporations in the 1970s against a background of more than 200 years of colonial exploitation by the English ruling class. In doing so, *The Cheviot* adopted a form which enabled it to make explicit connections between the past and the present, unlike *Days of Hope*, which invited the audience to make a connection between 'then' and 'now', the 1920s and the 70s, without making the parallels explicit in the drama. John McGrath felt that this was a weakness in *Days of Hope*:

> I had my only falling out with Raymond Williams over *Days of Hope* when I said that, although it was telling an important story, because it was using naturalistic techniques it wasn't really making its point properly. I said this publicly and then Raymond publicly said, 'Well, that may be true but, at the same time, because it's made in the dominant mode of television it's attracting mass audiences to parts of history which are glossed over, are not shown very often, therefore it's more valuable to get it on than not.' I still disagree with him, I still think they could have done a lot more to make the connection between *Days of Hope* then and *Days of Hope* now ... I suppose in another way Raymond was right, it was a good way of drawing attention to history. There's plenty of room for both. Or there was; there isn't any more.[38]

The examples of *The Cheviot* and *Days of Hope*, transmitted just over a year apart in the mid-1970s, offer different approaches to dealing with the representation of history in television drama. While they prompted considerable academic debate about history, realism and ideology in TV drama, they were isolated examples of progressive television programmes defining themselves against the dominant tradition of televising history, a tradition of which Downing was critical in his 1980 Edinburgh paper:

> History on television usually provides only one view of the past, based on a bourgeois conception of what history is, and only one sense of heritage, based on a specifically bourgeois historiography. There are alternatives but they are marginalised and often surrounded with controversy and so do not detract from the dominant impression of the past.[39]

The dominant tradition, as perceived by Downing, and also by Colin McArthur in his BFI monograph on *Television and History*, was based on an ideology of individualism, with the 'Great Man' notion of history featuring prominently. In the 1970s this type of historical drama was epitomised by the thirteen-part ATV series *Edward the Seventh* (April–July 1975) in which, according to McArthur, 'the central ideological project … is no less than the humanisation of the British monarchy'.[40] At the beginning of the decade the BBC had capitalised on the dual appeal of costume drama and the monarchy in two highly successful six-part series: *The Six Wives of Henry VIII* (BBC Two, January–February 1970), which attracted an average of 4 million viewers, followed by *Elizabeth R* (BBC Two, February–March 1971), the success of which brought an unprecedented early repeat on BBC One. The monarchy was also the subject of Thames TV's *Edward and Mrs Simpson* (November–December 1978), a seven-part serial which dramatised the events leading up to the abdication of the Prince of Wales in 1937.

Historical drama in the 1970s, however, was by no means confined to the monarchy. The Second World War was also a popular source for drama with London Weekend Television, the new ITV company which had taken over the London weekend franchise from Rediffusion (previously Associated Rediffusion) in 1968, producing twenty-six episodes of *Manhunt* (January–June 1970), featuring two members of the French resistance and a British fighter pilot on the run from the Nazis in occupied France. Meanwhile, Granada produced fifty-two episodes of *A Family at War* (1970–2), created by John Finch, a series about the middle-class Ashton family in Liverpool, which spanned the whole of the war. These popular ITV series were followed by three long-running series on the BBC: *Colditz* (BBC One, 1972–4), *Warship* (BBC One, 1973–7) and *Secret Army* (BBC One, 1977–9), each of which profited from the potential for action and suspense which their wartime scenarios afforded.

All of these series were made in colour. With the introduction of colour television on BBC One and ITV at the end of 1969, after BBC Two's earlier switch in 1967, colour became an important factor in the proliferation of historical drama during the 1970s, as was the increasing use of film for location shooting, although the studio-bound nature of many historical dramas did not seem to affect their popularity.

In addition to dramas about the monarchy and the Second World War, a variety of historical periods were plundered for their dramatic potential during the 1970s: ancient imperial Rome in *I, Claudius* (BBC Two, September–December 1976); eighteenth-century

Cornwall in *Poldark* (BBC One, 1975–7); nineteenth-century sea-faring in the BBC's long-running *The Onedin Line* (BBC One, 1971–80); the nineteenth- and early twentieth-century collapse of three European dynasties in *Fall of Eagles* (BBC One, March–June 1974); and the upheavals of the early twentieth century in *Upstairs Downstairs, The Duchess of Duke Street* (BBC One, 1976–7) and *When the Boat Comes In* (BBC One, 1976–81). Following *A Family at War*, John Finch wrote all thirty-nine episodes of the semi-autobiographical *Sam* (Granada, 1973–5), about life in a South Yorkshire mining village between the 1930s and the 70s.

The second half of the twentieth century was dramatised in two acclaimed drama serials: Frederic Raphael's six-part *The Glittering Prizes* (BBC Two, January–February 1976), which followed the lives of a group of Cambridge students from the early 1950s to the mid-1970s, and Arthur Hopcraft's seven-part dramatisation of John Le Carre's Cold War spy thriller *Tinker, Tailor, Soldier, Spy* (BBC Two, September–October 1979), featuring Alec Guinness as a lugubrious British spymaster, a role he reprised in the early 1980s sequel, *Smiley's People* (BBC Two, September–October 1982).

Some of these – such as *Upstairs Downstairs, A Family at War* and *Sam* – were original dramas devised for television, some were adaptations of novels. *I, Claudius* was adapted from two novels by Robert Graves while the material for *Poldark* was derived from four novels by Winston Graham. Other major productions in the mid-1970s included *The Pallisers* (BBC Two, January–November 1974), adapted from six novels by Anthony Trollope and very much in the tradition of quality BBC Two costume drama established in the late 1960s by *The Forsyte Saga*, while *Clayhanger* (ATV, January–June 1976), adapted from the trilogy by Arnold Bennett, reflected ITV's more populist approach to literary adaptation. Both *The Pallisers* and *Clayhanger* were transmitted over twenty-six episodes, while *Poldark*, on BBC One, ran to twenty-nine episodes, an indication of the huge investment being made in historical dramas in the mid-1970s.

The 1970s also saw a proliferation of adaptations of classic nineteenth-century novels, including Jane Austen's *Emma* (BBC Two, July–August 1972), Balzac's *Cousin Bette* (BBC Two, August–September 1971), a number of Dickens adaptations including *David Copperfield* (BBC One, December 1974–January 1975), *Our Mutual Friend* (BBC Two, March–April 1976) and *Hard Times* (Granada, October–November 1977), adaptations of Thomas Hardy's *The Woodlanders* (BBC Two, February–March 1970), *Jude the Obscure* (BBC Two, February–March 1971) and *The Mayor of Casterbridge* (BBC Two, January–March 1978), and a three-part adaptation of Dostoyevsky's *Crime and Punishment* (BBC Two, May–June 1979). However, it was the twenty-part dramatisation of another Russian literary classic, Leo Tolstoy's epic *War and Peace* (BBC Two, September 1972–February 1973), which consolidated BBC Two's reputation as the channel responsible for 'quality' literary drama. *War and Peace* was shown in twenty forty-five-minute episodes – fifteen hours of screen time – and was in production for three years, representing a major investment by the BBC which, along with the many other classic literary adaptations of the decade, firmly established the BBC's worldwide reputation for the production of quality costume drama.[41]

So why this major investment in historical drama and literary adaptation in the 1970s? In the 1960s the focus had been more contemporary, with both *The Wednesday Play* and drama series like *The Avengers* and *The Prisoner* attempting to capture the youthful zeitgeist of 1960s modernity. Although the BBC had always drawn from classic literature for its television drama, especially in the 1940s and 50s, historical costume dramas were less fashionable in the 'swinging 60s', until the *The Forsyte Saga* burst onto the scene in 1967 giving BBC Two its first big success and providing a successful template which numerous 1970s drama series tried to reproduce.

The cultural shift from the 1960s to the 70s, from liberalism to conservatism and from consent to coercion, was reflected in the television drama produced during the decade. The plethora of historical dramas arguably enabled an escape from the increasingly bitter conflicts of 1970s Britain. In some cases there were lessons to be learned from history – in the case of progressive dramas like *The Cheviot, the Stag and the Black, Black Oil* and *Days of Hope* this was part of their agenda. In most cases, however, this was not the main motivation – the attraction for the TV companies in producing multi-episode historical drama series residing more in their potential for maximising and retaining audiences.

Yet the question remains why certain periods, especially the late-Victorian, Edwardian and Georgian eras, were returned to so frequently, and proved to be so popular, in long-running serials such as *Upstairs Downstairs*, *The Pallisers* and *The Duchess of Duke Street*. A possible answer is offered by Colin McArthur although, as he admits, the supposition is 'speculative':

> It seems reasonable to suppose that a society going through a period of transition and finding it immensely painful and disorientating will therefore tend to recreate, in some at least of its art, images of more (apparently) settled times, especially times in which the self-image of the society as a whole was buoyant and optimistic. For post-war Britain, faced as it is with adjustment to being a post-colonial power, a mediocre economic performer, a multi-racial society and a society in which the consensus of acceptable social and political behaviour is fragmenting (all, of course, factors which are intimately inter-related), what better ideological choice, in its art, than to return to the period of the zenith of bourgeois and imperial power or to immediately succeeding periods in which the facade of that power appeared convincing.[42]

McArthur uses an episode from *Upstairs Downstairs* to illustrate and support his supposition. It is an episode called 'The Nine Day Wonder', from the fifth and final series in 1975, dealing with the General Strike of 1926 and its effect on the Bellamy household. As McArthur argues, while there are moments of friction and ideological conflict between the positions taken up by the various occupants of the house, the Bellamy family 'upstairs' and the servants 'downstairs', the episode is finally resolved in favour of the status quo and class relations are not unduly disturbed by the events. Where the ideological project of *Edward the Seventh* was that of 'the humanisation of the monarchy', the ideological project of *Upstairs Downstairs* becomes that of 'the valorisation of Social Democracy'.[43] In this respect there were connections to be made between the past and the present but, unlike the more controversial histories of *The Cheviot, the Stag* and the Black, Black Oil and Days of Hope, the representation of history offered in Upstairs Downstairs was designed to reassure at a time of similar industrial unrest.

Police series and crime drama

The police series underwent a transformation in the 1970s. While popular BBC stalwarts like Dixon of Dock Green, Z Cars and Softly, Softly continued well into the 1970s their portrayal of the police was being overtaken by events in the wider society. The consensus politics of the 1950s and early 60s had already begun to break down with the student protests of the late 1960s and, with increasing industrial unrest in the 1970s, the role of the state shifted as more coercive and authoritarian measures were introduced to deal with these more visible signs of dissent. This shift became more pronounced during the period of Conservative government, under the leadership of Ted Heath, in the early 1970s:

> The Heath government took recourse to the law as a means of confronting a range of situations from student protest to industrial action. The extension of the role of the state led to what the authors of Policing the Crisis called the 'exceptional state'. 'Exceptional' precisely because the power of the state which had remained so effectively concealed was being unmasked to shore up the position of the ruling bloc threatened from so many quarters it did not know what else to do. The old systems of policing were being challenged by the new role which the ever-increasing legislation was thrusting upon the police and new systems of policing were being developed to deal with this new emphasis.[44]

The introduction of new sections and squads within the police force was acknowledged in the fictional world of TV drama by the appearance of new police series in the late 1960s and early 70s: Fraud Squad (ATV, 1969–70), Special Branch (Thames, 1969–74), New Scotland Yard (LWT, 1972–4) and The Sweeney (Thames, 1975–8) – all ITV drama series. The BBC tacitly acknowledged that changes were taking place by adding the appendage Task Force to Softly, Softly in 1969, but generally the BBC was outmanoeuvred by the ITV companies in the development of new police drama in the 1970s. It is significant that each of the BBC's three long-running police series came to an end between 1976 and 1978, and although Target (BBC One, 1977–8) was developed by the BBC as a more hard-hitting police series it was generally regarded as a poor imitation of Thames Television's highly popular The Sweeney.

It is significant also that it was the two new London-based ITV companies, LWT and Thames TV, that were at the forefront in the development of these new series, for many of the new developments in policing were being initiated by the capital's Metropolitan Police Force. Special Branch, about an elite division within Scotland Yard set up to investigate international crime and espionage, was one of Thames TV's first productions. In 1972 the series became the responsibility of Euston Films, a subsidiary of Thames established in 1971 to make filmed drama for the ITV network, so, after two videotaped series, Special Branch moved over to film for its final two series – a significant aesthetic development in the evolution of a new kind of police drama in the 1970s.

While the second series of *Special Branch* was being filmed, Euston also began production on a series of single dramas, which were to go out under the series title of *Armchair Cinema*. When Thames took over the ABC franchise in 1968 it inherited the ground-breaking *Armchair Theatre* series of single plays. Thames produced another six seasons of *Armchair Theatre*, from January 1969–July 1974, but Euston's decision to produce single dramas on film brought an end to *Armchair Theatre* and contributed to the demise of the studio-based single play on the ITV network, until *ITV Playhouse* revived the studio play for a while from 1977–82.

Six *Armchair Cinema* films were transmitted between May 1974 and November 1975. That there were not more indicates that the priority for Euston Films, as for the ITV network generally, was the production of series and serial drama. Yet the *Armchair Cinema* films were very successful. The first, *The Prison* (Thames, 28 May 1974), topped the ratings and the second, *Regan* (Thames, 4 June 1974), was joint third. One of the main objectives of *Armchair Cinema* was to produce pilot episodes for possible series and with *Regan* Euston struck gold. The film featured John Thaw as Detective Inspector Jack Regan and Dennis Waterman as his partner, Detective Sergeant George Carter, police detectives in a special CID unit called the Flying Squad, aka 'The Sweeney' (short for 'Sweeney Todd', cockney rhyming slang for the Flying Squad), to give it the more familiar name by which it became known to millions over the next four years.

The first series of *The Sweeney* went into production even before *Regan* was transmitted, so confident was Euston of its series potential. Series one was transmitted from January–March 1975 and immediately proved popular, with all but one of the thirteen episodes featuring in the top twenty of the television ratings. By the second series (September–November 1975) *The Sweeney* was never out of the top ten, with seven of the thirteen episodes occupying the number one and two slots. Series three (September–December 1976) was even more popular and the programme was never out of the top five and by the time of the fourth and final series (September–December 1978) the average audience was 15 million.[45]

Clearly, *The Sweeney* succeeded in proving the popularity of a fast-paced contemporary drama series, going a long way to explain why series drama eclipsed the single play during the course of the 1970s. In a period of recession the drama series was more economically viable than the one-off play and it is no coincidence that the more cost-conscious ITV companies moved over to the production of series drama in a big way in the 1970s, virtually abandoning the single play.

Drama series were more economical because they could cut down on rehearsal time, with the same regular cast members and production personnel involved every week. Also the same sets could be used again and again. *The Sweeney*, for example, had a permanent set for the Flying Squad offices, with the bulk of each episode being filmed on location. However, series drama also brought constraints as a consequence of working within strict time limits and circumscribed production conditions. The following extracts from the format for the series, which producer Ted Childs wrote as a guide for writers, illustrate some of the constraints under which the series would be produced:

Each film is shot over ten days. We must, therefore, shoot an average of five
minutes edited screentime a day. This means we have to impose restrictions on
the number of locations we use. Normally ten locations, i.e. one per shooting day,
is enough ...

We normally schedule two days in the ten week shooting cycle in the office
composite set. This means we anticipate ten minutes of any film being set within
these Scotland Yard offices.

Since we are shooting through the summer months, exterior night shooting is
very expensive for us to undertake and we cannot normally anticipate more than
three minutes exterior night material in any script. Interior night scenes are not
normally difficult to contrive.[46]

With only two of the ten days (i.e., ten minutes of screen time) to be spent filming on
the studio set the priority was clearly to be given to location filming in order to achieve
the more realistic feel that was sought for the series. Most of the action was to take
place in real houses, flats, factories, clubs, warehouses and on the streets and the use of
a mobile 16mm film unit was to contribute significantly to the realisation of an action-
oriented police drama:

This series is based on the use of a film unit which moves very quickly across a
number of locations. The nature of our film operation itself very much
determines the style of our films. In general terms, we can cope with action more
readily than we can with multi-handed dialogue. Unlike television, where
extensive rehearsal facilities and the use of several cameras for any given scene
enable fairly complicated sequences involving several actors to be staged quite
easily, we have to light every shot individually for one camera. Also we cannot
enjoy the luxury of extensive rehearsal. This makes complicated dialogue
comparatively difficult for us.

On the other hand, the mobility of our equipment and the sophistication of
our editing and dubbing techniques allow us to produce action sequences which
can attain a considerable degree of pace and excitement. This is not to say that
we do not need good dialogue in our scripts. Clearly an investigatory police
thriller does depend, to no small extent, on good dialogue but in general terms it
is better to write uncomplicated story lines which deal straightforwardly with
crime and criminals where dialogue scenes are short and sharp rather than
intriguing.[47]

These extracts from the original format for *The Sweeney* give some indication of the constraints, and also the possibilities, of the series format within which the writers and
other members of the production team were required to operate, emphasising the
action-oriented focus of the series which shooting on film would facilitate.

Ideologically, *The Sweeney* was to tap into the new initiatives and methods being
introduced in the 1970s as the police had to deal with an increase in violent crime. This

New methods of policing in *The Sweeney*: John Thaw puts the boot in

was the Flying Squad's remit, rather than everyday petty theft, and the popularity of *The Sweeney* suggests that this more action-packed, American-style police drama was seen to be both more exciting and more relevant in the mid-1970s than series like *Dixon of Dock Green* and *Z Cars*, which were both appearing increasingly anachronistic.

Although *The Sweeney* bore the title of a squad within the Metropolitan Police, the ideology was more individualistic, with Regan representing a more ruthless and cynical police detective, one at odds with the new methods which his superiors were trying to introduce and someone who was not afraid to break the rules in order to apprehend the villains. Regan was cast in the mould of the 'rogue cop', a figure epitomised by 'Dirty Harry' in the 1971 Warner Bros. film, but modified in *The Sweeney* for a British context. Regan's partnership with Carter also cast *The Sweeney* in the genre of the 'buddy film', Carter having a grudging admiration for Regan, even though he might occasionally question his methods. Of course, Regan's methods were nearly always justified by the outcome. In an increasingly violent and lawless society, violent and unorthodox methods were seen to be necessary to overcome the threat posed to civil society.

While *The Sweeney* was greeted as a more realistic portrayal of the police, or at least that branch of the police that dealt with violent crime, its macho posturing and perfunctory dialogue left it open to parody and imitation. By the time of the fourth series, in 1978, its central characters were already beginning to seem like stereotypes and the action sequences were becoming clichéd. This impression may have been exacerbated by the appearance earlier that year of a four-part series called *Law and Order* (BBC Two, April 1978). Written by G. F. Newman, produced by Tony Garnett and directed by Les Blair, *Law and Order* adopted a documentary vérité style which immediately put the 'realism' of *The Sweeney* into perspective and which brought forth familiar objections that the documentary drama style obscured whether the series was 'fact' or 'fiction'.

In four eighty-minute films (the documentary approach and use of 16mm film cameras makes the term 'play' seem inappropriate here), *Law and Order* focused on police and judicial corruption in episodes entitled: 'A Detective's Tale' (6 April 1978), 'A Villain's Tale' (13 April 1978), 'A Brief's Tale' (20 April 1978) and 'A Prisoner's Tale' (27 April 1978). In a four-part series comparable to *Days of Hope*, except that this was resolutely contemporary, making its radical exposé of corruption in state institutions seem even more effective and relevant, Tony Garnett again demonstrated the advantage of a 'mini-series' approach to television drama, occupying four single-play slots but with the opportunity to develop a radical critique over more than five hours of screen time. While the series may have been relegated to BBC Two (a sign perhaps of the BBC's caution after the controversies surrounding *The Cheviot* and *Days of Hope*, not to mention the banning of *Brimstone and Treacle* and *Scum*) *Law and Order* once again demonstrated the radical potential of a drama documentary approach. The establishment outcry duly followed when, in an echo of the response of the Lancashire Constabulary to the portrayal of the police in the early *Z Cars*, the Prison Officers' Association, incensed at the portrayal of the legal institutions in *Law and Order*, banned the BBC from filming inside its prisons for a year.

After the more stylised, fictional realism of *The Sweeney*, the transparency of *Law and Order*'s naturalistic style seemed to offer the 'truth' about the police and judicial corruption, confirming doubts which many viewers may have held about the role of the police and the institutions of the law at the end of the 1970s.

Also in 1978 (surely a vintage year for British television drama), Euston Films produced *Out* (Thames, July–August 1978), a six-part serial written by Trevor Preston, directed by Jim Goddard (both of whom had worked on *The Sweeney*) and produced by Barry Hanson, who had been working as a script editor and producer at the BBC before moving over to ITV in the mid-1970s. *Out* shifted the focus from the police to the villains with its story of Frank Ross (Tom Bell), a convicted bank robber who, on being released from prison, begins a quest to find out who informed on him. The drama adopts the form of a melodramatic thriller, while retaining much of the iconography of social realism. In doing so, it was ground-breaking not only for making a working-class villain the central character, but for the convincing way in which it combined generic elements.

With an average audience of 10 million, *Out* demonstrated that a stylish, contemporary working-class drama could be hugely popular, despite (or perhaps because of) stretching the conventions of the crime genre by placing the villains centre stage. Perhaps the more 'realist' approach of *The Sweeney* had made this possible by setting its stories in ordinary working-class milieu and by showing that the police were often not that different from the villains in their respect for the law. The success of *Out* set a precedent, paving the way for more realist crime drama in the 1980s. It also represented a significant ideological development towards the end of a decade in which the issue of law and order had been put on the agenda as an important subject for television drama, the new police series and crime dramas of the 1970s not merely 'reflecting' what was going on in society at the time but contributing to the formation of ideas about, and attitudes towards, law and order in 1970s Britain.[48]

Non-naturalism

While the dominant aesthetic in 1970s television drama was still naturalism/realism, there were as many important departures from the aesthetic as there had been in the 1960s. One of them, The Cheviot, the Stag and the Black, Black Oil has already been discussed, but The Cheviot was not the only play to break with the tradition of social realism for which Play for Today is celebrated. In 1974 Alan Clarke, who with Scum and other work was to become known as a director of bleak realist drama, collaborated with the writer David Rudkin on Penda's Fen (BBC One, 21 March 1974), a filmed Play for Today which centres upon the fantasies of a boy growing up in the Malvern Hills. Barry Hanson, who was working as a script editor at BBC Pebble Mill in Birmingham, where the play was produced, helped to set it up:

> Penda's Fen is a play of mystical Olde English, a boy beset by angels and devils, and a pagan king emerging through an earth that held various appalling nuclear secrets. It also had Mary Whitehouse thinly disguised in it, and all sorts of obsessions and fears that were abroad in that early part of the 1970s. You name it, they all cropped up, and Alan [Clarke] was perfectly at home in that environment. I remember a marvellous matte shot where the aisle of a church was rent asunder. You'd never get away with it on the BBC now.[49]

Both the subject matter and treatment of Penda's Fen mark it out as a rare non-naturalistic drama within the history of Play for Today. Striking imagery, an impressionistic narrative involving a boy's growing awareness of his homosexuality, fantasy sequences, the evocation of myths and legends, all of these combine to make Penda's Fen a remarkable and unique film. Transmitted three months before The Cheviot, it is a totally different example of non-naturalistic drama to McGrath's play and one which the writer David Hare maintains could only have been made at Pebble Mill, under the auspices of producer David Rose:

> When I saw Penda's Fen, I just couldn't believe it. And that is the whole BBC Birmingham culture right there, which was David Rose letting people do what they wanted and nobody in London knowing what was going on. You know: 'The Earth splits open? Oh yeah?' There's just no way a London producer and script editor would have been having that. But my God, that film went out at nine-thirty at night on a majority channel, it's incredible – an hour and a half long. And how bold to do it![50]

Later the same year, the drama unit at Pebble Mill again went against *Play for Today* tradition with the production of *Gangsters* (BBC One, 9 January 1975). Written by Philip Martin, produced by Barry Hanson and directed by Philip Saville, *Gangsters* was a self-reflexive thriller with a multi-ethnic cast. As a thriller it was already a departure from the *Play for Today* norm, but the drama also made use of generic elements in an exaggerated and self-conscious way which had the effect of heightening and sometimes transgressing the conventions of the realist crime thriller. With its mixture of genres and discourses *Gangsters* was both pleasurable, inviting the audience to pick up on the generic and intertextual references, and provocative, stretching the accepted boundaries of the 'well-made play' and challenging the audience in a variety of ways. It was also progressive in its use of a multi-ethnic cast, a radical departure for the BBC, making good use of regional settings in and around Birmingham and ensuring that the drama genuinely reflected the multi-ethnicity of the city. For producer Barry Hanson, *Gangsters* was a deliberate departure from the conventions of serious social drama for which *Play for Today* was renowned:

> It did not fit into any known BBC television style of the time: its cue came from contemporary American urban crime movies. It was very much anti-*Wednesday Play* and *Play for Today* in that it did not have anything 'worthy' about it at all. We were approaching the mid-1970s now and we felt that the fare on offer at the time was too serious and too po-faced: we had heard enough about Sydney Newman. Poor old Cathy was still without a roof over her head, but *Gangsters* aimed to entertain the country through the glamorous exploitation of inner-city themes: illegal immigration, drug-related crime, all the impulses which kick-started the cop shows of the late 1970s and early 1980s, and which survive into the formats of today. *Gangsters* was a film that matched the city in its flashness, and in its new, raw talent. It was also a 'first' in that it used every ethnic minority in the city (Afro-Caribbean, Indian, Chinese, Pakistani, Sikh, and even the newly formed Bangladeshi population).[51]

The single play of *Gangsters* was followed by two six-part serials, in 1976 and 1978, which were also formally innovative. While the play was shot mainly on film, the serials were largely recorded on video in the studio, although with generous use of film inserts for the location sequences. Despite this change the serials retained many of the non-naturalistic features of the play, with the second serial stretching the conventions to breaking point until, at the end, the narrative is fractured when one of the leading characters turns to the camera, exclaiming, 'That's got to be the end!', before walking off the set, which we see from a high angle above the studio revealing the studio cameras and members of the production team. This is followed by the voiceover of the author, the writer Philip Martin, describing the return of one of the characters in the drama to Pakistan, fleeing the racism of England. In this final sequence, we actually see Martin dictating the final words of the script to a typist, on location in Pakistan. Then, with crowds looking on, Martin throws the script in the air and the serial ends on a freeze frame of the pages fluttering down.

BBC studio drama has traditionally been associated with naturalism, but, from time to time, as with *Storyboard* in the early 1960s, the studio has been used for non-naturalistic purposes, as in the two *Gangsters* serials. If Troy Kennedy Martin led the assault against naturalism in the early 1960s, Howard Schuman, an American writer who had moved to England in the late 1960s, was perhaps the leading exponent of studio-based non-naturalism in the 1970s. Unlike many television writers, Schuman was an advocate of the electronic studio, as his 1982 article 'Video-Mad: An American Writer in British Television' illustrates.[52] In 1973 Schuman wrote a one-off drama for a new series of television plays, commissioned by the BBC, which were to go out in a late-night slot. The play was *Censored Scenes from King Kong*, about the quest of a young journalist to unearth a missing 'censored' scene from the famous 1933 Hollywood film, a scene in which Kong makes love to Fay Wray. While the subject matter was perhaps risqué for the BBC, it was the realisation of Schuman's script by director Brian Farnham and designer Mike Porter which made it innovative for its time. Schuman set most of the action in a nightclub (a BBC studio was turned into a warehouse set by Mike Porter) and the narrative was interspersed with songs and music in almost Brechtian fashion. In addition, video technology was used as a means of breaking with naturalism, as Schuman explained in 1982:

> Mike Porter created the nightclub out of air and props and the scenes of Stephen's hallucinatory journey to track down the big story were done with Colour Separation Overlay using pop art collages as backgrounds. (CSO is a process in which actors are photographed against a blue background by a camera which does not pick up the colour blue, while another camera shoots the background, and then the two images are electronically mixed. Effective but frighteningly time-consuming.)
> The finished play mixed comedy, satire, songs, melodrama; it was shot and acted in a highly stylized way. It could only have been a video piece.[53]

While the video effects may have been time-consuming to achieve, the cost of producing the play in the studio was much cheaper than shooting it on film and the generic mixture, together with the play's use of video effects, marks it out as a 1970s equivalent of the *Storyboard* experiments. Unfortunately, the play became a victim of the industrial disputes of 1974 when the 10.30 pm shutdown of the television service prevented its transmission. While slots were subsequently found for three of the four plays that had been recorded for the series *Censored Scenes from King Kong* was never shown, according to Schuman because the Head of Plays, Christopher Morahan, disliked it and did nothing to help get it rescheduled. Two years before *Brimstone and Treacle*, therefore, an innovative drama fell victim to the BBC's inherent conservatism. *Censored Scenes from King Kong* was itself, effectively, censored:

> Kong was censored for aesthetic rather than overtly political reasons (but 'aesthetic' judgements in television are frequently political). It offended one man and so a highly original work, designed with great imagination (and on the cheap

Rock Follies: Howard Schuman's innovative musical drama

with many lessons for other designers), acted and directed with commitment and zest, was stored away (although, interestingly, it was not wiped but placed in the BBC vaults).[54]

Schuman subsequently applied the same formula to his 1976 series for Thames Television, *Rock Follies* (February–March 1976). Once again studio-based, *Rock Follies* charted the faltering progress of an all-woman rock group, interspersing its largely naturalistic narrative with musical numbers which were frequently non-naturalistic in their use of stylised sets and creative camerawork. These non-naturalistic sequences were even more pronounced in the second series, *Rock Follies of '77* (Thames, May–December 1977), with some scenes, such as the one which ends episode four, 'Loony Tunes', pushing towards abstraction in the use of 'solarised' video effects imagery.

Popular music from an earlier era played an important role in perhaps the most famous non-naturalistic drama of the 1970s, Dennis Potter's six-part serial, *Pennies from Heaven* (BBC One, March–April 1978). While Potter was clearly inspired by 1930s Hollywood musicals in the creation of *Pennies from Heaven* it is tempting to speculate that he may also have been influenced by *Rock Follies*, which immediately preceded his own musical drama. Although the 1930s period setting of *Pennies from Heaven* makes it far removed from the contemporary reality of *Rock Follies*, the use of popular songs as an imaginary means of escape for the central character, Arthur Parker (Bob Hoskins), from the grim reality of 1930s Britain is comparable to the way in which it is only through their music that the 'Little Ladies' in *Rock Follies* can keep their dream of stardom and success alive amid the dour reality of life on the road in a 1970s Britain also spiralling into recession. As John Cook has observed:

> It is chiefly in the musical numbers which constantly interrupt the narrative that *Pennies'* 'non-naturalism' resides. In their sheer number (eighty-two in all), the songs offer a constant alternative to 'naturalism' – the brightness and happiness of the melodies and choreography contrasting with the gloomy depiction of 'real life' in the Depression.[55]

Breaking the spell of naturalism in Dennis Potter's *Pennies from Heaven*

Potter's real innovation in *Pennies from Heaven* was to create non-naturalistic musical fantasy sequences in which the characters lip-synch to 1930s songs, while what we hear are the original recordings. This happens even when Arthur is lip-synching to the words of a female vocalist, as on the occasion in episode one when the technique is first used. Potter's aim in using this device was to disorient the viewer, to break the spell of naturalism through the abrupt intrusion of a non-naturalistic technique. At the Edinburgh International Television Festival in August 1977, Potter had presented a paper on 'Realism and Non-Naturalism' and had concluded with what might be seen as his defining statement on the merit of a non-naturalistic approach to television drama:

> Most television ends up offering its viewers a means of orientating themselves towards the generally received notions of 'reality'. The best naturalist or realist drama of the Garnett–Loach–Allen school for instance, breaks out of this cosy habit by the vigour, clarity, originality and depth of its perceptions of a more comprehensive reality. The best non-naturalist drama, in its very structure disorientates the viewer smack in the middle of the orientation process which television perpetually uses. It disrupts the patterns that are endemic to television, and upsets or exposes the narrative styles of so many of the other allegedly non-fiction programmes. It shows the frame in the picture when most television is busy showing the picture in the frame. I think it is potentially the more valuable, therefore, of the two approaches.[56]

The lip-synching of characters singing to popular songs from the 1930s, 40s and 50s was to become Potter's trademark. *Pennies from Heaven* broke new ground in this respect, utilising the device repeatedly to disrupt the narrative flow of the serial over its seven hours of screen time. *Pennies from Heaven* also marked an important shift for Potter away from the more specialised, and increasingly minority-interest, single play to the embracing of a more popular serial format. This was consistent with his original attraction to television as a mass medium which enabled him to communicate with 'large numbers of people in the working class'. That these words are those of Trevor Griffiths, rather than Dennis Potter, is an indication of the rich diversity of British television drama in the 1970s, when two such different writers were responsible for primetime drama serials, written for a mass, working-class audience and screened on the two main television channels.

Science fiction and horror

The genres of horror and science fiction in television drama have been paid little serious critical attention, yet not only have they been very popular but science fiction, in particular, has dealt with topical themes and issues as seriously as any *Wednesday Play* or *Play for Today*. At the beginning of the 1970s *Doomwatch* (BBC One, 1970–2) made a big impact as a popular science fiction series dealing with ecological and scientific issues such as pollution, human embryo research, the dumping of chemical warfare material at sea, and a variety of other illicit activities and experiments being undertaken by secretive organisations. The Doomwatch team was actually set up by the government – Doomwatch being a codename for the Department of Measurement of Scientific Work – but the team often came into conflict with its employers when its investigations unearthed activities that might prove embarrassing to the government. The quest of the Doomwatch team, which turned out to be more radical and zealous in its mission than the government ministers responsible for it may have wished, was to investigate all kinds of dubious scientific experiments. In so doing, *Doomwatch* brought topical issues to the attention of a mainstream television audience – an audience that might never have watched the more 'worthy' *Play for Today*.

Announcing the return of *Doomwatch* for a second series, the *Radio Times* described the ambition of the programme as being to present serious issues within the popular genre of the scientific thriller, with the aim of increasing awareness of those issues among a large audience:

> Kit Pedler, scientist, and Gerry Davis, dramatist, had an idea for a sci-fi thriller series with a difference. It was a bold idea, for the difference was that their stories were actually likely to come true.
>
> While having to succeed as exciting drama, each story in their series would be anchored in scientific reality, its writers projecting what could happen if a particular experiment or technology got out of hand.
>
> That was three years ago. *Doomwatch* finally reached the screen last February under producer Terence Dudley and made an immediate impact. By the time popular Toby Wren (Robert Powell) had been killed attempting to disarm a nuclear device in the last episode, the series had gained a record audience for a first run – 12 million viewers.[57]

An inquiry into the death of Toby Wren followed in the first episode of the second series, the incident being used in an (unsuccessful) attempt to discredit Dr Spencer Quist (John Paul), the Head of Doomwatch. The same episode also featured the grotesque consequences of genetic experiments on animals in a search for a 'human–animal hybrid', an experiment that presciently anticipated the successful cloning of animals, and the subsequent concerns about human cloning, nearly thirty years later.

The subversive credentials of *Doomwatch* were confirmed at the end of the series when what was to be the final episode, provocatively titled 'Sex and Violence', was banned following the inclusion of scenes of a real military execution. This act of BBC internal censorship, coming three years before the more celebrated censorship cases of the mid-1970s, set the seal on the programme's progressive reputation, proving 'that *Doomwatch* – a series that could, at its best, illuminate the deepest fears of the British public – never quite lost its power to shock'.[58]

In the mid-1970s the BBC, forging ahead of ITV in the production of science fiction series at this time, broadcast another prescient series, *Survivors* (BBC One, 1975–7). Created by Terry Nation, a leading writer on *Doctor Who* (and responsible for the 'Daleks'), *Survivors* was set in the aftermath of a worldwide biological plague which had wiped out 95 per cent of the human race – a chilling title sequence reminding viewers of this at the beginning of each episode. Focusing on a group of mainly middle-class survivors in Britain, the success of the series, which ran to thirty-eight episodes over three seasons, picked up on contemporary counter-cultural concerns about the excesses of the dominant culture, with the need for self-sufficiency and rural alternatives to the old city-centred, pre-apocalyptic society recurrent themes throughout the series.

Also on the BBC, *Doctor Who* continued throughout the 1970s, with a new Doctor (Jon Pertwee) and the introduction of Brigadier Lethbridge-Stewart (Nicholas Courtney) giving a more establishment-oriented bias to the series in the early 1970s. This emphasis, however, began to change with the replacement of Pertwee by Tom Baker as the fourth Doctor at the end of 1974, Baker steering the series through its most popular period with viewing figures peaking at 14 million in 1975–6. With a new producer and script editor joining the series at the same time as Tom Baker, *Doctor Who* underwent a change in the mid-1970s, with a strain of psychological horror being added to the successful science fiction mix:

> New producer Philip Hinchcliffe and script editor Robert Holmes began to steer the programme away from what they saw as comfortable SF 'Cowboys and Indians' and towards gothic, psychological horror. Influenced by Hammer, classic science fiction ('The Seeds of Doom' ripped off *The Thing from Another World* quite shamelessly) and ideas of possession and bodily mutation, the programme frightened viewers like never before.[59]

Like science fiction, the horror genre has also been neglected in television studies, yet there were a number of important horror series in the 1970s, programmes which are often categorised as science fiction because of their 'fantasy' elements. They include the final

series of *Out of the Unknown* (BBC Two, April–June 1971), which included an episode written by Nigel Kneale called 'The Chopper' (BBC Two, 16 June 1971) in which the spirit of
a dead motorcyclist manifests itself in the form of motorcycle noise. Kneale developed
this theme in the classic *The Stone Tape* (BBC Two, 25 December 1972), a ninety-minute
drama broadcast on Christmas Day 1972, the seriousness of which was in marked contrast to the light-hearted fare usually on offer at Christmas. The story concerned the
manifestation of a ghost in an old house where a team of electronics experts have just
arrived to begin a project testing new recording equipment. One of the group, Jill Greeley
(Jane Asher), has a psychic experience in an abandoned room, hearing footsteps and a
scream and then seeing the apparition of a woman:

> She and the team's director, Peter Brock, make enquiries about the house's history
> and discover stories of exorcism and mysterious death. When Brock, too, hears
> the scream he announces his plans to analyse and exorcise the ghost, using their
> modern technology. His theory is that traumatic emotions leave an impression
> trapped in the stone walls of the room. The team's first effort to 'play the Stone
> Tape', using amplified noise and ultra-violet light, appears instead to wipe it
> clean.[60]

Up to this point the story seemed like a conventional ghost story, but the inquisitive and
susceptible Greeley discovers that this 'haunting' conceals a deeper layer of psychic
phenomena, revealed towards the end in a dramatic sequence resulting in her death.
The creative use of video effects in the drama, together with the innovative use of
sound, elevate *The Stone Tape* above a run-of-the-mill ghost story, making it one of the
most imaginative and intelligent examples of the horror genre to appear on British television, a single play to rank alongside the best of *Play for Today*.

    Other 1970s horror series included *A Ghost Story for Christmas* (BBC One, 1971–8), an
anthology series which began in December 1971 and continued as an annual event for
most of the 1970s, plus seven horror stories shown under the series title of *Dead of Night*
(BBC Two, November–December 1972), while ITV screened two more Nigel Kneale series:
the six-part *Beasts* (ATV, October–November 1976) and a fourth *Quatermass* serial
(Thames, October–November 1979), the latter produced by Euston Films as a more
expensive filmed drama, twenty years after the BBC's studio-bound *Quatermass and the
Pit*.

Taking television drama seriously

The 1970s was not only a decade in which much 'serious' television drama was produced, dramas which, directly or indirectly, addressed the social and political issues of
the time, it was also a decade in which television drama itself began to be taken
seriously, by academics and others, as a significant cultural form.

    An early manifestation of this was the publication in a 1972 issue of *Screen*, the
theoretical journal published by the Society for Education in Film and Television (SEFT),
of an essay which attempted, as its title indicates, to develop 'A Methodology for

Television Analysis with Reference to the Drama Series'.[61] In 1975 SEFT held a weekend school on 'The TV Series' in which a number of popular television dramas were discussed, one of which, *Upstairs Downstairs*, was also the subject of an article published in the journal *Movie* in the same year.[62] The following year SEFT devoted an issue of its educational journal, *Screen Education*, to *The Sweeney*, presenting a number of different theoretical approaches which could be adopted by teachers in studying popular television drama series.[63] Also in 1976, John McGrath delivered an attack on naturalism in television drama in the founding MacTaggart Lecture at the first Edinburgh International Television Festival, reviving 'the case against naturalism' presented by Troy Kennedy Martin in his 1964 'Nats Go Home' polemic.[64]

In its first few years the Edinburgh International Television Festival provided an important forum for debating the cultural and ideological significance of television drama, with many academics attending and provoking an often bemused industry audience with critiques drawing on Marxist and feminist cultural theory. A prime example of this was the paper presented by Richard Dyer, Terry Lovell and Jean McCrindle on 'Soap Opera and Women' at the 1977 festival, which caused some eyebrow-raising among industry delegates not just for its serious focus on soap opera, a generally derided form of popular television, but also for its forthright Marxist-feminist ideological analysis. In a male-dominated industry and in a decade where so much of the drama appearing on British television was written, produced and directed by men, to shift the focus so radically, not only by taking soap opera seriously, but also by focusing on it as popular drama 'for and about women', was an important theoretical intervention which helped spark a sustained period of academic interest in soap opera (see Chapter 5). But this was only one of a number of important interventions made at the 1977 Edinburgh International Television Festival, with others coming from Raymond Williams and Dennis Potter on 'realism and non-naturalism', from Clive Goodwin and Anthony Smith on censorship, from Jerry Kuehl and Gus Macdonald on drama documentary and from Charles Barr on television drama criticism.[65]

As the decade closed, a number of books, articles and papers on television drama were in production and 1980–1 saw the publication of a new wave of serious critical writing on television, including another issue of *Screen Education* devoted to television drama, Carl Gardner and John Wyver's 1980 Edinburgh International Television Festival paper on the decline of the single play, and George Brandt's 1981 collection of essays on television dramatists.[66] As the boundaries for producing progressive television drama were closing in, a new era of television drama scholarship was, somewhat ironically, opening up.

5

Television Drama and Thatcherism, 1979–90

The industrial conflicts of the 1970s culminated in the so-called 'winter of discontent' at the beginning of 1979, in the wake of which Margaret Thatcher's Conservative government came to power with a mandate, albeit from less than half of the population, to 'solve the nation's problems' by pursuing stringent monetarist economic policies. The cost-cutting initiatives of the Tories produced a huge rise in unemployment as they set about systematically changing the social, industrial and political landscape of the British Isles. These policies undoubtedly benefited many, certainly enough of the population to ensure that the Tories were returned to power twice more during the 1980s. But they also disenfranchised large sections of the working class as the older industries, based largely in the Midlands and the north of the country, were closed down in favour of the new service industries, based mainly in the south. In this fashion, Thatcher polarised the nation, creating a North–South divide and a large underclass of socially deprived and disadvantaged communities.

The political philosophy pursued by the Conservatives under Margaret Thatcher, an ideology subsequently referred to simply as 'Thatcherism', was fundamentally different to the Conservatism of Ted Heath's early-1970s administration. Thatcher mounted an all-out attack on socialism, vowing to eradicate it from British society, and her government set about dismantling the liberal advances that had been achieved during the 'permissive' 1960s. Thatcher wanted a return to Victorian values, to values which she felt had made Britain 'Great', the values of Empire, when Britain was a 'civilising force' throughout the world.

The ideology of Thatcherism was diametrically opposed to the values of an egalitarian society, promoting instead a meritocratic system in which individual enterprise could flourish at the expense of those less able to help themselves, a system which favoured the strong over the weak and encouraged individualism over collectivism. The central tenet of this ideology, and one of Thatcher's most famous statements, was that 'society was dead'; there was, she insisted, no such thing as 'society', there were only individuals and families.

Thatcherism was responsible for a seismic shift in British society, affecting all aspects of British life. Television was no exception and, like most public services, television companies came under increasing pressure during the 1980s as the monetarist policies of the Tories were applied rigorously to all aspects of British culture and society. The BBC, with its tradition of liberalism in the 1960s and 70s, was a particular target and several attempts were made by the Tories to undermine its position as a bastion of public service broadcasting. By the end of the 1980s the BBC had been transformed from the more liberal institution which it had been for most of the 1960s and 70s and was in the process of being reinvented as a more commercially minded corporation under its new Director General, Michael Checkland, previously a BBC accountant, and his deputy, John Birt, who had been recruited from ITV.

Nevertheless, during the 1980s, there was considerable resistance to the Conservative attempts to 'tame' the BBC, as this chapter will illustrate. Some pressure may also have been taken off the BBC with the November 1982 launch of Channel 4, which immediately began to draw the ire of the conservative press with its uninhibited and often radical programming. Channel 4 had the advantage of coming into existence before the Thatcherite revolution was fully under way, as the new channel was the result of a process which had begun in the 1970s when Labour was still in power. In 1977 the Annan Committee had recommended that the proposed and long-awaited fourth channel should cater for a variety of different audiences and provide diversity in its programming, a recommendation which found its way into the 1980 Broadcasting Act which gave birth to Channel 4. These recommendations were supported by the traditional paternalist wing of the Conservative Party which valued the notion of public service, while the new Thatcherites favoured the competition of the free market. The latter contingent was placated by the recommendation that the channel should be a 'publisher' of programmes which it would commission from a variety of independent companies, thus conforming to the free enterprise philosophy of the Tories.

Yet among the plethora of independent production companies that were set up in the early 1980s, specifically to make programmes for Channel 4, were many people who had been involved in the Independent Film-Makers Association in the 1970s, an organisation representing radical and experimental film-makers. Many of the programmes, including some of the films and TV dramas that were made for Channel 4 in its early years, were therefore radical and oppositional, not at all what the Thatcherites, who really wanted a more commercial ITV 2, would have hoped for from the new channel. Channel 4 therefore ensured, along with the BBC, that a diverse and sometimes radical form of public service broadcasting continued into the 1980s, even though the climate in which it existed was, politically, more hostile to the whole concept of public service.

Boys from the Blackstuff (1982)

Of the many television dramas which attempted to address the impact that Thatcherism was having on the nation in the early 1980s none was more apposite and timely than the five-part series *Boys from the Blackstuff* (BBC Two, October–November 1982). The series was developed from a single play, *The Black Stuff* (BBC Two, 2 January

1980), which had been filmed on location in September–October 1978 but not transmitted until eight months after Thatcher came to power. *The Black Stuff* was about a group of workers from Liverpool who take on a job laying tarmac (the 'black stuff') in Middlesbrough where they do a 'foreigner', an illegal job, for which they get sacked by their boss. Immediately following the completion of filming of *The Black Stuff*, its author, Alan Bleasdale, wrote a letter to the producer, David Rose, and the script editor, Michael Wearing, outlining a proposal for 'at least five fifty-minute plays' which would develop some of the themes in the original play. Bleasdale emphasised in the letter the social concerns that lay behind the proposal:

> I think it is very important right now to write about the Dole as seen from the point of view of those who are on it, and to side with them against the people and papers who would like us to believe, despite the million and a half out of work and mass redundancies at every opportunity, that the majority of the unemployed are malingerers and rogues. It is my belief that at least ninety per cent of those who are out of work, want to work.[1]

Bleasdale's letter led to a commission from BBC English Regions Drama at Pebble Mill in Birmingham, who had produced some of his earlier work. The process of development of the plays, from November 1978 to the eventual transmission of the series in October 1982, was a lengthy one which saw one of the scripts that Bleasdale had written, 'McKenna's Story', developed and filmed as a separate *Play for Today* called *The Muscle Market* (BBC One, 13 January 1981). The decision to separate this play out from the rest of the series was a pragmatic one on behalf of producer Michael Wearing to keep Bleasdale interested while Wearing was trying to get the money from the BBC to make the rest of the series. In fact, *The Muscle Market* was different to the rest of the series in that it focused on the boss of an asphalt firm, rather than the 'boys' who worked for him, and worked perfectly well as a single play, with an excellent performance from Peter Postlethwaite as McKenna.

It proved easier for Wearing to get the money for a single play than it did to raise the money for the series, which was eventually budgeted at £860,000 in October 1981. In order to produce five fifty-minute plays on this budget a decision was taken to use outside broadcast (OB) video cameras for four of the episodes and to shoot one episode on film. Film is much more expensive than video and, while it was unlikely that the BBC would have put up the money to make the whole series on film, the use of OB video helped to keep the budget down.[2]

The decision to shoot on OB video was an important factor in Philip Saville being taken on to direct the series after Jim Goddard, who had directed *The Black Stuff*, became unavailable due to other commitments. Saville had been working in television since the 1950s, when he was a director on *Armchair Theatre*, and had a reputation for innovation. In 1964 he had directed the first OB drama recorded entirely on location, the BBC's *Hamlet at Elsinore* (BBC One, 19 April 1964), and in the 1970s had directed the first television drama to experiment with the new lightweight OB video cameras, a short play called

The Actual Woman (BBC Two, 11 March 1974), which was shown as part of BBC Two's *Second City Firsts*, a series of short dramas also produced by English Regions Drama at Pebble Mill.

In his original letter to Rose and Wearing, Bleasdale had gone on to say:

> This piece, whatever length it is, will, in parts, be a more sombre play than *The Black Stuff*. The images of urban decay, spiritual deprivation and death which I want to run throughout the whole length, will hopefully represent the hollowness and sense of worthlessness that a lot of people feel when they're on the Dole, on the estates, in the back of the bus.[3]

While Bleasdale qualified this by saying that the plays would be 'funny' too, it is clear that his main concern was to highlight the impact that mass unemployment was having on working-class people. In the interim, of course, a Conservative government had come to power and the stringent monetarist policies implemented by the Thatcher government had exacerbated the already severe unemployment situation, causing the number of those unemployed to double by the time that the series was completed, breaking the 3 million barrier for the first time since the 1930s. The delay in production, therefore, actually worked to the advantage of the series in that, when it was transmitted in October–November 1982, unemployment was at its highest level for over fifty years and had become a national issue:

> The effects of unemployment which the writer had observed in Liverpool in 1978, had also spread by 1981 far beyond the traditional geographical blackspots in the industrial north and were visible virtually everywhere. This alarming trend had far-reaching effects on society and arguably forced a re-shaping of attitudes to unemployment and its treatment in the media. For a time 'concern' over unemployment became the primary item on 'the nation's agenda' and the overriding political issue of the day. *Boys from the Blackstuff* was to contribute to expressions of general concern and feeling about unemployment and 'the right to work'.[4]

The series was initially scheduled in a late-night (10.30 pm) slot on BBC Two on Sundays, ghettoising it as serious 'arts' television. Despite this, the five episodes gained an average audience of over 4 million viewers and huge critical acclaim, earning it an unprecedented early repeat in January–February 1983 on BBC One, at 9.25 pm on Tuesdays (in the *Play for Today* slot). For the BBC One repeat the audience increased to an average of more than 6 million, with the last episode, 'George's Last Ride', attracting nearly 8 million viewers.

Boys from the Blackstuff quickly became a television 'event', tapping into the increasing public outcry about the social impact that Tory policies were having on working-class communities in the industrial heartlands of Britain. After the first episode, 'Jobs for the Boys', which introduced all of the central characters, the four subsequent parts were each based around one character's 'story'. Dixie (Tom Georgeson), in 'Moonlighter',

Boys from the Blackstuff: dramatising the social and economic consequences of Thatcherism

is supplementing his dole money with a nighttime security guard job at the Liverpool docks; Chrissie (Michael Angelis) is experiencing a crisis in his marriage to Angie (Julie Walters) in 'Shop Thy Neighbour' – an episode which Saville encouraged Bleasdale to write to redress the masculine bias in the series; Yosser (Bernard Hill), in the eponymous 'Yosser's Story', is in the throes of a dramatic breakdown following the departure of his wife and the loss of his children to social services; and, in the final episode, 'George's Last Ride', the death of the old Labour activist and trade unionist George Malone (Peter Kerrigan) enabled parallels to be drawn between past and present.

The series was character-based, rather than plot-driven, using the characters as a means to explore the condition of the working class, especially the Liverpudlian working class, in contemporary Britain. Yosser, immortalised by Bernard Hill in a haunting performance, became an iconic character in the series whose repeated refrain, 'Gizza job, I can do that', became a national catchphrase. Taken up and sung by thousands on the terraces of Liverpool Football Club, the phrase entered into popular currency, a defiant cry capturing the desperation and disenfranchisement of a whole class.

It was in the final episode that the profoundest statements were made about Britain's industrial decline and the 'death of socialism', represented by the death of George Malone, the trade unionist whose politics had been shaped in the Depression of the 1930s. There is an ambiguity about the portrayal of George's death in the abandoned setting of Liverpool's Albert Dock when, following the utterance of his dying words, 'I can't believe there's no hope ... I can't,' the camera zooms out to an extreme long shot of the derelict and deserted dock, a symbol of Liverpool's industrial decline. Like the final image of the series, of Chrissie, Loggo and Yosser walking forlornly past the Tate and Lyle factory which is under demolition, the image of the derelict dock seems to undermine the optimism of George's lament, suggesting little hope for the future.

Yet the bleakness of these images has to be balanced against the expressions of optimism uttered in the series by characters like George, not to mention the anger shown by two of the female characters in this male-dominated drama, the dramatically significant outburst of George's wife in reacting against the defeatism shown by her sons and the exasperation shown by Angie in trying to get Chrissie to fight back against the system which has emasculated him. Unlike George, the younger men have been ground down, lacking his resolution and his experience of fighting mass unemployment in the 1930s, and it is left to the women to try to rekindle some of that fighting spirit in their demoralised menfolk.

Nevertheless, the images of industrial decay all around them certainly provide grounds for the boys' pessimism, the all too visible destruction of Liverpool's industrial heritage providing a metaphor, for the television audience, of the systematic destruction of industrial Britain by the Tories. As Pawling and Perkins point out, the realistic style of the series enabled the actual industrial destruction that was taking place in Liverpool at the time to be conveyed in almost documentary fashion:

> The 'subject' of the drama was not simply the 'Boys', but Liverpool itself as a city under intense pressure. So the location shots of the derelict docks or the demolition of the Tate and Lyle refinery in 'George's Last Ride', were not just signifiers of a generalised backcloth of dereliction, but acted as specific records of the concrete destruction of people's working lives at that particular moment in time. This, then, was no dramatic recreation for visual effect, but actuality footage of Liverpool's devastation as it occurred, brick by brick.[5]

The use of video may have contributed to this look of 'actuality', video connoting 'immediacy' and 'the present' where film more often connotes 'the past', but the series was not a 'documentary' drama in the tradition of Loach/Garnett/Allen. Bleasdale made it clear that he did not see himself as a 'political' writer, in the Jim Allen mould – 'I have no tendencies to be Marxist' – and Michael Wearing has said that they wanted to adopt a different approach for Boys from the Blackstuff to the more partisan one adopted by Loach and Garnett in Cathy Come Home.[6]

While the 'realism' of the series was a major factor in its success, drawing audiences into recognition with situations and circumstances that were a part of their everyday lives, the comedy which Bleasdale injected into the series was also important, dramatically, in alleviating the grimness of the 'stories' that were being told, as well as confirming the verisimilitude of the series, as one Liverpudlian noted:

> There's a lot of humour in the series, a lot of tragedy. Someone once said, your life in Liverpool was a tragedy played as if it were a comedy. Well, the trouble with

that is that we tend to put a brave face on things if we can manage it, so we don't talk to each other about the problems we, as unemployed people, have. But since the series has been on, people have been saying, yes, we've been through that, I've thought like that, and it isn't just a question of individual characters. All of us have been, at some time or another, as desperate as Yosser, or feeling stripped of dignity as Chrissie. At times, maybe, we felt as optimistic as George, but it's like all the characters were facets of us put together; the kind of life all of us have, and that's a great achievement to make. He's given us words to communicate with each other about our own experiences.[7]

It was the blend of realism and humour, especially the use of black comedy as a 'stylistic device used to defuse the emotional intensity of a scene',[8] that made the series unique, not only contributing to the powerful and lasting effect that *Boys from the Blackstuff* had on its audience, but also marking a new development in British social realist drama. In its searing indictment of the effect that government policies were having on working-class communities, *Boys from the Blackstuff* demonstrated that it was possible, through television drama, to give a voice to those many millions of people who were suffering as a consequence of Thatcherite policies in the early 1980s.

Experiments in television drama

The contribution of director Philip Saville was crucial to the success of *Boys from the Blackstuff*, not only in the use of typically flamboyant camera shots, such as the pull-back from a close-up of George's dying words in the Albert Dock to an extreme long shot of Chrissie running to get help in the desolate, abandoned space of the dockyard, but also in the use of improvisatory exercises designed to get the actors to ease up on their fast-talking Scouse delivery in order to 'sit in their own space, their own panic, their own predicament',[9] in other words to create a space and a distance which would allow themselves, and the audience, to reflect on the social implications of their actions. John McGrath, writing in *The Listener*, saw Saville's creative contribution as one of the most important aspects of *Boys from the Blackstuff*:

> Had this series been made as straightforward television naturalism, it would have lost the distancing, and the creative boldness of the shooting, that are so much a part of its success. It is to Philip Saville's enormous credit that he has weathered the storms of philistine abuse poured on his constant need to experiment with form, pushed forward the frontiers of TV drama, and kept his own, and our, imaginations alive.[10]

One of Saville's more experimental dramas immediately preceded *Boys from the Blackstuff*. In 1980 Saville directed a drama for BBC Two's *Playhouse* series that made extensive use of video technology to bring to the screen a story developed by Saville in collaboration with novelist Beryl Bainbridge, about a trip that Adolf Hitler supposedly made to Liverpool in 1912, to visit his half-brother Alois, who was living there with his wife Bridget. *The Journal of Bridget Hitler* (BBC Two, 6 February 1981) was a dramatisation of those events as described by Bridget in her journal, but rather than filming the events in conventional manner as a historical narrative, Saville had the action take the form of an investigation played out in a television studio, with two interviewers questioning the now elderly Bridget Hitler (played by Siobhan McKenna) about the events described in her journal, some of which are shown as flashbacks on a large video screen in the studio. As Christopher Griffin-Beale explained in an article in *Broadcast* on the innovative approach employed for the drama:

> The enacted 'flashback' scenes are themselves stylised, often with photographic chromakey backgrounds. The Liverpool scenes are shot in sepia, the later 1930s Berlin in ultra-contrasty black-and-white.
> But one of the production's successes is that we are not distanced from the performances within these flashback scenes, even though in-between them we are constantly reminded about the question of their authenticity, constantly reminded that we are watching actors in a studio, and that the only non-actors are supposed to be Mrs Hitler (Siobhan McKenna), the interviewers and the floor manager (who is indeed an actor).[11]

The Journal of Bridget Hitler is a complex, self-reflexive production. Philip Saville appears in the drama as the director in the television studio and in a break during the recording of the 'investigation' Saville and Beryl Bainbridge are seen queuing for lunch in the BBC canteen along with other members of the TV production team and the 'real' Bridget Hitler. When the now out-of-character actor playing Adolf Hitler (Maurice Roeves) demonstrates a Hitlerian salute in the canteen it provokes a group of skinheads who are there for a recording of *Top of the Pops* and Bridget Hitler is visibly shocked at their response, remembering the 'real' events, forty years before, which have inspired this present-day scene. In this manner past and present, 'reality' and fiction, are interwoven in the drama.

The same kind of self-reflexivity is achieved in the television studio scenes where the investigation into the truthfulness of Bridget Hitler's journal is being conducted. Historical footage of Hitler declaiming is at one point intercut with a studio reconstruction of Roeves as Hitler at a podium, filmed against a backdrop of a stylised sky. The backdrop, however, is achieved electronically through a chromakey (or colour separation overlay [CSO]) technique by which any background can be electronically inserted into the image while an actor, in this case Roeves, performs in the studio in front of a blue screen. As Roeves, performing Hitler, declaims at the podium:

> His image freezes and expands in a hall of mirrors effect, and we cut to a long shot of the studio in colour, seeing the actor surrounded by blue. As he walks off and chats to the floor manager, background photos appear on some chromakey backgrounds, misaligned as on a rough night at 'News At Ten', except here the

effect is deliberate. Saville claims he was trying to demythologise the workings of the TV studio, and also making a point about the real Hitler, who himself adopted a persona and built up a performance for his public oratory.[12]

The Journal of Bridget Hitler was a bold experiment using the technology of chromakey and Quantel (a video effects mixer, more commonly used for special effects on Top of the Pops) to reveal the artifice in television drama production. The 'investigation' in The Journal of Bridget Hitler was as much an investigation into the creative potential of new video technology as it was an investigation into the claims contained within Bridget Hitler's journal in the fictional drama. Yet the mobilisation of this technology enabled the dramatic investigation to take place, rather than being merely a technical exercise. Saville saw the potential to utilise the technology to enhance the drama, to make it both original and distinctive. It was this directorial 'vision', rare in television directors, which made Michael Wearing turn to Saville when he was looking for someone who could make the most of Alan Bleasdale's scripts for Boys from the Blackstuff:

> Philip's an innovator and something of a visionary. He's always wanted to stretch the 'state of the art' of the current TV technology to serve his interpretation rather than the other way round. This often costs extra money, alters working methods, changes resource patterns – sometimes for work which is not likely to get easy public and professional acceptance. He's a highly controversial figure, but at least half the time he hits the bullseye with the audience.[13]

According to Griffin-Beale, The Journal of Bridget Hitler evolved as a 'studio-based format after an original plan to rely on location filming proved too expensive',[14] yet the technically challenging nature of the production, stretching the bounds of studio drama way beyond its naturalistic confines, represents a rare example of experimentalism in the history of British television drama. Indeed, The Journal of Bridget Hitler, coming as it did at a time when the possibilities for such experimentation were diminishing, turned out to be not the beginnings of a new kind of television drama but one of the last creative flourishes before the onset of a new commercially driven era in which economics, not aesthetics, was to be the determining factor.

Philip Saville was not the only director at this time interested in exploring the possibilities which the new video technology offered. In the 1970s, before his early death in 1974, James MacTaggart had made extensive use of CSO in his innovative TV dramatisation of Candide (BBC Two, 16 February 1973), with the characters moving through an entirely artificial, electronically generated world. CSO had also been used extensively in Howard Schuman's untransmitted Censored Scenes from Kong Kong and in some of the musical numbers in Rock Follies and Rock Follies of '77.

While Saville was working on The Journal of Bridget Hitler, John McGrath was also experimenting with the new video technology in a two-part Play for Today called The Adventures of Frank (BBC One, 4–11 November 1980). Developing a storyline which he and Troy Kennedy Martin had used as a basis for their 1964 non-naturalistic drama Diary of *a Young Man*, McGrath updated it to take account of the impact of Thatcherism on British society, transposing the material to the early 1980s with the aspirational Frank coming down to London from Sheffield to seek his fortune, lured by the promise of financial reward which the new Tory meritocracy offered.

Like *Diary of a Young Man*, *The Adventures of Frank* used photographic stills, voiceover narration and music to depart from the naturalistic conventions of mainstream drama. Frank, however, went further in deploying a variety of video effects as a means of interrupting the narrative flow, acting as a kind of Brechtian alienation device, constantly reminding the audience of the fact that they were watching a constructed drama, not a slice-of-life piece of naturalism. In this way, *The Adventures of Frank* was not dissimilar to *The Journal of Bridget Hitler*, but with *Frank* the objectives were more political. McGrath explained the intentions behind the drama in the *Radio Times*:

> Because it's an adventure story with lots of movement through it, there were possibilities for using still sequences, as we'd done in the 60s, but for using them in a totally different way with the new electronic devices. We were breaking completely new ground with some of these microchip and floppy disc devices, ways of storing computer information electronically. You can take the picture and reduce it in size or motor it out so that it blows out of the frame. You can take the picture and turn it round and put it into any shape by making the picture into computer information, feeding it into a microchip and then playing instructions on to a floppy disc. They use it on *Top of the Pops* all the time.
>
> In terms of drama, it says to the audience 'this is just a succession of images'. So, as the audience, you become aware that what you're watching is not a slice of life or a chunk of reality and therefore that somebody is creating it and there is a purpose to that creation. What it's capable of doing is to produce alienated television in the way that Brecht was aiming at alienated theatre. Not alienation in the sense that people stay away but that you step back a little bit from the picture and examine it more closely.[15]

Unfortunately, people did stay away. *The Adventures of Frank* was castigated by the critics and received a poor response from viewers, according to BBC Audience Research reaction profiles.[16] McGrath incorporated musical numbers into *The Adventures of Frank*, in typical 7:84 fashion, making use of alternative theatre performers rather than television actors because 'they have an approach, a boldness and a willingness to try things out that most safe television actors don't',[17] but the mix of alternative theatre, experimental video techniques and a 'political' narrative about the divisive ideology of the new Conservatism proved to be too alienating for a mainstream television audience. There were also production difficulties and constraints which prevented McGrath from putting right some of the problems that arose from experimenting with the new technology. Access to the Quantel equipment was limited and McGrath had only two days in which to do all the effects work on the two parts of the drama:

It was a bold attempt that didn't come off, partly for casting problems, partly I was trying to do far too much, to get too far ahead of the technology … Some of it worked, some of it's fine, I think probably more of the second part. It's shot in two parts because the cost of using Quantel was exorbitant, so they decided rather than cut it down they would do it as two plays which meant we'd get two budgets. That broke its back really.[18]

While *The Adventures of Frank* may have been a failed experiment, the fact that McGrath was given the opportunity to do it for the main BBC channel at peak-time shows that the possibilities for producing innovative, non-naturalistic drama still existed at the beginning of the 1980s. Three months later, Philip Saville's *The Journal of Bridget Hitler* was screened on BBC Two for a 'minority' audience and in 1986 Dennis Potter's formally ambitious and critically acclaimed *The Singing Detective* was also relegated to BBC Two. In the new 'era of cost-effectiveness', as Wyver and Gardner described it at the Edinburgh International Television Festival in August 1980, innovative and experimental dramas like *The Adventures of Frank* and *The Journal of Bridget Hitler* were likely to be marginalised, if they were made at all.[19]

The demise of the single play

The Adventures of Frank and *The Journal of Bridget Hitler* were shown within single-play anthology series on the BBC: the former as part of *Play for Today* on BBC One and the latter in the BBC Two *Playhouse* series. The fact that *The Adventures of Frank* was shown, unusually for *Play for Today*, in two parts was perhaps an early indication of a significant development in the 1980s which saw 'authored drama' relocating from the single play to the mini-series or serial. *Boys from the Blackstuff* was transitional in this respect. Alan Bleasdale's original single play, *The Black Stuff*, was developed as five plays, of which the first three were fifty-five to sixty minutes long with the final two stretching to seventy minutes. But while the five plays featured the same characters and explored the same theme, there was no developing narrative unfolding over the five parts. *Boys from the Blackstuff* was therefore a series of five plays, rather than a drama serial like Dennis Potter's *The Singing Detective* in which the complex, multi-layered narrative unfolded over six weekly episodes, totalling seven hours of screen time. With the six-episode serial, playwrights like Potter could apply themselves to a much broader canvas, as Potter had previously done with *Casanova* in 1971 and *Pennies from Heaven* in 1978. From the mid-1980s most of Potter's work was to take the form of four-part or six-part drama serials as the latter supplanted the single play in the schedules.

There were three reasons for the demise of the single play in the 1980s: aesthetic, economic and political. Aesthetically, the single play had been converging with the TV/cinema film since the 1960s as a consequence of the shift from electronic studio recording to location shooting on 16mm film. *Up the Junction*, as we have seen, marked the beginnings of this technological shift. While it was not the first television drama to be shot on film it was the first single play to use film extensively. A series of short dramas under the series title *Six* (BBC Two, December 1964–January 1965) had been shot on film before it, and Peter Watkins' *Culloden* was also shot entirely on film, but *Six* mainly comprised short films rather than single plays, while Watkins' dramatised documentary was made within the BBC Talks Division rather than the Drama Department.[20]

As we have seen, film was being used increasingly in the late 1960s and throughout the 70s on *The Wednesday Play* and *Play for Today*, although the extra cost of shooting on film meant that electronically recorded studio plays were still in the majority. As television drama entered the 1980s, however, the 'logic of convergence', as John Caughie describes it, between the television play and the cinema film (especially low-budget British feature films) became inexorable.[21] Social realism, arguably the dominant tradition in the single play from the mid-1960s onwards, dictated the use of film: real streets, real houses, real living rooms, not studio sets.

In 1977 Ken Trodd, who produced many of these social realist dramas, as well as much of the work of Dennis Potter, published a list of filmed television drama in the BAFTA journal *Vision*. Noting that Tony Garnett and Ken Loach had initiated the transition to filmed drama in the 1960s with plays like *Cathy Come Home* and *In Two Minds*, Trodd argued that these television plays were superior to the feature films that were being produced in Britain at the time:

> From these plays has developed what is probably the most healthy, thriving and varied incidence of fiction film-making in British movie history. Certainly the British feature films shown in public cinemas over the same period compare poorly with these TV films in terms of their overall quality, audience pleasure, the development of talented artists and technicians, and the honest reflection of contemporary life and crises.[22]

Technological change – from the electronic studio to filming on location – and the subsequent development of a different aesthetics for television drama, was one reason for the convergence of the television play and the feature film in this period, but it was not the only reason for the decline of the single play.

Economics – the cost of producing single plays in the new era of 'cost-effectiveness' – is possibly a more significant factor in charting the demise of the television play. The one-off nature of the prestigious single play, with its higher production values and larger budgets than other programmes, made it the most expensive form of television programming. In a period of recession, when budgets were being cut, the single play began to seem like a luxury the television companies could no longer afford. In such a climate, series and serial drama, where sets and props could be used again and again and where production costs could be spread over a number of episodes, were more 'cost-effective' as audiences could be built and retained over a longer period of time, especially in long-running drama series. With the single play, however, a production always had to start from scratch, making the play an expensive and increasingly risky financial investment.

The introduction of Channel 4 in 1982 was also significant in that it provided an opportunity for feature films, rather than television plays, to be made on higher budgets than TV drama departments could generally afford. Here there was the added incentive, for writers and directors, of making films that could gain a cinema release, rather than the solitary television screening that most single plays achieved. Film production was an important part of Channel 4's programming from the start and a significant proportion of the channel's budget (£6 million initially) was set aside for financing low- to medium-budget feature films to be shown in the channel's *Film on Four* slot on a Thursday evening.

Some of these films, including *The Draughtsman's Contract* (1982) and *My Beautiful Laundrette* (1985), were afforded a cinema release before their television screening, as a result of a new agreement between Channel 4 and the Cinema Exhibitors Association, while others, such as the opening-night film, *Walter* (Channel 4, 2 November 1982), starring Ian McKellen and directed by Stephen Frears, were only shown on television. Stylistically, many of these *Film on Fours* were indistinguishable from their *Play for Today* counterparts. Early 1980s *Play for Todays* such as Trevor Griffiths' *Country* (directed by Richard Eyre), Jim Allen's *United Kingdom* (directed by Roland Joffe) and Mike Leigh's *Home Sweet Home* (BBC One, 16 March 1982) were all shot on film and would have been equally at home on *Film on Four*. Once Channel 4 began, however, the number of filmed *Play for Todays* declined significantly. Over the last five seasons of *Play for Today*, the number of plays shot on film declined from fourteen in the 1979–80 season to seven in the 1981–2 season and to just three in the final 1983–4 season.

Home Sweet Home was the last *Play for Today* that Mike Leigh made for the BBC and his work in the 1980s is indicative of the convergence between the single play, the television film and the cinema film during this period. Leigh had 'devised' (the term he preferred to 'written and directed' at the time) seven plays for the BBC between 1974 and 1982, six of which were for *Play for Today*, with one other, *Grown-Ups* (BBC Two, 28 November 1980), made for BBC Two's *Playhouse*. After *Home Sweet Home*, Leigh's next film, *Meantime* (Channel 4, 1 December 1983), was produced by Central Television for *Film on Four*, in other words a television film rather than a single play. Stylistically, however, *Meantime* is no different from the BBC plays which preceded it (with the exception of the studio-recorded *Abigail's Party*) or from the single play which Leigh subsequently made for the BBC, the Northern Ireland drama, *Four Days in July* (BBC One, 29 January 1985). With the exception of *Abigail's Party*, all of Leigh's television work was shot on 16mm and all of it reflects his distinctive working methods which are designed to achieve a heightened social realism through an emphasis on characterisation and social interaction, achieved through extensive improvisation.

The same methods were applied to *High Hopes* (1988), Leigh's next film, but the difference with *High Hopes* was that, while it was funded by Channel 4 and shown in the *Film on Four* slot, it was shot on 35mm film for release in cinemas and its first television screening, on 1 March 1990, came more than a year after its cinema release. While the switch to 35mm did not unduly affect Leigh's concern to deal with indigenous subject matter – and in many ways *High Hopes* is the archetypal British film about Thatcherism – Leigh sees this development as significant in the transition from the single play to the television-funded feature film:

By the very dint of making them on 35mm and to motion picture standards, you got a different quality of material … The films at the BBC were made with total freedom from any kind of commercial pressure. There were no ratings wars. They weren't in competition with anybody. You had carte blanche to do whatever and therefore everybody was liberated to make indigenous subjects.

The minute Channel 4 started and the prospect came into existence, which it almost immediately did, of selling films overseas, then the American market became an issue, and the minute the American market became an issue, that started to inform the sort of films that people made.[23]

What took place in the 1980s, therefore, was a drift towards commercialism in television drama, of which the decline in production of the single play and its replacement by the television film was just one consequence. The larger budgets required for the television film and for the expensive drama serial led to more co-productions, often with American companies, and the freedom from editorial control that playwrights, directors and producers had previously enjoyed, especially at the BBC, was gradually eroded in this changing economy of television production.

Which brings us to the third factor to have a bearing on the demise of the single play in the 1980s: the political. In the more reactionary climate of Thatcherism a loss of editorial freedom had political consequences; it became increasingly difficult for radical or progressive drama to get commissioned in the 1980s and virtually impossible after *Play for Today* ended in 1984. In this climate, as Gardner and Wyver noted in the 1983 'Afterword' to their Edinburgh International Television Festival paper on the single play, those opposed to Thatcherite ideology ironically found themselves defending the Reithian ethos in broadcasting which they had spent years attacking for its 'elitism, paternalism, class-specificity and inaccessibility'.[24] In the new market-led broadcasting environment the political freedoms that writers, directors and producers had enjoyed for most of the 1960s and 70s came under threat and the opportunities for alternative voices to be heard were severely diminished:

There were important impulses and advantages in the Reithian system – in particular the attempt to generalise and popularise a range of dramatic, artistic and musical events and styles for a wider audience. It is this diversity and eclecticism, which occasionally opened up spaces for oppositional voices and contradictory meanings, which is threatened in the current wave of commercial homogenisation.

Against this background, it is depressingly predictable to note that the single play has in the last three years become more personal and less concerned with a social canvas.[25]

The main showcase for diversity and eclecticism in television drama, *Play for Today*, ended in August 1984. In the previous year the BBC's two other long-running single-play anthology series, *Play of the Month* (BBC One, 1965–83) and *Playhouse* (BBC Two, 1974–83), had also come to an end. Thereafter, the place of the single play in the schedules was occupied by the made-for-television film as the BBC introduced new showcases for feature-length filmed drama, first with *Screen Two* (BBC Two, 1985–97) and then *Screenplay* (BBC Two, 1986–93) and *Screen One* (BBC One, 1989–98).

In 1987, Alan Plater, one of the television playwrights most associated with originality and eclecticism in television drama, wrote what appeared to be an obituary for the single play:

> Who remembers television plays? They used to come one at a time, each gift-wrapped in a self-contained lump, under a banner heading like *The Wednesday Play* or *Armchair Theatre*.
>
> This is close to archeology, but in the early Sixties when we were all young and innocent, there were 300 plays a year on the two channels. Today, it is doubtful whether we have 100 on four channels, and many of those are small-scale movies.
>
> The reasons are obvious enough. Plays are unpredictable and dangerous: tricky qualities for a conformist society, and an industry increasingly market-driven, to use the American jargon. For writers there are two obvious consequences. It is six times as difficult for a new writer to find a way into television, and once he or she finds a space, it is quite likely to be on a long-running soap opera. We are in danger of breeding writers who can sing any tune except their own. For experienced writers, with a little street wisdom, the response is to cheat, albeit elegantly: write a play but pretend it's a genre series. When I feel an original statement coming on, I dress it up as a series and call it *The Beiderbecke Tapes* – and the smart money says a similar thought process lay behind *Edge of Darkness* and *The Singing Detective*.[26]

In marking the demise of the single play, Plater also highlighted the possibilities for original authored drama in the 1980s. The two-part *The Beiderbecke Tapes* (13–20 December 1987) was the second in a trilogy of comedy thrillers that Plater wrote for Yorkshire Television in the second half of the decade. It followed the six-part *The Beiderbecke Affair* (6 January–10 February 1985) and preceded the four-part *The Beiderbecke Connection* (27 November–18 December 1988), all featuring James Bolam as a Bix Beiderbecke jazz fan turned amateur detective. Along with Troy Kennedy Martin's six-part *Edge of Darkness* (1985) and Dennis Potter's six-part *The Singing Detective*, Plater's trilogy represented a shift in 'authored drama' away from the single play towards the drama serial as writers sought ways of adapting to and exploiting the changing ethos of drama production in the 1980s.

Edge of Darkness (1985)

While the shift to series and serial drama was largely commercially motivated, a response to the need to maximise audiences in an increasingly competitive marketplace, this change in the landscape of television drama was not without its positive

aspects. While it may have contributed
to the demise of the single play, for so
long the vehicle for original and progressive drama on television, series and
serial drama did enable some writers to
extend themselves by applying their
craft to a larger canvas. There is less
evidence of this in series drama simply
because for one writer to undertake a
multi-episode series is a huge commitment.[27] A long-running drama series
more commonly draws on the services
of a number of different writers who
are required to conform to the series
format, as in *The Sweeney*. So it is in the
mini-series or serial that 'authored'
drama is more likely to be found,
especially with the decline of the single
play in the 1980s.

Bob Peck as Ronnie Craven in *Edge of Darkness*:
a complex six-part nuclear thriller

   For television dramatists like Alan
Plater and Dennis Potter, who had both written many single plays in the 1960s and 70s,
the shift to serial drama was a natural development. Unlike Potter, whose reputation as
a television dramatist is based entirely upon single plays and drama serials, Plater, like
many aspiring playwrights, worked extensively on drama series such as *Z Cars* and
Softly, Softly in the 1960s before graduating to single plays and then serials. Troy Kennedy
Martin, on the other hand, started off writing single plays, but then transferred his
attention to series drama for most of the 1960s and 70s, devising and writing some of the
early episodes of *Z Cars*, contributing to the military police drama *Redcap* (ABC, 1964–6)
and then, after a period writing scripts for feature films such as *The Italian Job* (UK, 1969)
and *Kelly's Heroes* (USA/Yugoslavia, 1970), returned to British television with a situation
comedy for ITV called *If It Moves, File It* (LWT, 1970) and episodes for drama series such
as *Colditz* and *The Sweeney*. While writing scripts for *The Sweeney*, Kennedy Martin was
developing ideas for serials which were eventually to come to fruition in the 1980s. One
of these was a story about Sidney Reilly, who worked for British Intelligence in Russia in
the 1890s and early 1900s. This project was eventually picked up by Euston Films and
transmitted in 1983 as the twelve-part serial *Reilly – Ace of Spies* (Thames, September–
November 1983). In the same year Kennedy Martin's adaptation of Angus Wilson's novel
The Old Men at the Zoo (BBC Two, September–October 1983) was transmitted by the BBC
in five parts, but the serial which really tapped into the 1980s zeitgeist was the six-part
nuclear thriller *Edge of Darkness* (BBC Two, November–December 1985).

   Kennedy Martin had begun work on *Edge of Darkness* in the late 1970s and, during
the course of its long genesis, a plethora of ideas and influences were incorporated
into what became an extremely rich and complex narrative. As with Dennis Potter's

multi-layered *The Singing Detective*, the larger canvas afforded by the six-episode serial enabled Kennedy Martin to write a drama that was novelistic in its narrative scope. Before writing his first television drama, *Incident at Echo Six*, he had, in fact, written a novel, about the Indo-China war, and the return to long-form drama in the 1980s was really a return to a tradition in which he felt very comfortable:

> I've come out of a literary rather than a theatre tradition and my bent is towards the long form. Long-form drama is really what I do best and I do think the writer still has a major role to play in it. It's also one of the few areas where naturalism or realism still has a role to play. It links up with the nineteenth-century novel, it's a development of that. That's its heritage, not Terence Rattigan or the 1930s stage and not really cinema. So it's a kind of literary form, long convoluted stories and lots of characters.[28]

Edge of Darkness begins as a noirish detective drama. The serial's central character, Ronnie Craven (Bob Peck), is a Yorkshire police detective who is investigating the alleged rigging of a miners' union ballot (the serial followed the long-running miners' strike of 1984–5, the major industrial conflict of the 1980s during which the full force of the state was mobilised to crush resistance by the miners and their families to the National Coal Board's plans to close coal mines). From the beginning, therefore, Craven is identified as a member of the establishment, a role and a position which he is to question during the course of the narrative. The nighttime setting of the opening scenes, in pouring rain, establishes the iconography of film noir. Craven goes to collect his daughter Emma (Joanne Whalley) from a political meeting which she is chairing at a local college. The Labour MP Michael Meacher plays the politician addressing the meeting – an example of how the drama used real-life characters and events to lend a veneer of realism to the story, serving to authenticate the fictional narrative. As Craven and Emma arrive home they are confronted in the pouring rain by a hooded gunman who blasts them with a shotgun, killing Emma.

The death of Emma provides the initial disruption which is to motivate the rest of the narrative. Craven is told by his superior that the gunman, whom Craven once recruited as an informer in Northern Ireland, was waiting for him, but Craven is not convinced. He subsequently adopts the mantel of the classic noir detective, psychologically scarred because of the killing of his daughter (his wife has previously died from cancer), alienated from the political manoeuvring of those with whom he comes into contact and, in typical noir fashion, a detective increasingly at odds with his superiors as he undertakes his own investigation.

The narrative disruption caused by the killing of the protagonist's daughter early in the story, motivating his quest, is a familiar narrative strategy, typical of many Hollywood thrillers. Its narrative function, of course, is to hook the audience, even more important in television where there isn't a captive audience, as in the cinema, and where a drama has to compete with the programmes on offer on other channels. The epic scale of *Edge of Darkness*, however, three times longer than the average feature film, enabled not only a greater complexity than is often achieved in a feature film, but also the playing out of some scenes at greater length than one might normally expect.

Such is the case with Craven's reaction to the death of his daughter, which hangs heavy over much of the first episode. Shortly after she is killed, Craven goes into her bedroom, a scene which is described at great length in the script and which occupies five minutes of screen time. This is how Kennedy Martin describes the last part of the scene:

> He crosses to the bed. It is still blowing outside; still raining hard. Craven hears the gate creak and swing. He crosses to get the shotgun. He puts it beside the art nouveau bedside table and sits down again. He pulls open a drawer and takes out a Kleenex box first and then a cheque book, a passport and a wallet. He opens the wallet. It has some French francs in it; he puts it to one side, uninterested. He opens the passport, hoping to get one more glimpse of Emma. It is Emma's face all right. In the second drawer is a vibrator. He looks down at it, then kisses it gently. He puts it away with the other things. The third drawer is empty except for an automatic pistol. He takes it out. It is a 9mm Hungarian Firebird. He is completely taken aback by its presence.
>
> He lies back on the bed, gun in one hand and the battered old teddy in the other. Above him is the round orb of the earth, with a string of Mexican beads attached to one side.[29]

What is established in the first episode, 'Compassionate Leave', and underlined in subsequent episodes, is the near-incestuous relationship between Craven and Emma, which this scene makes explicit. The scene, and the closeness of the relationship, is dwelt on at great length in order to emotionally involve the viewer in Craven's grief, while the gun, maps and Geiger counter that he discovers in Emma's room provide the narrative enigmas which engage the viewer intellectually. Not only does Emma's death motivate Craven's narrative quest, it provides the human basis on which a drama of global significance is to unfold. Michael Wearing, who produced the serial, describes the process by which the drama starts on a human scale before opening out to encompass global issues:

> In simplistic terms, the story opens with the most sustained evocation of individual grief in bereavement that I can readily recall, and pushes outwards through these characters on a steadily widening canvas to a graphic recognition that, with the spectre of nuclear destruction hovering over contemporary life, the survival of our planet is at stake.[30]

For Kennedy Martin this was a deliberate strategy, facilitated by the serial form: 'The art is to start with a familiar idea and take the audience with you on a plane, so that when they look down they are thousands of miles above the Earth.'[31] The ingredients which anticipate this widening of the narrative scale are all present in the scene in Emma's bedroom, from the personal possessions which are all that Craven now has to remember her by, to the Geiger counter, maps, gun and the NASA poster of the Earth which hangs on Emma's wall (referred to in the script, although this does not appear in the scene as filmed).

Emma's death activates Craven's memories of the death of his wife from cancer ten years before. Before Craven goes into Emma's bedroom we are given flashbacks to his wife's funeral, followed by the young Emma telling her father that he should sleep with her now that Mummy isn't there (the first hint of the incest theme). The extremely close relationship Craven had with Emma helps to explain why he subsequently 'conjures her up' following her death, not only visualising her, but holding conversations with her – he literally cannot let her go. The original idea, apparently, was for Emma's voice to be heard after her death, conveying the idea that she continued to exist in Craven's mind, but the flashbacks to Emma as a child prompted the idea of having the adult Emma appear, for Craven only, as a material being who would suddenly appear as if from nowhere and then disappear again.

While clearly a departure from naturalism, Emma's appearances and disappearances are handled 'realistically', being introduced gradually and discreetly so that it seems 'natural' that Emma should reappear and have a continuing role in the story because of the close relationship between Craven and herself that has already been established. The key scene in this gradual process occurs in episode one when Craven is seen, with the young Emma in the car, driving down to London. However, this is not a flashback. Craven makes that journey following Emma's death and the young Emma appears, briefly, in the narrative present with Craven. By the middle of episode two, 'Into the Shadows', Craven is having on-screen conversations with the adult Emma and she continues, therefore, to have a narrative function to perform in the drama.

This narrative function also turns out to be an ideological function. Craven discovers that Emma was a member of Gaia, an ecological organisation which had infiltrated a nuclear waste plant called Northmoor, where they suspected plutonium was being manufactured illegally by its owners, International Irradiated Fuels (IIF). As a result of this incursion, and because the Gaia team had uncovered the truth of IIF's illegal activities, the company employed a hitman to kill the Gaia activists who had infiltrated Northmoor, including Emma.

Kennedy Martin got the idea for Gaia from the theory of the British scientist James Lovelock that the Earth is a self-regulating system, able to look after itself no matter what disasters might threaten its future. In the event of a nuclear explosion, for example, bacteria would process the radiation from the fallout and life would begin to evolve again. Lovelock's hypothesis is explained in his book *Gaia: A New Look at Life on Earth*, the title of which derives from the name of the Greek goddess of the Earth. After her death, Emma metaphorically assumes the role of the Earth Goddess as she instructs Craven on the ability of the planet to look after itself and this is the ideological position which he comes to adopt by the end of the drama. To complete Craven's transformation into a Celtic Green Man, Kennedy Martin wanted to go as far as having Craven turn into a tree at the end of the final episode, but this was vetoed by other members of the production team!

Emma's ideological position – the one taken up eventually by Craven – is contrasted to that adopted by the renegade CIA agent Darius Jedburgh (Joe Don Baker) who, like Craven, moves during the course of the narrative to adopt a more radical position, turning against his paymasters and stealing the plutonium from Northmoor in order to prevent it getting into the hands of the arch villain Jerry Grogan (Kenneth Nelson), president of the Fusion Corporation of Kansas which is planning to take over IIF in order to get hold of the plutonium being manufactured at Northmoor.

Grogan's company is engaged in research on the Strategic Defense Initiative, the controversial nuclear defence system proposed by the American government in the early 1980s and first announced in Ronald Reagan's 'star wars' speech in 1983. This narrative strand was a relatively late addition to the story but it proved to be the element which made *Edge of Darkness* especially relevant in the mid-1980s, focusing on the escalation in nuclear weapons and the 'special relationship' between Britain and America which led to the siting of American cruise missiles at US airbases in Britain. Kennedy Martin referred to these 'paranoid times' in his introduction to the published script:

> These were the years before detente, when born-again Christians and cold-war warriors seemed to be running the United States. It was the time when the White House changed its nuclear strategy from the thirty-year-old notion of mutually assured destruction (MAD) to the idea that a nuclear war was winnable. It was a time when 30,000 nuclear weapons were thought too old and too few and the whole armoury had to be modernized. And on top of that, 25 billion dollars was to be spent on space weapons. In March 1983 President Reagan made his 'star wars' speech allocating this money to the Strategic Defence Initiative: a defence umbrella which would safeguard America.[32]

So a drama serial which begins as a detective film noir opens out into a political thriller with international implications before evolving into a nuclear thriller with implications of global apocalypse. The epic scale of the narrative, unfolding over five hours of screen time, enabled *Edge of Darkness* to engage with a wide range of issues within an entertaining, at times gripping, storyline. Yet the drama succeeded in achieving an authenticity lacking in other thrillers, mainly through the way in which it incorporated references to the real world into its fictional narrative.

Michael Meacher's appearance in episode one is the first example of this, when he gives a talk to a student audience on the subject of 'the nuclear state', a subject with which Meacher was actively concerned as a Labour politician in the 1980s. Later in the same episode Craven watches Margaret Thatcher being interviewed on television by Robin Day about the government's investment in nuclear weapons. At another point there is a television news report about allegations of police violence following clashes between police and pickets, the subject of nightly news reports during the 1984–5 miners' strike, and in episode two Craven is interviewed at the BBC about Emma's murder, by the television presenter Sue Cook, playing herself.

Other examples of this blurring between the real and fictional worlds include the nuclear reprocessing plant at Sellafield being mentioned in the same breath as the fictional Northmoor, authenticating the latter while at the same time casting doubts about the former. Craven hears a news report on his car radio, read by the familiar voice of a real BBC newsreader, about the Commons inquiry into the proposed takeover of IIF by the Fusion Corporation of Kansas. Reagan, Carter, El Salvador, Nicaragua and the Falklands are all invoked as people and places that exist in the fictional world of *Edge of Darkness*. Might not, then, the fictional events portrayed in *Edge of Darkness* take place in the real world inhabited by the viewers?

Edge of Darkness has been described as the seminal 1980s nuclear thriller. When it was first screened on BBC Two in November–December 1985 it gained an average audience of 4 million viewers and huge critical acclaim, leading to a swift repeat on BBC One where the audience doubled to 8 million. In March 1986 it received six BAFTA awards, including that of Best Drama Serial, and by November 1986 the programme had been sold to nineteen countries.

As a contemporary thriller *Edge of Darkness* tapped into the key issues of the time: government secrecy, the future of the planet, the proliferation of nuclear weapons, the collusion between the Thatcher and Reagan governments, and the options for actively opposing 'the Dark Forces who would rule this planet'.[33] In a reactionary climate, when the possibilities for the production of 'social issue' drama were limited, *Edge of Darkness* proved that, by adapting to changed circumstances and adopting a serialised thriller format, it was still possible to produce ambitious and progressive television drama in Britain in the mid-1980s.

Crime drama

Edge of Darkness was sufficiently broad in its generic scope to be included in a section on 'crime drama' in *The Guinness Book of Classic British TV* while also meriting an entry in Roger Fulton's encyclopedia of science fiction programmes.[34] In reviews the serial was described as both a 'political thriller' and a 'nuclear thriller', and given its investigatory structure it could also be classified as a 'detective drama' (references to it as a film noir were also common). Generic hybridity was increasingly evident in 1980s television drama, not least in the crime genre itself where a blurring began to take place between programmes which might previously have been classified unambiguously as police series (e.g. *Z Cars*) or detective drama (e.g. *Sherlock Holmes*) or crime drama (e.g. *Gangsters*).

Such was the case with *Minder* (Thames, 1979–94), a comedy drama where the focus was on the petty criminal activities of Arthur Daley (George Cole) and his minder Terry McCann (Dennis Waterman). Developed by Euston Films as a replacement for *The Sweeney*, *Minder* was much softer, a light-hearted crime drama that was able to present criminals as the affectionate central characters precisely because they were not a serious threat to the social order. While the police regularly featured in the series they were usually comic, ineffectual foils to the stars of the show, repeatedly failing to apprehend Arthur for his incursions of the law. While Terry provided the muscle when and where necessary (as Waterman often had as the sidekick to John Thaw's Regan in *The*

Sweeney), the Waterman/Cole pairing was generally played for its comic potential, with George Cole emerging as the charismatic focus of the drama, despite the series' title.

Towards the end of the 1980s John Thaw re-emerged in a more upmarket police detective drama to the one in which he had featured as Detective Inspector Jack Regan in the 1970s. In *Inspector Morse* (Central, 1987–2000) Thaw this time played a Chief Inspector with a taste for classical music as well as classic cars. Partnered with the working-class Detective Sergeant Lewis (Kevin Whately), who could provide the physical force if required, Morse was more cerebral than Regan, the emphasis in the two-hour dramas being on deduction rather than action. Adapted from the novels of Colin Dexter and set amid the gleaming spires of Oxford, *Inspector Morse* proved to be a successful amalgam of the police/crime drama and investigative detective genre. As a two-hour drama (minus commercial breaks), presented in short seasons varying in length from three to five dramas, *Inspector Morse* also provided the pleasures of the one-off single play/TV film within a series format: self-contained stories with regular, familiar central characters. More leisurely and stylish than most police/crime drama, more contemporary than Sherlock Holmes (of which there were two more series in the 1980s[35]), *Inspector Morse* was a huge ratings success, gaining an audience of 13.9 million for the first episode, rising to 15 million plus by the fifth series.[36] Its critical and popular success was an indication of how audience tastes were changing in the late 1980s and its hybridity (not just police/crime/detective drama, but also heritage drama – see below) was illustrative of how the television companies were seeking to maximise audiences by broadening the appeal of their generic drama, including a variety of elements for a diversity of tastes.

This diversity was also evident in the new police series that appeared in the early 1980s. After the machismo of 1960s and 70s police dramas, the effect of the women's liberation movement finally began to be felt in television drama in the 1980s with two new series featuring women as central characters. In *The Gentle Touch* (LWT, 1980–4) Detective Inspector Maggie Forbes (Jill Gascoine) made history as the first woman to feature as the central character in a police series, shortly followed by Inspector Jean Darblay (Stephanie Turner) and her successor Inspector Kate Longton (Anna Carteret) in *Juliet Bravo* (BBC One, 1980–5). When *The Gentle Touch* ended, Jill Gascoine graduated to detective drama when her character, Maggie Forbes, joined a team of three women to form the Eyes Enquiry Agency, a front for a Home Office special intelligence team known as Covert Activities, Thames Section (C.A.T.S.). *C.A.T.S. Eyes* (TVS, 1985–7) was both a feminist response to the machismo of *The Professionals* (LWT, 1977–83) and a British equivalent to the successful American series *Charlie's Angels* (ITV, 1977–82). With the demise of macho series like *The Sweeney* and *The Professionals*, these three female-centred series marked the beginnings of an improvement in the representation of women in British television drama in the 1980s, both on screen and as industry employees.

Ethnic diversity was also in evidence in the early 1980s with *The Chinese Detective* (BBC One, 1981–2), featuring David Yip as the eponymous Chinese Detective Sergeant John Ho, and the short-lived *Wolcott* (ATV, 13–15 January 1981), featuring George William Harris as an Afro-Caribbean cop. The presence of these non-white police officers in leading roles led, inevitably, to racism being confronted as an issue in these dramas, both within the police force and outside of it. Although both *Wolcott* and *The Chinese Detective* attempted to offer positive representations of black and Asian characters to counter the more typical representation of blacks and Asians as villains, the fact that these dramas were short-lived, compared to the female-centred dramas, leaves a question mark against their social effectivity. While *The Chinese Detective* lasted for two series, *Wolcott* got no further than its three-part pilot.

A new 1980s series which did survive, and which was destined to become the longest-running police series on British television, was *The Bill* (Thames, 1984–2010). Developed from an episode of Thames TV's *Storyboard* series called 'Woodentop', *The Bill* attempted to update the police series for the 1980s, following in the tradition of periodic renewal represented by *Z Cars* in the 1960s and *The Sweeney* in the 70s. In its second series, in November 1985, *The Bill* introduced a black policeman to the programme, enabling it to deal with issues of racism in the police force while, at the same time, attempting to counter the accusation that black characters only ever appeared in police/crime drama as villains.

However, as other series have discovered, there is a limit to which this progressive project – in this case to provide a positive representation of a black character and to confront institutional racism – can be taken in a popular genre like the police series without fracturing the ideological basis on which the genre is founded, namely the maintenance of law and order. When, in July 1988, *The Bill* moved from a weekly one-hour drama series, presented in twelve-episode seasons, to an ongoing twice-weekly half-hour series, moving it closer to the format of a television soap, the dominant ideological function of 'reassurance' performed by police series was inevitably consolidated. Thereafter, the character of the black police constable Malcolm Haynes (Eamonn Walker) was 'deracialised', as Jim Pines puts it: 'a cue for PC Haynes to do what all TV cops are supposed to do, catch criminals'.[37]

Perhaps the most significant development in crime drama in the 1980s, at a time when the state was becoming increasingly coercive under Thatcher's Conservative government, was a notable increase in dramas featuring criminals as central characters, rather than the usual focus in the crime genre on the enforcers of law and order. Euston Films was in the vanguard here, as it was in so many aspects of series and serial drama in the 1970s and 80s. Trevor Preston had set a precedent for this with his 1978 serial *Out* and he followed it with *Fox* (Thames, March–June 1980), a thirteen-part serial about a south London family headed by Billy Fox (Peter Vaughan), an ex-criminal with many underworld connections. While the serial was more of a family saga than a crime drama, it conformed to the ethos which Preston had explored in *Out*, presenting a sympathetic portrayal of a working-class fraternity in south London. Like *Out* it also marked a shift towards long-form drama, as the director of both serials, Jim Goddard, noted:

It was about loyalty – working-class loyalty, working-class villain loyalty ... And it was an attempt by all of us to say, OK the single play may be dead but we now see the possibility of starting something, if you like, called the television novel. Because they are novelistic in their structure – *Fox* was a novel.[38]

The fraternal ethos within a working-class south London community was also central to *Minder*, although the generally petty crimes of Arthur Daley were given a more light-hearted treatment. The structural difference between *Minder* as a series and *Out* or *Fox* as serials is significant here in terms of a more limited narrative canvas, with *Minder* leaning towards the structure of a situation comedy, in which each episode's story is resolved so that Arthur and Terry can begin the next episode in the same basic situation that they are always in, and it is this which makes *Minder* more conservative than the crime serials which Euston were producing at the same time. Yet it is still possible to argue that *Minder* was progressive in its portrayal of a small-time criminal who repeatedly outwits the forces of law and order. While Leon Griffiths, who devised *Minder*, by no means set out to write a radical drama and while Arthur was in many ways a working-class conservative and a Thatcherite, the sympathetic portrayal of his petty criminal activities can be seen as progressive in the context of a mainly conservative genre and a reactionary political climate. As *Minder*'s script editor Linda Agran said of the series in the early 1980s:

> I think the more our society is going the way it is, the more people are understanding and identifying with the little men trying to fiddle, or whatever, their own success and somehow get an edge. Actually I've got a feeling that under a Labour government *Minder* might have been completely different – under this government you have to show that you can survive.[39]

The most radical crime drama of the 1980s, and another Euston Films production, was Lynda La Plante's *Widows* (Thames, March–April 1983), produced by Linda Agran and directed by Ian Toynton. After a number of male-centred dramas, many of which were aggressively macho in orientation, Linda Agran, Head of Scripts and Development at Euston, and Verity Lambert, Head of Drama at Thames, the parent company, were looking for something which might attempt to redress the balance. Agran explained the problem in a 1984 interview:

> I've had lots of feminist groups attack me for the way that women are portrayed in some of our films. I think the problem is that series writing in this country is completely dominated by men. All the male writers I work with are terribly concerned people and genuinely think that women get a raw deal, but some of them talk about women as though they're Martians. They're afraid of getting them wrong, so they leave them out or drop in a stereotype just in order to get a point across. Thus there's no possibility of redressing the balance while there are so few women writers.[40]

When Lynda La Plante came along with the idea for *Widows* both Agran and Lambert were very keen to produce it and encouraged La Plante, who had been working as the character actress Lynda Marchal, to develop it as a serial, even though this was her first script. It ended up as a six-part serial lasting over five hours, the same length as *Out*. Starting with a failed heist, in which three men are killed, *Widows* told the story of how

Widows by Lynda La Plante: breaking the mould of the crime drama

the men's wives, the eponymous widows, get together with a fourth woman to plan and execute the same robbery, succeeding where their husbands had failed.

What was radical about *Widows* was not only that it focused on four working-class women as criminals, detailing their preparations for the robbery and their evasion of both the police and a gang which wants the ledgers Dolly Rawlins (Ann Mitchell) has inherited, but that it also showed the women getting away with the crime. La Plante had not originally written it this way, but both Lambert and Agran wanted to show the women getting away with it:

> I know that some people think that the end is morally very questionable and Lynda said to me they can't get away with it, can they – the IBA wouldn't allow it. And I said, 'Nuts. Sure I'll talk to the IBA if necessary. If people are really going to get involved with it – and it is fiction – of course they're going to want them to get away with it.'[41]

Widows therefore broke the mould in more ways than one. It was also a ratings success and an unusual one in that it gained viewers as the serial proceeded, a rare occurrence in serial drama, building from 11 million viewers for the first episode to 12.5 million in episode six – the fourth most watched programme on British television that week, getting a larger audience than both *Dallas* and the *Eurovision Song Contest!*[42]

The first series was followed by a sequel in 1985, *Widows II* (Thames, April–May 1985), but the second series could not maintain the ground-breaking impact of the original and, after daring to show the women getting away with it in the first series, was resolved far more negatively, with two of the women dead and Dolly in prison (leaving an opening for a further sequel, *She's Out*, in 1995).

Soap opera

If crime drama, until *Widows*, had primarily been a male genre, soap opera, since its beginnings on 1930s American radio, has always been primarily a female genre. As such, it was often a source of ridicule and not considered worthy of serious attention. In the late 1970s, as we have seen, this began to change with the growth of the women's movement and the emergence of cultural studies as an academic discipline, leading to the appearance of a feminist television criticism, of which the Dyer, Lovell and McCrindle paper on 'Soap Opera and Women' at the 1977 Edinburgh International Television Festival was an early example. This 'feminist turn' in television criticism and the focus on soap opera as a genre worthy of attention went hand in hand, leading to a number of publications in the early 1980s including books on *Coronation Street* and on *Crossroads*, the most popular British soaps at the time.[43]

The 1981 BFI monograph on *Coronation Street* was a collection of essays exploring different theoretical approaches to the Granada serial and included contributions from two of the authors of the Edinburgh paper, Richard Dyer and Terry Lovell, with an essay also by Christine Geraghty, who was to make a leading contribution to the study of television soap opera in the 1980s. This monograph was followed by Dorothy Hobson's study of *Crossroads*, published in 1982, in which she examined both the production and consumption of the Central TV serial, providing an early ethnographic study of a soap opera with viewers being interviewed about the pleasures they derived from watching the programme.

Another notable academic contribution was Charlotte Brunsdon's 1981 *Screen* article, 'Crossroads: Notes on Soap Opera', examining the way in which the serial was gendered as feminine. Unlike male-oriented television programmes, such as crime drama, for example, Brunsdon argued that:

> *Crossroads* is in the business not of creating narrative excitement, suspense, delay and resolution, but of constructing moral consensus about the conduct of personal life. There is an endless unsettling discussion and resettling of acceptable modes of behaviour within the sphere of personal relationships.[44]

Brunsdon's article contributed to an influential feminist discourse on popular television which was attempting to redress the balance of critical attention which had previously privileged the 'serious' genres of news, current affairs and documentary.[45] Like the other analyses of soap opera appearing at the time, Brunsdon's article echoed a key principle of 1970s feminism that 'the personal is political' and this new wave of feminist criticism saw a shift in emphasis in television studies away from a preoccupation with questions of balance and bias in news and current affairs towards a focus on gender and sexual politics. In the field of popular television drama, Brunsdon argued, soap operas not only targeted the female viewer but required different kinds of (feminine) reading skills to other forms of drama:

> The argument is that the narrative strategies and concerns of *Crossroads* call on the traditionally feminine competencies associated with the responsibility for 'managing' the sphere of personal life. It is the culturally constructed skills of femininity – sensitivity, perception, intuition and the necessary privileging of the concerns of personal life – which are both called on and practised in the genre.[46]

Unlike crime drama, which is gendered as stereotypically masculine, goal-oriented and action-based, soap opera is gendered as feminine because it privileges feelings, personal issues and family relationships in a discursive, open-ended manner, the ongoing structure of the continuous serial enabling storylines and issues to be returned to again and again in 'an endless unsettling discussion and resettling of acceptable modes of behaviour'.

    While the advent of a feminist approach to popular television was an important and influential development in television studies in the early 1980s, the impact of Thatcherism on British society was to bring a reassessment of the nature and composition of soap opera as a popular form as the genre adapted to a changing audience demographic. As Thatcherite policies decimated the older, male-dominated heavy industries and unemployment rose in the early 1980s, there was a change in patterns of employment and leisure in British society during the decade which had a significant impact on both the composition of the television audience and the issues and representations which popular programmes like soap opera engaged with. As Christine Geraghty has noted, this involved a shift from the previous focus on 'the personal' to an increased engagement with social issues. It also had an effect on the status of soap opera as a 'woman's genre', as men began to feature more prominently in storylines in recognition of the changes in gender roles which were happening in the wider society. These changes were especially evident in the new soaps that were introduced during the decade:

> It was not until the 1980s when *Brookside* (1982) and *EastEnders* (1985) were both launched that British soap operas took up social issues more overtly and handled social problems in a more direct way that went beyond the plight of individual characters and dealt with the public sphere as well as the personal. In doing so, the new programmes sought to engage an audience which included those not normally attracted to soaps – young people, men, those concerned about political and social issues.[47]

When Channel 4 started in 1982, the new channel recognised the importance of having a continuous serial in its schedules in order to attract and build an audience. It commissioned *Brookside* from Mersey Television, an independent production company run by

Confronting social issues head-on in *Brookside*: Channel 4's alternative soap opera

Phil Redmond who had previously developed the children's drama *Grange Hill* for the BBC. *Brookside* was to be a Liverpool-based twice-weekly soap which would reflect its regional setting with its array of Scouse accents, while also dealing with contemporary national issues. While the programme did not challenge *Coronation Street* or *Crossroads* in terms of audience size, *Brookside* immediately proved itself to be the most popular programme on Channel 4, conforming to the alternative remit of the channel by adopting a more 'realist' style, utilising single-camera filming on location (a cul-de-sac of thirteen houses purchased by Mersey Television) instead of multi-camera recording in the studio, while striving also to be more realistic in the language used and the issues that it dealt with, such as unemployment, redundancy, strikes, homosexuality, AIDS, rape, criminality and the ethics of private medicine as opposed to the National Health Service.

While not all of the issues *Brookside* engaged with were unique to the 1980s, they were certainly issues which were topical at the time, many of which, such as the 'privatisation' issues, were a direct consequence of Thatcherite policies. The decision to base the drama on a new housing estate and not to have a local pub as a meeting place was a direct result of the determination to reflect social change, as Phil Redmond explained:

> At the time, in the early 1980s, approximately 58 per cent of homes were owner-occupied, approximately 15 per cent were private rented accommodation and the rest was council-owned accommodation. In the mid to late 1980s the owner-occupying percentage has risen to about 62. Therefore it seemed more realistic and more logical to have a residential drama serial reflecting such owner-occupation.[48]

EastEnders followed *Brookside's* example in dealing with social issues, including the 1980s 'crisis in masculinity'

While this may have reflected changing social trends in the acquisitive 1980s, it did, however, cause some dramatic problems and it was not long before a row of shops was introduced as a place where characters could meet and exchange gossip, instead of meeting at the local postbox which featured rather heavily in early episodes! The quest for realism, therefore, in setting the drama on a housing estate, had to be weighed against the dramatic needs of the genre, in this case the need for a meeting place where characters could 'realistically' come together so that dramatic storylines and situations could be enacted.

While social issues were often foregrounded in the new 1980s soaps, this was also sometimes problematic within the conventions of the genre, the problem arising from the fact that, as Christine Geraghty has observed, both *Brookside* and *EastEnders* were based around the family unit, rather than the community:

> This may be a surprising assertion in the light of their apparent emphasis on family breakup and tensions. Family life was an important element in the network of relationships in *Coronation Street* but in the main it was the community which sustained its individual members whether they were part of a family or not and ensured no one was without support. *Brookside* and *EastEnders* specifically turned their back on what were seen to be nostalgic notions of neighbours turning to each other for help. In *Brookside* the Close was divided on

class lines and it was rare for the boundaries to be breached ... In *EastEnders*, the notion of community was certainly invoked, but it was not always seen to be effective; it belonged to the 'good old days' about which the older women reminisce but whose very existence is questioned by the younger characters. The notion of the community was thus rendered problematic and a vacuum left in *Brookside* and *EastEnders* which had to be filled; somewhat ironically, it was the family which emerged as the model.[49]

This development does not seem surprising at a time when Thatcherism was demanding a return to 'family values' and arguing against the notion of 'community' and 'society' in favour of 'privatised' family units, though this conservative ideology was still undermined within *Brookside* and *EastEnders* by the stress on tensions and splits within the family unit. The emphasis on the family, however, did limit the extent to which the new soaps were able to engage with social issues as these issues always had to be dealt with in the context of the family, rather than the wider society. This is, perhaps, the fundamental structural limitation of soaps, for in developing a realistic world within which both personal and social dramas can be played out, soaps cut themselves off from the real world of social and political agencies. While *Brookside* and *EastEnders* were progressive in dealing with contemporary issues and in offering a wider representation of social groups, the extent to which they could engage with social issues and different representations was ultimately limited by the conventions of the genre.

Heritage drama and the 'quality' debate

At the other end of the 'quality' spectrum to soap opera were those dramas, usually lavish serials with big budgets, which have come to be described as 'heritage' drama. This is not the industrial heritage of coal mines, factories or shipyards celebrated in some of the work of Loach/Allen/Garnett, the decline of which was lamented in *Boys from the Blackstuff*, but the upper-class and aristocratic heritage of country houses and stately homes which features in the work of novelists from Jane Austen to Evelyn Waugh.

As with the historical dramas discussed in Chapter 4, these serials were usually literary adaptations, evoking a period of history when Britain was still 'Great', possessing an Empire, and where everyone not only knew their place in the social hierarchy but where everyone was also (apparently) content with their lot. As in the 1970s, when British society was undergoing a similar period of social and economic upheaval, such dramas performed an ideological function of reassurance, evoking nostalgia for a lost age, a time when things were (apparently) more settled.

Andrew Higson has discussed this in relation to British films of the 1980s such as *Chariots of Fire* (1981), *Another Country* (1984), *A Passage to India* (1985) and *A Room with a View* (1986), arguing that they constitute a cycle of films which are essentially conservative and nostalgic in their mode of address. Unlike other British films of the period, some of which were the Channel 4-funded films which displaced the single play, such as *The Ploughman's Lunch* (1983) and *My Beautiful Laundrette*, which were set in the present and addressed contemporary social issues:

The heritage films ... provide a very different response to developments in
Thatcherite Britain. By turning their backs on the industrialized, chaotic present,
they nostalgically reconstruct an imperialist and upper-class Britain ... The films
thus offer apparently more settled and visually splendid manifestations of an
essentially pastoral national identity and authentic culture: 'Englishness' as an
ancient and natural inheritance, Great Britain, the United Kingdom.[50]

Television also contributed to this heritage cycle, most famously with *Brideshead Revisited*
(Granada, October–December 1981) and *The Jewel in the Crown* (Granada, January–April
1984), prestigious drama serials which, between them, amounted to twenty-five hours
of screen time. If *Chariots of Fire* marked the beginning of a cycle of heritage cinema in
the 1980s, *Brideshead Revisited*, transmitted in the same year that *Chariots* was released,
did the same for television drama. Adapted by John Mortimer from the novel by Evelyn
Waugh, the eleven-part serial, in thirteen hours of screen time, told the story of the
encounter of Charles Ryder (Jeremy Irons) with the aristocratic Marchmain family,
whose family home was Brideshead Castle. The serial begins in the mid-1940s, with
Ryder, a captain in the army, stationed at Brideshead towards the end of the Second
World War, the return to which nostalgically triggers memories of his first visit there
with Lord Sebastian Flyte (Anthony Andrews), the son of Lord Marchmain (Laurence
Olivier), when they were both students at Oxford in the 1920s. The serial proceeds to
describe, in flashback, the passage of Ryder's encounters through the 1920s and 30s,
returning us to a 'golden age' signified by the golden hues of Oxford, Venice, Paris and
the other romantic locations that feature in the serial.

With a star-studded cast (John Gielgud, Claire Bloom and Diana Quick also featured),
lavish sets, exotic locations (in addition to Oxford, Paris and Venice there were scenes in
New York, North Africa and London, with the palatial Castle Howard in Yorkshire providing the setting for Brideshead Castle) and a total budget of £4 million, *Brideshead
Revisited* was cited, along with the equally exotic *The Jewel in the Crown*, as a prime
example of the quality drama which British television excelled in. Such programming,
it was argued later in the decade, was threatened by the Conservative government's
plans to apply free-market principles to broadcasting, proposals for which were
announced in a government White Paper published in 1988.

The title of the White Paper was 'Broadcasting in the 1990s: Competition, Choice and
Quality' and it put the question of 'quality' in broadcasting firmly onto the political
agenda. The fact that 'competition' preceded 'quality' in the title was thought by many
commentators to be an indication of the government's priorities. This concern was
heightened by the proposal that, when the ITV franchises came up for renewal, they
should be awarded to the highest bidder, an initiative that was clearly in line with the
competitive free-market philosophy of the Conservative government.

This sparked off a major debate about the threat to public service broadcasting
posed by the proposals. While the immediate threat to the BBC was deferred until 1996,
when the BBC's Charter was due for renewal, the proposal that the ITV companies
should bid for their licences in a multi-million-pound 'auction' raised the spectre of new

Heritage drama: images of Englishness in Granada's lavish serial *Brideshead Revisited*

companies gaining licences purely on the grounds of their financial muscle, with no guarantees that they would fulfil a public service commitment to inform, educate and entertain, as the existing ITV companies had done. With the government favouring competition and a free market, it was feared that there would be nothing to stop future ITV companies going completely downmarket in their programming and jettisoning the public service commitment to supply less popular programmes to minority audiences in pursuit of the large audiences they would need to attract sufficient advertising revenue to finance their franchise bids.

In anticipation, perhaps, of the opposition that this proposal would generate, a 'quality threshold' was outlined in the White Paper. This was intended to ensure that some element of a public service commitment would have to be guaranteed by the successful bidders:

> The 'threshold' consisted of three key requirements for the Channel 3 licensees: to provide regional programmes; to show 'high quality news and current affairs … in main viewing periods', and 'to provide a diverse programme service calculated to appeal to a variety of tastes and interests'.[51]

Between the publication of the White Paper and the eventual passage of the 1990 Broadcasting Act through parliament, intense lobbying took place, led by organisations like the Campaign for Quality Television, to ensure that this quality threshold was raised to include a wider range of programmes and also to ensure that an 'exceptional circumstances' clause was added to the Bill that would enable the ITC, which would oversee the issuing of the new licences, to veto a higher bid if it was not satisfied that the quality threshold could be fulfilled.

In these circumstances, the ITV companies were concerned to demonstrate the quality of their existing programming and it was significant that lavish and expensive drama serials like *Brideshead Revisited* and *The Jewel in the Crown* were cited as prime examples of the kind of programmes that would be under threat as a result of the government's proposals. Not only were these prestigious serials seen by many as encapsulating 'quality' in ITV programming, they were also very popular, with *Brideshead* gaining an average audience of 10 million viewers and *The Jewel in the Crown* gaining an average of 8 million. Furthermore, because of their focus on an aristocratic and upper-class notion of British heritage and their sumptuous visual aesthetic, they were very lucrative in terms of overseas sales and their success may explain the production of numerous other ITV period dramas in the late 1980s, such as *Paradise Postponed* (Thames, September–November 1986), *The Charmer* (LWT, October–November 1987), *Hannay* (Thames, 1988–9) and *Agatha Christie's Poirot* (LWT/ITV, 1989–2013), as well as the 'contemporary' heritage drama, *Inspector Morse*.

In her 1990 article 'Problems with Quality' Charlotte Brunsdon examined some of the aspects of this debate about quality in broadcasting, identifying four 'quality components' characterising heritage drama on British television.[52] The first signifier of 'quality' she identified as the literary source, whether it be 'highbrow' literature, such as Jane Austen, or 'middlebrow', such as Evelyn Waugh, both lend prestige to the more 'vulgar' medium of television. Second, the best of British acting: prestigious actors with a theatrical background whose presence lends 'class' to television drama. Third, money: enabling high production values, the presence of a large budget being clearly evident on the screen. Fourth, heritage export: the representation of 'a certain image of England and Englishness (with little reference to the rest of Britain), in which national identity is expressed through class and imperial identity'.[53]

These 'quality components' suggest a combination of 'high culture' values and high production values, representing both a Reithian concept of quality (bringing 'high' culture to the masses) and a post-Reithian public service concept of quality (where 'quality' is determined primarily by high production values). Yet there is a third definition of 'quality' in broadcasting which is more in tune with the Thatcherite free-market philosophy. 'Quality' here is determined by the public and measured in terms of ratings – a 'quality' programme being one that gets a big audience. In contrast to the famous Reithian credo: 'few know what they want and very few what they need',[54] the free-market definition of quality is based on giving the public what they want, rather than what broadcasters think they need.

Brideshead Revisited and *The Jewel in the Crown* can be seen to conform to each of these definitions of quality: not only did they have 'high culture' values and high production values, but they were also very popular, gaining huge audiences. What their success showed, and what the success of *Inspector Morse* with its contemporary heritage iconography, its high production values and its high ratings also showed later in the decade, was that notions of 'quality' in television drama were changing as British society was being transformed under Thatcherism.

Where once 'quality' had been synonymous with a narrow elite, by the end of the 1980s quality in television drama had come to mean different things to different people. On the one hand it was the heritage drama of *Brideshead Revisited* and *Inspector Morse*; on the other it was socially committed, progressive drama such as *Boys from the Blackstuff* and *Edge of Darkness*. In each case, quality drama was also popular drama, drama that was watched and enjoyed by millions of people. The concern at the end of the decade, as Rupert Murdoch's satellite television service Sky TV began transmitting, was whether such programmes would continue to get made in a more competitive, multi-channel environment.

6

Reinventing Television Drama, 1990–2002

The passing of the 1980s saw the end of an era in more ways than one. In November 1990 Margaret Thatcher was ousted as the leader of the Conservative Party, forced to resign by a coalition of her own senior ministers who recognised that their leader's increasing unpopularity had made her an electoral liability, a fact exacerbated by the implementation of the Poll Tax in 1990. Thatcher was replaced by the somewhat less strident John Major, a move which enabled the Tories to gain re-election in 1992. Though less radical than the Thatcher administrations, the Major government consolidated the social and political revolution wrought under Thatcher's leadership and extended the Tory hegemony for another five years.

Thatcher had presided over fundamental and lasting changes to British society and the consequences of the Thatcherite revolution were to be felt throughout the 1990s and beyond. In order to overturn the Tories in 1997 the Labour Party had to reinvent itself as a party of the centre which would appeal to middle-class voters as well as its traditional working-class supporters, many of whom had abandoned the Labour Party in the 1980s. With socialism temporarily defeated the political radicalism of the 1960s and 70s, which had spawned so much progressive television drama, was supplanted in the 1980s and by the consumer culture of the new capitalism.

elevision, the 1990 Broadcasting Act saw the culmination of Thatcher's efforts to y free-market principles to broadcasting.[1] Its most contentious clauses included the renewal of ITV franchises by competitive tender, awarding new contracts to the highest bidder in a multi-million-pound auction. This resulted in four ITV franchises changing hands, of which the most significant was the ending of Thames Television's franchise when it was outbid for the London weekday contract by Carlton Television. Many saw this as Thatcher gaining revenge on a more liberal broadcaster which had angered her with programmes like *Death on the Rock* (1988), an investigative documentary about the killing of three unarmed IRA activists by the SAS in Gibraltar in March 1988. Thames had held its franchise since 1968 and had developed a reputation as a producer of quality programmes, not least in the realm of drama where its wholly owned subsidiary Euston Films had played a leading role in television drama production since the early 1970s.

The Broadcasting Act also introduced a quota for independent production on the BBC and ITV, extending the free-market philosophy which lay behind the establishment of Channel 4 as a publisher-broadcaster. Meanwhile, Channel 4 was to sell its own advertising from 1993, a move which raised concerns that the channel would be forced to abandon its innovative public service remit in order to compete with the other commercial television companies for advertising revenue, a concern that, in many aspects of its programming, was subsequently proven to be well founded. With a gradual increase in the number of satellite and cable channels, plus the introduction of a fifth terrestrial channel in 1997, competition between an increasing number of television channels for a diminishing share of the audience was the pattern throughout the 1990s.

The BBC was not exempt from this more competitive ethos and in its new Director General John Birt, who officially took over from Michael Checkland in 1992 but was effectively in charge from 1991, the corporation was led by someone who was quite prepared to embrace free-market economics, implementing a new policy initiative, 'Producer Choice', which was designed to introduce a more 'cost-effective' approach to BBC programme-making. Widely disliked by those working at the BBC, the new initiative considerably increased bureaucracy while bringing no significant improvement to programme standards. On the contrary, the majority view was that a consequence of the new commercial ethos at the BBC was to take the initiative away from the creative staff and put it into the hands of a new legion of administrators and bureaucrats whose priority was cost-effectiveness rather than the production of distinctive, public service programmes.

These fundamental changes in both the provision and consumption of television made the 1990s the most significant decade for change in British television since the arrival of ITV in the 1950s. It marked the beginnings of a 'postmodern' shift away from the idea of a producer-led culture, in which the broadcasters delivered to a mass audience what, on the whole, they felt the public needed, towards a consumer-led culture where the broadcasters were forced to compete with an increasing number of competitors for a share of the audience. In this more competitive climate many broadcasters, including the BBC, were seemingly more than willing to give the public what it wanted, leading to accusations of a 'dumbing down' in broadcasting and a significant decline in the production of challenging, social-issue drama for which British television was renowned in the 1960s and 70s.

Confronted with these changed circumstances, television drama producers faced new challenges in the 1990s. While channel controllers and commissioning editors were increasingly concerned to play safe and win audiences with tried and tested formats, a few progressive producers, writers and directors rose to the challenge of 'reinventing' television drama in the 1990s, finding new ways to work the system in order to produce what Tony Garnett has described as 'Trojan Horse' drama:

> Throughout history people like us have had to use existing structures and make them work for us as best we can. If forced to work in a particular form or genre, then we must try to subvert it, or put new wine in old bottles, or find other ways of creating 'Trojan Horse drama'.[2]

From producer-led to consumer-led drama

In his 1997 book *TV Drama in Transition* Robin Nelson identified a paradigm shift in television drama production in the 1990s.[3] Where, before the 'dislocations of postmodernity', television drama had been 'writer- and producer-led', with writers having the autonomy to produce original and often controversial drama, aided and abetted by sympathetic producers and directors, in the post-Thatcher, postmodern 1990s the onus shifted to the audience, or to the 'consumer' to use the new market-driven terminology, as the television companies became increasingly conscious of the need to win and retain audiences in a fragmenting broadcasting environment.

Nelson cites the example of *Heartbeat* (ITV, 1992–2010), a popular rural police drama set in the 1960s, as a prime example of a 1990s consumer-led drama series. After a successful first series, shown at 9 pm on Friday evenings, which attracted an audience of 10–13 million, the second series was moved to primetime on Sunday evening, where its audience increased to an average of 15 million to become the most popular non-soap drama on British television.[4] Nelson explains how the series was developed as a product for audience consumption, being subject to market research in order to establish which elements of the drama would be popular with viewers:

> *Heartbeat* serves as an example of the development of a drama series in part through the application of the methods of market research undertaken by Audience Planning at the ITV Network Centre. The approach clearly marks a shift from the writer- and producer-led, supply-side aesthetics in drama production of the past.[5]

The original concept and a pilot episode were tested on focus groups to establish what the most popular elements of the drama were, and adjustments were made accordingly to suit the needs of the audience, or rather the target groups, the market research having established that there were three distinct audience groupings who were attracted to different elements of the drama. These three groups were characterised as 'East-End girls', 'lager-lads' and 'green mums':

> The 'East-End girls' were attracted to watch by the centrality of Nick Berry playing the role of PC Rowan and bringing, as noted, a following from his role in *EastEnders*. Notwithstanding the poor showing of police series as such in the concept-testing, 'lager-lads', a second identifiable audience group, proved to be attracted to the police story-lines and the 1960s soundtracks. Thirdly, 'green mums' were drawn by 1960s nostalgia, the rural context of the series and its 'soft' approach to social issues.[6]

For Yorkshire Television, which had bid an enormous £37.7 million to secure its franchise in the 1992 franchise auction, a successful ratings-winning programme was essential. Yorkshire Television's subsequent merger with Tyne Tees Television, which had itself bid £15 million to renew its franchise, meant that Yorkshire-Tyne Tees was faced with

annual repayments to the Exchequer of
£52.7 million. With nearly all of the ITV
companies now facing far higher rev-
enues than ever before the pressure to
produce ratings-winning programmes
which would attract sufficient advertising revenue to pay for their inflated
franchise bids was greatly increased. In
these circumstances, the move from a
producer-led to a consumer-led culture
was hardly surprising.

In television drama, of course,
especially in the realm of the single play
and the serial, the prevailing culture
had been author-led, with writers such
as David Mercer, Dennis Potter, Trevor
Griffiths and Alan Bleasdale leading the
roll-call of television dramatists who
had helped to establish British television drama as 'the best in the world'
during the 1960s, 70s and 80s. With the
decline of the single play and the tran-

Heartbeat: a product of the new consumer-led
drama

sition to a consumer-led drama in the 1990s, however, the position of the writer, once pre-
eminent, was now downgraded. Or rather, the position of the writer with an 'authorial
vision' was now considered to be a luxury that most television companies could no
longer afford.

Instead, what was required in the market-driven context of the 1990s were writers
who could develop marketable projects which would win and retain audiences. Indeed,
the concept to be developed might not be an original idea brought to a producer by a
writer but a concept developed by TV drama commissioners, perhaps in collaboration
with a writer who might then be invited to develop the idea if it was deemed potentially
marketable.

In these new circumstances, the death, in June 1994, of Dennis Potter, undoubtedly
Britain's most celebrated television dramatist, signalled the end of an era for British television drama. Coming at a time when the transition to consumer-led drama was already
under way, Potter's death took on a greater significance, symbolically representing the
'Death of the Author' in British television drama. In the wake of his death much was
made of the fact that Potter had emerged at a time when there was a great deal of freedom for writers, especially on the BBC where, in the mid-1960s when he made his debut
as a television dramatist, Potter had seven full-length plays produced in the space of
little more than two years.

When Potter was invited to give the 1993 MacTaggart Lecture at the Edinburgh
International Television Festival, he mounted a searing attack on the new 'management

culture' at the BBC, famously ridiculing Director General John Birt and the Chairman of
the Board of Governors, Marmaduke Hussey, as 'a pair of croak-voiced Daleks'[7] before
proceeding to attack both Rupert Murdoch and Margaret Thatcher for their advocacy of
a deregulated broadcasting system which privileged cost-effectiveness and private
enterprise over creativity and public service:

> Our television has been ripped apart and falteringly reassembled by politicians
> who believe that value is a monetary term only, and that a cost-accountant is
> thereby the most suitable adjudicator of what we can and cannot see on our
> screens. And these accountants or their near-clones are employed by new kinds
> of media owners who try to gobble up everything in their path.[8]

The references to Thatcher, to Michael Checkland, who had been an accountant at the
BBC before being promoted to Director General in 1987, and to Rupert Murdoch as the
head of a global media corporation were unmistakeable, but the public accusation of
their betrayal of public service broadcasting was a heartfelt plea by a writer whose
experience of television had been formed in more liberal times. Early the following year,
in February 1994, Potter was diagnosed with terminal cancer and given only a few weeks
to live. In a final valedictory television interview, recorded for Channel 4 and transmitted in April 1994, two months before his death, Potter bemoaned the current state of
British television, lamenting the fact that there would be little or no opportunity for
him, or for writers like him, to break into television in the 1990s as he and others had in
the 1960s:

> I was given the space to grow into, and I gave, I gave my working life to it as a
> result, and I have, I have stayed with television to such a large extent because of
> that. Whereas if I was starting now, where would I get that chance? Who would
> cosset and look after me? Where is the single play? And the series, you can punch
> the numbers in the predictability ... You can call the shot numbers out in
> advance. The formula-ridden television is because of sales ... The pressure upon
> creators, whether they're writers, directors, designers, actors, producers,
> whatever, that pressure will be all the time until you maximize your audience at
> any given point, which is the very antithesis of discovering something you didn't
> know. It's the very antithesis of the kind of broadcasting on television which was
> such a glory in British life.[9]

Born out of a lifetime's creativity, of giving audiences something they had not previously experienced, Potter's emotional final interview summed up the consequences
of the consumer-led approach to making television drama. Consumer research is
designed to increase sales, or in this case to increase ratings, but by asking audiences
what they like, with a view to giving them more of it, the possibility is denied of giving
the audience something beyond their experience, something that they did not know
that they wanted. What the consumer-led approach to television drama produces is

bland, audience-pleasing, undemanding drama like *Heartbeat*, drama which is a pale reflection of the challenging, provocative, author-led drama of previous decades like *Cathy Come Home*, *Pennies from Heaven*, *Boys from the Blackstuff* and *The Singing Detective*, dramas which had made British television 'such a glory in British life'.

Costume drama and literary adaptations

The market-led approach to television drama was also a factor in the revival of interest in costume drama in the 1990s. Where, in the 1970s, the return to the past in television drama merited the description of 'historical drama', and in the revisionist 1980s that of 'heritage drama', in the 1990s the ahistorical and all-embracing 'costume drama' became the preferred term for describing the abundance of literary adaptations that populated British television screens throughout the decade.

While early 1990s manifestations might include ITV's popular *The Darling Buds of May* (Yorkshire TV, 1991–3), based on the novels of H. E. Bates, and the BBC's *The House of Elliott* (BBC One, 1991–4), not an adaptation but an original idea from the creators of *Upstairs Downstairs*, the new cycle of costume dramas is most readily associated with a series of adaptations from classic English literature beginning, in 1994, with George Eliot's *Middlemarch* (BBC Two, January–February 1994) and Charles Dickens' *Martin Chuzzlewit* (BBC Two, November–December 1994) and *Hard Times* (BBC Two, December 1994), followed in 1995 by Jane Austen's *Persuasion* (BBC Two, April 1995) and the hugely popular six-part serialisation of *Pride and Prejudice* (BBC One, September–October 1995). The critical and popular success of these adaptations paved the way for a wholesale plundering of the canons of English literature with further adaptations from Austen, Dickens, Hardy and the Brontë sisters, extending to include other European literary 'greats' such as Dostoyevsky, Flaubert, Peake, Swift, Thackeray and Tolstoy as the seemingly insatiable thirst for costume drama continued into the twenty-first century.[10]

In the deregulated, competitive climate of the 1990s such a plethora of 'high-culture' adaptations on British television screens (mostly, but not exclusively, on the BBC) might seem curious. Yet, as we have seen in the debate about 'quality' drama in the late 1980s, 'heritage export' has been an important factor in the production of literary adaptations since the international success of *The Forsyte Saga* in the late 1960s. In the context of a more commercially minded BBC and the ratings-driven broadcasting environment of the 1990s the investment in costume drama made financial sense, and not only for the BBC – the larger ITV companies and Channel 4 have all invested in the production of expensive costume dramas since the mid-1990s.

While some of these productions have been single or two-part dramas, the most lavish and expensive adaptations have extended to six-part serials, enabling something of the epic sweep of the novels to be captured and approximating to the serial form in which some of the novels first appeared. Yet, as many commentators have noted, the subtleties of the novels do not easily translate to the visual medium of television, resulting in an often superficial treatment of social complexities and a privileging of the glamorous visual surface over the social messages contained in the novels. John Caughie is

not alone in noting the difficulties faced by film and television adaptations in transposing the social subtext to the screen:

> It seems to me an irony in itself that British quality film and television
> adaptation is drawn, like a butterfly to a flame, to a literature which is itself
> deeply ironic, to texts whose central defining ironic trope resists easy translation
> into the visual. The nineteenth-century novels of Austen, Eliot, Dickens, the
> twentieth-century novels of E. M. Forster or Evelyn Waugh are sown through
> with an ironic discourse which continually nudges the reader into judgement,
> assigning to him or her an understanding of the social which the characters do
> not have.[11]

Drawing on Fredric Jameson's theorisation of the 'nostalgic mode' in postmodernism
and the manner in which history is effaced by historicism in postmodern representations of the past, Caughie discusses how history is 'emptied out' in television's adaptations of classic literature, so that what we get is a series of seductive images of
country houses, period furniture, pastoral landscapes and extravagant costumes, but
without any attempt to locate this wealth of visual detail within any fully understand-
able social or political context:

> History becomes the present in costume, showing us only human continuities
> and lingering generalities of tone and style – the seduction of the image – without
> the formal distance and the historical particularity which might enable us to
> experience difference and change.[12]

In most 1990s costume drama the past is 'de-historicised' as classic literature is popularised for contemporary consumption, which may explain why costume drama was
such a popular genre in the 1990s. In his skilful adaptation of *Pride and Prejudice*, the prolific screenwriter Andrew Davies, responsible for many TV adaptations, foregrounded
those elements which might appeal to a postmodern audience, in a manner not dissimilar to the selection of marketable elements for different target groups in *Heartbeat*.
The country houses, landscapes, furniture and costumes that are put on display in the
serial may have provided the necessary qualities for 'heritage export', but what the story
in *Pride and Prejudice* boiled down to was a good old-fashioned love story, a high-culture
soap opera with its romance updated for a 1990s audience:

> Romance ... remains the heart of the matter, but in the mid-1990s TV 'costume
> drama', a modern sexual chemistry is required to be anachronistically displayed
> through casting, costuming, location and cinematography. The decolletage
> revealing Jennifer Ehle's ample bosom as Elizabeth Bennett in *Pride and Prejudice*
> has more to do with the anticipated viewing pleasures of a heterosexual male
> segment of the contemporary audience than Regency English manners. Likewise,
> Firth/Darcy's dip in the lake had a strong appeal to heterosexual women.[13]

The success of *Pride and Prejudice* was
evident from the huge audience of 10
million viewers that it drew, ensuring
that it fulfilled the criteria for 'quality
drama' on all counts. As a Jane Austen
adaptation it met the criteria of high
culture, its £6 million budget guaranteed high production values and its
success in the ratings fulfilled the
free-market definition of quality: television which is popular with a mass
audience.

Not that all costume drama necessarily de-historicises the past for popular
consumption. John Caughie singled out
the two-part adaptation of Anne Brontë's
The Tenant of Wildfell Hall (BBC One, 17–24
November 1996) as an example of a
classic adaptation that went beyond an
ahistorical 'heritage' representation of
the past:

Pride and Prejudice marked the pinnacle of the
renaissance in costume drama in the 1990s,
attracting 10 million viewers

> In the BBC's 1996 serialization of *The Tenant of Wildfell Hall* detail stands out,
> thrown into relief by a photographic style which very clearly frames its shots. A
> highly composed and beautifully lit shot of three women seated on a chaise
> longue, dressed in evening gowns of contrasting colour and vivid texture, sipping
> tea, is held static for long enough for its pastness to register as something
> different. The exquisitely composed framings of the Bronte landscape recall
> Victorian landscape painting in a way which situates the drama in a time, an
> ethos and a way of seeing. This precise location in time makes all the more
> shocking the theme of sexual and physical domestic abuse, giving us the same
> sense of horror which the novel gave to the Victorians, and, at the same time,
> historicizing domestic violence.[14]

Robin Nelson makes a similar point about *Middlemarch* which, despite a tendency to shift
the focus 'from the broader historical and intellectual context of the action of the novel
on to the personal romantic relationships',[15] a tendency which the serial shares with
other costume dramas, does nevertheless succeed, through its much slower narrative
pace and more considered *mise en scène*, in 'affording viewers time to respond to and
reflect on emotional and intellectual complexity'[16] in much the same way that the long
static shot Caughie refers to in *The Tenant of Wildfell Hall* encouraged viewers to see the
drama's representation of the past as 'something different'. Nelson describes the filming of the sequence in *Middlemarch* in which Dorothea (Juliet Aubrey) finds her husband,

Casaubon (Patrick Malahide), dead in the garden as an example of the slow and deliberate visual aesthetic which differentiates costume drama from the increasingly fast cutting to be found in other forms of popular drama. The scene is central to the narrative but also crucial to an understanding of the complexity of Dorothea's feelings at this moment. In a novel complex feelings can be described at length but in a television adaptation they need to be conveyed essentially through visual means:

> Two minutes at the end of the episode are afforded to Dorothea from her entering the garden to the fade to black and the credits at the end of the episode. Almost half of that time is taken up with a Close Two-Shot, foregrounding the top of the deceased husband's head, but showing Dorothea full-face to camera speaking just a few words slowly and softly in a fruitless effort to rouse him as the truth of the situation slowly dawns on her. This is an exceptionally long time for a TV camera to linger on inaction involving no further plot information or dialogue. It demands an active and imaginative response from viewers to engage with the complex web of Dorothea's thoughts and feelings. It is this aspect of the series which, with some success, attempts to retain the textures and moral seriousness of the novel, whatever the motivations of the production overall and the difficulties of the transposition of codes.[17]

The adaptation of classic literature for television always presents problems of transposition and the classic serial is often criticised for abbreviating the source material, losing much of the social complexity of the novels in the process. With the added tendency to de-historicise in the postmodern costume drama the weaknesses of the genre are evident. Yet, as the examples from *Middlemarch* and *The Tenant of Wildfell Hall* demonstrate, it is possible for costume drama to avoid this de-historicising tendency by turning the characteristic visual aesthetic of the genre to productive use. The popular success of costume dramas in the 1990s, however, may have had more to do with their heritage qualities, the seductiveness of the imagery and the romantic intrigue of the narratives than their ability to historicise and produce active and imaginative responses from viewers.

Social-issue drama

Given the increased pressure on television drama producers to deliver ratings success on the main channels and 'cost-effective' drama even on the minority channels, it is no surprise that there was a decline in 'social-issue' drama in the 1990s. As we have seen, the pressures on progressive drama grew throughout the 1980s as the single play disappeared from the schedules and the opportunities for dealing with social issues in other genres became increasingly subject to political, institutional and economic constraints.

An indication of the difficulties facing progressive writers and producers during this period is provided by the example of *Our Friends in the North* (BBC Two, January–March 1996), an epic nine-part serial following the personal and political experiences of four friends from the north-east of England over four decades, from 1964–95. That the serial

was made at all was testimony to the
perseverance of writer Peter Flannery,
who had originally written the drama
as a stage play at the beginning of
the 1980s (it was staged by the Royal
Shakespeare Company in 1982) and
then produced several more versions of
it for television, encouraged by Michael
Wearing, who eventually executive-
produced the serial, with each version
increasing in length as its protracted
on–off development dragged on for
fourteen years, undoubtedly the longest
production period ever in the history of
British television drama.[18]

Originally covering the period from
the election of Harold Wilson's Labour
government in 1964 to Margaret
Thatcher's victory in 1979, the serial
was extended to take in the miners'
strike in 1984 and the 1987 General

Our Friends in the North: flying the flag for
social realism in the 1990s

Election, with a ninth part being added to bring the saga up to date. By focusing on key
political moments over a thirty-year period the serial announced itself as a socio-pol-
itical drama in the Allen/Garnett/Loach mould and shared their concern, as expressed
in *Days of Hope*, to focus on the lives of ordinary people and to look at the past in order
to learn about the present. That seemed to be the reason why Michael Jackson, the new
Controller of BBC Two, wanted to recommission *Our Friends in the North* in the mid-1990s:

> I wanted to do the serial because it is so pertinent, with an election coming up
> and another new Labour Party making promises. The parallels are so much there
> with 1964. There had been 13 years of a Tory administration and a youthful
> Labour leader in Harold Wilson. Now it is 16 years of Tories and Blair with his New
> Labour.[19]

Aesthetically, the serial is in the tradition of social realism but without adopting Loach's
naturalistic visual style. Instead, it adopts a melodramatic approach and the characters
are more foregrounded in *Our Friends in the North*, inviting the viewer to identify with
their personal narratives and to experience the social and political history as they
experience it. If the serial has a weakness it is that the political events can sometimes
seem like a dramatic backdrop to the real drama of the characters' personal lives and
Flannery admitted that by the time *Our Friends in the North* was eventually produced,
when he had rewritten it for a third time, he was less interested in the politics than in
the personal lives of the characters:

Originally it was much more about the politics than the personal. I belonged to
that generation of writers and I began on the question of why it was that people
were so hostile and apathetic about the political process. By the time I wrote it for
the third time I was in my forties and my concerns were different. There's no loss
of the political stuff, we are talking about something that became twice as long,
but there's much more about growing to middle age, much more about fathers
and children, mothers and children, because those became my concerns as I grew
older.[20]

While Flannery's concerns may have changed during the course of the drama's long
gestation, the dramatic scope of *Our Friends in the North* is undeniably impressive and
it can be argued that to present a social and political history of Britain over a thirty-
year period in the less favourable political climate of the mid-1990s, when so much
television drama was both ahistorical and apolitical, was a significant achievement in
itself. That it was commissioned and screened on BBC Two was an indication of the
extent to which the broadcasting climate had changed from the period in which the
first few episodes of the serial are set, when such a drama would have been screened
at peak viewing time on BBC One. As it was, the serial gained an average audience of
4.6 million, very respectable for BBC Two, and was critically acclaimed, winning a
BAFTA award for Best Drama Serial in 1997. Given a less conservative BBC than the
1990s one *Our Friends in the North* might have been screened on BBC One and doubled
its audience, but that it was made at all, at a cost of £7 million (a record for BBC Two),
was an indication that there were still opportunities for producing progressive, political, authored drama in the 1990s.

One dramatist who emerged as a leading representative of this tradition during the
decade was Jimmy McGovern. Having begun as a writer on *Brookside*, where he had the
opportunity to contribute to the issue-based agenda of the soap opera in its early days,
McGovern went on to develop *Cracker* (Granada, 1993–6), a crime drama featuring the
wise-cracking criminal psychologist Fitz (Robbie Coltrane) whom the police recruit to
help them track down the perpetrators of various grim and grisly crimes.

One three-part *Cracker* story, 'To Be a Somebody' (Granada, 10–24 October 1994), featured Robert Carlyle as a skinhead serial killer whose crimes are motivated by the
trauma of the 1989 Hillsborough stadium disaster, when ninety-six Liverpool supporters were killed due to overcrowding at the FA Cup semi-final between Liverpool and
Nottingham Forest. The anger and demand for vengeance expressed by the central character in 'To Be a Somebody' was something that the families of the Hillsborough victims
could identify with, feeling a strong sense of injustice at the failure to hold a public
inquiry into the causes of the tragedy. Because of this, McGovern, a Liverpudlian himself, was encouraged by the Hillsborough Families' Support Group to write a drama
about the event. The result was *Hillsborough* (Granada, 5 December 1996), a drama documentary in the campaigning tradition of *Cathy Come Home* and the more recent *Who
Bombed Birmingham?* (Granada, 28 March 1990), the latter dramatising the events surrounding the conviction of six Irishmen for the IRA pub bombings in Birmingham in

1973. Like *Cathy Come Home*, which supported the campaigning work of Shelter, the new charity for the homeless, *Who Bombed Birmingham?* was part of a campaign which led to the release of the Birmingham Six within a few months of the screening of the drama, when the Court of Appeal overturned their 1974 conviction as unlawful.

McGovern's *Hillsborough* did not shirk from laying the blame for the disaster squarely at the feet of the South Yorkshire police force and, in particular, their commanding officer on the day, whose decision to open the gates at the Leppings Lane end of the ground led to the overcrowding which caused the tragedy. This direct accusation predictably provoked controversy, elevating *Hillsborough* to the pantheon of controversial television drama documentaries. McGovern, however, denied accusations of bias in his portrayal of the police: 'The police were so bloody incompetent there was no need for us to exaggerate for dramatic effect ... The bald facts are enough. If anything we toned it down, because nobody would believe some of the things that went on.'[21]

Although *Hillsborough* was screened on ITV, and was therefore subject to interruption by commercial breaks, even this was not allowed to detract from the powerful emotional effect of the drama. Having mainly written for Channel 4 and ITV, McGovern was used to structuring his scripts to take commercial breaks into consideration and on *Hillsborough* he cleverly used the breaks in order to heighten the emotional effect rather than allowing them to defuse the intensity of the drama:

> When the first ad break arrived, halfway through the match-day narrative, it felt initially that the momentum, so carefully built up, had been destroyed. But McGovern was freeze-framing the action to consider the key moment in the disaster. After the break, an actor playing a father of one of the dead said to camera: 'All they had to do was close off the tunnel like they normally did and we would have all had to go round the sides into pens with plenty of space. They didn't. And we all went down that tunnel into two pens that were already chocker and no way out.' This device served both McGovern's didactic end of indicting the senior police officers responsible for crowd control that day, and denying us what perhaps we expected and feared – the dramatised representation of the crush against the fence.[22]

In previous decades controversial drama documentaries had been the prerogative of the BBC, but *Hillsborough* and *Who Bombed Birmingham?* were both produced by Granada Television, one of the main ITV companies. At a time when commercial pressures were dictating a shift towards safer, populist drama it was reassuring that an ITV company was prepared to commission such a potentially controversial drama as *Hillsborough*. Of course, the ITV companies still needed to balance their populist dramas with 'quality' product and in this respect social-issue dramas like *Who Bombed Birmingham?* and *Hillsborough* helped the ITV network to fulfil a public service remit in the 1990s and to counter accusations that ITV was 'dumbing down' in the pursuit of ratings.

Like *Our Friends in the North*, *Hillsborough* won a BAFTA award in 1997, for Best Single Drama. In the following year, Peter Kosminsky's *No Child of Mine* (Meridian, 25 February

1997), a drama about child sexual abuse, produced by one of the smaller ITV companies after Yorkshire-Tyne Tees had backed away from the project because of its controversial subject matter, won a BAFTA award for Best Single Drama. In 2000, another ITV production won a BAFTA for Best Single Drama: *The Murder of Stephen Lawrence* (Granada, 18 February 1999) dramatised the murder in April 1993 of the black teenager Stephen Lawrence by a group of white racist youths, against whom the police had failed to gain a conviction. All of these dramas were based on controversial, real-life subject matter, all adopted the conventions of drama documentary, although in different ways, and all reaffirmed British television's reputation for progressive, social-issue drama.

The surprise was that it was the ITV companies, together with Channel 4 (which screened *The Colour of Justice* [Channel 4, 21 February 1999], a courtroom dramatisation of the Stephen Lawrence trial, and *Dockers* [Channel 4, 11 July 1999], on which Jimmy McGovern worked with dockers involved in the long-running Liverpool dock strike), which seemed to have assumed responsibility for commissioning and producing progressive drama in the 1990s, rather than the BBC, whose natural territory this had previously been.

The BBC did make the occasional contribution to social-issue drama in the 1990s, such as Jimmy McGovern's *Priest* (BBC Two, 18 November 1995), about homosexuality in the priesthood, which was screened in the same year that *Our Friends in the North* finally went into production, but it was significant that these dramas were shown on BBC Two (*Priest* was shown in the *Screen Two* slot) rather than on the main channel. Under John Birt the BBC largely abandoned social-issue drama in the 1990s, ploughing its resources instead into the safer, tried and trusted costume dramas which were suddenly back in vogue.

The emergence of a postmodern aesthetic

While the popularity of costume drama, traditionally naturalist in form, might suggest a return to orthodoxy in British television drama in the 1990s, there were some quite significant formal and stylistic developments during the decade which suggest the emergence of a new, postmodern aesthetic. Where costume drama has always depended to a large extent on a transparency in its form, enabling its sumptuous *mise en scène* to be emphasised, the success of other genres in the 1990s depended to a certain extent on a manipulation of narrative conventions in order to enhance the potential for maximising audiences.

While the 'quality components' of classic literary adaptations – 'best of British' acting and high production values (facilitated by expensive budgets) – may have been sufficient in themselves to win audiences to costume drama, with mainstream contemporary drama other strategies were deemed necessary in order to maximise audiences in an increasingly competitive marketplace. In an age of shortened attention spans, arising partly from the increased competition for the attention of viewers, new strategies were required not only to hook audiences, but also to retain them for the duration of a drama and to get them to return for the next episode.

The exposition–complication–resolution structure of the traditional single play, also that of a typical series drama episode from the 1960s or 70s, conventionally modelled on a single storyline, was no longer deemed appropriate for the more 'sophisticated' 1990s viewer seeking a greater degree of narrative complexity and distraction. Increasingly, therefore, the multiple narratives and cliff-hanger endings of the most successful (in ratings terms) television drama form – soap opera – were adopted for drama series and serials. This new narrative strategy was characterised as 'flexi-narrative' by Robin Nelson, acknowledging the way in which popular drama series adopted looser, more flexible narrative structures as a means of catering for a wide variety of viewing tastes and interests:

> 'Flexi-narrative' denotes the fast-cut, segmented, multi-narrative structure which yields the ninety-second sound-and-vision byte form currently typical of popular TV drama. As noted, the narrative structure derives in part from soaps but cross-cutting to gain pace and to juxtapose incidents and images has long been a cinematic device.[23]

As Nelson indicates, the principle of intercutting between different storylines and situations to increase pace and complexity is not new, but with flexi-narrative in television drama the process is taken much further, with a more rapid and sustained intercutting between an increased number of narrative strands. In the example Nelson gives in *TV Drama in Transition*, from a 1993 episode of *Casualty* (BBC One, 1986–), there are four separate storylines 'and a narrative fragment exclusive to the episode'.[24] Nelson illustrates how these narrative strands are broken down into sixty-two narrative bytes in the episode, a narrative byte being defined as 'the time and space given to a particular narrative strand before cutting to a byte of another narrative strand'.[25] In the fifty-minute episode this means that each narrative byte lasts, on average, forty-eight seconds, with some bytes lasting less than ten seconds while others last over a minute. The shortest narrative bytes may be only one shot, whereas the longer narrative bytes, involving greater complexity and longer exchanges between characters, will almost certainly be made up of multiple shots.[26]

As Nelson's analysis indicates, the length of narrative bytes shortens at moments of dramatic tension and lengthens during periods where greater exposition is needed. The adoption of this flexi-narrative structure generally results in a quickening of the narrative tempo as the drama moves swiftly and flexibly between the different narratives, ensuring that the 'dramatic temperature' is maintained over the fifty minutes of the drama, thus retaining the interest and involvement of viewers and reducing the possibility that they might be tempted to switch to another channel:

> … once the strands of the narratives are established, it is possible to cut to the high points in the action of each, thus keeping up – if not always at fever pitch – the dramatic temperature. Extending viewers' increasing ability to fill in the narrative gaps … all but the most dynamic or dramatically intense moments of a story can be omitted.[27]

This might imply that flexi-narrative dramas eschew psychological depth in favour of the more superficial attractions of dramatic highpoints designed to attract audiences, a criticism which accords with the view that series drama has become subject to the 'dumbing down' that is a consequence of the move towards a market-led broadcasting culture.

This need not, however, be an inevitable consequence of the flexi-narrative form as there is the potential for an enhanced narrative complexity arising out of the multiple plot strands, with the possibility of complex relationships being established between them. Such possibilities could suggest the opposite of a 'dumbing-down' process, with audiences being required to actively and pleasurably participate in the unravelling and decoding of a variety of thematic inter-relationships between a number of narrative strands. However, as Nelson acknowledges, the production circumstances of popular drama series probably militate against such complexity:

> Writers are usually under pressure to produce scripts to tight deadlines and therefore lack the time to work on the thematic, multiple-plot construction of scripts. On occasion they find by design or accident that such an organic complex emerges, but it is not a high priority. It is a possibility of the flexi-narrative form, not its defining characteristic.[28]

A drama which could be said to have achieved such complexity within a multi-narrative form is Tony Marchant's *Holding On* (BBC Two, September–October 1997). This eight-part serial ambitiously interweaved the lives of multiple characters living, working and trying to survive in London in the late 1990s. While featuring an ensemble cast, *Holding On* differs from the ensemble casts of dramas such as *Casualty* or *Cold Feet* (Granada, 1997–2003) in that the lives of the characters are lived quite separately, not coming together because of a shared workplace or mutual friendship. Instead, the drama builds a kaleidoscopic picture of life in London through the multiple narratives that it interweaves, featuring a cross-section of class and ethnic groups. Gradually, during the course of its eight-hour duration, connections are made between the different narratives, but not in order to move towards a final collective resolution of issues and problems. Instead, the connections are more tenuous, illustrating the possibility of lives coming into contact in an arbitrary way in the metropolis, while the resolutions to the individual narratives cover the spectrum from tragic to hopeful, in most cases showing characters just 'holding on', trying to get their lives together.

Holding On is a multi-narrative serial drama which includes dramatic highpoints but which is not intent on maintaining the dramatic temperature within each episode to the extent of a flexi-narrative series such as *Casualty*. The multi-narrative structure of *Holding On* enhances the possibilities for dramatic and thematic complexity arising from its different narrative strands, encouraging viewers to make thematic links while denying the satisfaction of traditional narrative resolutions. Needless to say, *Holding On*, unlike a popular drama series such as *Casualty*, is an 'authored' drama, its writer, Tony Marchant, being one of the few distinctive and original voices to emerge on

British television during the 1990s. It was also significant that the serial was screened on BBC Two, rather than the main BBC channel.

While the emergence of flexi-narratives can be seen as part of the 'reinvention' of television drama in the 1990s, the form is not unique to the 1990s, the flexi-narrative structure deriving in part from soap opera where multiple interwoven narrative strands have always been a convention of the genre. What was new to the 1990s was that this structure became more prevalent in mainstream drama as popular drama series sought to replicate the elements within soap opera which enabled them to top the ratings. The most obvious element in this respect was the continuous narrative structure of soap opera which required viewers to keep returning to the programme. Flexi-narrative offered a variation on this by having some narratives, involving the regular characters, continue over episodes, perhaps over a period of weeks, while other narratives, involving guest characters, are resolved within the episode in which they feature. In this respect the 'postmodern' drama series represents a hybrid of the traditional drama series, where stories are resolved within episodes on a weekly basis, and that of the drama serial, where a storyline continues over a number of episodes.

Flexi-narratives are advantageous to the television companies in that their multiple narratives can target a broad spectrum of audience groupings, an essential requirement in the pursuit of high ratings. In the episode of *Casualty* analysed by Nelson he notes the presence of characters of all ages, of different ethnic and sexual identities, among both the regular and the 'visiting' characters. Furthermore, the multiple narratives offer a variety of different social and narrative possibilities, enough to cater for a wide range of different audience tastes:

> Flexi-narrative series would appear to have achieved an accommodation between traditional viewer interest in stories presented in the familiar naturalist mode and a market-driven need to maximize an audience with a short span of attention. It has achieved a narrative structure which combines the allegedly 'masculine' preference for action and narrative resolution with the supposedly 'feminine' fluidity and open-endedness in story-telling with an emphasis on human interest. By combining a number of stories in one episode, it is indeed possible to appeal to a range of audience segments.[29]

Nelson acknowledges the influence of American television dramas such as *Hill Street Blues* (NBC, 1981–7) in the development of a flexi-narrative style in British television. *Hill Street Blues* was an innovative ensemble-based police series which incorporated multiple narratives within each episode, often eschewing narrative resolutions. It has been cited as the progenitor of an exciting new wave of television drama in America, including series such as *NYPD Blue* (ABC, 1993–2005), *Homicide: Life on the Street* (NBC, 1993–9), *ER* (NBC, 1994–2009) and *The West Wing* (NBC, 1999–2006). Grant Tinker, co-founder of MTM, which produced *Hill Street Blues*, suggests that the move towards ensemble drama and multiple narratives in American television drama stemmed from the need to cater for shorter attention spans, evident as early as the 1970s:

> At one time in television Jackie Gleason could sit out there and practically do it all by himself. But by the 1970s the attention span of the viewers had shortened. They were spoiled. You had to come at them from all directions to keep their attention. An ensemble could do that.[30]

This suggests that the process Nelson identifies as an important feature of the 'postmodern' television drama series in Britain in the 1990s occurred twenty years earlier in America, possibly because a more commercial and deregulated broadcasting system was already in existence there, whereas in Britain the increased competition arising from deregulation did not begin until much later. Consequently, American TV drama often seems much faster, glossier and more exciting than its British counterpart, which has been steeped for much longer in a naturalist/social realist tradition and which is still largely dependent on a studio *mise en scène* in its regular popular drama series.

Nevertheless, flexi-narrative has now become prevalent in British television drama series, to the extent that the form has become the new orthodoxy, certainly as far as popular drama is concerned. That the narrative tempo of British television drama has quickened can be seen when comparing the ASL and number of scenes in the first episode of *Coronation Street*, transmitted in December 1960, with that of a more recent episode. In 1960 the ASL was 9.7 seconds, with 144 shots and only nine scenes in the episode. In the episode screened on 28 January 2002 the ASL was 6.3 seconds, with 209 shots and twenty scenes in an episode that was over a minute shorter than the 1960 one. The transition from live to pre-recorded drama and the development of digital editing technology has certainly facilitated an enhanced narrative tempo, but, as some of the examples discussed below illustrate, the adoption of a flexi-narrative style and a faster tempo was not determined by technological development alone but was an aesthetic choice made in response to the increased competition to engage and retain the attention of viewers in the new postmodern culture.

Consequently, British television dramas in the 1990s increasingly adopted a faster narrative pace, incorporating new stylistic features which indicated a desire to loosen the shackles of naturalism. This may have been a consequence of the influence of American drama series, or it may have been in recognition of the need to find a style that would attract younger viewers. From the mid-1990s a 'new wave' of British television drama began to emerge which epitomised the shift to a postmodern aesthetic, providing another example of the 'reinvention' of television drama in the period from 1990–2002.[31] Many of these dramas, perhaps not coincidentally, were produced by independent production companies which tended to be at the cutting edge of new drama production in the 1990s–2000s. One of the leading independents during this period was Tony Garnett's World Productions, responsible for *Cardiac Arrest* (BBC One, 1994–6), *This Life* (BBC Two, 1996–7), *The Cops* (BBC Two, 1998–2001) and *Attachments* (BBC Two, 2000–1), among many others. The Manchester-based Red Production Company, formed in 1998 by Nicola Shindler, also produced a number of innovative dramas, most notably *Queer as Folk* (Channel 4, 1999–2000) and *Clocking Off* (BBC One, 2000–3), while Tiger Aspect Productions produced *Births, Marriages and Deaths* (BBC Two, 1999) and

Teachers (Channel 4, 2001–4) as two of its more stylistically innovative dramas. These 'new wave' dramas utilised a range of postmodern stylistic features including fast cutting, unusual shot transitions, hand-held camerawork, montages, fantasy sequences and surreal inserts in an attempt to create a new form of television drama for a new postmodern audience, an audience that had not been reared on studio naturalism and which, with a shorter attention span than previous generations, was inclined to be more impatient with the slow narrative development and 'realist' *mise en scène* traditionally associated with British television drama.

This Life (1996–7)

Among this new wave of British television drama it was *This Life* which set the trend for a new kind of upmarket, youth-oriented television drama. Over two series, *This Life* acquired a cult reputation, growing in confidence and popularity as it developed, to the extent that there was a huge outcry when it did not return for a third series.

Based around an ensemble of young twenty-something aspiring lawyers, the series tapped in to a lifestyle that many young people could identify with. Ostensibly a work-based drama, like many recent series, the dramatic focus in *This Life* was on the social lives of the five central characters, all living in the same house in south London. It was their 'permissive' lifestyles, with plenty of drink, drugs and sex – gay and heterosexual – which attracted the attention of the popular press and contributed to *This Life*'s popularity with younger viewers, rather than the legal backdrop against which the drama was set. This was not, generically, a legal drama but a 'lifestyle' drama, in which the social lives of the characters were the main dramatic interest.

Created by twenty-nine-year-old Amy Jenkins, who brought a youthful vitality to the drama which was taken up by subsequent writers on the series, *This Life* followed *Our Friends in the North* onto BBC Two in March 1996, making an immediate impression, if not always a favourable one, with reviewers unable to work out whether it was a legal drama or a 'middle-class soap opera'. In addition, some reviewers were clearly irritated by the 'distracting' camerawork and shocked by the language and the nudity.

Where *Our Friends in the North* represented 'old-style' BBC social realism, *This Life* represented the fast-paced 'new realism' of flexi-narrative drama, neither a series in the traditional sense, with self-contained stories in each episode, nor a conventional serial, with one narrative extending over a number of episodes. Instead, the first series was made up of eleven forty-minute episodes, with multiple narrative strands extending over the whole series, some continuing into the subsequent twenty-one-episode second series, to be joined by new narratives and new characters.

Narrative, however, did not provide the main impetus for the series, which was more character- than narrative-based. It was the astute casting of fresh new faces, all of whom worked well together in front of the camera, allied to lively scripts and an inventive visual style, which made *This Life* such a ground-breaking series. A product of Tony Garnett's World Productions company, *This Life* was made for BBC Two, yet another indication of the importance of BBC Two in commissioning innovative drama in the 1990s.

Following his involvement with the production of many seminal television dramas in the 1960s and 70s, Tony Garnett had kept a low profile during the Thatcher years, spending most of the 1980s in America. On returning to Britain, Garnett set up World Productions as an independent production company and began making drama series, recognising that this was where the potential for innovative drama resided following the decline of the single play and the marginalisation of the progressive drama serial. An early critical and popular success was *Between the Lines* (BBC One, 1992–4), a series about the activities of the Criminal Investigation Bureau, a unit set up to investigate complaints against the police which enabled issues of police corruption to be explored within a mainstream primetime drama. This was followed by *Cardiac Arrest*, an issue-based hospital drama which addressed the crisis in the National Health Service.

Unlike *Between the Lines*, which was shot on film and was therefore more expensive to produce, *Cardiac Arrest* was shot on video, reducing the cost while resulting in a style which anticipated that of the docu-soaps which were to become popular in the late 1990s. This style was developed in *This Life*, which was filmed using digital Betacam video cameras, enabling greater mobility and versatility in the filming, as well as increasing the amount of screen time which could be achieved in a day from the three to four minutes of *Between the Lines* to an exceptional eleven minutes, effectively enabling an episode to be filmed in four days.

This approach was a radical departure for television drama in Britain. Eschewing the traditional studio aesthetic, which Garnett has always been antipathetic towards (hence the ground-breaking *Up the Junction* and *Cathy Come Home* in the mid-1960s), the World Productions series of the mid- to late 1990s, especially *Cardiac Arrest*, *This Life* and *The Cops* which were all filmed on digital Betacam and all low budget, represented a significant development in the history of British television drama, comparable to the social and technological revolution of the mid-1960s. Unlike the more expensive American dramas of the 1990s, which were shot on film, Garnett opted for a low-budget aesthetic, acknowledging the financial constraints within which his company had to work, but recognising the possibility of turning that to his advantage:

> If you're writing a novel, the economics don't come into it, but whenever you're doing a dramatic fiction for the screen economics always come into it, whether it's 100 million dollars in Hollywood, or a tiny amount of money for the BBC, because you always have to allocate resources, finite resources, in a finite amount of time. And every money decision is an artistic decision, I think, and almost all artistic decisions are money decisions. So on the economic side of it, yes, first of all I've always traded budget for creative freedom. So I'll work on a smaller budget if that will buy me some creative freedom.[32]

Having developed a working relationship with Michael Jackson, when he was BBC Two Channel Controller, and subsequently Mark Thompson and Jane Root, Garnett saw the opportunity to make an intervention in British television drama in the 1990s, comparable to that which he and others had made under Sydney Newman in the 1960s. But the market-led television industry of the 1990s was a completely different beast to that of the 1960s, when there was more freedom to produce challenging, cutting-edge drama. In the 1990s it took someone of Garnett's creative ability, with his astute knowledge of the business, to recognise the opportunity to do something similar to what he had achieved in the 1960s, to produce innovative drama quickly and cheaply without having to make artistic compromises in order to achieve high ratings:

> This Life was eleven minutes of screen time a day, single camera. The Cops, and there are an enormous number of location movements in The Cops, all over town, is between seven and eight minutes a day, cut show, single camera. Now that's a lot. Between the Lines was three or four minutes. But the creative freedom I got was enormous, because I'm on a lower budget, because I'm on a minority channel. The broadcaster has never interfered in who was going to be in them, who's going to direct them, who's going to write them, what the content was. I'll do something very cheap for that kind of creative freedom. If I'd wanted twice that amount of money, they'd start wanting to tell me who's going to be in them.[33]

In the case of This Life, therefore, economic constraints were turned to positive advantage. The low budget brought a degree of independence from editorial control and the use of digital Betacam video cameras, coupled with limited filming time, resulted in a new style of television drama.

This Life was progressive not just because it stretched the boundaries of what was acceptable on television, in terms of sexuality, language and the depiction of drug-taking as an everyday activity, but also because of its formal and stylistic innovations, which resulted from a combination of the economic circumstances of production, the technical possibilities offered by digital video and the aesthetic choices made by the production team.

What is immediately striking about the drama is its energy, the fact that it moves along at a very fast pace while still enabling the viewer to get involved with the characters and to identify with them. This is made possible by a combination of rapid, elliptical editing, which maintains a fast narrative tempo; hand-held camerawork, which helps to give the drama much of its energy and vitality; and close-up photography, which draws the audience into an empathetic engagement with the personal and professional experiences and dilemmas of the characters.

That the narrative tempo of This Life is much faster than most contemporary drama can be seen when comparing the ASL in the first episode with that of other contemporary British television drama. With an ASL of 4.6 seconds, the tempo of This Life is faster than both Coronation Street and Casualty, which have ASLs of over six seconds, and much faster than Heartbeat, which has an ASL of over nine seconds.[34]

A comparison of the opening sequence of the first episode of This Life with the opening sequence of an early episode of Heartbeat will help to illustrate the formal and stylistic differences between mainstream and innovative British television dramas in the 1990s. While one might expect a sedate Sunday evening series like Heartbeat, set in the

Yorkshire Dales in the 1960s, to adopt a more leisurely narrative pace than a youth-oriented urban drama like *This Life*, the comparison illustrates the extent to which *This Life* adopts a completely different televisual style, with faster cutting, greater use of elliptical editing and much tighter framings on characters.

In the episode of *Heartbeat* ('Dead Ringer', Yorkshire TV, 17 October 1993), fairly conventional establishing shots are used, with more long shots than close-ups, a tracking camera on a dolly or a crane and several dissolves, rather than straight cuts, between shots, all serving to emphasise the *mise en scène* and slow down the narrative tempo. In contrast, the first episode of *This Life* ('Coming Together', BBC Two, 18 March 1996) starts with close-ups, eschewing the convention of establishing shots. There are, in fact, ten close-ups before the first establishing shot and it is only after further establishing shots, some way in to the opening sequence, that it becomes clear that the action is taking place in three different locations. All of the opening shots are quite short in length and there are straight cuts between the characters in the different locations, rather than dissolves or fades, ensuring that a fast narrative tempo is established and maintained.

In its narrative structure *This Life* conforms to that of flexi-narrative, with an ensemble cast and multiple narrative strands, between which the drama moves freely, adding new narratives and discarding others as each episode proceeds. The difference with *This Life* is that the drama moves much more rapidly between different characters, different locations and different narrative strands than in other dramas, such as *Casualty* or *EastEnders*, where the intercutting between characters and situations is not usually as rapid as it is in *This Life*.

This Life is also far less concerned about resolving its narrative strands and in that it leans more towards the continuing narratives of soap opera, rather than an episodic series like *Casualty*, which is why many reviewers described *This Life* as BBC Two's new 'middle-class soap'. Because *This Life* is less concerned with narrative than it is with character, the style that was developed for the series was designed to enable characterisation to be developed as fully as possible and for the actors to be able to concentrate on developing their characters without the distractions which accompany the filming process, as far as that is possible.

For Tony Garnett, the decision to shoot quickly and cheaply on *This Life*, using digital Betacam, which resulted in a more elliptical, vérité style, was not just an economic decision but an ideological one:

> No, it wasn't just an economic decision. It's my impatience with the
> paraphernalia and the rigmarole of film-making, where actors get sacrificed to
> technology … I'm interested in two things really, one is how an individual is in a
> social and economic setting and how an individual is inside. Because those are
> my two great interests in life, I suppose, in these days when there are no more
> grand narratives, in these postmodern days, I suppose I'm just an old relic of the
> enlightenment, so Marx and Freud are very important to me. I want to have
> characters who are in their real environment and see the environment's effect on
> them and their effect on the environment, and I want to be able to be close in

enough on them where you don't see the acting, where they're not doing, they're being. So every bit of help you can give the actor is to be had. And any way you can help the actor to be 'in the moment', so that what's going on on that actor's face is authentic, we'll go for, and a lot of things follow from that.[35]

So the formal and stylistic innovations of *This Life* were developed with the objective of enabling the actors to be as authentic as possible within their social environment, an objective which *This Life* shares with *Up the Junction*, *Cathy Come Home* and many of the dramas with which Garnett has been associated. With *This Life*, therefore, there was an ideological reason for using minimal equipment, natural lighting and a vérité style. The 'distracting' hand-held camerawork and elliptical editing was not just a stylistic affectation, which it sometimes appears to be in the American dramas, like *NYPD Blue*, with which *This Life* was compared by many reviewers. Garnett is quite adamant that, stylistically, *This Life* was not influenced by Steve Bochco-style American drama, even though he admires those dramas, and he described the thinking behind the *This Life* style in the following terms:

When we're coming up with a style, obviously you say, now, what's important? Now, on those kind of budgets are you going to spend half the day lighting it and come out with a show that has DP-itis, and have hardly any time to spend with the actors and getting the performances, or are you going to go for what interests me, which is the human face? For me the screen is about a close up and I hate the way most television drama and most movies are shot because they're all sort of boring mid-shots with too many people in them. The only landscape that really interests me is the human face.

So we create a style which allows us to be very flexible in what we shoot, to be shooting a lot of the day, and the aesthetic behind it is what the actors do is what's important and we'll do everything we can to facilitate an actor being 'in the moment', in character. So actors are not put on marks and it's the camera's job to find them and to catch them. So that means, with that amount of time, there's no tracks, there's no dollies, it's steady hand-held because then you can just adjust for the movement of the actors. They don't have to think about doing exactly the same thing on the next take.[36]

Two scenes from episode five of series one, 'Fantasy Football', provide contrasting examples of the stylistic strategies used on *This Life*. A scene featuring Egg and Millie discussing the problems in their relationship opens with whip pans between the two characters, who are seated at a table, before cutting in to frame each character separately in tight close-ups, cutting between the two during the conversation. The whip pans at the beginning of the scene are an example of the 'distracting camerawork' for which the series was criticised by some reviewers and which led many commentators to compare it to American dramas like *NYPD Blue*. Tony Garnett agreed that this kind of camerawork, used early in the series when they were still searching for the right style, *was* distracting and he had this to say about this particular scene:

Our introduction to Anna (Daniela Nardini) in *This Life* illustrates the drama's close-up televisual style

> Those whip pans, we thought that's how the eye moves, but of course it doesn't. The eye does move like that, but it's like a cut with your eye, and those whip pans I think became a mannerism and got in the way of the show, so they got fewer and fewer as the show went on.[37]

The whip pans draw attention to the camerawork, whereas the close-ups used for the remainder of this short scene enable the viewer to concentrate much more on what Egg and Millie are saying. Those big close-ups provide a good illustration of the intention to get in close enough so that the viewer is not conscious of the actors acting and can concentrate on the drama of the moment, just as the actors can concentrate on being 'in the moment'. It is also worth noting that, once again, the scene does not start with an establishing shot but ends with one, reversing the normal convention.

This and the opening scene discussed so far are slightly unusual in that, for most of the time, the positions of the actors are fixed – they are sitting down. An earlier scene in the 'Fantasy Football' episode provides an example of a more typical scene, in the kitchen of the house which the main characters share, where there is a lot of movement, both of the actors and of the camera. This is a very busy scene, encompassing a number of different narrative strands, many of which are ongoing from previous episodes, but the different storylines are not emphasised as they might be in a more conventional drama through the rhetoric of *mise en scène*. Instead, a more observational style is employed which puts the onus on the viewer to pick up on the narrative significance of what is being said and the exchanges of looks between characters. Meanwhile, the camera simply tries to catch aspects of the action as it unfolds, almost as though this was a *vérité* documentary.

This scene illustrates the working method on *This Life* very well. The kitchen is evenly lit, so that the actors can move about in the space, leaving the camera operator to focus on them as and when he or she chooses. One of the features of this style is that it puts the onus on the operator to follow the action and make decisions that, on more expensive and more rehearsed productions, would be the responsibility of the director or the director of photography. While the camerawork may be observational, as in cinéma vérité, *This Life* differs from a documentary in that there is a lot of cutting, including 'disguised' cuts on action, as two different takes, shot on different focal lengths, have been edited together. The nature of the editing indicates an assemblage of material gathered from many different takes – according to Tony Garnett as many as ten or twelve takes of this scene may have been filmed (digital Betacam allowing greater flexibility here because of the lower cost of filming on video) – with the intention of putting it all together in the edit. With thirty-six shots in a scene which lasts just over two minutes, giving an ASL of 3.4 seconds, this is a highly constructed scene.

With its positive representations of a range of 'minority' characters and alternative lifestyles (alternative, that is, to those portrayed in most television drama), together with its formal and stylistic innovations and use of new technology, *This Life* offered a model for progressive television drama in the more 'cost-conscious', market-led climate of the 1990s. The series showed the advantages of working on a low budget, enabling a degree of creative freedom while also demonstrating the possibilities for formal and stylistic innovation using new digital technology. At a time when broadcasters and producers were more conscious of cost than ever, *This Life*, together with *Cardiac Arrest* and *The Cops*, provided a model for the continuation of a tradition which Tony Garnett did much to initiate in the 1960s.

Clocking Off (2000–3)

Another example of the way in which British television drama was reinvented during this period, with an independent production company again playing a leading role, was *Clocking Off*, a factory-based series created by Paul Abbott. Unlike *This Life*, which self-consciously tapped into the new postmodern zeitgeist with its focus on young people trying to succeed as barristers in London, *Clocking Off* seemed like a throwback to an older tradition of social realism with its northern setting, its focus on working-class relations in a Manchester textiles factory and its issue-based storylines. This description might, in fact, suggest a 'serious' television drama from the 1960s or 70s, written perhaps by Jim Allen or Jeremy Sandford and directed by the likes of Jack Gold or Ken Loach, the kind of drama which would have been shown as a *Wednesday Play* or a *Play for Today*. The comparison is not superfluous. Nicola Shindler, whose Manchester-based Red Production Company produced the series, made the allusion directly:

> It was an opportunity to write really big quality stories for a massive populist audience. We talked a lot about *Play for Today* and the *Wednesday Play* which more often than not were good blue-collar stories, told properly. They used to get the nation talking.[38]

The new social realism of *Clocking Off*

The fact that *Clocking Off* was commissioned by the BBC, rather than ITV, was significant given the BBC's track record in producing realist, issue-based drama, from *Cathy Come Home* in the 1960s to *Boys from the Blackstuff* in the 1980s. That there had been little such drama produced since *Boys from the Blackstuff* was a result of the shift towards a more competitive climate in television in the 1990s, resulting in an aversion to risk-taking on behalf of the television companies and a preference for drama series and serials designed primarily to maximise audiences. This led the BBC to try to emulate ITV's success with bland, middle-of-the-road dramas like *Heartbeat* by commissioning equally unadventurous soap-star vehicles such as *Sunburn* and *Harbour Lights* (both BBC One, 1999–2000), featuring Michelle Collins and Nick Berry respectively, both of whom had established themselves in *EastEnders*, which Nick Berry left to become the leading actor in *Heartbeat* from 1992–8. In contrast to these series, *Clocking Off* provided the BBC with an opportunity to return to its traditional strengths with a northern working-class drama intent on updating social realism for a new 'postmodern' television audience.

In the ratings-driven climate of the late 1990s when *Clocking Off* was being developed (under its original title of *The Factory*), Paul Abbott recognised that the BBC was a more likely home for such an unfashionable concept than ITV, for whom he had previously worked as a writer on *Coronation Street* (from 1989–94), *Cracker* (two stories in 1995), *Reckless* (1997–8) and *Touching Evil* (1997). Not only did the BBC have a track record for producing social realist drama, but also the series needed a backer prepared to spend enough money to ensure it was both stylish and original:

> I took the idea to the BBC because at that time, if you mentioned northern working-class textile drama to anyone else, each word knocked the budget down by about 50 grand per episode. I knew it had to be done on a large scale, otherwise the stories would look like soap.[39]

Part of the originality of *Clocking Off* as a series (and one of the ways in which it revived an earlier tradition in series drama) was that it offered self-contained stories in each episode, rather than conforming to the increasing tendency in series drama towards serialisation, carrying storylines over from one episode to the next. Although a number of guest actors (John Simm, Christopher Eccleston, David Morrissey, Marc Warren, Denise Black, Tom Georgeson) made one-off appearances in the series, taking leading roles in single episodes, one of the novelties of *Clocking Off* was the way in which regular characters would also feature as the leading character for an episode while other factory employees played secondary or subsidiary roles. In subsequent episodes, a background character might take the lead while the previous week's leading character would slip into the background.

The first series began with John Simm making a guest appearance as Stuart Leach, one of three Leach brothers working for Mackintosh Textiles. Paul Abbott's opening sequence provided an intriguing, attention-grabbing premise, with Stuart arriving home from a normal working day only to be met by the shocked and puzzled reactions of his wife and young son who have not seen him for thirteen months. Abbott gradually reveals that Leach has lost his memory and his bemused response to what has happened is conveyed so naturalistically that a series of enigmas are established without the expositional predictability one might find in a more formulaic drama. Abbott adds layers of complexity to the plot as it is revealed that Leach, a lorry driver with Mackintosh Textiles, had, during his long absence, met and married a woman in Sheffield with whom he has a child, only to be found out by the woman's brother who viciously beats him up, causing the loss of memory. On coming round, he leaves hospital and goes home but, in a narrative twist typical of Abbott's writing, Leach, remembering nothing of the last thirteen months, goes to his old home in Manchester, not his new one in Sheffield, thus initiating the events which motivate the plot. To add a further complication, Leach returns to find that his older brother Martin (Jason Merrells) has, in his absence, developed a relationship with Stuart's wife.

John Simm disappeared from the series after the first episode, the absence of his character being explained in episode two when Stuart's wife and child move to Sheffield, where he has been imprisoned for bigamy. Meanwhile, both Jason Merrells as Martin and Jack Deam, as the third Leach brother Kev, remained as central characters, with Kev featuring as the leading character in the first episode of series two, while Martin was to feature as the leading character in the final episode of the second series where his relationship with Sue, Stuart's wife, is reprised when she returns from Sheffield eight months pregnant, bearing Martin's child. Both of these episodes were written by Abbott, who shared the writing on the second series with three other writers, having written all six episodes of the first series himself.

In episode two of the first series Christopher Eccleston was brought in to play the leading role alongside factory worker Yvonne Kolakowski (Sarah Lancashire). While Lancashire had been a background character in episode one and would continue as such in subsequent episodes in the first series, Eccleston made only one further appearance. That such a recognisable television actor as Sarah Lancashire, best known at the time for her role as sexy barmaid Rita in *Coronation Street*, was prepared to appear in episodes of *Clocking Off* as a secondary character, a machine-worker who might simply be glimpsed in the background, was one of the features of the series which greatly enhanced its appeal. Referring to Eccleston's walk-on part in episode four of the first series, Abbott stressed that such appearances were important in lending weight to the drama, even if it meant a star actor appearing only briefly in the background: 'He just strolls through. And it must have cost 10 grand for him to do that but it's really important because he dignifies the story that is currently being told. It's the opposite of what normally happens, and it's great.'[40]

The first series of *Clocking Off* attracted an average audience of 8.2 million, winning BAFTA and Royal Television Society (RTS) awards for Best Drama Series, while Paul Abbott won the RTS Writer's award for the series. The support of Nicola Shindler, founder of Red Production Company, for writer-led (rather than producer-led) drama was crucial to *Clocking Off*'s success. Red was founded in 1998 as a Manchester-based company, working out of offices rented from Granada TV, and its commitment to producing innovative regional drama was confirmed with its first commission, *Queer as Folk* (Channel 4, 1999–2000), a colourful, fast-paced drama about Manchester's gay community. Russell T Davies' ground-breaking series established Red as a progressive company which was prepared to champion risk-taking, writer-led drama with a strong regional flavour. *Clocking Off* cemented that reputation.

Clocking Off can be viewed as an amalgamation of two traditions in British television drama. On the one hand, Nicola Shindler's reference to 'good blue-collar stories, told properly', the sort of stories that 'used to get the nation talking', locates the series in the Loach/Garnett/Allen tradition of *The Wednesday Play* and *Play for Today*. On the other hand, the 'domestic' qualities of *Clocking Off*, its emphasis on the camaraderie of the factory workers, the 'ordinariness' of the characters and their social situations, the element of serialisation that is present as a result of the personal relations between regular characters, all suggests an affinity with the popular social realism of a soap opera such as *Coronation Street*, a factor which may help to explain the popularity of such an unfashionable twenty-first-century concept as a drama series set in a northern textiles factory. The blending of these two traditions in *Clocking Off* is indicative of a postmodern shift in the representation of social realism in twenty-first-century television drama. The cultural divide between the 'serious' social realism of *The Wednesday Play* and *Play for Today* and the 'popular' social realism of *Coronation Street* was gradually eroded in the 1980s and 90s, enabling a series such as *Clocking Off* to embrace both traditions, being at the same time both 'popular' and 'serious'.

In trying to present 'sophisticated adult programming' for a twenty-first-century audience, *Clocking Off* reworked social realism in a number of ways. First, instead of the politics of the workplace which feature in a *Wednesday Play* such as *The Big Flame*, *Clocking Off* presented a series of 'morality tales', eschewing the overt politics of classic social realism and focusing instead on the moral dilemmas of the central characters as they confront a variety of social problems which impinge on their personal lives, problems such as alcoholism, drugs, male violence, paedophilia and racism. For Paul Abbott the variety in the episodes was one of the series' strengths, distinguishing it from other series where the pursuit of ratings success tends to result in a generic uniformity: 'I love the fact that one strand will be a romantic comedy, then the next week is more like a thriller. It has that flexibility.'[41] This variety and difference between episodes, while dealing with single-issue storylines within them, is one way in which Clocking Off departed from the 'flexi-narrative' approach adopted in other contemporary drama series, placing it more in the single-play tradition of anthology series like The Wednesday Play or Play for Today.

A concession to postmodernity in Clocking Off was the introduction of stylistic features which differentiate the series from its more sombre and sometimes pedantic social realist predecessors. The greatly increased tempo of Clocking Off is immediately evident. The short title sequence sets the tone: a colourful visual montage of images from inside the factory, including hand-held camera shots moving past factory machines, cut together with abstract images providing a blur of colour and movement, an effect creating the impression of frenzied activity, reinforced by a driving 'rhythm and blues' soundtrack.

Following the title sequence each episode followed a similar pattern, usually a montage of factory scenes: employees arriving for work, or already occupied in the factory, or sometimes knocking off at the end of the working day, the familiar music track reinforcing the mood of activity prior to the initial equilibrium being disrupted and the week's story put into motion. The first episode is typical, starting off at a cracking pace with scenes at the factory taking place at some undisclosed time during the working day, intercut with Stuart Leach travelling on the metro in Manchester on his way home. After the shock of his unexpected reappearance, Sue (Alison Swann), his wife, telephones the factory and we see Trudy (Lesley Sharp), the assistant to Mack (Philip Glenister) the factory owner, taking the call and delivering a message to Martin who rushes off to Sue's house. Martin comes face to face with his brother almost exactly five minutes into the episode, in which time there have been eighty-one shots, an ASL of 3.7 seconds. This is very fast for British television drama and while the pace inevitably slows after this brisk opening the narrative tempo of the episode as a whole is considerably faster than most contemporary drama.

To give another example, the first episode of the second series (featuring Stuart's brother Kev, who develops suspicions that a workmate who moves into the house opposite may be a paedophile) has only forty-eight shots in the first five minutes, an ASL of 6.25 seconds. Yet the opening sequence of this episode seems just as fast as that of the first episode of series one because of the amount of camera movement within it. In Clocking Off the camera is rarely still and in the opening sequence of 'Kev's Story' (episodes in the second series were given such titles) the camera is very restless, its perpetual movement contriving to create the same impression that rapid editing did in the opening episode of the first series, generating a mood of ceaseless activity and capturing the attention of the viewer through the sheer vitality of its exposition.

Traditionally, social realism has been associated with a dour look, especially when the location has been the factories and terraced houses of the industrial north, as if this iconography was synonymous with dark colours and an absence of vitality. The role of cinematographer Peter Greenhalgh was crucial to the creation of a more colourful *mise en scene* for *Clocking Off*, executive producer Nicola Shindler asking him 'to make it look "beautiful" not grimy and industrial like one would expect'.[42] Among Greenhalgh's previous credits was the stylish contemporary vampire series *Ultraviolet* (Channel 4/World Productions, 1998) and Shindler wanted a similarly glossy look for *Clocking Off*. According to Greenhalgh, 'She was looking for a lot of colours, tight shots and moving images,' while, for the second series, he went 'a little further in trying to achieve an enhanced look. I've gone for a lot of out of focus colours. I would often just put a fluorescent tube with a colour on it, well in the back of the shot, just to give the depth.'[43] This enhancing of the colour scheme is clearly evident in the first episode of series two where the opening sequence is replete with colour, especially in the factory scenes where the fabrics are all vivid primary colours. Many of the factory employees are also dressed in brightly coloured clothes with Kev, the focus of attention, wearing a bright orange T-shirt (with 'Sex-God' in large lettering on the front and back, a neat summation of his 'laddish' character which Greenhalgh highlights with a camera movement drawing attention to it). The enhanced colours of the factory interior are maintained as the shift comes to an end, Kev going out to his van – bright yellow with a blue stripe running along the side – and more brightly coloured clothing is in evidence as he drives past workers outside the factory.

The use of primary colours is one of the most distinctive features of *Clocking Off* and one of the several ways in which it 'updates' social realism for a new audience. While Peter Greenhalgh played an important part in enhancing the colourful, vibrant look of the series, it was production designer Chris Wilkinson who was primarily responsible for the colour scheme, having received instructions from Shindler to be as inventive with colour as possible:

> I went to him and said that just because these characters were working-class didn't mean their houses were all grey and small and horrible. These days everybody is obsessed with interior design and trying to make their surroundings as attractive as they can – just look at *Changing Rooms*. So he brought colour into every home and location.[44]

Nicola Shindler acknowledged the influence of American series such as *Ally McBeal* (Fox, 1997–2002) and *ER* in wanting to create a stylish look for *Clocking Off*, seeking to jettison the sombre look of classic social realism in a drama which is, nevertheless, set amid the industrial heartlands of the north-west of England: 'I think sometimes English people have a fear of making things look too good because they think it will look glossy and unreal. What we've tried to do with this is make it look real, but also make it look good.'[45]

Paul Abbott also acknowledged the influence of American series on the style of *Clocking Off*:

> They set an example for the rest of the world to follow. Of course you want your own shows to be as fast, good-looking and fantastically well done as *The West*

Wing. I think that influence can be seen in *Clocking Off.* One way you see it is in the editing. We cut mercilessly. Once a line is over, we move on.[46]

For a series like *Clocking Off* which is in the tradition of British social realism, set in a factory in the north-west of England and featuring predominantly working-class characters, the adoption of a faster, glossier style was a radical departure, an acknowledgment that British television drama could no longer continue to tell stories using the old naturalist/realist forms prevalent in the 1960s and 70s, but needed to update those forms in order to take account of different audience tastes at the beginning of the twenty-first century.[47]

Slow television

Not all British television drama in the 1990s and early 2000s succumbed to the pressure to produce faster narratives and shorter scenes. Two drama serials written by Stephen Poliakoff, *Shooting the Past* (BBC Two, 10–24 January 1999) and *Perfect Strangers* (BBC Two, 10–24 May 2001), together with the ten-part *In a Land of Plenty* (BBC Two, January–March 2001), adapted by Kevin Hood from a novel by Tim Pears, demonstrated a stubborn refusal to conform to the new orthodoxy by adopting more leisurely narrative structures. Each of these languorous drama serials resists dramatic urgency in favour of a much slower unfolding of complex narrative histories. While not costume dramas, in the traditional sense, each is concerned with the past and its relation to the present, their serial form being used as a means to reflect on this relationship, often replaying scenes, sometimes in slow motion, in a manner more typical of art cinema than television drama.

In an article on *Shooting the Past*, Amy Holdsworth discusses Poliakoff's concern to 'slow down television', quoting from a BBC documentary in which Poliakoff described the serial as a reaction to the increasingly fast pace of television dramas in the 1990s:

> *Shooting the Past* was written as a sort of experiment really. I became very interested in how short scenes had become on television so I thought, right, I will slow television down to the point that it stops … I mean leave scenes so long that they seem ridiculous and try to compel people in that way.[48]

The three-part, three-hour serial was about a photographic library on the outskirts of London which has been bought by new American owners who want to sell off or dispose of the contents of the library and turn this idiosyncratic English institution into a high-tech business school for the twenty-first century. True to his promise, Poliakoff adopted a leisurely style for the drama with long scenes which often dwell on the photographs in the collection, 'freezing' the narrative flow and underlining where his sympathies reside in this clash between old and new cultural values. But, having persuaded the BBC to take a chance with his three-hour 'experiment', Poliakoff still encountered some opposition from people within the BBC who thought the drama was too slow:

I wanted to fight the idea that people couldn't concentrate for long, and when it was finished all hell did break loose. By now they did try to tell you how to write, and some relatively junior executives thought it should be cut and made quicker, which would have ruined the whole point of it. I went bananas and eventually won the battle. So it wasn't a question of being invited by the BBC to do what I liked. People did try to interfere, but I resisted them and was ultimately proved right.[49]

Poliakoff's belief in the virtues of 'slow television' was vindicated. *Shooting the Past* was a critical success and initiated what Robin Nelson has described as a 'second starburst' of acclaimed television dramas written and directed by Poliakoff in the late 1990s–2000s, following his earlier period of writing television plays in the 1970s–80s.

Generically, *Shooting the Past*, *Perfect Strangers* and *In a Land of Plenty* represent 'art television', a self-consciously slow and reflective narrative form, incorporating elements of a modernist or non-naturalistic *mise en scène*. These 'art television' serials demand attention and commitment in a way that flexi-narrative dramas do not and their pleasures are consequently of a different order. They offer a form of television drama much less in evidence in recent years, outside of the heritage television of costume drama, appealing perhaps to an older, more middle-class audience, their success measured not so much in terms of ratings but critical acclaim and industry awards, which in turn brings kudos to the television companies that commission them, underlining their determination to produce 'quality drama' in a more competitive broadcasting environment.

The television work of Alan Bennett can also be seen as a reaction to the predilection for fast-paced, flexi-narrative dramas in this period, especially his two series of *Talking Heads* monologues (BBC One, 1988 and 1998) and the autobiographical *Telling Tales* (BBC Two, 2000),[50] although much of his previous work is, by its nature, more leisurely than most television drama. Like Poliakoff, Bennett started writing plays for television in the 1970s and continued to do so in the 1980s, alongside his work for theatre and the cinema, but *Talking Heads* represented a new departure in his work, away from the evocations of Englishness in such dramas as *A Day Out* (BBC Two, 1972), *The Old Crowd* (LWT, 1979), *One Fine Day* (LWT, 1979) and *An Englishman Abroad* (BBC One, 1983), towards a more intimate and personal mode of storytelling. According to Michael Brooke:

> *Talking Heads* ... lifted Bennett's television writing onto a higher plane. The title was inspired by the adage that 'talking heads' made bad television, but Thora Hird, Maggie Smith, Stephanie Cole, Julie Walters, Patricia Routledge and Bennett himself comprehensively countered it, painting unforgettable portraits of damaged lives and thwarted expectations.[51]

It has been noted (in Chapter 1) how the combination of small television screens and live transmission in the 1930s–40s led to a stylistic concentration on 'talking heads' and extended takes in early television drama, contributing to a slow tempo and limited movement, but Bennett, in his television monologues, turns this 'limitation' to his advantage in crafting intimate narratives delivered in the form of direct personal address with the viewer. In doing so, as Kara McKechnie observes, Bennett 'reinvented the monologue for television and stage by creating a generic composite. The result is a format that seems familiar, but is innovative and tailor-made to suit its author's and its performers' strengths.'[52] Once again, this time in the form of 'art television', intimate narratives and autobiographical monologues, television drama was busy reinventing itself as the twentieth century gave way to the twenty-first.

Gender, genre and representation

The reinvention of television drama in the 1990s extended also to the domain of representation. If a characteristic of postmodernism is the destruction of old certainties and the erosion of cultural hierarchies, this was increasingly evident in British television drama in the 1990s as new representations emerged to challenge the hegemony of traditional gender stereotypes.

An early 1990s manifestation of this occurred in that most traditional of male genres, the police/detective/crime drama when, in *Prime Suspect* (Granada, 7–8 April 1991), Detective Chief Inspector Jane Tennison (Helen Mirren) led a male-dominated murder squad in the successful pursuit of a serial killer, after overcoming the initial scepticism and hostility of a team more accustomed to the masculine bravado of their previous boss. Written by Lynda La Plante, whose 1980s series *Widows* had broken the mould of the male-dominated crime series, *Prime Suspect* was an attempt to subvert the police/detective genre, where the detective is traditionally male, by introducing a woman to the role. The result was criticised by some feminist writers on the grounds that, in order to achieve success, the character of Tennison had to be 'masculinised'. While this may be true to some extent – the adoption of conventionally masculine characteristics being a necessary prerequisite for success in this male-dominated environment – it is eventually through her feminine insight, showing an understanding of the female victims which the male detectives are incapable of, that Tennison is able to make the breakthrough that leads to the apprehension of the killer. In doing so, she is ably supported by a female police constable, who Tennison had insisted be on the team, whose insight at a key moment in the narrative is also based on specifically feminine knowledge and which is crucial in helping Tennison to solve the murders.

In *Prime Suspect*, therefore, La Plante not only introduces a strong female protagonist to challenge the masculine hegemony in police drama, she achieves a breakthrough in the genre itself by showing that a female detective can possess attributes that enable her to succeed where male detectives have failed. As Glen Creeber has argued:

> Tennison's detective techniques uncover and reveal the dynamics by which the murder case (as partly representative of a wider masculine genre) is decoded and gradually deconstructed. Her understanding and respect for the prostitutes and her refusal to turn them into sexualized or objectified objects finally enable her to solve the crime and perhaps even interrogate the genre in which she

unconsciously acts. In contrast, the male detectives appear to belong to a tradition of detection that is no longer able to successfully uncover the true identity of the murderer or their victims.[53]

While it is suggested that there is a price to be paid for Tennison's success – in failed relationships and, later on in the series, an abortion – *Prime Suspect* nevertheless broke the mould of the male-dominated police detective series as dramatically as *Widows* had broken the crime genre mould in the previous decade. The series, which ran from 1991–6 and was revived from 2003–6, paved the way for other female-centred dramas such as *Chandler and Co* (BBC One, 1994–5), *The Governor* (Yorkshire, 1995–6), *Ambassador* (BBC One, 1998–9), *Scott & Bailey* (ITV, 2011–) and *Vera* (ITV, 2011–).[54]

    Silent Witness (BBC One, 1996–) was also a female-centred drama, based on Professor Helen Witwell, a forensic pathologist who series creator Nigel McCrery knew when he worked as a murder detective in the Midlands. For the first eight series (1996–2004), forensic pathologist Professor Sam Ryan (Amanda Burton) took a leading role in the criminal investigations that she was called to advise upon, providing a female counterpart to Fitz in the equally dark and disturbing *Cracker*. *Silent Witness* was progressive not only in assigning a woman to a leading role in a crime drama but also by showing her to be professional, authoritative and in total control when engaged in her work, particularly when examining and dissecting the bodies of the victims. This was a new departure for crime drama in the 1990s, not just the detailed visceral examination of the corpses but the placing at the centre of the drama of a female pathologist whose detached and clinical examinations of the bodies placed her in a position of power and authority rarely enjoyed by female protagonists. Robin Nelson has discussed how this positioning subverts the stereotypical representation of women in television drama, reversing the terms by which women are often objectified and subordinated within the narrative:

> As a forensic pathologist employed by the Coroner's Office in Cambridge, England, where she is located, Sam Ryan works in hi-tech laboratory conditions. In virtually every episode she is imaged undertaking an autopsy in this environment. To take a typical example, Sam is shown to be screened off by plate glass from the detectives urgently awaiting the outcome of her investigation of the suspected murder victim. Sam Ryan is dressed in a white surgical suit with a green plastic surgeon's apron over it. On her head she wears a surgeon's 'hard hat' with visor over a skull cap and nose and mouth mask. Only her eyes are visible. Her hands are gloved. She literally handles the brain and lungs of the dead man on the slab without a flinch, in marked contrast with the 'can't bear to look' reaction of the case-hardened woman detective behind the glass partition. She speaks aloud into an overhead microphone. Her voice is steady, calm, 'professional'. She is the surveyor of the male body, not a body to be surveyed by the male gaze. She is no longer there to be looked at, or is at least not simply so.[55]

Like Jane Tennison, Sam Ryan was one of a new breed of female protagonist in British television drama. Professional, career-minded, glamorous and intelligent, these postmodern protagonists were an important ingredient in the reinvention of television drama in the 1990s, providing strong, positive images for female viewers, but with qualities of aggression and glamour sufficient to appeal also to male viewers. In the new market-led televisual economy these characters were successful on several levels: in terms of ratings, in helping to revitalise old genres and in offering new postmodern identities for the television audience.

In this they were not alone. A number of new drama series appeared in the late 1990s and early 2000s – many of them written by women – which offered new, more forceful and more

Amanda Burton as Dr Sam Ryan in *Silent Witness*: one of a new breed of postmodern female protagonist in the 1990s

confident female characters. *This Life* featured several strong women, including the brash and outspoken Anna (Daniela Nardini) who was to become an icon of 1990s British TV drama; the writer and actor Kay Mellor created a number of ensemble dramas with strong, independent female characters, including *Band of Gold* (Granada, 1995–6), *Playing the Field* (BBC One, 1998–2002) and *Fat Friends* (ITV, 2000–5); Debbie Horsfield has also written gritty northern-based dramas with strong female roles such as *Making It* (BBC One, 1989–91), *Sex, Chips and Rock'n'Roll* (BBC One, 1999) and *Cutting It* (BBC One, 2002–5); while *Clocking Off*, *Linda Green* (BBC One, 2001–2) and the popular ensemble drama *Cold Feet* all contained female characters who were at least the equal of their male counterparts and often more interesting than them.

Perhaps the most radical series of the 1990s, however, in terms of representation and the shattering of sexual taboos, was Russell T Davies' *Queer as Folk*. With a punning title referencing the northern working-class adage, 'There's nowt as queer as folk', this Manchester-based series caused an uproar when it was transmitted in February 1999 because of its uninhibited representation of the lifestyles of a group of gay men, centred upon the extrovert Stuart (Aidan Gillen), the inhibited Vince (Craig Kelly) and the schoolboy Nathan (Charlie Hunnam). It was Stuart's seduction of the fifteen-year-old Nathan in the first episode which caused the initial controversy, with 160 people complaining to the ITC about the episode, more complaints than any television programme previously broadcast.[56]

What seemed of particular concern to the ITC was the 'celebratory tone' of the series, a concern which ironically highlighted what, for more than 4 million viewers (an

Queer as Folk: reaffirming Channel 4's original radical remit through a celebration of gay sexuality

audience share exceeding Channel 4's expectations), was so fresh and exciting about the series. With a 'postmodern' televisual style far removed from the social realism of other issue-based series – rapid cutting between scenes, a vibrant and colourful *mise en scène*, lively camerawork and a pounding soundtrack – *Queer as Folk* was, indeed, a celebration not only of Manchester's gay scene, but also of its more radical and confrontational elements. This radicalism was indicated by the provocative use of the word 'queer' in the series title, the radical reclaimed meaning of the word signifying a more overt and politicised expression of gay politics and identity.

The outrageous, charismatic figure of Stuart was, literally, the mouthpiece for the expression of this queer sensibility. It is no coincidence that it is he who seduces the underage Nathan in the first episode, taking him back to his expensive designer loft apartment, where they have sex (a scene portrayed more explicitly than gay sex had previously been on British television). Stuart celebrates his sexuality in language and deeds which embarrass his close friend Vince who, in comparison to Stuart, is more restrained and inhibited in his gay identity, which he initially conceals from his workmates until Stuart's goading eventually forces him to come out.

Stuart has no such inhibitions about expressing his identity, not just as gay but as queer – except, that is, to his family, to whom he eventually comes out in a scene which encapsulates both his confrontational nature and that of the series as a whole. In response to an attempt by his ten-year-old nephew, Thomas, to blackmail him, following Thomas' discovery of a gay porn website on Stuart's computer, Stuart decides to call Thomas' bluff by coming out to his family in typically outrageous fashion:

Because I'm queer, I'm gay. I'm homosexual. I'm a poof. I'm a bum-boy batty-boy backside-artist bugger, I'm bent, I am that arse bandit, I lift those shirts, I'm a fudge-packing shit-stabbing uphill gardener, I dance at the other end of the ballroom, I dine in the downstairs restaurant, I'm Moses and the parting of the Red Cheeks, I fuck and I'm fucked, I suck and I'm sucked, I rim them and wank them and every single man's had the shag of his life, and I am not – (beat) – a pervert. If there's one twisted bastard in this family, it's that little blackmailer, so congratulations, Thomas. I've officially just outed you.[57]

The scene is deliberately shocking, for Stuart's family and the audience, with its uninhibited rendition of a litany of homophobic euphemisms for homosexuality. At the same time, for Stuart it is a defiant assertion of his sexuality in response to the latent homophobia of Thomas, the outburst achieving an almost poetic quality in the writing of Russell T Davies and the charismatic performance of Aidan Gillen as Stuart. In many ways this speech encapsulates the spirit of the series: shocking, outrageous, liberating, colourful, uninhibited.

That Channel 4 was brave enough to screen the series was a reaffirmation of the original radical remit of the channel, at a time when it was beginning to seem that the channel's 'alternative' remit had been abandoned. In an article in the *Observer*, prior to the screening of the second series, Michael Collins praised *Queer as Folk* for its positive representation of gay sexuality and cited the contention of Gub Neal, the Head of Drama at Channel 4 at the time, that, notwithstanding the concerns of the ITC, what they had hoped to achieve with the series was a celebration of gay sexuality:

> As regards the promotion of a positive view of homosexuality, it doesn't come any more positive than *Queer as Folk*. Never has the case for promiscuity and Gloria Gaynor's back catalogue been put so exuberantly, so proudly – particularly in the character of cocksure Stuart, the 30-year-old well-dressed, well-paid, warehouse-living, pill-popping gay man whose only concern in life is where the next penis is coming from. 'The culture of the world in the series thrives on sexual experiences', says Gub Neal. 'This is what happens, and we wanted to celebrate it, not restrain it.'[58]

Each of the dramas discussed in this section illustrates the way in which, in the 1990s and early 2000s, British television attempted to revitalise old genres and 'reinvent' television drama by offering new representations of gender and sexuality. There are many other examples, in mainstream and minority-interest drama, in soap operas and in sitcoms. This 'reinvention' even extended to ethnic-minority representations, beyond the token black and Asian characters to be found in series such as *Casualty*, *The Bill*, *EastEnders* and *London's Burning* (ITV, 1988–2002). More concerted and interesting efforts in this regard were to be found in series such as *Hope and Glory* (BBC One, 1999–2000), featuring Lenny Henry as a 'progressive' secondary school headteacher; *Metrosexuality* (Channel 4, 2001), a sort of black *Queer as Folk*, set in west London, which attempted to redress the balance as far as the absence of black gay men in *Queer as Folk* was concerned; and *Babyfather* (BBC Two, 2001), a four-part drama featuring an all-black cast, with a black writer and a black director.

While most of these developments were positive, they by no means represented a revolution in British television drama at the turn of the century. On the contrary, these few instances of 'progressive' dramas have to be seen in the context of an increasingly cautious television industry where the majority impulse was towards the production of safer, more formulaic drama designed to maximise audiences. In this context, the commissioning of risky, innovative drama that might extend boundaries and challenge preconceptions was dependent on the enlightened decisions of executives on the minority channels and the willingness of enterprising writers, producers and independent production companies to rise to the challenge to do something different.

'A Shrinking Iceberg Travelling South ...'

A report published in 1999 took a more jaundiced view of the state of British television at the end of the twentieth century. Commissioned by the Campaign for Quality Television, 'A Shrinking Iceberg Travelling South ...': Changing Trends in British Television described an apparent decline in the quality of British television drama from the 1970s to the 90s.[59] The authors of the report, Steven Barnett and Emily Seymour, produced a comparative analysis of the content of selected dramas from the late 1970s, late 80s and late 90s and interviewed senior industry figures involved in the commissioning and production of television drama. One such (unidentified) figure offered a typically pessimistic view of the situation in the late 1990s which provided the authors with the title of the report: 'There's no long term commitment to anything – no Lew Grade type character developing great pools of talent, nowhere for writers and directors to grow up. The quality end is a shrinking iceberg travelling south.'[60]

The content analysis revealed the extent to which the single play, traditionally the outlet for original drama, had disappeared from the schedules between the late 1970s and the late 90s, with the number of such productions declining by more than half. Meanwhile, series drama during the same period had increased from 47 per cent of all drama on British television in 1977–8 to 63 per cent in 1997–8, while soap operas had increased from 10 per cent in the late 1970s to 29 per cent in the late 1990s. The content analysis also revealed the extent to which the police/detective/crime genre had consolidated its dominance of television drama, increasing from 27 per cent of all drama in the late 1970s to nearly a third of all drama (excluding soap opera) in the late 1990s.

Interestingly, home-produced drama was seen to dominate the schedules of the main channels, BBC One and ITV, while imported drama, especially American drama, dominated the minority channels. The most telling statistic here was the reduction of British drama on BBC Two from over 90 per cent in the late 1970s to less than 40 per cent in the late 1990s, a significant reduction which did not bode well for independent producers whose hopes of getting more innovative work onto British television resided largely with BBC Two and Channel 4.

Television drama executives and practitioners interviewed for the report noted the greater pressure which a more competitive environment had brought and the tendency to play safe when there was so much pressure, especially on BBC One and ITV, to maximise ratings:

> You become cautious if your priority is to get very big ratings for something. You tend to stick with the middle range, which is white, working class, lower-middle class people ... I'm not interested in making art-house stuff, but I think there is an immense and exciting cultural diversity in this country, which is good material

for drama, but I suspect that would be quite difficult to move, and it's a result of caution brought on by commercial pressure.[61]

This concern was frequently expressed by the more creative producers, directors and writers, who complained about the power wielded by channel controllers as a result of the structural changes that had taken place in British television in the 1980s and 90s, a period during which the autonomy previously enjoyed by programme-makers had been considerably eroded:

> I think what's really happened over the last ten years is that the power is held really with the controllers of BBC 1 and BBC 2, and they make all the creative decisions. Now, there's nothing wrong in that, except that it narrows it down to one single point of view, which I don't think is particularly good for diversity of viewing.[62]

Over four decades John McGrath was one of the most radical practitioners in British television, theatre and film, responsible not only for bringing a new style to police drama with *Z Cars* in the early 1960s and for such non-naturalistic experiments as *Diary of a Young Man* (see Chapter 3), *The Cheviot, the Stag and the Black, Black Oil* (Chapter 4) and *The Adventures of Frank* (Chapter 5), but also for writing, directing and producing several radical dramas for Channel 4 in the 1980s and early 90s and two dramas for BBC's *Screen Two* series: *The Long Roads* (1993) and *Half the Picture – Scenes from the Scott Arms to Iraq Inquiry* (1996). When I interviewed him in April 2000 he gave a concrete example of how the new regime of executive control was stifling creativity in television drama in the late 1990s:

> Quite recently I had a situation where I submitted an idea for a three-part serial to the BBC and I had to wait five or six months until the Controller of BBC Two had actually read the novel that it was going to be based on and then has given a green light. Then I'd got – I was working as a producer at this time – a very good writer who wrote the three episodes, three hours or whatever it was, and we then had to wait another five or six months while the Controller of BBC Two read the three episodes and at the end of it he came back and said, 'Well, three "sixtys" are no longer fashionable, couldn't you get it to be two "ninetys"?'
> So I went back to the writer and I said, 'Look this guy wants two "ninetys",' so he very reluctantly said, 'Well, you know I've constructed it this way, I'm going to have to rethink the whole bloody thing.' But he did. We then put it back in. Every time the BBC Head of Department was all for it and accepted it but had to wait for the Controller of BBC Two to actually read it. [We] put in the two 'ninetys' and it came back three or four months later, 'Oh, I think this would be better as a one-off.' Then the Head of Series and Serials, Mike Wearing, said, 'Okay, but can I still have it in my department?' He [the BBC Two Controller] said, 'No no no, it has to go to One' ... and then it was inherited by Single Drama who said, 'What's this? We don't want this.'[63]

This cautionary tale is not untypical of the hurdles which writers and producers have to negotiate in trying to get original drama onto television and the more radical the project, the more difficult it can be to get it made. In the market-led climate of the 1990s–2000s originality was, to a large extent, squeezed out of the schedules. In its place, channel controllers and commissioning editors wanted a reliable product which would bring in an audience, especially on the two main channels.

In an echo of Dennis Potter's complaint about the predictability of contemporary television drama, the following quote from the Campaign for Quality Television's report illustrates the lack of ambition and originality in British television drama in the late 1990s:

> You switch on and you know what's going to happen ... 'Sunburn', 'Harbour Lights', I mean we could all spew out the plots ourselves, or variations on them. But something that is allowing something really profound to be said, in however an entertaining or interesting way, there is very little of that ... there is very little now which is making any sort of social comment or talking about the state of the nation or the state of the world.[64]

The competition for ratings success on the main channels in the 1990s led to a narrowing in the range and diversity of drama available on British television. As the Campaign's report showed, police/detective/crime drama and soap opera dominated the schedules, with hospital and historical drama also well represented. Original contemporary drama, however, especially if non-generic, was much less in evidence. In the pursuit of ratings the presence of a 'star name', such as John Thaw, David Jason or Amanda Burton, or a popular actor from a soap opera, such as Nick Berry, Michelle Collins or Ross Kemp, became an essential prerequisite for success. But this strategy can easily lead to greater conformity and a narrowing of choice as star actors present slight variations (sometimes very slight) on their previous roles. Meanwhile, the opportunities for new talent to emerge, in different kinds of roles, are significantly reduced.

As the shift to a more competitive, market-led broadcasting environment took place the complaints about the deterioration in quality and lack of originality in British television increased. It was not only writers, producers and directors of the 1960s generation, such as Dennis Potter, John McGrath and Tony Garnett, who bemoaned the drift towards predictable, formulaic drama, but also leading industry figures of a younger generation, such as David Liddiment, Director of Programmes at ITV from 1997–2002, and Mark Thompson, Director of Television at the BBC from 2000–2, when he left to succeed Michael Jackson as Chief Executive of Channel 4 (before returning to the BBC as Director General in 2004). Liddiment and Thompson both used the annual MacTaggart Lecture at the Edinburgh International Television Festival to deliver trenchant critiques of the state of British television at the beginning of the twenty-first century.

Liddiment's target, in August 2001, was the obsession with ratings in British television:

> The soul of British television is in danger. Numbers now seem to be the only universal measure for excellence that we have: how many, how much, how often.

> We're losing sight of the innate value of programmes in our fixation on the
> success that can be measured by profit, profile or performance.[65]

Liddiment's speech found favour with many in the industry and outside of it, echoing a
general concern about the obsession with ratings at the expense of originality in British
television. For such sentiments to be expressed by an ITV executive was unusual and
an indication that concerns about profit taking priority over quality in programming
were not restricted to the old guard.

In August 2002, Mark Thompson's concern was the lack of creativity in British television, especially in relation to American TV:

> In many ways, production quality and professionalism are higher than they've
> ever been. The problem is that so much of it just feels dull, mechanical and
> samey. There's a pervasive sense of predictability. When you're looking for
> ambitious, complex and above all modern TV, you find yourself watching not
> British, but American pieces: *Six Feet Under*, say, or *24*. There are exceptions but the
> idea that British television is teeming with that kind of creative risk is a joke.[66]

In accounting for this perceived lack of creativity in British television Thompson pointed
to an inherent conservatism in British television culture:

> When you add this broader conservatism to the more recent risk-aversion that
> has resulted from centralised decision-making and a move from instinct towards
> analysis, you have a cocktail that is nearly lethal for creativity. British television
> used to be famous for its risk-taking. Now, we're trailing behind American TV, and
> our own viewers.[67]

Thompson's claim that British television at the beginning of the twenty-first century
was 'dull, mechanical and samey' compared to American television was not an isolated
refrain. It became almost commonplace in the early 2000s to hear people within the
British television industry and outside of it praising the virtues of American TV, such as
Paul Abbott wanting *Clocking Off* to be 'as fast, good-looking and fantastically well done
as *The West Wing*'. *The West Wing* was just one of many American series admired for its
style, pace, performances and writing. Mark Thompson, later the same year, cited *Six
Feet Under* (HBO, 2001–5) and *24* (Fox, 2001–10) as examples of 'ambitious, complex and
above all modern TV'.

Each of these series contributed to a 'second phase' of quality television drama in
the USA, following closely on the heels of the first phase which the American academic
Robert J. Thompson discussed in his 1996 book, *Television's Second Golden Age: From Hill
Street Blues to ER*.[68] But the benchmark for quality television in the early 2000s was
undoubtedly the series being produced by the American subscription channel HBO. In
addition to *Six Feet Under* there was *Oz* (1997–2003), *Sex and the City* (1998–2004), *The
Sopranos* (1999–2007), *The Corner* (2000) – the precursor to *The Wire* (2002–8) – and *Band of*

Brothers (2001, co-produced with the BBC). As Robert Thompson wrote in 2007, these series 'went beyond anything imaginable in the old network era in terms of content, narrative complexity, language and lots more'.[69]

In his 2002 MacTaggart Lecture Mark Thompson did acknowledge that there were exceptions to the 'pervasive sense of predictability' in British television, but the conservative nature of British television in the 1990s did not encourage the kind of risk-taking that might have produced British equivalents of *The Sopranos*, *Six Feet Under* and *The Wire*, even if budgets had allowed for such programmes, which they generally did not. Among his 'exceptions' Thompson might have acknowledged the stylistic innovation of series such as *This Life*, *Queer as Folk* and *Clocking Off*; the social engagement of issue-based dramas such as Jimmy McGovern's *Hillsborough* and *Sunday* (Channel 4, 28 January 2002), as well as Paul Greengrass's *Bloody Sunday* (Granada, 20 January 2002); the originality of crime dramas such as *Prime Suspect*, *Cracker* and *Waking the Dead* (BBC One, 2000–11); and the literary quality of period dramas such as *Middlemarch, Pride and Prejudice* and *The Tenant of Wildfell Hall*, but his observation that British television was not 'teeming with that kind of creative risk' in the 1990s and early 2000s was generally sound.

The comments from industry figures contained in the Campaign for Quality Television report highlighted the degree of pessimism about the possibilities for producing quality television drama in a cost-cutting, market-led industry. While the advent of a more competitive, multi-channel environment in the 1990s did not lead to the demise of public service broadcasting in Britain, there were genuine concerns about whether there was the will among executive decision-makers to commission original, innovative, quality drama on the main channels, or whether such work would be restricted to much smaller audiences on minority digital channels, if indeed it survived at all.

7

British Television Drama in the Digital Age, 2002–14

The post-1990 'reinvention' of British television drama did not end in 2002, but continued during the first decade of the twenty-first century, aided and abetted by the transition from an analogue to a digital television environment. Digital technology, as we have seen, was a spur to innovation in the production of television drama from the mid-1990s, but the proliferation of digital channels in the first decade of the new century gave a boost to the production of new drama, just as the introduction of ITV, BBC Two and Channel 4 had in previous decades.

The BBC launched its first digital channel, BBC Choice, on 23 September 1998, followed by BBC Knowledge on 1 June 1999; these channels were relaunched in 2002–3 as BBC Three and BBC Four, respectively, as part of a reorganisation of the BBC's digital provision, which also saw two digital children's channels launched in 2002. BBC Four was launched on 2 March 2002 with BBC Three being launched nearly a year later, on 9 February 2003, the launch of BBC Three having been delayed because of concerns that it would be competing with two commercial digital channels: ITV2, launched on 7 December 1998, and E4, launched by Channel 4 on 18 January 2001, both of which, like BBC Three, were targeting a younger audience demographic.

Having launched FilmFour as a digital film channel in 1998 (rebranded Film4 in 2006) and E4 in 2001, Channel 4 also launched More4, for an older demographic, on 10 October 2005. Meanwhile, ITV launched ITV3 on 1 November 2004 and ITV4 on 1 November 2005, both channels targeting an older audience with a mixture of drama repeats, movies, lifestyle programmes and sport. Channel 5, which had been launched as the fifth terrestrial UK channel in 1997, introduced its own digital channels in October 2006: Five Life (later Fiver and then 5*) and Five USA, while Sky introduced Sky Arts on 1 March 2007, after taking over Artsworld (2000–7) in 2005, and Sky Atlantic on 1 February 2011, to add to the plethora of digital television channels being launched during this period. While some of these digital channels were launched before 2002, no drama was produced for digital channels until 2002, when BBC Four commissioned and broadcast several new dramas. Consequently, 2002 could be seen as the year in which a new era of British television drama began: the digital age.

At the end of 2003, a new broadcasting regulator, Ofcom (the Office of Communications), was introduced, replacing several existing regulators, including the Independent Television Commission (ITC), and paving the way for a single ITV company to be formed, following the mergers and takeovers that had been taking place in independent television since 1992. On 2 February 2004, the two largest ITV companies, Carlton and Granada, merged to form ITV plc, with Scottish TV, Grampian, Ulster and Channel TV remaining separate from the newly consolidated company. The implications of this development in commercial television were already becoming apparent, with fewer regional dramas being produced by ITV as the new company began to reinvent itself as an international broadcaster, capable of competing in the new global marketplace.

That the broadcasting environment was already changing in 2002 was evident from the lack of any clear distinction between BBC One and ITV1 in terms of programming.[1] This was highlighted by the screening of a new version of *The Forsyte Saga* (Granada, April–May 2002) not on the BBC but on ITV, thirty-five years after Galsworthy's saga was first screened on BBC Two. Not only did this indicate the extent to which cultural divisions between these channels had been eroded over that period, but also the extent to which audiences had been eroded, with Granada's new version attracting a similar-size audience (an average of 7 million) to the 1967 BBC Two version and a far smaller audience than the 18 million that watched the original serial when it was shown on BBC One in 1968. This despite the advantage of a bigger budget, higher production values and location filming in the ITV remake.

Another example of this cultural exchange between the BBC and ITV in 2002 was BBC One's new serialisation of *Auf Wiedersehen, Pet* (BBC One, April–June 2002), the comedy drama based on the escapades of a group of Geordie labourers which was first screened on ITV in the 1980s (Central TV, 1983–6). In this case, the average audience of 10.7 million for the 2002 serial was closer to the huge audience which the drama attracted in the 1980s, with up to 15 million viewers for the second series in 1986. Indeed, the first episode of the new BBC version attracted 12 million viewers and was number two in the ratings that week, second only to *Coronation Street*.

The popular success of the BBC's *Auf Wiedersehen, Pet* provided an illustration of the increased competitiveness of the BBC under its new director general, Greg Dyke (appointed 1 January 2000), who, as an ex-ITV executive, was prepared to challenge ITV on its own populist territory in the new deregulated broadcasting environment. The switching of channels between the earlier and later versions of the dramas also highlights the changing cultural values of the two main broadcasters in this new postmodern televisual era. Not only was there no longer a clear cultural distinction, in terms of programming, between the BBC and ITV, between 'public service' and 'commercial' broadcasting, it was also becoming more difficult for the two broadcasters to predict audience tastes and preferences, between, for example, a working-class ensemble drama like *Auf Wiedersehen, Pet* and a middle-class literary serial like *Pride and Prejudice*, which had also attracted 10 million viewers on BBC One in the mid-1990s.

Historical drama and literary adaptations

The cultural exchange and blurring between 'public service' and 'commercial' channels has been particularly evident in historical drama and literary adaptations in the first decade of the twenty-first century. In 2005, ITV transmitted a feature-length, two-part production of *Colditz*, a Second World War drama previously screened by the BBC in 1972–4. This was followed, in 2007, by three Jane Austen adaptations – *Mansfield Park* (18 March 2007), *Northanger Abbey* (25 March 2007) and *Persuasion* (1 April 2007) – plus E. M. Forster's *A Room with a View* (4 November 2007) and Charles Dickens' *The Old Curiosity Shop* (26 December 2007), all on ITV, where once they would have been seen as traditional BBC material. Then, in 2010–12, the BBC resurrected a classic ITV series, *Upstairs Downstairs*, continuing the story in 1936, six years after the conclusion of ITV's 1971–5 version, with Jean Marsh, the original series co-creator, reprising her role as Rose, now promoted from the rank of housemaid to housekeeper.

What was noticeable with the new versions of *Colditz* and *Upstairs Downstairs*, however, was how abbreviated they were compared to the long-running 1970s series. In the new ITV version, *Colditz* was restricted to two episodes, whereas the original BBC series comprised twenty-eight episodes; meanwhile, the BBC presented their new version of *Upstairs Downstairs* in a three-episode first series in 2010, followed by a six-part second series in 2012, whereas the original ITV series ran for five years and sixty-eight episodes. The difference highlights the changed ecology of British television drama production between the 'golden age' of the 1970s and the situation forty years later. Outside of the soaps and the continuing or returning series, such as *Casualty*, *Silent Witness*, *Holby City* (BBC One, 1999–), *Doc Martin* (ITV, 2004–) and *Doctor Who* (BBC One, 2005–), recent drama series have been considerably shorter, in comparison to their 1950s–70s equivalents. This is partly a result of the shift from studio production to high definition location filming, with its consequent escalation of costs, but is also a result of a greater timidity on behalf of drama commissioners and channel controllers, who are far more hesitant about commissioning long-running or extended series, preferring to stick with the established brands in a far more competitive marketplace.

Nevertheless, there has been no shortage of historical drama and classic literary adaptations since 2002. The primary reason for the popularity of period drama or costume drama, to use the terms more often associated with these productions, is probably much the same as it was in the 1970s and 90s, during the previous cycles of popularity: a longing to return to the past and to more apparently settled times during a period of social and political uncertainty following the Al-Qaeda attacks on New York and Washington in September 2001 and the subsequent 'War on Terror'. There is also an economic incentive for the television companies, with these 'heritage' dramas proving perennially popular in overseas markets, making them a sound financial investment despite their high production costs. Allied to this is the fact that, in this high-tech digital age, they can be produced in high definition and widescreen ratios, enhancing their attractiveness to domestic consumers and overseas markets alike.

Historical dramas during this period range from Andrew Davies' one-off, feature-length drama about the Celtic queen *Boudica* (ITV, 2003) who led an uprising against the

Romans in the first century AD, to a host of dramas set in the sixteenth and seventeenth centuries, such as Peter Morgan's two-part *Henry VIII* (ITV, 2003), Nigel Williams' two-part *Elizabeth I* (Channel 4, 2005), with Helen Mirren playing the eponymous queen, Paula Milne's four-part *The Virgin Queen* (BBC One, 2006), with Anne-Marie Duff as Elizabeth I, Jimmy McGovern's two-part *Gunpowder, Treason and Plot* (BBC Two, 2004), which focused on Mary, Queen of Scots (in part one), and James I and the Gunpowder Plot (in part two), Peter Flannery's four-part *The Devil's Whore* (Channel 4, 2008), set during the English Civil War, and Adrian Hodges' four-part *Charles II: The Power and the Passion* (BBC One, 2003) which begins, historically, where *The Devil's Whore* ends.

More recently, the ten-episode *The White Queen* (BBC One, 16 June–18 August 2013) dramatised Philippa Gregory's historical novels about the Wars of the Roses, telling the story from the viewpoint of the women caught up in this fifteenth-century struggle for the English throne. The eighteenth century was the setting for Tony Marchant's series *Garrow's Law* (BBC One, 2009–11), about the pioneering barrister William Garrow, and the early nineteenth century was the setting for Channel 4's four-part drama *The Mill* (Channel 4, 28 July–18 August 2013), about the lives of child labourers in England during the Industrial Revolution. Two more BBC One series, *The Paradise* (2012–) and *Ripper Street* (2012–) are set in the late nineteenth century, the former about the first English department store and the latter a crime drama set in the East End of London shortly after the Jack the Ripper murders.

The early twentieth century is the setting for ITV's *Mr Selfridge* (2013–), a series about the eponymous department store magnate, created by Andrew Davies and based on the biography *Shopping, Seduction and Mr Selfridge* by Linda Woodhead. But one of the most successful of these historical series, in terms of ratings, critical acclaim and overseas sales, has been Julian Fellowes' *Downton Abbey* (ITV, 2010–), a lavish period drama that replicated the success of ITV's *Upstairs Downstairs*, spanning a similar historical period, with the first series beginning in 1912, the day after the sinking of the *Titanic*, and continuing through the First World War into the 1920s. Unlike *Upstairs Downstairs*, however, which was originally intended to be told from the point of view of the servants downstairs, *Downton Abbey* paid more attention to the aristocratic Crawley family, a strategy which proved to be a popular success, with audiences averaging over 9 million. By November 2013 the series had proved to be a global success, having been sold to more than 220 countries and with an estimated global audience of 120 million.[2]

It may be no coincidence that *Downton Abbey*'s huge success followed the election of a Conservative-led coalition government in the UK in 2010, in which the Prime Minister, David Cameron, and several of his cabinet had attended Eton and other independent fee-paying schools and were, therefore, a product of the hierarchical social structure which *Downton Abbey* celebrates. As always with this kind of historical drama, the world that it depicts has echoes in the present. *Downton* is a reminder that the British class system still survives in the twenty-first century and its popularity cannot simply be explained as a nostalgic longing for a long-lost social and political order.

As a rebuttal to *Downton Abbey*, the BBC produced *The Village* (BBC One, 2013–), another series set in the early years of the twentieth century but focusing, in this case, on the working class in a Derbyshire village. Following a similar historical trajectory to *Downton Abbey*, the first series begins in 1914 and ends in 1920. Writer Peter Moffat said that he wanted to create a British *Heimat* (1984–2013), referring to the epic German TV serial which followed one family from 1919–82. Whether he succeeds in doing so with an unremittingly bleak drama which eschews the romantic melodrama of *Downton Abbey* for a social realist approach remains to be seen.

More recent history has been dealt with in the four-part *Cambridge Spies* (BBC Two, 2003), about the activities of Kim Philby, Guy Burgess, Donald Maclean and Anthony Blunt during the 1930s and 40s, when they were recruited as spies by the Soviet Union while they were at Cambridge University, and in two Second World War dramas: *Dunkirk* (BBC Two, 2004), a three-part drama about the British retreat from Dunkirk in 1940, and *The Sinking of the Laconia* (BBC Two, 2011), a two-part drama written by Alan Bleasdale about the torpedoing of a British ocean liner by a German U-boat off the coast of Africa in 1942 and its aftermath, when the captain of the U-boat stayed to rescue the passengers from the sunken liner, only to be attacked by American aircraft.

BBC Two was a major contributor to the genre of historical drama during this period. In April 2011, a feature-length drama about the Munich air crash, which killed many of Manchester United's promising young football team – the 'Busby babes' – was the subject of *United* (24 April 2011), while, in July 2011, the first series of Abi Morgan's drama about a fictional 1950s BBC current affairs programme, *The Hour* (2011–12), began, to be followed by a second series in 2012. Also on BBC Two in 2012, Paula Milne's six-part *White Heat* (8 March–12 April 2012) charted some of the major social and political events of the period from 1965–90, as experienced by a group of young people sharing a house in north London. In its historical trajectory and focus on a group of friends, set against a backdrop of significant social change, the series was similar to Peter Flannery's *Our Friends in the North*, but Milne wanted to focus more on the role of women, race and sexual politics during the period, whereas Flannery's serial was more masculine, and white, in its emphasis. Milne's series, one of nine dramas written or adapted by her during this period, took its title from Harold Wilson's famous 1963 speech about the 'white heat of technology' forging a new social and industrial revolution.

BBC Two continued its strong showing with historical drama in 2013, when Stephen Poliakoff's six-part *Dancing on the Edge* (February–March 2013), about a black jazz band in London in the 1930s, was followed by the first series of *Peaky Blinders* (2013–), a crime drama about the activities of a gangster family in Birmingham set just after the First World War. Both dramas were stylish and well received by the critics, consolidating BBC Two's renaissance as a commissioner of quality drama during this period.[3]

One of the biggest ratings successes of this period was the BBC One series *Call the Midwife* (2012–), about midwives working in the East End of London in the 1950s. Based on the memoirs of Jennifer Worth, the series was written by Heidi Thomas, who had previously written the eight-part period drama *Lilies* (BBC One, January–March 2007), set in Liverpool in the 1920s, the five-part *Cranford* (BBC One, November–December, 2007), adapted from Elizabeth's Gaskell's novellas, and the new series of *Upstairs Downstairs*, all for the BBC.

Call the Midwife was hugely popular, with audiences equalling and occasionally exceeding those of *Downton Abbey*, with which it was in competition on Sunday evenings. The two series offered sharply contrasting representations of the past, with *Downton* celebrating a hierarchical social structure in which the working classes 'knew their place' as servants to the aristocratic Crawley family, while *Call the Midwife* celebrated the collective struggles of a largely female community in the East End of London during the early years of the new National Health Service (NHS). The contrast between the 1920s and the 50s, in terms of class and social differences, was brought into sharp focus through the juxtaposition of *Call the Midwife* and *Downton Abbey*, and the dramas, as Estella Tincknell has argued, could be seen to be performing contrasting ideological functions in Britain in 2012–13, with *Call the Midwife* showing the virtues of a welfare system that the Conservative-led government was actively seeking to dismantle:

> Against the romantic spectacle offered by *Downton Abbey*, *Call the Midwife* offers a compelling defence of socialised medicine as central to the transformation of the health and happiness of ordinary people. By staging the past it calls attention to a present in which the NHS is under attack from the same kind of Conservative-led coalition whose cultural antecedents seem so seductive when bathed in *Downton Abbey*'s dappled light, and this intervention represents a reassertion of not simply the importance of the NHS but of what might more broadly be called women's values.[4]

During a period in which 'political' drama on television was almost non-existent, the ideological work being performed by popular series such as *Call the Midwife* should not be underestimated.

Sharing many characteristics with historical drama – period settings, lavish attention to costumes and *mise en scène*, well-known actors, high production values – literary adaptations were also much in evidence during this period. Andrew Davies continued to be ubiquitous with his adaptations of many novels, both classic and modern, having established himself during the 1990s with adaptations of classic novels by Austen, Eliot, Gaskell and others. In addition to his scripts for *Boudica* and *Mr Selfridge*, Davies' television work during this period included a three-part adaptation of Sarah Waters' 1998 debut novel, *Tipping the Velvet* (BBC Two, October 2002), a lavish, three-part adaptation of *Doctor Zhivago* (ITV, November–December 2002), a four-part adaptation of Anthony Trollope's *He Knew He Was Right* (BBC One, 2004), a feature-length adaptation of Elizabeth Jane Howard's 1999 novel *Falling* (ITV, 6 March 2005) and an adventurous fifteen-part adaptation of Charles Dickens' *Bleak House* (BBC One, October–December 2005), delivered in one fifty-five minute and fourteen half-hour episodes, replicating the episodic form in which Dickens originally delivered the story. Davies' adaptation of *Bleak House* was a conscious attempt to popularise Dickens by presenting the drama in the form of a soap opera, with weekly half-hour episodes and a 'flexi-narrative' structure, moving rapidly from one narrative strand to another in order to heighten and maintain audience involvement. The adaptation was highly praised and *Bleak House* received a BAFTA award for Best Drama Serial in 2006.[5] Davies repeated the strategy in 2008 with a fourteen-part adaptation of Dickens' *Little Dorrit* (BBC One, October–December 2008), screened in two sixty-minute and twelve half-hour episodes, eight hours in total (like *Bleak House*), representing a major undertaking for one writer.

There was little respite from Andrew Davies' prolific output during this period. In between the two Dickens adaptations he wrote a ninety-minute drama, *The Chatterley Affair* (BBC Four, 20 March 2006), about the obscenity trial which followed the publication of D. H. Lawrence's *Lady Chatterley's Lover* in 1960, a three-part adaptation of Alan Hollinghurst's 2004 Booker prize-winning novel, *The Line of Beauty* (BBC Two, May 2006), the adaptations of *Northanger Abbey* and *A Room with a View* mentioned above, a four-part adaptation of George and Weedon Grossmith's *Diary of a Nobody* (BBC Four, April–May 2007), a two-part adaptation of *Fanny Hill* (BBC Four, October 2007) and a three-part adaptation of Jane Austen's *Sense and Sensibility* (BBC One, January 2008), not to mention his screenplay for the cinema version of *Brideshead Revisited* (2008). After a three-year gap in which he concentrated on movie screenplays, Davies returned to television with a three-part adaptation of Winifred Holtby's 1936 novel, *South Riding* (BBC One, February–March 2011).[6]

Other classic literary adaptations during this period included ITV's 2007 adaptation of Dickens' *The Old Curiosity Shop* and a three-part adaptation of *Great Expectations* (BBC One, December 2011), with Gillian Anderson, who was a superb Lady Dedlock in *Bleak House*, as Miss Havisham. There was also a *Jane Austen Season* (ITV, March–April 2007) on ITV which included *Mansfield Park* and *Persuasion* in addition to Andrew Davies' adaptation of *Northanger Abbey*, a two-part adaptation of Thomas Hardy's *The Mayor of Casterbridge* (ITV, December 2003) and six modern-day versions of Chaucer's *The Canterbury Tales* (BBC One, September–October 2003), from writers including Peter Bowker and Sally Wainwright, who both contributed to a similar updating of four Shakespeare plays, presented under the series title: *ShakespeaRe-Told* (BBC One, November 2005). Peter Bowker also adapted Emily Brontë's *Wuthering Heights* (ITV, August 2009) during a prolific period in which he wrote several original dramas (see below). Sally Wainwright, who was also very prolific during this period, had previously written *Sparkhouse* (BBC One, 2002), a three-part modern-day version of *Wuthering Heights*.

Sandy Welch was another prolific adapter during this period, rivalling her husband Stephen Poliakoff's output with adaptations of Elizabeth Gaskell's *North and South* (BBC One, November–December 2004), Charlotte Brontë's *Jane Eyre* (BBC One, September 2006) and Jane Austen's *Emma* (BBC One, October, 2009), all in four parts, plus a ninety-minute dramatisation of Henry James' *The Turn of the Screw* (BBC One, 30 December 2009). With Lizzie Mickery adapting John Buchan's *The 39 Steps* (BBC One, 28 December 2008), Paula Milne adapting Andrea Levy's *Small Island* (BBC One, 6–13 December 2009) and Sarah Waters' *The Night Watch* (BBC Two, 12 July 2011), and Abi Morgan adapting Sebastian Faulks' First World War novel *Birdsong* (BBC One, 22–9 January 2012), women writers showed that Andrew Davies did not have a monopoly on literary adaptations in this period.

The First World War was also the subject of Ford Madox Ford's *Parade's End* (BBC Two, August–September 2012), adapted for television in five parts by Tom Stoppard. Another early twentieth-century adaptation was *Twenty Thousand Streets Under the Sky* (BBC Four, April 2005), adapted in three parts by Kevin Elyot from Patrick Hamilton's trilogy. This was one of several outstanding dramas on BBC Four, which emerged as an important new outlet for quality drama following the channel's launch in 2002. Other literary adaptations on BBC Four included: two ghost stories by M. R. James, *A View from a Hill* (BBC Four, 23 December 2005) and *Number 13* (BBC Four, 22 December 2006); *Wide Sargasso Sea* (BBC Four, 9 October 2006), adapted by Stephen Greenhorn from the 1966 novel by Jean Rhys; *Who Killed Mrs De Ropp?* (BBC Four, 2 May 2007), based on stories by Saki; and *Women in Love* (BBC Four, March 2011), adapted by William Ivory from two D. H. Lawrence novels, *The Rainbow* and *Women in Love*.

Although Channel 4 tended to specialise in original dramas rather than literary adaptations, the channel was responsible for an award-winning four-part adaptation of William Boyd's *Any Human Heart* (Channel 4, November–December 2010), which won a BAFTA award for Best Drama Serial in 2011.

There were also a few theatre adaptations during this period, although these were negligible in comparison to the number of literary adaptations. Most were on BBC Four, the new channel transmitting TV versions of successful stage plays as part of a strategy to distinguish itself from the other digital channels. An early example was Michael Frayn's play *Copenhagen* (BBC Four, 26 September 2002), about a meeting in 1941 between the physicists Niels Bohr and Werner Heisenberg, which ran for 300 performances at the National Theatre in the late 1990s. This was followed by another National Theatre production, *Vincent in Brixton* (BBC Four, 20 March 2003), about the time Vincent van Gogh spent living in London when he was twenty years old. Peter Nichols' 1967 play *A Day in the Death of Joe Egg* (BBC Four, 28 October 2003) was also screened in 2003 and, the following year, BBC Four transmitted Kwame Kwei-Armah's *Elmina's Kitchen* (21 January 2004) and Chekhov's *Three Sisters* (22 February 2004). In 2008 the channel screened a TV version of Joe Penhall's play *Blue/Orange* (BBC Four, 14 October 2008), which had premiered at the Cottesloe Theatre in 2000, and transmitted a new play for television by Kwame Kwei-Armah, *Walter's War* (BBC Four, 9 November 2008), about the wartime experiences of black footballer Walter Tull.

Meanwhile, Channel 4 produced a TV version of the Royal Shakespeare Company's 2007 production of *King Lear* (More4, 25 December 2008), directed by Trevor Nunn, which was first shown on the digital channel More4 on Christmas Day 2008 and repeated on Channel 4 the following day.[7] Finally, in 2009, Sky TV made an attempt to revive the live television play in a season of six short plays, broadcast under the anthology title *Theatre Live!* (Sky Arts 1, 2009), the first time that plays had been shown live on British television since 1983, when five plays were broadcast live by the BBC under the series title *Live from Pebble Mill* (BBC Two, February–March 1983).[8]

Social-issue drama post 9/11

The Al-Qaeda attacks in America on 11 September 2001, when four aeroplanes were hijacked by Islamic terrorists and flown into the Twin Towers of the World Trade Center in New York and the Pentagon in Washington, leading to the collapse of the towers and

Spooks: social-issue drama post-9/11

the deaths of nearly 3,000 people, changed the nature of social-issue/political drama in the twenty-first century. In America, the political thriller 24 tapped into the mood of fear and paranoia engendered by the 9/11 attacks and the subsequent 'War on Terror'. Its British equivalent, though without the 'real-time' scenarios of the American series, was *Spooks* (BBC One, 2002–11), about a group of counter-terrorist agents working for MI5 in London. The series was developed by independent production company Kudos, which emerged as one of the leading television drama producers in this period, and was already in development, with four scripts written, at the time of the 9/11 attacks. Acknowledging the significance of the attacks, some changes were made to the scripts and future episodes were written in the context of the new American-led 'War on Terror', with which Britain became inextricably involved when the UK joined with US forces in attacking the Taliban regime in Afghanistan, from where the 9/11 attacks had been planned, and, in 2003, invading Iraq in order to depose the regime of Saddam Hussein.

Spooks was created by David Wolstencroft, who wrote the first two episodes and co-wrote the final episode of the first series with Howard Brenton, who also wrote two episodes in the first series and was one of the main writers on the first four series. Brenton had a reputation as a radical playwright in the 1970s–80s, not least for his controversial National Theatre play, *The Romans in Britain* (1980), but he had not written for television since the mid-1980s, when his remarkable *Play for Today*, *Desert of Lies* (BBC One, 13 March 1984) was followed by the four-part crime thriller, *Dead Head* (BBC Two, January–February 1986). *Spooks*, however, gave Brenton the opportunity to return to the political fray with a glossy drama series that proved to be a popular success, the first series averaging 7.49 million viewers.[9]

The storylines in the first series included the opening one about an American pro-life group conducting a bombing campaign in the UK, a right-wing fanatic planning to instigate a race war in Britain (episode two), an attempt by a terrorist group to kill US President George Bush on a visit to the UK (episode four – Brenton's first episode) and, in the sixth and final episode, a double threat from an Irish terrorist group which plants a bomb in London and a Sudanese terrorist group planning an attack on a nuclear power station. The final episode finished with a cliff-hanger when MI5 agent Tom Quinn (Matthew Macfadyen) receives a telephone call from the leader of the Irish terrorist group telling him that the laptop he has given him (containing details of the Sudanese terror attack) is loaded with explosives. Tom has taken the laptop home and, as a result of a problem with his new security system, Tom's partner Ellie and her daughter are trapped inside. With the explosives timed to go off, Tom stares helplessly at Ellie from outside as the episode comes to an end.[10]

The cliff-hanger ending capped a successful series which delivered its topical and suspenseful storylines in a stylish manner, with high production values, fast cutting and the use of split-screen (as in 24) to heighten the suspense and facilitate the delivery of complex narratives. While the series was accused of glamorising the activities of MI5 agents (applications to join the service increased considerably after Spooks was screened), the series was not afraid to upset audience expectations by killing off central characters, a tactic introduced as early as episode two when Helen Flynn (Lisa Faulkner), who had been introduced as one of the central characters in episode one, was shockingly killed by having her head plunged into a deep fryer of boiling oil by the aforementioned right-wing fanatic, Robert Osbourne (Kevin McNally).[11]

The first series of Spooks won a BAFTA award for Best Drama Series in 2003 (ahead of Clocking Off, Cutting It and Teachers) and it returned as a ten-episode series in 2003 (reduced to eight episodes for series seven to nine and six episodes for the final series). The manner in which Spooks drew on real-life international developments was evident in the second series from storylines such as David Wolstencroft's opening episode, when a bomb goes off killing the Secretary for State in Northern Ireland and a top secret military base in the south of England is also bombed, by a Serbian General. In the second episode, written by Howard Brenton, an Afghan mullah is training young suicide bombers in a Birmingham mosque and a sixteen-year-old boy blows himself up before MI5 are able to intervene. In Brenton's second episode for the series (episode four), a member of the Russian mafia is attempting to launder 20 billion dollars of stolen US aid money through the UK and, in episode five, Brenton wrote a story about a nerve gas attack in London which causes MI5 to be sealed off, only for the whole incident to be revealed as a drill to test the team at the end of the episode.

After the first episode of series two, episodes two to nine were shown first on BBC Three and repeated a week later on BBC One (with one episode being shown two weeks later) in an attempt to get viewers to watch the new digital channel. The first and final episodes of the series were only shown on BBC One; this strategy continued for the next six series. Kudos also produced a spin-off series in 2008, Spooks: Code 9 (BBC Three, August–September 2008), targeted at a younger audience on BBC Three. The series involved a scenario in which there had been a nuclear attack on London during the opening ceremony of the Olympic Games (which took place, within the story, in London in July–August 2008), following which the government relocates to Manchester and a new, younger generation of MI5 operatives are recruited to prevent further attacks. However, the series was not well received and a second series was not commissioned.

By 2008 the viewing figures for Spooks had started to fall and the seventh series was reduced to eight episodes. It continued to engage with contemporary issues, however, with stories about Al-Qaeda kidnapping a British soldier in an attempt to get the Remembrance Sunday service called off and, in a subsequent episode, a plan to mount a series of attacks using suicide bombers. The resurgence of Russia as a world power generated several stories, including one about a Russian submarine in British waters which threatens a cyber attack, while a continuing storyline throughout the series culminates, in the final episode, with a Russian agent attempting to detonate a nuclear bomb in London. Adam Carter (Rupert Penry-Jones), one of the main MI5 characters since series three, is killed at the beginning of the series when he drives a car rigged with explosives away from a memorial service where it is timed to go off. The series ended with a cliff-hanger when MI5 counter-terrorism head Harry Pearce (Peter Firth) is kidnapped by the Russian Secret Service.

Fast-moving, stylish and action-packed, Spooks engaged with the new twenty-first-century 'War on Terror' throughout its ten series in a variety of ways. In doing so, as Paul Cobley argues, the series dramatised social anxieties which were very real post 9/11:

What Spooks has done is to maintain a tense balance of glamour (young, attractive actors, bracketing quotidian realities such as social class) and, through verisimilar currency, to pull back on the fantasy world of surveillance and state secrets, foregrounding homeland security, political crime and the safety of the populace in an everyday (western) world supposedly threatened by terror.[12]

Glamorised it may have been, but the series' engagement with contemporary events reinforced its verisimilitude, as the opening two-part story of the fourth series, about a terrorist attack on the transport system in central London, demonstrated. Produced several months before the suicide bombings which killed fifty-six people (including the four suicide bombers) and injured over 700 more on the London transport system on 7 July 2005, the similarity between the opening story and the real-life bombings caused the BBC to consider dropping the episodes, but, in a decision which reinforced the contemporary significance of the series, they were screened on 12 September 2005 on BBC One (a day after the 9/11 anniversary) and 13 September 2005 on BBC Three, two months after the London bombings, with a warning that viewers might find some of the scenes disturbing.

Over ten series and eighty-six episodes, from 2002–11, Spooks provided an important counter-balance to the plethora of historical dramas and literary adaptations being produced in the same period. Topical and stylish, the series showed that American series did not have a monopoly on quality 'high-end' drama. With its ability, whether serendipitous or otherwise, to engage with contemporary realities and social anxieties Spooks reestablished the BBC's reputation for cutting-edge social-issue drama, reinvented for a post-9/11 audience.

Several other dramas engaged with post-9/11 issues during this period, albeit not as extensively as Spooks did over its nine-year run. Dirty War (BBC One, 24 September 2004) was a drama documentary about an Islamic terrorist attack on central London in which a 'dirty bomb' – a mixture of conventional explosives and radioactive material – is detonated. Co-written by Lizzie Mickery and director Daniel Percival, the ninety-minute drama showed the inadequacy of the emergency services in dealing with the attack, in a hypothetical situation analogous to the aftermath of the 9/11 attacks three years earlier. *Dirty War* was co-produced with HBO Films, as was the BBC's *House of Saddam* (BBC Two, July–August 2008), a four-part drama which charted the rise and fall of the Iraqi leader, Saddam Hussein, made two years after he had been captured and sentenced to death following the American-led invasion of Iraq. *House of Saddam* was preceded by *Saddam's Tribe* (Channel 4, 10 May 2007) on Channel 4, a single drama made by Tony Garnett's World Productions company about Saddam Hussein's family, which ruled Iraq for more than a quarter of a century.

Channel 4 was prominent in the production of political drama post-9/11, contemporary social-issue drama being the channel's forte. Peter Kosminsky was a key figure here, first of all with his dramatisation of the David Kelly affair, *The Government Inspector* (Channel 4, 17 March 2005), which examined the events leading up to the death of the British scientist and former United Nations weapons inspector Dr David Kelly who became caught up in the controversy over whether Iraq really did possess weapons of mass destruction prior to the invasion of Iraq in 2003. Kelly was interviewed by a BBC journalist, Andrew Gilligan, who subsequently reported that a claim in a government dossier that Iraq was capable of firing biological and chemical weapons within forty-five minutes, which Kelly was sceptical about, had been fabricated by the government in order to justify the invasion of Iraq. The identification of Kelly as the source for Gilligan's claim put him under intense pressure and led to his suicide. The subsequent inquiry into his death resulted in the BBC being criticised for its report and led to the resignation of both the BBC chairman, Gavyn Davies, and the director general, Greg Dyke. The events surrounding the death of David Kelly, therefore, had wider ramifications, involving Tony Blair's Labour government and the BBC, making the controversy one of the major issues of the period. *The Government Inspector* received a BAFTA award for Best Single Drama in 2006.

Kosminsky's next post-9/11 project was *Britz* (Channel 4, October–November 2007), a two-part drama about a brother and sister, the children of Pakistani immigrants, who respond differently to the political climate in Britain after 2001, which saw Muslims subjected to discrimination and violence following the 9/11 attacks and the London suicide bombings in July 2005.[13] In Kosminsky's drama, Sohail (Riz Ahmed), the brother, who is studying law in London, decides to join MI5 because he believes he needs to do something to help prevent further terrorist activities, while his sister Nasima (Manjinder Virk), who is studying medicine in Leeds, grows increasingly disenchanted with the attitude towards Muslims in Britain, leading her to make contact with a terrorist group in Pakistan after her family have sent her there for an arranged marriage when they discover she is in a relationship with an African man. The drama ends with Nasima apparently about to carry out a suicide bombing on her return to Britain.

Britz was written and directed by Kosminsky as a response to the 2005 Prevention of Terrorism Act, which saw the introduction of new control orders which increased the powers of the police to retain individuals suspected of being involved in terrorist activities. The control orders were widely used to restrict the activities of people from Muslim communities and were seen by many to be an infringement of civil liberties.

Also in 2007, Tony Marchant's *The Mark of Cain* (Channel 4, 12 April 2007) was about young British soldiers implicated in the torture and sexual abuse of Iraqi insurgents who they believe to be responsible for the death of their commanding officer. One of the soldiers photographs the abuse, in an echo of the real-life abuse perpetrated by American military personnel on Iraqi insurgents at Abu Ghraib prison in 2003–4, but the drama was as much about the culture of bullying in the army which forces soldiers to collude in the nefarious actions of their colleagues. Following its screening, the British Defence Secretary, Des Brown, expressed concerns that *The Mark of Cain* might increase hostility towards British forces abroad and endanger the lives of British soldiers. This was, perhaps, an indication of the drama's success in raising questions about British involvement in Iraq and at the BAFTA awards in 2008 *The Mark of Cain* won the award for Best Single Drama.

Peter Bowker wrote a similar drama about British soldiers in Iraq which was given a more extended treatment in the three-part *Occupation* (BBC One, 16–18 June 2009). Presenting three different points of view on the war, from the perspective of the three central characters, *Occupation* illustrated some of the complexities of the war. All three soldiers are seen in action with the army in Iraq in episode one and all three return to Iraq, but for different reasons, in episodes two and three. Sergeant Mike Swift (James Nesbitt) falls in love with an Iraqi woman, a doctor who is looking after a young girl Swift has heroically rescued; Corporal Danny Peterson (Stephen Graham) returns as a mercenary, providing 'security' to foreign contractors; and Lance Corporal Lee Hibbs (Warren Brown) returns because he genuinely wishes to contribute to the 'rebuilding' of Iraq.

Occupation was well received by the critics and won a BAFTA in 2010 for Best Drama Serial. However, in an article entitled '"Terrible things happen": Peter Bowker's *Occupation* and the Representation of the Iraq War in British Television Drama', Stephen Harper criticised the drama for its 'failure – despite certain powerfully oppositional moments and its generally sceptical register – to challenge official justifications for the invasion'.[14] Harper argued that, while *Occupation* contained an implicit critique of western involvement in Iraq and could be considered to be a progressive text, it was not a radical drama because it did not provoke the kind of controversy that such 'oppositional' dramas did in the 1960s and 70s, and which *The Mark of Cain* did when the Defence Secretary expressed concerns about it. Rather, Harper suggests, *Occupation* was symptomatic of the kind of cautious approach the BBC was adopting in its programming following the criticisms made of the corporation by the Hutton inquiry:

> Six years after the beginning of a war whose prosecution provoked widespread public dissent, the limited nature of *Occupation*'s critique of the war may suggest

something of the BBC's difficulty in creating contestatory drama in what some
have argued to be the conservative moment of post-Hutton public service
broadcasting.[15]

This caution on behalf of the BBC may explain why it took four years for *Occupation* to
reach the screen.

No such caution was apparent in Channel 4's production of post-9/11 and other
social-issue drama during this period. In addition to *The Government Inspector*, *The Mark
of Cain*, *Saddam's Tribe* and *Britz*, Channel 4 also screened Alistair Beaton's satirical drama
The Trial of Tony Blair (More4, 15 January 2007) which, like Beaton's earlier *A Very Social
Secretary* (More4, 10 October 2005), about New Labour Home Secretary David Blunkett,
was first shown on More4 before being shown on Channel 4. In *The Trial of Tony Blair*, the
ex-prime minister (played by Robert Lindsay) is brought before an international tribu-
nal to face charges of war crimes for taking Britain into the Iraq War. Acknowledging
Blair's strong Christian faith, Beaton speculated that his troubled conscience about Iraq
made him try to convert to Catholicism. In a case of life imitating art, it was revealed in
December 2007 that Tony Blair had, indeed, converted to Catholicism.

Complicit (Channel 4, 17 February 2013), another Channel 4 post-9/11 drama, focused
on a black MI5 operative's obsessive pursuit of a British Muslim who he suspects is planning a terrorist attack. Written by Guy Hibbert, who also wrote (with Paul Greengrass)
the BAFTA-winning *Omagh* (Channel 4, 27 May 2004), a drama documentary about the
1998 Omagh bombing which killed twenty-nine people, and *Five Minutes to Heaven* (BBC
Two, 5 April 2009), another Northern Ireland drama which won Hibbert a BAFTA writer's
award, *Complicit* controversially showed the MI5 agent, Edward Ebuko (David Oyelowo),
agreeing to the torture of Waleed (Arsher Ali) in an attempt to extract information. More
than ten years after the 9/11 attacks, *Complicit* showed that the 'War on Terror' was still
a topical political issue in television drama and that the issues involved were no longer
simply black and white, a question of 'good versus evil', as they often were in *Spooks*, but
were rather more complicated than that.

Not all social-issue drama post-9/11 was preoccupied with the 'War on Terror'. Abi
Morgan's two-part drama *Sex Traffic* (Channel 4, 2004) used a thriller format to explore
the trafficking of women from Eastern Europe to London, where they are forced to work
as prostitutes by the men operating the trafficking ring. A co-production between
Granada, Big Motion Pictures and the Canadian Broadcasting Corporation, *Sex Traffic* was
a powerful drama which received a BAFTA award for Best Drama Serial in 2005, contributing to Channel 4's impressive portfolio of social-issue drama during this period
and establishing Abi Morgan as an important writer.

Morgan's next projects were a BBC/HBO co-production about the 2004 South Asian
tsunami, *Tsunami: The Aftermath* (BBC Two, 28 November 2006), a feature film adaptation
of Monica Ali's novel *Brick Lane* (2007) and the award-winning *White Girl* (BBC Two, 10
March 2008), about a young Catholic girl's conversion to Islam following her family's
move to an Asian area of Bradford.[16] Other noteworthy Channel 4 dramas in this period
include Paula Milne's *Endgame* (4 May 2009), based on Robert Harvey's book *The Fall of*

Apartheid, about the secret talks that led to the end of apartheid in South Africa; *I Am Slave* (30 August 2010), about a case of modern-day slavery, largely based on the real-life case of a Sudanese woman kept in slavery in Sudan before being brought to London, where she managed to escape; and *The Promise* (2011), Peter Kosminsky's four-part drama about the British Mandate in Palestine, told from the point of view of a young woman visiting present-day Israel who learns about the pre-history of the Israeli/Arab conflict by reading the diary of her grandfather, a soldier in the British Army in Palestine shortly before the end of the British Mandate in 1948. Her reading is accompanied by flashbacks showing the British forces struggling against a Jewish insurgency in Palestine after the Second World War, a struggle which eventually led to the establishment of the state of Israel in 1948 and the beginning of the protracted conflict between Jews and Arabs following the departure of the British.

Having made his mark in the 1970s–80s with controversial social-issue dramas such as *Law and Order* and *The Nation's Health* (Channel 4, 1983), G. F. Newman reinvented himself during this period as a writer of popular television drama with *Judge John Deed* (BBC One, 2001–7), about a liberal judge who takes on the establishment while presiding over cases concerning topical social issues such as the MMR vaccine, GM crops and the potential health hazards of telephone masts, medical and environmental issues about which the health-conscious Newman felt passionately. More melodramatic than social realist, *Judge John Deed* proved very popular, running for six series and averaging over 6 million viewers. Having Martin Shaw play the eponymous judge contributed significantly to the popular appeal of the drama, which pulled off the remarkable feat of being radical, for a primetime television drama, while occasionally stretching belief beyond the realms of plausibility, which may be why the series did not prove to be quite as controversial as some of Newman's previous work.

Other social-issue dramas on BBC One included Paul Abbott's six-part political thriller *State of Play* (May–June 2003), about a journalist investigating political corruption in a complex plot involving collusion between the British government and the oil industry. The serial was a departure for Abbott from his previous character-based work and was highly acclaimed, even being given the dubious accolade of being made into a Hollywood feature film. Lizzie Mickery's *The State Within* (BBC One, November–December 2006) was also a six-part political drama, this time with an international post-9/11 plot involving a diplomatic crisis between the British and US governments after a plane is blown up in America by a British Asian suicide bomber. A co-production with BBC America, the plot included a right-wing US Defense Secretary pushing for US military intervention in a 'rogue' state in Central Asia, in a clear allusion to American involvement in Iraq and Afghanistan.

Also in the political thriller/conspiracy genre was Channel 4's *A Secret State* (7 November 2012), a four-part drama based on Chris Mullin's 1982 novel, *A Very British Coup*, previously made as a four-part drama by Channel 4 in 1988. In this new version, the British Prime Minister is killed in suspicious circumstances when the plane on which he is travelling crashes in the Atlantic as he returns from a visit to a US petrochemical company, where he has been seeking compensation for the deaths of nineteen people following an accident at the company's UK industrial plant. Deputy Prime Minister Tom Hawkins (Gabriel Byrne) conducts an investigation which uncovers a conspiracy between government, the military and big business. Mullin's book was believed to be inspired by rumours that the British Secret Service had tried to depose Harold Wilson's Labour government in the 1970s, a story which was itself dramatised in *The Plot Against Harold Wilson* (BBC Two, 16 March 2006).

Like BBC One and Channel 4 (but unlike ITV, whose production of social-issue drama was virtually non-existent during this period), BBC Two's contribution to social-issue drama since 2002 was also significant. Apart from *Tsunami: The Aftermath*, *House of Saddam* and *White Girl*, there was *The Day Britain Stopped* (BBC Two, 13 May 2003), a drama documentary about the potential for collapse of Britain's transport system, illustrated in a devastating chain of events following a fictional train crash, which provokes a national strike by the rail unions over safety concerns, and *Shoot the Messenger* (BBC Two, 30 August 2006), a controversial drama about a black teacher (played by David Oyelowo) who suffers a mental breakdown which manifests itself in a hatred of black people (the drama was originally entitled *Fuck Black People!*). Despite being written and produced by black women, *Shoot the Messenger* was described by an African media campaign group as 'one of the most racist, demeaning and misrepresentative films ever broadcast and commissioned by the BBC'.[17] This condemnation of the drama was not an isolated example. Sarita Malik, however, argued that *Shoot the Messenger*, despite its problematic elements, could actually be interpreted as a radical drama which provides a critique of social inequality: 'The drama's ambiguous orientations, stylistic innovations, the critical work it demands of its viewers, and ultimately the heterogeneous interpretations that the production makes possible – essentially through the theme of Black mental illness – all cement its radical credentials.'[18]

In contrast to the period from 1990–2002, when ITV was a significant producer of social-issue drama while the BBC poured its resources into 'safer' genres which were more likely to attract audiences, since 2002 this situation has been reversed, with ITV becoming more conservative in the wake of its consolidation into one large company while the BBC, post-John Birt, has been more adventurous in the production of social-issue drama, despite a period of caution following the Hutton inquiry. Meanwhile, Channel 4 saw something of a return to its radical roots under its new Head of Film and Drama, Tessa Ross, with a wide range of left-field drama being produced. An early indication of the progressive commissioning policy that would be adopted by Ross came with Peter Morgan's *The Deal* (Channel 4, 28 September 2003), directed by Stephen Frears, which was about the deal struck between Tony Blair and Gordon Brown over the leadership of the Labour Party in 1994. ITV had originally commissioned the drama but pulled out due to concerns about its political sensitivity at a time when the company was seeking approval from the New Labour government for the merger between Carlton and Granada. Channel 4 had no such concerns and with subsequent dramas including *Sex Traffic*, *Omagh*, *Yasmin* (13 January 2005), *The Government Inspector*, *The Mark of Cain*, *Saddam's Tribe*, *Britz*, *I Am Slave*, *The Promise*, *Secret State* and *Complicit* Channel 4 made a significant contribution to social-issue drama post-9/11.

Authored drama

In addition to the resurgence in social-issue drama post 9/11 there was also a renaissance in authored drama during this period. While many dramatists found it difficult to get original work produced in the 1990s, due to the preference for generic drama in a more competitive marketplace, writers such as Alan Bleasdale, Howard Brenton, Peter Flannery, Jimmy McGovern, Paula Milne, G. F. Newman and Stephen Poliakoff, who had established themselves as television writers before the 1990s, all had significant work produced in the 2000s. In addition, a new generation of writers emerged, or established themselves, during this period including Peter Bowker, Guy Hibbert, Jed Mercurio, Lizzie Mickery, Peter Moffat, Steven Moffat, Abi Morgan, Peter Morgan, Dominic Savage and Sally Wainwright.

The recent work of Bleasdale, Brenton, Flannery, McGovern and Newman has been mentioned in previous sections, although it should be noted that Flannery, in addition to his English Civil War drama, *The Devil's Whore*, also developed *Inspector George Gently* (BBC One, 2007–)[19] from the novels by Alan Hunter, while G. F. Newman, in addition to *Judge John Deed*, developed another legal drama series (with Matthew Hall) called *New Street Law* (BBC One, 2006–7), but unlike *Judge John Deed*, for which Newman wrote all twenty-nine feature-length episodes, he only wrote two of *New Street Law*'s twelve episodes. Meanwhile, Jimmy McGovern, in addition to *Gunpowder, Treason and Plot*, developed three themed anthology series in this period: *The Street* (BBC One, 2006–9), based around the lives of residents of a Manchester street, with each hour-long drama focusing on a different resident, successfully revived the anthology drama series and won a BAFTA award for Best Drama Series in 2007 and 2008; *Moving On* (BBC One, 2009–) was a daytime series of forty-five-minute dramas which succeeded *The Afternoon Play* (BBC One, 2003–7); and *Accused* (BBC One, 2010–12) was an anthology series in which each hour-long drama focused on a different character as they await the verdict on their court case. While McGovern wrote, or co-wrote, most of the episodes for *The Street* and *Accused*, *Moving On* was a vehicle for new writers and all three series demonstrated McGovern's concern to nurture new writers during this period, something that Paul Abbott also did with *Clocking Off*, *Linda Green*, *Shameless* (Channel 4, 2004–13) and *Hit & Miss* (Sky Atlantic, May–June 2012).[20]

Paul Abbott, in fact, was more often credited as the creator and executive producer of series in this period than the writer, a development suggesting a shift towards the American 'showrunner' model of television drama production which problematises the traditional notion of authorship in television drama. Throughout the 'golden age' of British television drama, from the late 1950s to the early 80s, it was the writer who was generally considered to be the author, but with the shift towards series and serials, written by a team of writers, this idea began to be eroded and it was only in a diminishing number of original dramas that the idea of authorship as the province of one writer persisted. Whereas Abbott was both the creator and writer on *State of Play* and the two-part *Alibi* (ITV, 2003), on the long-running *Shameless*, after writing all seven episodes of the first series and the feature-length Christmas special (Channel 4, 23 December 2004), he wrote just three of the ten episodes in series two and only one episode in the next five series as he handed over the writing to other writers. This followed the pattern established with *Clocking Off*, where he wrote all of the episodes on the first series but then gradually handed over the writing of individual episodes to other writers, withdrawing from writing episodes altogether by the fourth and final series. On *Linda Green*, which ran for two series, Abbott wrote six of the ten episodes in the first series, but then only two of the ten episodes in the second series.

Once *Shameless* was established as a popular and successful brand (the first series won a BAFTA for Best Drama Series in 2005; by series five it had increased to sixteen episodes and to twenty-two episodes in series eight), Abbott turned his attention to adapting it for television in the USA, where it was subjected to the American model of team-writing with eleven writers contributing to the first three series. He also created the three-part *Exile* (BBC One, 2011), produced by his own company, AbbottVision, but this was written by Danny Brocklehurst, one of the writers Abbott had nurtured on *Clocking Off* and *Linda Green*, while the six-part *Hit & Miss*, the first original drama series to be shown on Sky Atlantic, was conceived by Abbott but written entirely by Sean Conway.[21]

Stephen Poliakoff's 'second starburst'[22] continued in this period with *The Lost Prince* (BBC One, 2003), a two-part drama about the youngest child of King George V and Queen Mary, who was hidden from the world because he suffered from epilepsy, dying at the age of thirteen. This and Poliakoff's subsequent work was well served by the advent of the digital television era; indeed, his renaissance and success in this period may well be as a result of the development of high-quality, 'cinematic' aesthetics in television drama facilitated by new digital technology. This was certainly a feature of his dramas that was praised by the critics in his work from *Shooting the Past* onwards. Yet this predilection for stately, slow-moving dramas which privilege a rich and colourful *mise en scène* could sometimes seem overly self-indulgent, with more attention paid to the lavish surface detail and not enough to depth of character and narrative clarity. In his book on Poliakoff, Robin Nelson expresses such reservations about the feature-length *Friends and Crocodiles* (BBC One, 15 January 2006):

> Having argued that this phase of television work marks the high point of Poliakoff's career to date precisely because it brings together his playwright's capacity for character and dialogue with a film-maker's eye for fluid images in motion in a way that is perfectly suited to the digital TV medium, it may be that, in *Friends and Crocodiles*, Poliakoff veers to the cinematic at the expense of clarity of narrative and deep exploration of character which is still required, even of the most successful 'high-end' television drama.[23]

The feature-length *Gideon's Daughter* (BBC One, 26 February 2006), transmitted just a few weeks later, was a sequel to *Friends and Crocodiles* which continued 'the reflective commentary on the political times by picking up where *Friends and Crocodiles* left off, in the early years of "New Labour" following the success of Tony Blair's campaign in May 1997'.[24] With the narrative this time covering months rather than the decades of *Friends and Crocodiles*, the drama was more focused, providing an implicit critique of New Labour under Tony Blair which echoed the political concerns of some of Poliakoff's earlier work.

Another pair of dramas followed in 2007. *Joe's Palace* (BBC One, 4 November 2007) and *Capturing Mary* (BBC Two, 12 November 2007) were both set in the same large west London house and shared the same central character, Joe (Danny Lee Wynter), the young caretaker employed to look after the now empty house. Both dramas adopt the familiar Poliakovian theme of exploring the past in order to see how it has shaped the present, in this case by having characters remember events associated with the house. Lacking the contemporary political commentary of *Friends and Crocodiles* and *Gideon's Daughter*, *Joe's Palace* and *Capturing Mary* were more dependent on the 'art television' tropes characteristic of much of Poliakoff's recent work. These tropes were also evident in his 2009 feature film, *Glorious 39*, and the six-part *Dancing on the Edge*, both of which were set in the 1930s. While the narrative of *Dancing on the Edge* involved the murder of one of the singers in the black jazz band, the serial could hardly be described as a thriller, its languorous pace and exquisite attention to period detail exemplifying Poliakoff's authorial style.

Paula Milne was hardly inactive in the 1990s, having had three original serials produced: *Die Kinder* (BBC Two, 1990), *The Politician's Wife* (Channel 4, 1995) and *The Fragile Heart* (Channel 4, 1996), as well as the female detective series *Chandler and Co* (BBC One, 1994–5), plus three feature films and the untransmitted *Thursday the 12th*. She continued to be equally productive in the 2000s. In addition to *The Virgin Queen*, *Endgame*, *White Heat* and the adaptations of *Small Island* and *The Night Watch*, all previously mentioned, there was *Second Sight* (BBC One, 2000–1), an unconventional crime drama starring Clive Owen as a police detective who is losing his sight; the two-part psychological thriller *State of Mind* (ITV, 2003); *Whatever it Takes* (ITV, 26 July 2009), a single drama about celebrity culture; and, taking her into her fifth decade as a television dramatist, *The Politician's Husband* (BBC Two, April–May 2013), a three-part sequel to the earlier *The Politician's Wife*, and *Legacy* (BBC Two, 28 November 2013), a Cold War drama set in the 1970s in which a trainee British spy tries to recruit a Russian diplomat he knew at university. Having begun her career as a television writer in the 1970s, by 2013 Paula Milne was firmly established as the pre-eminent female dramatist in British television.

Whereas both established and new writers found it difficult to get original work commissioned in the 1990s, many new writers first having to establish themselves writing for soaps and popular series before they were given a chance to do anything original, a new generation of talented writers emerged in the 2000s, contributing to the diversity of drama produced in this period. Peter Bowker was one such writer. He started off writing for *Casualty*, *Medics* (Granada, 1990–5), *Out of the Blue* (BBC One, 1995–6) and *Peak Practice* (ITV, 1993–2002) in the 1990s before writing the four-part science fiction series, *The Uninvited* (ITV, 1997); the six-part *Undercover Heart* (BBC One, 1998); three feature-length dramas: Dickens' *A Christmas Carol* (LWT, 20 December 2000), *Hidden Treasure* (LWT, 14 October 2001) and *Flesh and Blood* (BBC Two, 25 September 2002); *The Miller's Tale* (BBC One, 11 September 2003), part of the modernised *Canterbury Tales* series;

and the six-part series, *Single* (ITV, October–December 2003). But it was the six-part musical drama, *Blackpool* (BBC One, November–December 2004) which really brought him to critical attention. Drawing comparisons with the innovative work of Dennis Potter, *Blackpool* differed in that it had the actors singing the musical numbers, rather than having them lip-synch to songs as in Potter's musical dramas. In this respect *Blackpool* was perhaps less original than Potter's work but it was, nevertheless, an engaging and well-crafted serial, enlivened by excellent performances from David Morrissey, Sarah Parish and David Tennant as the three central characters. It spawned a one-off sequel, *Viva Blackpool* (BBC One, 10 June 2006), two years later.

In addition to *A Midsummer Night's Dream* (BBC One, 28 November 2005), part of the *ShakespeaRe-told* series, *Occupation* and his adaptation of *Wuthering Heights*, Bowker also wrote the six-part *Desperate Romantics* (BBC Two, July–August 2009), loosely based on Franny Moyle's book about the Pre-Raphaelite Brotherhood; *Eric and Ernie* (BBC Two, 1 January 2011), a biographical drama about Eric Morecambe and Ernie Wise; and the three-part *From There to Here* (BBC One, May–June 2014), which covers four years at the end of the twentieth century, beginning with the IRA bomb which caused widespread damage in central Manchester in 1996. Not only has Bowker been very prolific, an indication in itself of the greater opportunities available to writers in this period, his oeuvre is also very diverse, embracing science fiction, original dramas, adaptations, modern-day versions of Chaucer and Shakespeare, historical drama, biographical drama, contemporary drama about Iraq and Britain under New Labour and a musical murder mystery.

Peter Moffat has been less eclectic than Bowker but almost as prolific. As a former barrister it is not surprising that he made his television debut with an episode of *Kavanagh QC* (ITV, 1995–2001) before creating the underrated legal drama series *North Square* (Channel 4, October–December 2000) for which he wrote seven of the ten episodes. In 2003, his four-part drama on the *Cambridge Spies* was transmitted, followed by *Hawking* (BBC Two, 13 April 2004), a single drama about the physicist Stephen Hawking, and his modern-day version of *Macbeth* (BBC One, 14 November 2005), shown as part of the *ShakespeaRe-told* series. Further legal dramas followed with *Criminal Justice* (BBC One, June–July 2008), shown over five consecutive nights – an innovation which proved very successful, enhancing the emotional intensity of the drama – which won a BAFTA award for Best Drama Serial and the Best Writer award for Moffat. After a single drama about the development of Albert Einstein's theory of relativity, *Einstein and Eddington* (BBC Two, 22 November 2008), Moffat wrote a second series of *Criminal Justice* (BBC One, October 2009), again shown over five consecutive nights, and created *Silk* (BBC One, 2011–), a legal drama focusing on a group of barristers. *The Village* (previously discussed) marks a departure from Moffat's preoccupation with legal drama, but is no less serious in its focus on rural working-class life in the early twentieth century. In contrast to the frivolity and superficiality of some recent drama, Peter Moffat is a leading advocate for serious drama in the digital age. It may be no coincidence that, since *North Square*, all of his work has been for the BBC.

Apart from her two-part debut, *My Fragile Heart* (ITV, 2000), the four-part *Murder* (BBC Two, May–June 2002) and the feature-length *Royal Wedding* (BBC Two, 17 May 2010), which took the 1981 wedding of Charles and Diana as its subject but showed it from the perspective of a Welsh mining village, most of Abi Morgan's work for television has already been mentioned. With her other work including *Sex Traffic*, *Tsunami: The Aftermath*, *White Girl*, *The Hour* and *Birdsong*, it is clear that Morgan is a writer with a considerable range. In addition to her television work she has also written four successful screenplays since 2007, including *The Iron Lady* (2011) and *Shame* (2011), and her work for the theatre has been significant, with thirteen plays produced since 1998.

Peter Morgan's work for television, in addition to the previously mentioned *The Deal*, *Henry VIII* and *Colditz*, includes the six-part *The Jury* (ITV, February–March 2002), which was followed by a second series in 2011; *Longford* (Channel 4, 26 October 2006), about Lord Longford's visits to the Moors Murderer, Myra Hindley, which won Morgan a BAFTA Best Writer award; and *The Special Relationship* (BBC Two, 18 September 2010), the third part of Morgan's 'Tony Blair trilogy', which began with *The Deal* and continued with the feature film, *The Queen* (2006). Throughout this period Peter Morgan has also written for the theatre and, increasingly, for the cinema.

Like Stephen Poliakoff, who since the 1990s has written and directed all of his television work, Dominic Savage is also a writer/director, but there the resemblance ends. Whereas Poliakoff's work is largely concerned with revisiting the past and is imbued with 'art television' tropes, Savage's work is resolutely contemporary and realist in style. Significantly, his first television drama, *Nice Girl* (BBC Two, 11 May 2000), won him the BAFTA Best New Director award, rather than a writer's award, while his next, *When I Was 12* (BBC Two, 26 September 2001), won a BAFTA for Best Single Drama. *Out of Control* (BBC One, 15 September 2002) was the third in a loose trilogy of dramas about social deprivation, a theme of much of his work. The feature film, *Love + Hate* (2005) was about interracial love in a northern English town, while the feature-length drama *Born Equal* (BBC One, 17 December 2006) comprised several inter-related narratives about poverty, homelessness, race and immigration. *Freefall* (BBC Two, 14 July 2009) was about the consequences of the 2008 financial crisis, while both the two-part *Dive* (BBC Two, 2010) and the five-part *True Love* (BBC One, 2012) explored issues around relationships in a slight departure from the social-issue imperative informing his previous work. *True Love* was also developed through improvisation, an approach which associates him with earlier writer/directors such as Mike Leigh and Les Blair, but it was less successful than his previous social realist work and was criticised for its use of sentimental music which detracted from the drama. Whereas the authorial voice in television drama has mostly been that of the writer, Dominic Savage represents a different tradition of authorship where the authorial signature is associated with a writer/director working closely with the actors to develop a more 'realist' form of drama.

Kay Mellor continued to be a prolific writer in this period. After *Band of Gold*, *Playing the Field* and *Fat Friends*, which she created but on which she shared the writing with several other writers, Mellor wrote the six-part *Between the Sheets* (ITV, November–December 2003) about the relationships and affairs of several inter-related couples, and *Strictly Confidential* (ITV, November–December 2006), a six-part series about a bisexual ex-police officer, now working as a sex therapist while acting as a consultant for the police on a series of sex murders. Mellor also wrote the veterinary drama *The Chase* (BBC One, 2006–7), with five other writers contributing to the eleven-part second series, the two-part *A Passionate Woman* (BBC One, 2010), based on her 1992 stage play, and *The Syndicate* (BBC One, 2012–), about a group of supermarket workers (in the first series) and hospital workers (in the second series) who have big lottery wins, with ensuing complications. Like Sally Wainwright, who wrote four episodes of *Playing the Field*, Kate Mellor is a northern writer (she is from Leeds) who writes popular dramas and specialises in roles for women.

Like Kay Mellor, Sally Wainwright began her television writing career on *Coronation Street* and other soaps before making her authorial debut with *At Home with the Braithwaites* (Yorkshire, 2000–3) in 2000. Her prolific output since has included the previously mentioned *Sparkhouse* and episodes for *The Canterbury Tales* and *ShakespeaRe-told*, the six-part comedy drama, *Jane Hall* (ITV, July–August 2006) about a female bus driver (based on Wainwright's own experience as a bus driver in the 1980s), *The Amazing Mrs Pritchard* (BBC One, October–November 2006), about an ordinary woman with no political experience who becomes prime minister, the feature-length *Dead Clever* (ITV, 1 January 2007) and the three-part *Unforgiven* (ITV, 2009), both about women who have been convicted of, or are implicated in, past crimes. Her best work is arguably her most recent: the highly successful *Scott & Bailey* (ITV, 2011–), about a female police detective partnership, *Last Tango in Halifax* (BBC One, 2012–), a romantic drama about the relationship between two childhood sweethearts who meet again in their seventies and announce to their families that they plan to get married, and *Happy Valley* (BBC One, April–June 2014), an accomplished crime drama starring Sarah Lancashire as a no-nonsense police officer investigating a kidnapping in a small northern town. With many of these dramas produced by the Manchester-based independent, Red Production Company, Wainwright, who was born in Yorkshire, is firmly associated with northern, working-class drama, usually featuring women as the central characters, with a compelling blend of humour and pathos, making for drama which is popular with a broad demographic.

The wide range of writers, and writer/directors discussed in this section reflects the diversity of authored drama in the digital age, a period in which established writers have been given a new lease of life, albeit sometimes with less radical drama than might have been commissioned in the 1970s–80s, while a number of new writers have graduated from the experience of writing for soaps and generic drama in the 1990s to create their own original drama in the 2000s. In their breadth and creative diversity these British television writers, and the many others not mentioned here, have contributed to a renaissance in authored drama in the digital age which, while it may not be on the same scale as that of the 1960s–70s, could be described as a 'new wave' of British television dramatists.

Generic hybridity

Peter Bowker's *Blackpool* is just one example of an increasing hybridity in television drama in recent years. While the mixture of a musical drama and a detective/murder mystery was unusual, contributing to the originality of the drama, the blending of elements from different genres has become more frequent as television companies seek ways to maximise audiences in an increasingly fragmented and competitive market-place. Another unusual but highly successful example of this was *Life on Mars* (BBC One, 2006–7) which mixed elements of science fiction with the police procedural by having a present-day police detective travel back in time to find himself part of a police division which had more in common with *The Sweeney* than a modern, twenty-first-century police force. The time-travelling element was the result of an accident when Detective Chief Inspector Sam Tyler (John Simm) is knocked down by a speeding car and wakes up to find himself in 1973 rather than 2006.[25] Whether this is a fantasy and he is really in a coma is never really made clear, but it made for a fascinating culture clash with Tyler having to adjust to the cruder methods employed by his new police colleagues in 1973. James Chapman has summarised the generic blending that resulted from this original premise:

> *Life on Mars* exemplifies the erosion of traditional genre boundaries that has become a significant trend in contemporary television drama. It is, at once, both a realist text, dealing with social issues and problems including crime, racism and sexism, and an example of telefantasy in that it is posited on a fantastic premise: that of a policeman from the present (2006) who suddenly finds himself living and working in the past (1973).[26]

Life on Mars was particularly successful because it combined two of the most popular contemporary genres: the police series, which maintained its popularity in the 2000s but which was given a retro twist here by invoking a classic police series of the 1970s (and thus broadening its potential audience by attracting older viewers with memories of *The Sweeney*), and fantasy, a genre more popular with younger viewers which was given a new lease of life in this period, partly through the relaunch of *Doctor Who* in 2005. The suggestion of time-travel in *Life on Mars* could be seen as a direct allusion to *Doctor Who*, but the idea for *Life on Mars* was actually first pitched by its creators, Matthew Graham and Ashley Pharoah, in 1998, when *Doctor Who* had been absent from British television screens for nine years. In 1998, however, Graham and Pharoah found that TV commissioners were not prepared to take a chance with such an unlikely-sounding premise. That *Life on Mars* was eventually commissioned, by Jane Tranter, Head of Drama at the BBC, and produced by BBC Wales in Cardiff, home of the revived *Doctor Who*, is a sign of the more progressive attitude being adopted by TV drama commissioners in the 2000s.

A sequel to *Life on Mars*, called *Ashes to Ashes* (BBC One, 2008–10) after another David Bowie song, had a similar theme, this time with policewoman Alex Drake (Keeley Hawes) as the central character who, after being shot in 2008, inexplicably regains conscious-ness in 1981, enabling a similar culture clash to be played out, but this time with the focus on Thatcher's Britain in the early 1980s. Repeating the unusual narrative dis-placement of *Life on Mars* risked stretching an original idea too far, but it did not prevent *Ashes to Ashes* running for three series – one more, in fact, than *Life on Mars*.

Generic hybridity was most evident in the police/detective/crime genre which, following the success of *Silent Witness* in the UK and *CSI: Crime Scene Investigation* (CBS, 2000–) in the USA, grew increasingly forensic in nature, partly as a consequence of the availability of new technology unknown to crime investigators in the 1970s–80s (part of the success of *Life on Mars* was the conflict between Sam Tyler, with his knowledge of forensics, and the old school police detective Gene Hunt [Philip Glenister], to whom forensics was anathema and whose approach to solving crimes was largely instinctive). So integral has forensics become to police/crime/detective drama in the 2000s that it has almost become a genre in its own right. Like the American series *CSI*, which expanded into a franchise with *CSI: Miami* (CBS, 2002–) and *CSI: New York* (CBS, 2004–), the popularity of *Silent Witness* shows no sign of abating. It has also survived the departure of its lead character, Professor Sam Ryan (Amanda Burton), who was replaced with a new forensic pathologist, Dr Nikki Alexander (Emilia Fox), in 2004. While the police do have a presence in *Silent Witness*, their role is often marginal to that of the forensic pathologists, who effectively take on the task of personally investigating crimes and apprehending suspects, making them the central characters and forensic pathology (rather than routine detective work) the driving force of the narrative.

Forensics was also integral to *Waking the Dead*, a police/detective/crime drama created by Barbara Machin, featuring a special police unit set up to investigate 'cold cases', unsolved deaths from the past which forensics now offers a means of solving. The special police unit comprised a team led by Detective Superintendent Boyd (Trevor Eve) and included psychological profiler Dr Grace Foley (Sue Johnston) as well as a forensic pathologist (originally Dr Frankie Wharton, played by Hollie Aird). The series was very popular, averaging more than 8 million viewers. A spin-off, *The Body Farm* (BBC One, September–October 2011), featuring Tara Fitzgerald as forensic pathologist Dr Eve Lockhart, who appeared in *Waking the Dead* from 2007–11, lasted for just one series, suggesting that it was the concept of a specialised team investigating 'cold cases' that was the secret of *Waking the Dead*'s success, not just the contribution of the forensic pathologist.

New Tricks (BBC One, 2003–) is also based around the concept of a special police unit set up to investigate unsolved crimes and has proved to be even more popular, often exceeding 9 million viewers with a formula which is less 'dark' than that of *Waking the Dead* and with a cast of well-known actors – Alun Armstrong, James Bolam, Amanda Redman and Dennis Waterman forming the original team – of a certain age (mid-forties to sixties) attracting an older audience demographic. Indeed, the difference with this team is that, apart from the Amanda Redman character (replaced by Tamzin Outhwaite in 2013), they comprise retired police officers who bring their previous experience as 'old dogs' to solving past crimes. As the adage which gives the series its title goes: 'you can't teach an old dog new tricks' and this premise has clearly struck a chord with an ageing television audience who may well remember the actors from such popular 1960s–80s programmes as *The Likely Lads* (BBC Two, 1964–6), *Whatever Happened to the Likely Lads?* (BBC One, 1973–4), *The Sweeney*, *When the Boat Comes In*, *Minder* and the *Beiderbecke* trilogy (Yorkshire, 1985–8).[27] Not only does *New Tricks* combine elements of the police/detective series with the cold case/unsolved murders sub-genre, it also injects a lot of humour into what is essentially a crime drama, maximising its audience by blending the old and the new, past and present.

Law and Order: UK (ITV, 2009–) is a police series/legal drama hybrid, giving equal time to the legal proceedings which follow the investigation of a crime which takes place in the first half of each episode. Based on the popular US *Law and Order* franchise, *Law and Order: UK* is a relatively rare example of a successful British version of a popular American series. It is not uncommon for American television to remake successful British series, which usually turn out to be less successful when transposed to an American context. It is much less common for a British company, in this case Kudos Film and Television (responsible for *Spooks*, *Life on Mars*, *Ashes to Ashes*, *Occupation* and *The Hour*, among many others), to produce a successful remake of an American series.

There have also been crime/supernatural hybrids in this period with *Marchlands* (ITV, February–March 2011) and *Lightfields* (ITV, February–March 2013). Both serials were based on a similar idea of three families living in the same house in different time periods: 1968, 1987 and 2010 in the case of *Marchlands*, 1944, 1975 and 2012 in the case of *Lightfields*. In each case, a mysterious death at the house in the earlier period has repercussions for the families living there in later decades when the spirit of the dead person appears to certain members of the household. The serials were murder mysteries with a supernatural element played out at different historical moments, a combination which, once again, was designed to maximise the audience through its genre blending while also targeting a wide age range by setting the action in different periods.

Other series such as *Ripper Street* and *Whitechapel* (ITV, 2009–13) hybridise past and present by combining the crime genre and historical drama. *Ripper Street* is set in Whitechapel in 1889, shortly after the Jack the Ripper murders, but gives the period a particularly 'modern' treatment,[28] whereas *Whitechapel* is set in London's East End in the present-day but references the Jack the Ripper murders of 1888, even investigating a copycat Ripper murderer in present-day Whitechapel. Rebecca Williams has discussed *Whitechapel* as 'Gothic horror', highlighting another aspect of generic hybridity, and argues that the series' references to the past, far from offering reassurance, in the way that costume drama often provides a nostalgic representation of the past, suggest that history 'seems doomed to repeat itself':

> Eschewing straightforward depictions of the past as instructive or as a way of reflecting on the conditions of the present, *Whitechapel* presents the area's violent, bloody past in a more complicated way. Here, history seems doomed to repeat itself in vicious cycles of murder and violence, and information about what has occurred before does not necessarily lead to the prevention of further crimes or to a conclusive resolution of the narrative.[29]

While generic drama continued to be popular throughout this period, with continuing series including the police/detective dramas *Midsomer Murders* (ITV, 1997–), *Inspector George Gently*, *DCI Banks* (ITV, 2010–), *Vera*, *Scott & Bailey*, *Death in Paradise* (BBC One, 2011–),

Line of Duty (BBC Two, 2012–) and *Broadchurch* (ITV, 2013–), and medical dramas such as *Casualty*, *Holby City* and *Doctors* (BBC One, 2000–), the tendency towards hybridisation, a characteristic of postmodernism which persists into the digital age, has made contemporary television drama both more interesting and less predictable, mixing up previously self-contained genres and generic traits as part of the continuing reinvention of British television drama in the twenty-first century.

New forms of TV drama

One very positive outcome of the digital age has been the increase in digital channels which has enabled television companies to target different audience segments with new forms of television drama. This is most apparent with BBC Three and E4, both digital channels targeting the fifteen to thirty-five age group with a variety of youth-oriented programming. Channel 4 also rediscovered the innovatory remit of its early years with a number of youth-oriented dramas in the 2000s, including *As If* (2001–4), a series based around the exploits of a group of young people sharing a house in London. *As If* was, in some ways, a younger version of *This Life* and, where the stylistic innovations of that mid-1990s drama were made possible by new digital technology, *As If* similarly made full use of digital cameras and digital editing to create a flamboyant visual style distinguished by rapid cutting, unusual camera angles, zooms, slow motion and a colourful *mise en scène*, complemented by a soundtrack replete with a variety of pop and indie music.

Teachers was another Channel 4 drama targeting the fifteen to thirty-five-year-old audience which utilised non-naturalistic stylistic motifs, including rapid cutting and unusual shot transitions, as well as surreal imagery and fantasy sequences, to differentiate itself from the naturalistic drama generally targeted at a mainstream audience.[30] With *Shameless*, which mixed social realism with some new stylistic innovations, Channel 4 started screening episodes on E4, its digital channel, a week before they were screened on Channel 4, with the exception of the first episode of each series which was only shown on Channel 4. A similar strategy was adopted for *Sugar Rush* (Channel 4, 2005–6), a teen drama based on Julie Burchill's novel about a fifteen-year-old lesbian, with the first and last episode of the first series debuting on Channel 4 while the remaining episodes were first shown on E4. With the second series (June–August 2006) every episode was shown first on E4 and then repeated a week later on Channel 4.

Dubplate Drama (Channel 4, 2005–9) was an 'interactive' drama based around a young female rapper (played by Shystie) trying to make it in the urban music business. Targeting a young black audience, the interactive element involved viewers voting (by text) at the end of each episode on how the narrative should proceed, based on two possibilities. The first series (November–December 2005) consisted of six fifteen-minute episodes and was followed by a second series (September–October 2007) comprising six thirty-minute episodes. It concluded with a feature-length two-part series in June–July 2009. The series was also shown on E4 and was available to download to mobile phones.

Skins: teenage drama in the digital age

Skins (E4, 2007–13) was a fully fledged E4 drama, the first series not being shown on Channel 4 until seven months after its E4 debut. Susan Berridge has discussed the significant role Channel 4 has played in the development of youth television programmes and especially dramas aimed at a teenage audience.[31] *As If* and *Sugar Rush* are two examples of this, but it was the introduction of E4 as a digital youth-oriented channel that really gave a boost to the production of British youth dramas, enabling Channel 4 to re-establish through its new digital channel some of the reputation it had in the 1980s for challenging, cutting-edge representations. As Berridge observes:

> the legacy of the early days of Channel 4 is evident in the ethnic, racial, sexual
> and class diversity of the teenage characters in *Skins*. For example, the core
> teenage cast of series 1 and 2 features a black female, a Muslim male and a
> homosexual male. While US teen dramas also often feature central non-white or
> homosexual characters, this tends to be an either/or matter. Moreover, the
> centrality of an openly gay teen can be seen as part of a longer tradition of overt
> homosexual portrayals on Channel 4.[32]

Skins was developed by the father/son team of Brian Elsley and Jamie Brittain, and the latter was instrumental in persuading his father that the series should not portray teenagers as seen by adults. Consequently, young writers were recruited to ensure that the series reflected the interests and concerns of young people, 'free from a moralising adult agenda'.[33] In order to keep the series fresh the cast was replaced after the second and fourth series, so that three generations of teenagers appeared over the first six series, with some of the former cast members returning for the seventh and final series, which took the form of three two-part stories, each featuring a character from the earlier series. The success of *Skins* led to it being remade for MTV in America in 2011, but the portrayal of sex and drug use among teenagers, although possibly tamer than that in the original British series, proved controversial, with accusations of 'child por-nography' causing many of the advertisers to withdraw from the programme. As a result the US *Skins* lasted for only one series.

Dead Set (E4, 2008) was a five-part series, shown on E4 over five consecutive nights in October 2008, ending on Halloween, which satirised the reality TV show, *Big Brother* (Channel 4, 2000–10) by having a hoard of zombies surround the *Big Brother* house, trap-ping the contestants and production staff inside. The series was written by Charlie Brooker, whose vitriolic *Screenwipe* (BBC Four, 2006–8) review programme had already made clear his loathing for reality shows such as *Big Brother*. *Dead Set* was Brooker's revenge, ending with the zombies breaking into the house and killing the contestants, who subsequently turn into zombies. *Dead Set* was unequivocally 'horror TV',[34] and Brooker followed it up with *Black Mirror* (Channel 4, 2011–), which might be described as science fiction in that it presented a dystopian view of new technology. Original and innovative, *Black Mirror* went beyond satire to present a futuristic warning about tele-vision as 'the "black mirror" … on every wall, on every desk, in the palm of every hand: the cold, shiny screen of a TV, a monitor, a smartphone'.[35]

Misfits (E4, 2009–13) could also be described as science fiction as it featured a group of young offenders doing community service who acquire supernatural powers when they are caught in an electrical storm. Filmed largely on the Thamesmead estate in south-east London, with its concrete brutalist architecture, the iconography of the series is both social realist and futuristic, with the supernatural powers of the central charac-ters realised through special effects which introduce an element of telefantasy into the narrative, providing a generic mix which made for a very original drama. That originality was recognised in 2010 when *Misfits* received a BAFTA award for Best Drama Series, the first time that a series screening on a digital channel had won the award.

In 2012 the BAFTA for Best Drama Series went to another drama from a digital channel, *The Fades* (BBC Three, 2011), Jack Thorne's six-part series about a seventeen-year-old who is able to see vengeful spirits of the dead, known as the Fades, who are seeking to break back into the world and destroy the human race. Another series that showed the popularity of supernatural drama with young audiences, *The Fades* was imaginative and original, illustrating the extent to which, by 2011, the digital channels, BBC Three and E4, had become the home of innovative drama.[36]

Since its launch in 2003, BBC Three has been responsible for a number of innovative dramas, including Russell T Davies' three-part *Casanova* (2005) – a subject previously dramatised by Dennis Potter in 1971 – which featured David Tennant as the young Casanova and Peter O'Toole as the old Casanova. This was followed, later the same year, by *Funland* (BBC Three, October–November 2005), an eleven-part comedy-thriller (made up of one fifty-minute episode and ten half-hour episodes) set in Blackpool, written by Jeremy Dyson and Simon Ashdown, which contained much of the dark humour of *The League of Gentlemen* (BBC Two, 1999–2002), which Dyson had previously created with Mark Gatiss, Steve Pemberton and Reece Shearsmith.

The *Doctor Who* spin-off *Torchwood* (BBC, 2006–11) was introduced on BBC Three, where its first series screened from October 2006–January 2007, before graduating to

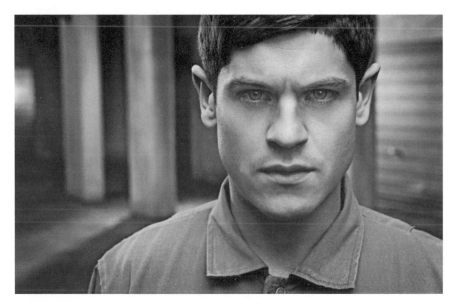

Social realism meets the supernatural in *Misfits*

BBC Two and then BBC One as it became more popular. The creator of *Misfits*, Howard Overman, wrote *Dis/Connected* (BBC Three, 31 March 2008) as the pilot for a BBC Three series which was not commissioned, perhaps because the subject matter – teenage suicide – was too realist, lacking the supernatural element which made *Misfits*, *The Fades* and *Being Human* (BBC Three, 2008–13) so successful. *Being Human* was created by Toby Whithouse and featured three people sharing a flat who are all trying to be human, although one is a ghost, one a werewolf and one a vampire. The series was another generic hybrid, combining the supernatural and moments of bloody horror with comedy, an unlikely mix but one which, as in *Misfits*, proved to be a successful combination with its youthful audience. The series was one of the most successful on BBC Three, with series two and three regularly attracting over a million viewers. *Being Human* was twice nominated for Best Drama Series at BAFTA, losing out to *Misfits* and *Sherlock* (BBC One, 2010–), but was voted Best Drama Series at the Writers' Guild of Great Britain Awards in 2009, 2010 and 2012.

Being Human, *Skins* and *Misfits* all ended in 2013 but new dramas were introduced to replace them. *In the Flesh* (BBC Three, 2013–) was another supernatural drama with an intriguing premise involving the rehabilitation of people who turned into zombies in 2009 when 'The Rising', a zombie apocalypse, occurred. Kieren Walker (Luke Newberry), a teenager who committed suicide and was buried the day before 'The Rising', returns to his parental home following his rehabilitation, wearing contact lenses to disguise his 'partially deceased' appearance and having daily injections which help to maintain his PDS (partially deceased syndrome) status. He meets up with other PDS patients in his home village, but they face prejudice from other villagers, some of whom are part of a local vigilante group who want to kill the 'rotters', as they describe PDS sufferers. Like many dramas about outsiders, In the Flesh could be seen as a metaphor for the hatred and oppression of 'the other', whether blacks, Muslims, homosexuals, or teenagers rebelling against social conformity.

Black teenagers formed the cast of Youngers (E4, 2013–), which began an eight-episode run on E4 shortly after In the Flesh made its debut on BBC Three. Set on an estate in south-east London, Youngers is about a group of friends trying to succeed on the urban music scene, but as they become more successful their problems increase. Like the earlier Dubplate Drama, but without the 'interactive' element, Youngers was attempting to cater for a black teenage audience, a group not well served on British TV.[37]

Utopia (Channel 4, 2013–) was a conspiracy thriller about a group of people in possession of a cult graphic novel which is rumoured to have predicted the worst disasters of the last century and which is being sought by a shady organisation called 'The Network'. Visually striking and controversial because of its violence, Utopia contributed to Channel 4's impressive schedule of original drama during this period. In addition to the series already mentioned, other new Channel 4 dramas included Red Riding (2009), a three-part adaptation of David Peace's Red Riding Quartet (1999–2002), set against the backdrop of the Yorkshire Ripper murders in the late 1970s; This Is England '86 (2010) and This Is England '88 (2011), sequels to Shane Meadows' feature film, This Is England (2006); Dates (June–July 2013), a series of nine half-hour dramas, created by Brian Elsley, featuring the first dates between people who meet through an online dating agency; and Southcliffe (2013), a four-part drama written by Tony Grisoni about a series of shootings in a small market town.

While many of the cutting-edge dramas in this period were on the new digital channels, leading Ben Dowell to write on the Guardian website in 2011: 'channels which target the under 35s are emerging as among the best places for boldness and innovation in UK TV drama',[38] innovation in television drama was not restricted to the minority channels. Although there was not much evidence of innovation on ITV, BBC One transmitted several series which showed that dramas could be both innovative and popular. Hustle (BBC One, 2004–12), a slick crime drama about a group of con artists, produced by Kudos Film and Television, incorporated non-naturalistic techniques such as characters talking to camera or scenes in which time stops and the action is frozen while the characters talk about the nature of the con, either to the audience or among themselves. The technique was used to illustrate how the con, which was often complex, would be achieved, when the characters were working it out for themselves, or had been achieved, when it was explained for the benefit of the audience. Hustle also incorporated other non-naturalistic elements, such as fantasy sequences, illustrating the extent to which even popular mainstream drama was utilising new digital technology in order to interrupt the narrative flow and address the audience in new ways.

Perhaps the most significant development in British television drama in this period was the revival of the longest-running science fiction series in the world, Doctor Who (BBC One, 1963–89, 1996, 2005–). Apart from a one-off, and fairly poorly received, TV movie in

1996, *Doctor Who* had been absent from British television screens for fourteen years when Russell T Davies was commissioned to write a new series to be produced by BBC Wales in Cardiff. The first episode of the new series premiered on 26 March 2005, with Christopher Eccleston as the ninth Doctor and Billie Piper as his companion, Rose Tyler. The episode attracted an audience of 10 million and the series was a huge success, winning a BAFTA award for Best Drama Series in 2006. Christopher Eccleston, an established actor who made his name in the 1990s with *Our Friends in the North* and *Hillsborough*, brought a darker, more serious quality to the new series which enabled it to be established as a serious drama for adults, as well as telefantasy for younger viewers.

Not wanting to get typecast, however, Eccleston decided to leave at the end of the series, to be replaced by David Tennant as the tenth Doctor, through the established precedent of 'regeneration', a narrative conceit which has enabled *Doctor Who* to negotiate numerous changes and extend its life over six decades. David Tennant was also an established actor but with a less 'serious' persona than Eccleston and his charismatic performance as the tenth Doctor helped the series to maintain and build on its success. With Russell T Davies masterminding the revival and Steven Moffat contributing some excellent scripts, the new *Doctor Who* made full use of digital technology that was not available in the 1980s, when the series was criticised for its 'low-tech' appearance, leading to it being axed.[39] With a bigger budget and access to better special effects, plus being placed in the hands of writers who were self-confessed fans of *Doctor Who*, the new series was a triumph and has become the most written-about programme on British television.[40]

In November 2013 *Doctor Who* celebrated its fiftieth anniversary with a seventy-five-minute episode, 'The Day of the Doctor' (BBC One, 23 November 2013), written by Steven Moffat, who took over from Russell T Davies as *Doctor Who*'s lead writer in 2009. The broadcast was a major event, being transmitted in 2D and 3D, screened simultaneously in ninety-four countries and in 3D in selected cinemas. The episode had an audience of 10 million viewers in the UK, which rose to nearly 13 million when 'time-shifted' viewings were taken into account, and it had an audience appreciation index figure of eighty-eight, which is very high. The episode featured Matt Smith, who had taken over from David Tennant in 2010, as the eleventh Doctor, David Tennant as the tenth Doctor, John Hurt as the 'War Doctor', Billie Piper as an incarnation of her Rose Tyler character, and there was a small role for the fourth Doctor (Tom Baker, who featured in the series from 1974–81). There was also a fleeting appearance by Peter Capaldi as the new twelfth Doctor, who officially took over from Matt Smith in the next episode, a Christmas special called 'The Time of the Doctor' (BBC One, 25 December 2013), which was also *Doctor Who*'s 800th episode.

So successful was the revived *Doctor Who* that it gave rise to two spin-offs: *Torchwood* and *The Sarah Jane Adventures* (CBBC, 2007–11), the latter featuring Sarah Jane Smith (Elisabeth Sladen), a former companion of the Doctor in the 1970s, plus a documentary series, *Doctor Who Confidential* (BBC Three, 2005–11), about the making of each episode in the new series, which was shown on BBC Three immediately after the screening of the episode on BBC One.

The new *Doctor Who*: Peter Capaldi as the twelfth Doctor

Another mythical character was given a twenty-first-century makeover when Steven Moffat and Mark Gatiss reworked *Sherlock*, with Benedict Cumberbatch playing the eponymous detective and Martin Freeman as his assistant, Doctor Watson. As with the new *Doctor Who*, *Sherlock* was also stylistically innovative, making creative use of new digital techniques, including text superimposed on screen to illustrate Sherlock's deductive processes as an alternative to what would have been a more pedantic voiceover. The stories were also updated by having Holmes make use of the internet, mobile texting and GPS (Global Positioning System) to solve crimes. Restricted to just three feature-length episodes per series, *Sherlock* has been a great success, winning a BAFTA award for Best Drama Series in 2011, and growing in popularity, with ratings rising from 7 million in the first series to 8 million in the second series and nearly 12 million in the third series. In the case of *Sherlock*, less (fewer episodes) has proved to be more (higher quality and growing popularity), demonstrating one of the strengths of British television drama compared to the long-running series on American TV, which are often recommissioned for commercial purposes despite the exhaustion of their original premise.

While British television drama cannot compete with the budgets and scale of American television drama, the undoubted quality of recent British television drama is a result of original ideas being concentrated into fewer episodes and series, not being played out until they are exhausted. The degree of innovation in British television drama in the digital age is evident in the originality and variety of the new forms of drama that have been screened since 2002, both on the new digital channels and on the established mainstream channels.

Internet drama

Another feature of the digital television age has been the convergence between television and the internet. This has taken two forms: the use of websites as an adjunct to broadcast dramas and the development of web dramas made specifically for the internet. Many new television dramas, especially those targeted at younger viewers, now have a website where viewers can access further information and interact with the characters and storylines. The audience for *Dubplate Drama* could watch the series on Channel 4, but also on the social networking site MySpace, and download episodes to mobile phones. Subsequently, the episodes were uploaded to YouTube, which was launched in February 2005, a few months before *Dubplate Drama* was produced, and which has since become the premier site for internet dramas.

Skins, as Glen Creeber notes, had a website presence right from the beginning which offered more than simply watching the episodes online:

> Each series of *Skins* … was launched on MySpace, with previews of the first episodes aired a few days before they were broadcast. Videos were also released exclusively on the show's website, including character profiles and 'Unseen *Skins*' mini-episodes. There was also an official *Skins* internet bot (web robot, a software application that runs automated tasks over the internet) for Windows Live Messenger, which allowed users to receive automated messages throughout the airing of each episode with music credits, trivia and behind-the-scenes gossip.[41]

The new *Doctor Who* also took advantage of the opportunities which the internet offered for connecting with its audience when it returned to UK TV screens in 2005. *Doctor Who* had an unofficial internet existence even before the official relaunch in 2005, with audio episodes being made available as webcasts, accompanied by slides, but with the official BBC relaunch *Doctor Who* had a continuous presence on the BBC website. In 2006, this extended to the production of 'Tardisodes', short one-minute videos made to accompany each episode in the 2006 series which could be accessed via the BBC website or downloaded to mobile phones.[42]

In 2010 the BBC released a series of interactive games called *Doctor Who: The Adventure Games* which could be accessed and downloaded free of charge from the BBC website. They proved to be hugely popular, with 1.6 million downloads within three months of the first two games being made available.[43] The first four games were released between June and December 2010, with a fifth released in October 2011. *The Adventure Games* were a spin-off from the new *Who* which capitalised on the success of the television series, extending its reach beyond the medium of broadcast television into the realm of new media.

The BBC also produced an internet spin-off from another of its most popular programmes in 2010. *EastEnders: E20* (BBC Online, 2010–11) was made to tie-in with the twenty-fifth anniversary celebrations of the soap and was targeted at a teenage audience which was more likely to watch episodes on the internet than on broadcast television. Accordingly, *E20* featured a teenage cast, some of whom had appeared, or were appearing, in *EastEnders*, and was written by young writers who were recruited through a BBC writing competition. As such, not only was *E20* intended to attract younger viewers but also to be a training ground for young writers, actors and other members of the production team. Filmed on the *EastEnders* set, *E20* (named after the postal district in which the fictional Walford is set) was stylistically different, using hand-held cameras and faster cutting in order to give it a fresher style and make it more appealing for a younger audience. Thirty-seven episodes, varying in length from three to sixteen minutes, were released on the BBC website between January 2010 and June 2011 and omnibus editions were screened on BBC Three.

E20 was by no means the only internet drama with which the BBC was involved. In 2007 Endemol, the producers of *Big Brother*, produced an interactive online drama for the BBC called *Signs of Life* which was launched on BBC Switch, a cross-platform initiative producing programmes for a teenage audience on BBC Two, Radio 1 and BBC Online. As Meg Carter wrote in the *Guardian* in 2007:

> *Signs of Life* is a thriller set in a fictional Suffolk town with a look and tone inspired by *Twin Peaks* and *Buffy the Vampire Slayer*. Unlike in previous interactive drama, however, viewers won't be able to alter the plot. Instead, they will be encouraged to engage more deeply with content in a variety of ways, such as playing games, completing puzzles, or doing personality tests relating to plot content, the results of which they can post directly on to their own page on MySpace or elsewhere online.[44]

Made with a budget of £800,000, *Signs of Life* was a professional production which differed from other internet dramas made with a low-budget or no-budget aesthetic. Its production qualities were high and its difference from broadcast television drama was not as great as in some non-professional internet dramas. What is more, it had an interactive dimension that was not possible with broadcast drama.

One of the first web dramas to be made and now one of the most famous is *lonelygirl15* (YouTube, 2006–8), which began life as a series of videos posted on YouTube in June 2006 about a 'lonely girl' called Bree who seemed to be posting short video blogs using a webcam in her bedroom. The series achieved notoriety in September 2006 when it was revealed that it was not just another video blog, but was, in fact, an elaborate fiction which, as Jon Dovey relates,

> gradually became a more and more compelling story, as Bree, the main character, seemed to be recording her descent into a dark and cult-like urban nightmare. It became a YouTube hit, gathering an active and speculative fan base. The Lonely Girl was eventually exposed as an actress by journalists and the whole project revealed as a brilliantly staged promotion by a group of aspiring film-makers and producers. The ambiguous status of the reality of *lonelygirl15* is typical of web aesthetics. The webcam blog carries the feel of authenticity and one-to-one communication that makes a strong dramatic 'proposition' to the viewer sitting at home on their own in front of the computer screen.[45]

lonelygirl15 (also known as *LG15*) was produced in the USA and should not, strictly speaking, have a place in a book on British television drama, but it is the nature of internet dramas that they are not confined to national boundaries when they are uploaded to the World Wide Web, even if they have been produced in one particular country. *LG15* and its various spin-offs were not only viewed by internet audiences around the world, but were also produced in different countries, even by fans of the original series. Among the spin-offs *LG15* generated was *KateModern* (Bebo, 2007–8), which was produced in the UK and filmed mainly in east London. Produced by the same team responsible for *LG15*, *KateModern* had a similar scenario: Kate is a video blogger who has an unusual blood type which makes her the target of a secret organisation called The Order. At the end of the 2007 season she is killed and in the 2008 season her friends try to find out who was responsible.

As an internet drama, there were opportunities for viewers to interact with *KateModern* in various ways, including through online communication with the characters and even by meeting up and participating in the filming, as in the episode entitled 'Carnaby Street, Saturday 18 August, 10 am', when fans were invited to go along to Carnaby Street in London to witness and participate in the filming of the episode. The second season included two twelve-hour 'marathons', when twelve videos were posted over a period of twelve hours and viewers were invited to interact with the drama by communicating online with the characters, and with the rest of the *KateModern* 'community', during the course of each marathon viewing session.[46]

The *KateModern* webisodes were first shown on the social networking site Bebo and then uploaded to YouTube twenty-four hours later. While individual webisodes may have been short, usually only two to three minutes long, over the two years that *lonelygirl15* and *KateModern* were running they both clocked up a significant number of screen hours, equivalent to a thirteen-hour television series in the case of *KateModern* and nearly twice that in the case of *LG15*.[47] There was also an American-produced sequel to *LG15* and *KateModern* called *LG15: The Resistance* (September–December 2008) and three further series: *N1ckola* (January–June 2009), produced in Poland, *LG15: The Last* (January–July 2009), produced by Australian fans of the series, and *LG15: Outbreak* (January–March 2010), produced by American fans of the series.

Like *KateModern*, *Sofia's Diary* (2008–9) was also shown on Bebo but, unlike *KateModern*, *Sofia's Diary* was also bought for television by Channel 5 and shown on their digital channel, Fiver, from April 2008–June 2009. Clearly influenced by *lonelygirl15* and *KateModern*, *Sofia's Diary* lacked the darker elements of those web dramas, which probably made it more attractive to Channel 5, but season two did contain a storyline about gun crime after a character was killed at the end of the first season and teenage viewers were invited to call a helpline to report gun crime. *Sofia's Diary* was subsequently released on a two-disc DVD containing alternative endings 'letting the viewer decide what Sofia should do in her daily situations'.[48]

The Cut (BBC Two, 2009–10) was another BBC Switch production for a teenage audience. Described in a BBC press release as a 'soap for teens' it was shown online each day in five-minute episodes and repeated in a twenty-five-minute omnibus on BBC Two at weekends. As Geoffrey Goodwin, Head of BBC Switch, said:

This series reflects the way many young people want to consume content. We've united top British writing talent with the freshest and newest interactive ideas to make appointment to view content for soap loving British teens.

The story is fast paced and relevant to young audiences, with secret crushes, family dramas and plenty of intrigue. The writing is quick, witty, and knowing, rich with pop culture references and with storylines suggested by teens themselves.[49]

Not all internet dramas are targeted at teenage audiences, however. *Crisis in the Credit System* (2008) was a four-part British web drama about the 2008 financial crisis, produced by Artangel, a London-based arts organisation. Written and directed by Melanie Gilligan, the drama is described on the website, where it can still (at the time of writing) be accessed:

A major investment bank runs a brainstorming and role-playing session for its employees, asking them to come up with strategies for coping with today's dangerous financial climate. Role-playing their way into increasingly bizarre scenarios, they find themselves drawing disturbing conclusions about the deeper significance of the crisis and its effects beyond the world of finance.

Using fiction to communicate what is left out of documentary accounts of the crisis, the short, TV-style episodes reflect the strangeness of life today in which the financial abstractions that govern our lives appear to be collapsing.

Crisis in the Credit System, commissioned and produced by Artangel Interaction, is the result of extensive research and conversation with major hedge fund managers, key financial journalists, economists, bankers and debt activists.[50]

Crisis in the Credit System demonstrates the potential for internet dramas to move beyond the intimate webcam aesthetic of early online dramas to produce something closer to the 'serious' drama of the BBC's *Play for Today*. The attraction of internet drama for producers and film-makers is that they can bypass the commercial and editorial restrictions of the television companies to produce truly independent dramas that can be viewed anytime, anywhere, by anyone. Deploying a variety of aesthetic styles and narrative strategies, internet dramas have a degree of flexibility in how they tell stories that is often not available to broadcast television dramas, given the restrictions of scheduling and the requirements of advertisers. Furthermore, web dramas are often designed to be viewed in short segments on a variety of different screens, including mobile phones, increasing the possibility of anyone accessing them anytime, anywhere.

With MySpace launching in 2003 and both Bebo and YouTube launching in 2005 it is clear that social networking sites have been instrumental in the development of internet drama, but the television companies, especially the BBC, recognise the importance of the internet as another platform for drama and have taken steps towards producing product specifically for that platform. While it would be unwise to suggest that television is migrating to the internet, for there is still a demand for 'high-end' dramas made on big budgets, for big screens and, perhaps, for an older audience less interested in accessing drama online, internet drama is emerging as an important form in its own right, complementing, rather than competing with, the myriad forms of drama being produced for broadcast television.

What the above examples illustrate is that internet drama is eroding national boundaries through being distributed on the World Wide Web. While this book has charted the rich and varied history of British television drama, from 1930 to the present, the concept of 'national' television drama, already problematic given the make-up of the British Isles, is likely to become even less tenable in future as international co-productions increase and new technology such as the internet dissolves national boundaries. Meanwhile, as this chapter hopefully illustrates, British television drama, contrary to those who bemoan a decline in quality, seems to be enjoying something of a renaissance in the new digital age. While the quantity of drama produced may not be as great as it was in the 1960s–70s, there seems to be no decline in the quality of the dramas that have been made since the turn of the century. On the contrary, it could be argued that the advent of digital channels and the internet has increased the outlets for drama and that the range, variety and quality of British television drama is now as great, if not indeed greater, than it was in the mythical 'golden age' of the 1960s–70s.

Notes

Introduction

1. The expanded Bibliography in this edition, enlarged to include articles and book chapters as well as a range of new books, gives some indication of the increased interest in British television drama since the first edition was published.

2. See Robin Nelson, *State of Play: Contemporary 'High-end' TV Drama* (Manchester: Manchester University Press, 2007).

3. While this final chapter is dated 2002–14 this is not to suggest that the 'digital age' begins and ends in this period, simply that I completed work on this edition in 2014. The review of television drama produced since 2002, while wide-ranging, is by no means comprehensive, any more than it is in the rest of the book.

4. Note, however, the University of Westminster 'Screen Plays: Theatre Plays on British Television' project which is 'concerned with all plays written for the theatre produced for British television since 1930', http://screenplaystv.wordpress.com (accessed 6 February 2014). An article by the project's principal investigator, John Wyver, on the pre-war television director Dallas Bower is listed in the Bibliography.

5. The Kaleidoscope British television drama research guides, now available as downloads, exhaustively list every episode of every television drama made by the BBC since 1936 and by ITV since 1955. They are invaluable resources for anyone interested in British television drama history (see the Bibliography: Catalogues and Reference Books). The late Tise Vahimagi's *British Television: An Illustrated Guide, 2nd Edition* (Oxford: Oxford University Press, 1996) remains a very useful resource, although it stops in 1995.

6. For children's drama, see Mark J. Docherty and Alistair McGown, *The Hill and Beyond: Children's Television Drama – An Encyclopedia* (London: BFI, 2003), which is useful but in need of updating.

7. John Caughie, *Television Drama: Realism, Modernism and British Culture* (Oxford: Oxford University Press, 2000).

8. George Brandt (ed.), *British Television Drama* (Cambridge: Cambridge University Press, 1981), and *British Television Drama in the 1980s* (Cambridge: Cambridge University Press, 1993).

9. Carl Gardner and John Wyver, 'The Single Play: From Reithian Reverence To Cost-Accounting and Censorship', Edinburgh International Television Festival 1980, Official Programme published by *Broadcast*, reprinted in *Screen*, vol. 24, no. 4–5, July/October 1983, p. 115. This article is discussed in Chapters 1 and 4.

10. John Ellis, *Seeing Things: Television in the Age of Uncertainty* (London: I.B.Tauris, 2000), p. 39.

11. See Robin Nelson, *State of Play*, p. 7.

12. Dave Rolinson, *Alan Clarke* (2005), Stephen Lacey, *Tony Garnett* (2007), Lez Cooke, *Troy Kennedy Martin* (2007), Julia Hallam, *Lynda La Plante* (2005), Steve Blandford, *Jimmy McGovern* (2013) (all Manchester: Manchester University Press).

13. Christine Geraghty, *Bleak House* (2012), Stephen Lacey, *Cathy Come Home* (2010), Mark Duguid, *Cracker* (2009), Kim Newman, *Doctor Who* (2005), John Caughie, *Edge of Darkness* (2007), Charlotte Brunsdon, *Law and Order* (2010), Mick Eaton, *Our Friends in the North* (2005), Deborah Jermyn, *Prime Suspect* (2010), Glyn Davis, *Queer as Folk* (2007), Glen Creeber, *The Singing Detective* (2007) (all London: BFI).

Chapter 1

1. John Caughie, 'Before the Golden Age: Early Television Drama', in John Corner (ed.), *Popular Television in Britain* (London: BFI, 1991); Charles Barr, '"They Think It's All Over": The Dramatic Legacy of Live Television', in John Hill and Martin McLoone (eds), *Big Picture, Small Screen: The Relations Between Film and Television* (Luton: University of Luton Press/John Libbey, 1997); Jason Jacobs, *The Intimate Screen: Early British Television Drama* (Oxford: Oxford University Press, 2000).

2. In his *History of Broadcasting in the United Kingdom*, Asa Briggs cites a Listener Research Report of 26 June 1939 which 'suggested that 280 sets had been sold by the end of 1936', *The History of Broadcasting in the United Kingdom, Volume II: The Golden Age of Wireless* (Oxford: Oxford University Press, 1995) p. 566.

3. Ibid., p. 573.

4. Stuart Hood and Thalia Tabary-Peterssen, *On Television* (London: Pluto Press, 1997), p. 30.

5. In *The Intimate Screen*, Jason Jacobs attributes the term 'photographed stage plays' to Carl Gardner and John Wyver's 1980 Edinburgh International Television Festival paper, 'The Single Play: From Reithian Reverance to Cost-Accounting and Censorship' (Jacobs, 2000, pp. 2–3). Yet Gardner and Wyver never actually use this term, referring instead to 'televised stage plays' (Edinburgh International Television Festival 1980, Official Programme published by *Broadcast*, reprinted in *Screen*, 24/4–5, July/October 1983). At the beginning of ch.3 of *The Intimate Screen*, Jacobs quotes from a 1947 *BBC Quarterly* article by Val Gielgud, one of the first directors of BBC television drama, in which Gielgud asked whether television drama aimed 'to be no more than a photographed stage play' (p. 77).

6. For more on this see Steve Bryant, *The Television Heritage* (London: BFI, 1989). Also Barr, '"They Think It's All Over"'; Caughie, 'Before the Golden Age'; and Jacobs, *The Intimate Screen*.

7. Tim O'Sullivan is one of the few people to have undertaken research into television viewing habits in the post-war period, based on oral histories. See 'Television Memories and Cultures of Viewing 1950–65' in John Corner (ed.), *Popular Television in Britain* (London:

BFI, 1991), and 'Researching the Viewing Culture: Television and the Home, 1946–1960', in Helen Wheatley (ed.), *Re-viewing Television History: Critical Issues in Television Historiography* (London: I.B.Tauris, 2007).

8. Mark Aldridge, *The Birth of British Television: A History* (Basingstoke: Palgrave Macmillan, 2012)

9. '*The Man with the Flower in his Mouth*: The First British Television Play – 1930', www.tvdawn.com/earliest-tv/the-man-with-the-flower-in-his-mouth (last accessed 4 June 2014). However, Aldridge notes that Baird had previously transmitted a version of John Maddision Morton's 1847 one-act farce *Box and Cox* from his studio in Long Acre, London, on 15 December 1928 (Aldridge, *The Birth of British Television*, p. 217, n. 6). The source of this information appears to be Denis Gifford's unpublished British Television Catalogue: 1923–1939 and Aldridge provides a link to the British Vintage Wireless Society website, where there is further information about Gifford's catalogue on the archived 405 Alive website: 'The author's painstaking research also reveals numerous "firsts" in television history, thus correcting the establishment's handed-down history – for example, that the first televised play was John Maddison Morton's *Box and Cox* (15th December 1928), nearly two years earlier than previously thought', www.bvws.org.uk/405alive/faq/prog_further_reading.html (last accessed 4 June 2014). However, Don McLean, curator of *The Dawn of TV* website, is cautious about considering *Box and Cox* as the first televised play: 'I would not make a big thing of the "first". Dec 15 1928 was the transmission date and it was not the whole play, and it was effectively amateur dramatics. It would also appear to have been vision/sound alternating. Also any audience it had comprised enthusiasts who could make their own receiver/displays. ... The BVWS page seems to suggest that Denis discovered *Box and Cox* as the first play. I don't think that's strictly correct. It's been known about for decades, but because it was amateur, in part, and those scenes alternating video-only and audio-only, it hardly met the criteria. In fact refer to Moseley and Barton-Chapple (2nd ed.): they flag "the first play" by television as TMWTFIHM. Baird mentions putting out *Box and Cox* – "a little play" in his autobiography and then refers to TMWTFIHM as the BBC's first play by television', emails to the author, 24 and 26 May 2014.

10. See Aldridge, *The Birth of British Television*, p. 37.

11. The play was remade in thirty lines in 1967, in an edited version, in consultation with the original producer, Lance Sieveking, using the original artwork by C. R. Nevinson and the original music. This reconstruction can be viewed on *The Dawn of TV* website (see note 9), www.tvdawn.com/?s=the+man+with+the+flower+in+his+mouth (last accessed 29 October 2014).

12. Jacobs, *The Intimate Screen*, pp. 32–3.

13. Caughie, 'Before the Golden Age', p. 25.

14. See Jacobs, *The Intimate Screen*, pp. 28–32.

15. Andrew Crissell, *An Introductory History of British Broadcasting* (London: Routledge, 1997), p. 72.

16. Gardner and Wyver, 'The Single Play'. Jason Jacobs takes issue with Gardner and Wyver, setting out to 'revise significantly, rather than refute completely' the model of early TV

drama that Gardner and Wyver propose (Jacobs, *The Intimate Screen*, p. 3). Through a detailed examination of the aesthetics of early TV drama, Jacobs sets out to disprove the suggestion that all early television drama was as static and theatrical as Gardner and Wyver imply. This partially misses the point of Gardner and Wyver's critique however, which was that the adherance to theatrical values in early TV drama was a direct consequence of the paternalistic Reithian project that pervaded the BBC during the period in which early television drama developed

17. Tise Vahimagi, *British Television: An Illustrated Guide, 2nd Edition* (London: BFI, 1996), p. 5.

18. Jacobs, *The Intimate Screen*, p. 36.

19. 'Probably' because, without visual records of the transmissions, we cannot be entirely sure how these early productions appeared to the television audience at the time.

20. Quoted in Jacobs, *The Intimate Screen*, p. 35. The play was *When We Are Married*, by J. B. Priestley, transmitted live from St Martin's Theatre in London on 16 November 1938, 8.30–10.40 pm.

21. First produced for radio in 1932, the television version of *Ann and Harold* was shown at varying times between 9.00 and 10.00 on Tuesday evenings, each episode lasting between fifteen and twenty minutes.

22. Jacobs, *The Intimate Screen*, p. 48.

23. Ibid., pp. 52–3.

24. Jan Bussell, *The Art of Television* (London: Faber & Faber, 1952).

25. *Radio Times*, 3 March 1939, p. 15.

26. John Caughie, *Television Drama: Realism, Modernism and British Culture* (Oxford: Oxford University Press, 2000), p. 35.

27. Vahimagi, *British Television*, p. 18.

28. See Kate Harris, 'Evolutionary Stages: Theatre and Television, 1946–56', in Dominic Shellard (ed.), *The Golden Generation: New Light on Post-War British Theatre* (London: British Library, 2008), p. 156.

29. Jacobs, *The Intimate Screen*, p. 103.

30. See ibid. for a consideration of the 1947 and 1950 television versions, pp. 103–8.

31. Ibid., p. 107.

32. Vahimagi, *British Television*, p. 23.

33. Quoted in Jacobs, *The Intimate Screen*, p. 127.

34. Quoted in ibid., p. 97.

35. Vahimagi, *British Television*, p. 39.

36. Asa Briggs, *The History of Broadcasting in the United Kingdom, Volume IV: Sound and Vision* (Oxford: Oxford University Press, 1995), p. 221.

37. Quoted in Jacobs, *The Intimate Screen*, p. 125.

38. Jacobs, *The Intimate Screen*, p. 92.

39. Ibid., p. 130.

40. Ellen Baskin, *Serials on British Television 1950–1994* (Aldershot: Scolar Press, 1996), p. 4.

41. Vahimagi, *British Television*, p. 37.

42. Jeff Evans, *The Guinness Television Encyclopedia* (London: Guinness, 1995), pp. 232–3.

43. BBC Written Archives Centre, Programme File T12/137/5, 1954.

44. It is perhaps a sign of the BBC's disdain towards a popular series like *The Grove Family* that only two of the 146 episodes have survived.

45. Extracts from the 1990 interview were included in a tribute to Cartier, screened on BBC Two on 1 July 1994, shortly after his death.

46. This analysis of the first scene is based on a viewing of the first episode at the BFI National Archive. Since publication of the first edition of this book, the two surviving episodes of *The Quatermass Experiment*, together with *Quatermass II* and *Quatermass and the Pit*, have been released on DVD by the BBC (BBC Worldwide, 2005).

47. Quoted by Julian Petley in 'The Quatermass Conclusion', *Primetime* no. 9, Winter 1984/5, p. 23

48. Four *Sunday Night Theatre* plays were telerecorded between February and July 1953, the first of which was *It Is Midnight, Dr Schweitzer* (26 February 1953).

49. Jacobs, *The Intimate Screen*, pp. 112–13.

50. Barry Salt gives the ASL in films at this time as eleven seconds, in *Film Style and Technology: History and Analysis* (London: Starword, 1983), p. 317

51. Jacobs includes a seventeen-page analysis of *Nineteen Eighty-Four* in *The Intimate Screen* which is greatly enhanced by the availability of a viewing copy in the BFI National Archive. The play was screened on BBC Two in July 1994 as a tribute to Rudolph Cartier, who died in April 1994.

52. Jacobs, *The Intimate Screen*, p. 143.

53. See Lez Cooke, *Style in British Television Drama* (Basingstoke: Palgrave Macmillan, 2013), ch. 1, for a more detailed discussion of this scene.

54. Quote from a tribute to Rudolph Cartier screened on BBC Two, 1 July 1994.

55. Caughie, *Television Drama*, pp. 49–50.

Chapter 2

1. In 1955, the number of combined TV and radio licences issued was 4,503,766, compared to 9,476,730 radio licences. By 1961, the number of combined TV and radio licences had risen to 11,267,741, while the number of radio licences issued had fallen to 3,908,984. (Source: Asa Briggs, *The History of Broadcasting in the United Kingdom, Volume V: Competition* [Oxford: Oxford University Press, 1995], p. 1005.) Cinema admissions fell from 1,180 million in 1955 to 449 million in 1961. (Source: Eddie Dyja [ed.], *BFI Film and Television Handbook 2000* [London: BFI, 1999], p. 30.)

2. See Tise Vahimagi, *British Television: An Illustrated Guide, 2nd Edition* (Oxford: Oxford University Press, 1996), p. 29, for details of when the different ITV franchises began operating.

3. Andrew Crissell, *An Introductory History of British Broadcasting* (London: Routledge, 1997), p. 102.

4. See John Caughie, 'Before the Golden Age: Early Television Drama', in John Corner (ed.), *Popular Television in Britain: Studios in Cultural History* (London: BFI, 1991), p. 39.

5. Joan Hooley in Jim Pines, *Black and White in Colour: Black People in British Television Since 1936* (London: BFI, 1992), pp. 99–100.

6. Marion Jordan, 'Realism and Convention', in Richard Dyer, Christine Geraghty, Marion Jordan, Terry Lovell, Richard Paterson and John Stewart, *Coronation Street* (London: BFI, 1981), p. 28.
7. For a detailed stylistic analysis of the dinner-table scene in the Barlow household, see Lez Cooke, *Style in British Television Drama* (Basingstoke: Palgrave Macmillan, 2013), ch. 2.
8. Richard Paterson, 'The Production Context of Coronation Street', in Dyer *et al.*, *Coronation Street*, p. 56.
9. Jordan, 'Realism and Convention', p. 28.
10. Richard Dyer, 'Introduction', in Dyer *et al.*, *Coronation Street*, p. 2.
11. Raymond Williams, *Culture and Society 1780–1950* (London: Penguin, 1966), p. 16; first published 1958.
12. Dyer, 'Introduction', p. 4.
13. *TV Times*, 20 September 1955, p. 18.
14. Stuart Laing, *Representations of Working-Class Life 1957–1964* (London: Macmillan, 1986), p. 147.
15. ABC Television, *The Armchair Theatre* (London: Weidenfeld & Nicolson, 1959), p. 102.
16. John Russell Taylor, *Anatomy of a Television Play: An Inquiry into the Production of Two ABC Armchair Theatre Plays* (London: Weidenfeld & Nicolson, 1962), p. 9
17. Philip Purser, 'Landscape of TV Drama', *Contrast* vol. 1 no. 1, Autumn 1961, p. 18.
18. *Emperor Jones* was telerecorded at the time of transmission – a viewing copy of the production is held by the BFI National Archive and the play is available on DVD in the collection: *Armchair Theatre Vol.4* (Network, 2013).
19. From *And Now For Your Sunday Night Dramatic Entertainment: The People Behind Armchair Theatre* (Microcraze Productions for Channel 4, 8 February 1987).
20. Taylor, *Anatomy of a Television Play*, pp. 13–14.
21. Philip Saville, 'Director and Writer', *Contrast* vol. 2 no. 2, Winter 1962, p. 136.
22. From *And Now For Your Sunday Night Dramatic Entertainment*.
23. Ibid.
24. Ibid.
25. Ibid.
26. Irene Shubik, *Play for Today: The Evolution of Television Drama* (London: Davis-Poynter, 1975), p. 94.
27. Purser, 'Landscape of TV Drama', pp. 18–19.
28. *Lena, O My Lena* was recorded on Ampex videotape on Thursday, 15 September 1960, in the ABC Television Studios at Didsbury, from 7.30–8.40 pm, with a ten-minute break between Acts 1 and 2 for the 're-setting of sets' (from the camera script held by the BFI Library). The play was transmitted on Sunday, 25 September 1960, 8–9 pm.
29. *And Now For Your Sunday Night Dramatic Entertainment*.
30. Jason Jacobs, *The Intimate Screen: Early British Television Drama* (Oxford: Oxford University Press, 2000), p. 144, emphasis original.
31. In the first edition of this book I described this as a 'tracking' movement, but it is not strictly a tracking movement (which implies a camera moving on purpose-built tracks) because, if it was, the movement would be smoother than it is and the reverse shot that

follows would reveal the tracks leading into the warehouse yard. Rather, it is a camera mounted on a dolly which is being pushed by grips (technicians whose job this was), resulting in some camera shudder as the dolly moves across the studio floor.

32. This calculation is based on dividing the running time given in the camera script by the total number of camera shots (276) listed on the script. However, the camera script has two different running times, written in pencil (58.43 seconds) and in ink (58.06 seconds), which may be the difference between the run-through and the actual recording. It is worth noting that the camera script indicates forty shots in the first five minutes of the play, whereas there are only thirty-two shots in the first five minutes of the play as recorded. It is unlikely, therefore, that the total of 276 shots given on the camera script is the same as the number of shots in the final recording – a reminder that in live television drama decisions are taken by the director while a play is being transmitted, or in this case recorded, which may cause the play to depart from the script, both in terms of camera movement and cuts from one camera position to another, as the director makes adjustments for reasons of running time, position and movement of the actors, etc.

33. Jacobs, *The Intimate Screen*, p. 145.

34. Caughie, *Television Drama*, p. 77.

35. An account of this is given by Charles Barr in ' "They Think It's All Over": The Dramatic Legacy of Live Television', in John Hill and Martin McLoone (eds), *Big Picture, Small Screen: The Relations between Film and Television* (Luton: University of Luton/John Libbey, 1997), pp. 63–4.

36. Howard Thomas, quoted in Laing, *Representations of Working-Class Life*, pp. 144–5.

37. For an account of the production of both *The Rose Affair* and *Afternoon of a Nymph*, see Taylor, *Anatomy of a Television Play*.

38. Ted Willis, 'Dock Green through the Years', *Radio Times*, 17 September 1964, p. 7.

39. See Steve Bryant, *The Television Heritage* (London: BFI, 1989).

40. Joy Leman, 'Wise Scientists and Female Androids: Class and Gender in Science Fiction', in Corner, *Popular Television in Britain*, p. 122.

41. Paul Kerr, 'F for Fake? Friction over Faction', in Andrew Goodwin and Garry Whannel (eds), *Understanding Television* (London: Routledge, 1990), p. 78.

42. Rowan Ayres, 'Incident at Echo Six', *Radio Times*, 5 December 1958, p. 5.

43. Ibid.

44. Troy Kennedy Martin, interviewed by the author, 25 September 1998.

45. For more on Troy Kennedy Martin and *Incident at Echo Six*, see Lez Cooke, *Troy Kennedy Martin* (Manchester: Manchester University Press, 2007).

46. Bernard Sendell, *Independent Television in Britain Volume 1: Origins and Foundation, 1946–62* (London: Macmillan, 1982), p. 346.

47. Ian Atkins, memorandum to Anthony Pelissier, 22 February 1956, BBC Written Archives Centre, T31/292.

48. Anthony Pelissier, letter to Michael Barry, 22 February 1960, BBC Written Archives Centre, T31/292.

49. For more on *Three Ring Circus*, see Lez Cooke, '*Three Ring Circus*: The Ur-text of Modernist Television Drama', *Screen* vol. 50 no 4, Winter 2009.

50. Troy Kennedy Martin, interviewed by the author, 27 March 1986.

51. Troy Kennedy Martin, 'Sharpening the Edge of TV Drama', *The Listener*, 28 August 1986, pp. 9–10. The MacTaggart Lecture was established in honour of James MacTaggart, who died in 1974.

52. For a more extensive discussion of the Pilkington Committee Report, see Caughie, *Television Drama*, pp. 79–85.

Chapter 3

1. Quoted in Stuart Laing, *Representations of Working-Class Life 1957–1964* (London: Macmillan, 1986), p. 170.

2. It is worth noting that Tony Garnett appeared as an actor in several early *Z Cars* episodes and that Ken Loach, who directed the first *Wednesday Plays* to be shot on film, also directed three episodes of *Z Cars*.

3. Peter Lewis, 'Z Cars', *Contrast* vol. 1 no. 2, Summer 1962, p. 309.

4. Ibid., p. 307.

5. Ibid., p. 314.

6. Quoted in Laing, *Representations of Working-Class Life*, p. 179.

7. Quoted in Peter Lewis, 'Z Cars', p. 315.

8. Ibid.

9. John R. Cook, ' "Between Grierson and Barnum": Sydney Newman and the Development of the Single Television Play at the BBC, 1963–7', *Journal of British Cinema and Television* vol. 1 no. 2, 2004, p. 214.

10. Philip Purser, 'Head of Drama', *Contrast* vol. 2 no. 1, Autumn 1962, p. 36.

11. Irene Shubik, *Play For Today: The Evolution of Television Drama* (London: Davis-Poynter, 1975), p. 55.

12. John R. Cook, 'Adapting Telefantasy: The *Doctor Who and the Daleks* Films', in I. Q. Hunter (ed.), *British Science Fiction Cinema* (London: Routledge, 1999), pp. 115–16.

13. Verity Lambert, quoted in John Tulloch and Manuel Alvarado, *Doctor Who: The Unfolding Text* (London: Macmillan, 1983), p. 39.

14. Troy Kennedy Martin, 'Nats Go Home: First Statement of a New Drama for Television', *Encore* vol. 11 no. 2, March–April 1964, p. 21.

15. Troy Kennedy Martin, interviewed by the author, 27 March 1986.

16. Kennedy Martin, 'Nats Go Home', p. 25.

17. Ibid.

18. Ibid., p. 32.

19. Ibid., p. 31.

20. The idea of a 'golden age' in television drama in the 1960s was a recurrent theme at a conference held at the University of Reading in April 1998: 'On the Boundary: Turning Points in TV Drama 1965–2000', organised as part of a research project on 'The BBC Wednesday Plays and Post-War British Drama'. A collection of essays, based on papers and presentations at the conference, was subsequently published: Jonathan Bignell, Stephen Lacey and Madeleine Macmurraugh-Kavanagh (eds), *British Television Drama: Past, Present and Future* (Basingstoke: Palgrave, 2000). For more on the shift to a 'cost-conscious'

television drama in the 1970s, see Carl Gardner and John Wyver, 'The Single Play: From Reithian Reverence To Cost-Accounting and Censorship', Edinburgh International Television Festival 1980, Official Programme published by *Broadcast*, reprinted in *Screen*, vol. 24 no. 4–5, July–October 1983.

21. Shubik, *Play for Today*, pp. 39–41.

22. Ibid., p. 75.

23. Ken Trodd, quoted in Humphrey Carpenter, *Dennis Potter: A Biography* (London: Faber & Faber, 1998), p. 141.

24. For the full list see Shubik, *Play for Today*, pp. 60–2.

25. Madeleine Macmurraugh-Kavanagh, ' "Drama" into "News": Strategies of Intervention in "The Wednesday Play" ', *Screen* vol. 38 no. 3, Autumn 1997.

26. Madeleine Macmurraugh-Kavanagh, 'The BBC Wednesday Play 1964–1970: Researching and Interpreting a Formative Moment in British Television Drama', *Media Education Journal* no. 23, Winter 1997/8, p. 13. That women are a token minority in this list, being responsible for only sixteen out of the total of 176 *Wednesday Plays* that were produced between 1964 and 1970, is an issue that Macmurraugh-Kavanagh addresses in 'Boys on Top: Gender and Authorship on the BBC Wednesday Play, 1964–70', *Media, Culture & Society* vol. 21 no. 3, May 1999; and in 'Too Secret for Words: Coded Dissent in Female-Authored Wednesday Plays', in Bignell, Lacey and Macmurraugh-Kavanagh, *British Television Drama*.

27. Macmurraugh-Kavanagh, 'The BBC Wednesday Play', pp. 11–12.

28. Graham Fuller (ed.), *Loach on Loach* (London: Faber & Faber, 1998), p. 13.

29. Tony Garnett, interviewed by the author, 29 February 2000.

30. Troy Kennedy Martin, 'Up the Junction and After', *Contrast* vol. 4 no. 4/5, Winter 1965/ Spring 1966, p. 141.

31. Tony Garnett, interviewed by the author, 29 February 2000.

32. Fuller, *Loach on Loach*, p. 15.

33. Tony Garnett, interviewed by the author, 29 February 2000.

34. Fuller, *Loach on Loach*, p. 14.

35. Tony Garnett, interviewed by the author, 29 February 2000.

36. For more on the controversy resulting from the screening of *Up the Junction*, see Macmurraugh-Kavanagh, ' "Drama" into "News" '.

37. Ken Loach's *The End of Arthur's Marriage* (BBC One, 17 November 1965), shown as a *Wednesday Play* two weeks after *Up the Junction* (but actually filmed before it), was also impressionistic in style and shot largely on film (see John Hill, *Ken Loach: The Politics of Film and Television* [London: BFI, 2011], pp. 19–22); *The Bond* (BBC One, 1 December 1965), another *Wednesday Play*, transmitted four weeks after *Up the Junction*, was also very elliptical in its opening twenty minutes, before reverting to a more conventional studio naturalism (see Lez Cooke, *Style in British Television Drama* [Basingstoke: Palgrave Macmillan, 2013], ch. 3).

38. For more on *Up the Junction*, see John Caughie, *Television Drama: Realism, Modernism and British Culture* (London: Oxford University Press, 2000), pp. 114–20; Hill, *Ken Loach*, pp. 36–50; and Jacob Leigh, *The Cinema of Ken Loach: Art in the Service of the People* (London: Wallflower, 2002), pp. 26–39.

39. Quoted in Michael Tracey, 'A Nightmare Vision that Shook the BBC', *Guardian*, 1 September 1980, reprinted in Andrew Goodwin, Paul Kerr and Ian McDonald (eds), *BFI Dossier 19: Drama-Documentary* (London: BFI, 1983), p. 81.

40. Alan Lovell, 'Television Playwright: David Mercer', *Contrast* vol. 2 no. 4, Summer 1963, p. 258.

41. Ibid., p. 257.

42. David Mercer, interviewed by Paul Madden, April 1975, from the NFT programme notes for *And Did Those Feet?*, reprinted in *Film Dope* no. 42, October 1989, p. 27.

43. Glen Creeber, *Dennis Potter: Between Two Worlds* (Basingstoke: Macmillan, 1998), pp. 53–4.

44. Caughie, *Television Drama*, p. 169.

45. George Melly, *Observer*, 9 October 1966.

46. Hopkins had previously written a three-part adaptation of Ford Maddox Ford's *Parade's End* for *Theatre 625* (BBC Two, 6–20 December 1964).

47. John Hopkins, interviewed in Paul Madden (ed.), *British Television Drama* (London: BFI, 1976).

48. Christopher Morahan, email to the author, 1 October 2004.

49. George Melly, *Observer*, 10 March 1968.

50. Charlotte Brunsdon, 'Problems with Quality', in *Screen Tastes: Soap Opera to Satellite Dishes* (London: Routledge, 1997), pp. 142–3, first published in *Screen* vol. 31 no. 1, 1990.

51. Dave Rogers, *The Ultimate Avengers* (London: Boxtree, 1995), p. 201.

52. Toby Miller, *The Avengers* (London: BFI, 1997), p. 10.

53. Alain Carraze and Helene Oswald, *The Prisoner* (London: Virgin, 1995), p. 5. Other books on *The Prisoner* include: Chris Gregory, *Be Seeing You … Decoding The Prisoner* (Luton: University of Luton Press, 1997); Ian Rakoff, *Inside The Prisoner: Radical Television and Film in the 1960s* (London: Batsford, 1998); and Steven Paul Davies, *The Prisoner Handbook* (London: Boxtree, 2002).

54. David Buxton, *From The Avengers to Miami Vice: Form and Ideology in Television Series* (Manchester: Manchester University Press, 1990), p. 94.

55. Ibid., p. 97.

Chapter 4

1. George Brandt, *British Television Drama* (Cambridge: Cambridge University Press, 1981), p. 20.

2. Shaun Sutton, 'Sydney Newman and the "Golden Age"', in Jonathan Bignell, Stephen Lacey and Madeleine Macmurraugh-Kavanagh (eds), *British Television Drama: Past, Present and Future* (Basingstoke: Palgrave, 2000), p. 56.

3. This total includes two trilogies of short films and two plays which were shown in the same *Play for Today* slot but which were by different writers – Barrie Keefe's *Gotcha* and Brian Clark's *Campion's Interview* (12 April 1977); it does not include plays that were commissioned for *Play for Today* but not shown as part of the series: for example, Dennis Potter's *Brimstone and Treacle*, recorded in 1976 but not shown until 1987; Roy Minton's *Scum*, made in 1977 but not shown until 1991; Alan Bleasdale's *Blackstuff*, made in 1978 but not transmitted until 2 January 1980, on BBC Two; and Paul Copley's *Pillion*, recorded

in 1979 but never transmitted. It also does not include plays that were first shown in other series and repeated as a *Play for Today*. For a list of these plays see the *Play for Today* section on the *British Television Drama* website: www.britishtelevisiondrama.org.uk/?page_id=1724 (accessed 4 July 2013).

4. One of these six films was *Orkney* (13 May 1971), a trilogy of three short films adapted by John McGrath from stories by George Mackay Brown, directed by James MacTaggart.

5. Fourteen plays were shot on film in the tenth season of *Play for Today* and another fourteen recorded in the studio, but one of these, *Pillion*, was never transmitted. Source: Simon Coward, Richard Down and Christopher Perry (eds), *The Kaleidoscope British Television Drama Research Guide 1936–2011*, first digital edition (Dudley: Kaleidoscope, 2011).

6. It is worth noting that all of the twenty plays listed here were written by men. Out of 298 *Play for Todays* only thirty-three were written by women, while one was co-written by a woman. The single play has traditionally been dominated by male writers.

7. For more on the wiping, and preservation, of television programmes see Steve Bryant, *The Television Heritage* (London: BFI, 1989).

8. Mike Leigh, interviewed by the author, 14 July 2000.

9. Ibid. I think Leigh must be referring to the first repeat of *Abigail's Party* here, as the second repeat was not until 1992, and the BBC audience record does not support his claim that the play had an audience of 16 million when it was repeated. Rather, the BBC *Daily Viewing Barometer* records an audience of 4,332,600 (8.3 per cent of the population), dropping to 3,915,000 by the end of the play (BBC WAC, R9/37/15). On its first broadcast in November 1977, the play had an audience of 9,342,500 (18.5 per cent of the population), dropping to 8,888,000 by the end (BBC WAC, R9/37/13).

10. Quoted in John R. Cook, *Dennis Potter: A Life on Screen* (Manchester: Manchester University Press, 1995); rev. edn 1998, p. 100.

11. Caryl Churchill and director Roland Joffe removed their names from *The Legion Hall Bombing* after the BBC made cuts to the play. See www.screenonline.org.uk/tv/id/557937 (accessed 3 July 2013).

12. Carl Gardner and John Wyver, 'The Single Play: From Reithian Reverence to Cost-Accounting and Censorship', Edinburgh International Television Festival 1980, Official Programme published by *Broadcast*, reprinted in *Screen* vol. 24 no. 4–5, July–October 1983.

13. Ibid., p. 47.

14. Ibid., p. 48.

15. Cook, *Dennis Potter*, p. 88.

16. Ibid., p. 94.

17. Ibid., p. 99.

18. Quoted in Richard Kelly (ed.), *Alan Clarke* (London: Faber & Faber, 1998), p. 105.

19. Quoted in Janet Wolff, 'Bill Brand, Trevor Griffiths, and the Debate about Political Theatre', *Red Letters* no. 8, 1978, p. 57.

20. Quoted in Mike Poole and John Wyver, *Powerplays: Trevor Griffiths in Television* (London: BFI, 1984), p. 73.

21. Quoted in Wolff, 'Bill Brand, Trevor Griffiths, and the Debate about Political Theatre', p. 57.

22. Quoted in Paul Madden, 'Jim Allen', in Brandt, *British Television Drama*, p. 48.

23. Colin MacCabe, 'Realism and the Cinema: Notes on Some Brechtian Theses', *Screen* vol. 15 no. 2, Summer 1974.

24. Colin McArthur, 'Days of Hope', *Screen* vol. 16 no. 4, Winter 1975/6.

25. Colin MacCabe, 'Days of Hope: a Response to Colin McArthur', *Screen* vol. 17 no. 1, Spring 1976.

26. John Caughie, 'Progressive Television and Documentary Drama', *Screen* vol. 21 no. 3, 1980, pp. 33–4.

27. Colin McArthur, *Television and History* (London: BFI, 1978), p. 51.

28. John McGrath, *The Cheviot, the Stag and the Black, Black Oil* (London: Methuen, 1981), p. 76.

29. Ibid., p. 77.

30. John McGrath, interviewed by the author, 27 April 2000.

31. Ibid.

32. Ibid.

33. Chris Pawling and Tessa Perkins, 'Popular Drama and Realism: The Case of Television', in Adrian Page (ed.), *The Death of the Playwright?* (Basingstoke: Macmillan, 1992), p. 51.

34. McGrath, *The Cheviot, the Stag and the Black, Black Oil*, pp. 72–3.

35. Ibid., pp. 73–4.

36. John McGrath, interviewed by the author, 27 April 2000.

37. Taylor Downing, 'Tele-History Is Bunk – or Is It?', Edinburgh International Television Festival 1980, Official Programme, p. 19.

38. John McGrath, interviewed by the author, 27 April 2000.

39. Downing, 'Tele-History Is Bunk – or Is It?', pp. 18–19.

40. McArthur, *Television and History*, p. 36.

41. For more on *War and Peace* and the other classic adaptations mentioned, see Robert Giddings and Keith Selby, *The Classic Serial on Television and Radio* (Basingstoke: Palgrave, 2001), ch. 2.

42. McArthur, *Television and History*, p. 40.

43. Ibid., p. 45.

44. Alan Clarke, '"This Is Not the Boy Scouts": Television Police Series and Definitions of Law and Order', in Tony Bennett, Colin Mercer and Janet Woollacott (eds), *Popular Culture and Social Relations* (Milton Keynes: Open University, 1986), p. 223. See also, Alan Clarke, '"You're Nicked!": Television Police Series and the Fictional Representation of Law and Order', in Dominic Strinati and Stephen Wagg (eds), *Come On Down? Popular Media Culture in Post-War Britain* (London: Routledge, 1992), p. 238.

45. See Lucy Douch, 'Audience Measurement in the UK', in Manuel Alvarado and John Stewart, *Made for Television: Euston Films Limited* (London: BFI, 1985), pp. 190–210. By the fourth series of *The Sweeney* the audience was being measured in terms of millions of viewers, rather than millions of homes.

46. Ibid, p. 59.

47. Ibid., p. 61.

48. See Stuart Hall, Charles Chrichter, Tony Jefferson, John Clarke, Brian Roberts, *Policing the Crisis: Mugging, the State, and Law and Order* (London: Macmillan, 1978), ch. 9, for more on the development of a law and order society in Britain in the 1970s.

49. Kelly, *Alan Clarke*, p. 68.

50. Ibid., p. 69.

51. Barry Hanson, 'The 1970s: Regional Variations', in Bignell, Lacey and Macmurraugh-Kavanagh, *British Television Drama*, pp. 62–3.

52. Howard Schuman, 'Video-Mad: An American Writer in British Television', in Frank Pike (ed.), *Ah! Mischief: The Writer and Television* (London: Faber & Faber, 1982).

53. Ibid., p. 84.

54. Ibid., p. 86.

55. Cook, *Dennis Potter*, p. 180.

56. Dennis Potter, 'Realism and Non-Naturalism 2', Edinburgh International Television Festival 1977, Official Programme published by *Broadcast*, 22 August 1977, p. 37.

57. Peter French, 'Presenting the Deadly Dangers of Today …', *Radio Times*, 10 December 1970, p. 60.

58. Paul Cornell, Martin Day and Keith Topping, *The Guinness Book of Classic British TV 2nd Edition* (London: Guinness, 1993), p. 307.

59. Ibid., p. 301.

60. Roger Fulton, *The Encyclopedia of TV Science Fiction* (London: Boxtree, 1990), p. 571.

61. Ashley Pringle, 'A Methodology for Television Analysis with Reference to the Drama Series', *Screen* vol. 13 no. 2, Summer 1972.

62. Charles Barr, Jim Hillier and V. F. Perkins, 'The Making of Upstairs, Downstairs: A Television Series', *Movie* no. 21, Autumn 1975.

63. 'The Sweeney: TV Crime Series', *Screen Education* no. 20, Autumn 1976.

64. John McGrath, 'TV Drama: The Case against Naturalism', *Sight & Sound*, Spring 1977, pp. 100–5.

65. Richard Dyer, Terry Lovell and Jean McCrindle, 'Soap Opera and Women'; Raymond Williams, 'Realism and Non-Naturalism 1'; Potter, 'Realism and Non-Naturalism 2'; Clive Goodwin, 'Censorship and Drama 1'; Anthony Smith, 'Censorship and Drama 2'; Jerry Kuehl, 'Drama Documentary 1'; Gus Macdonald, 'Drama Documentary 2'; Charles Barr, 'Criticism and TV Drama'; Edinburgh International Television Festival 1977, Official Programme.

66. *Screen Education* no. 35, Summer 1980; Gardner and Wyver, 'The Single Play'; Brandt, *British Television Drama*.

Chapter 5

1. From a letter dated 22 November 1978, sent by Alan Bleasdale to David Rose and Michael Wearing, reproduced in Richard Paterson (ed.), *BFI Dossier Number 20: Boys from the Blackstuff* (London: BFI, 1982), p. 21; also in Bob Millington and Robin Nelson, *Boys from the Blackstuff: The Making of TV Drama* (London: Comedia, 1986), p. 179.

2. The budget for shooting four episodes on video was £590,000, whereas the budget for the one episode shot on film was £266,000. See ibid., p. 71.

3. Paterson, *BFI Dossier Number 20*, p. 21.

4. Millington and Nelson, *Boys from the Blackstuff*, p. 51.

5. Chris Pawling and Tessa Perkins, 'Popular Drama and Realism: The Case of Television', in Adrian Page (ed.), *The Death of the Playwright?* (Basingstoke: Macmillan, 1992), p. 54.

6. See Bob Millington, 'Making Boys from the Blackstuff: A Production Perspective', in Paterson, *BFI Dossier Number 20*, p. 11.

7. Alan O'Toole, interviewed by BBC producer John Archer on 16 December 1982, for an edition of *Did You See ...?* (BBC Two, 7 January 1983), from Paterson, *BFI Dossier Number 20*, p. 49

8. Millington, 'Making Boys from the Blackstuff', p. 18.

9. Philip Saville, quoted in ibid.

10. John McGrath, 'The Boys Are Back', in Paterson, *BFI Dossier Number 20*, pp. 63–4.

11. Christopher Griffin-Beale, '"Bridget Hitler": A Key Advance for Post-Production Techniques', *Broadcast*, 2 February 1981, p. 14.

12. Ibid., p. 15.

13. Michael Wearing, quoted in Millington and Nelson, *Boys from the Blackstuff*, p. 50.

14. Griffin-Beale, '"Bridget Hitler"', p. 14.

15. John McGrath, quoted in Stephen Gilbert, 'Comedy with Chips', *Radio Times*, 1–7 November 1980, p. 11.

16. BBC Audience Research, Selected Television Programmes: Reaction Profiles, Weeks 45–6, 1980, BBC Written Archives Centre. *The Adventures of Frank, Part 1: Everybody's Fiddling Something* (4 November 1980) had a reaction index (RI) of thirty, which was very low, while *Part 2: Seeds of Ice* (11 November 1980) was more favourably received with an RI of fifty-one, but still below average.

17. John McGrath, quoted in Gilbert, 'Comedy with Chips', p. 11.

18. John McGrath, interviewed by the author, 27 April 2000.

19. For a fuller discussion of *The Adventures of Frank*, see Lez Cooke, 'An Experiment in Television Drama: John McGrath's *The Adventures of Frank*', in Laura Mulvey and James Sexton (eds), *Experimental British Television* (Manchester: Manchester University Press, 2007).

20. The series *Six* was produced by John McGrath. The films in the series were thirty to sixty minutes long and included Ken Russell's *Diary of a Nobody* (BBC Two, 12 December 1964) and Philip Saville's *The Logic Game* (BBC Two, 9 January 1965).

21. John Caughie, 'The Logic of Convergence', in John Hill and Martin McLoone (eds), *Big Picture, Small Screen: The Relations between Film and Television* (Luton: University of Luton/ John Libbey, 1997). See also John Caughie, *Television Drama: Realism, Modernism and British Culture* (Oxford: Oxford University Press, 2000), ch. 7.

22. Kenith Trodd, 'Introduction to Trodd Index', in Jayne Pilling and Kingsley Canham (eds), *The Screen on the Tube: Filmed TV Drama* (Norwich: Cinema City, 1983), p. 53.

23. Mike Leigh, interviewed by the author, 14 July 2000.

24. Carl Gardner and John Wyver, 'The Single Play: An Afterword', *Screen* vol. 24 no. 4–5, July–October 1983, p. 127.

25. Ibid.

26. Alan Plater, 'Langham Diary', *The Listener*, 17/24 December 1987, p. 48.

27. John Finch, who wrote all thirty-nine episodes of *Sam*, is a rare example of someone writing every episode of a long-running series.

28. Troy Kennedy Martin, interviewed by the author, 27 March 1986. Kennedy Martin's novel was *Beat on a Damask Drum* (London: Panther, 1959).

29. Troy Kennedy Martin, *Edge of Darkness* (London: Faber & Faber, 1990), p. 16.

30. Michael Wearing, quoted in the *Morning Star*, 4 November 1985, p. 4.

31. Troy Kennedy Martin, quoted in the *Sunday Times*, 3 November 1985, p. 38.

32. Kennedy Martin, *Edge of Darkness*, p. vii.

33. Ibid., p. 142.

34. Paul Cornell, Martin Day and Keith Topping, *The Guinness Book of Classic British TV 2nd Edition* (London: Guinness, 1993), pp. 248–51; Roger Fulton, *The Encyclopedia of TV Science Fiction* (London: Boxtree, 1990), p. 159.

35. *The Adventures of Sherlock Holmes* (Granada, 1984–5) and *The Return of Sherlock Holmes* (Granada, 1986–8).

36. See Mark Sanderson, *The Making of Inspector Morse* (Basingstoke: Macmillan, 1991), p. 113.

37. Jim Pines, 'Black Cops and Black Villains in Film and TV Crime Fiction', in David Kidd-Hewitt and Richard Osborne (eds), *Crime and the Media: The Post-Modern Spectacle* (London: Pluto Press, 1995), p. 71.

38. Jim Goddard, quoted in Manuel Alvarado and John Stewart (eds), *Made for Television: Euston Films Limited* (London: BFI, 1985), p. 83.

39. Linda Agran, quoted in Alvarado and Stewart, *Made for Television*, p. 97.

40. Linda Agran, quoted in James Saynor, 'Minder's Keepers', *Stills*, November 1984, p. 42.

41. Agran, quoted in Alvarado and Stewart, *Made for Television*, p. 109.

42. See Alvarado and Stewart, *Made for Television*, pp. 207–8.

43. Richard Dyer, Christine Geraghty, Marion Jordan, Terry Lovell, Richard Paterson, John Stewart, *Coronation Street* (London: BFI, 1981); Dorothy Hobson, *Crossroads: The Drama of a Soap Opera* (London: Methuen, 1982).

44. Charlotte Brunsdon, 'Crossroads: Notes on Soap Opera', *Screen* vol. 22 no. 4, 1981; reprinted in Charlotte Brunsdon, *Screen Tastes: Soap Opera to Satellite Dishes* (London: Routledge, 1997), p. 16.

45. See Charlotte Brunsdon, 'The Role of Soap Opera in the Development of Feminist Television Scholarship', in Robert. C. Allen (ed.), *To Be Continued … Soap Operas Around the World* (London: Routledge, 1995); also Brunsdon, *The Feminist, the Housewife and the Soap Opera* (Oxford: Oxford University Press, 2000).

46. Brunsdon, 'Crossroads', p. 17.

47. Christine Geraghty, 'Social Issues and Realist Soaps: A Study of British Soaps in the 1980s/1990s', in Allen, *To Be Continued …*, pp. 66–7.

48. Phil Redmond, quoted in George Brandt (ed.), *British Television Drama in the 1980s* (Cambridge: Cambridge University Press, 1993), p. 57.

49. Geraghty, 'Social Issues and Realist Soaps', pp. 69–70.

50. Andrew Higson, 'Re-presenting the National Past: Nostalgia and Pastiche in the Heritage Film', in Lester Friedman (ed.), *British Cinema and Thatcherism* (London: UCL Press, 1993), p. 110.

51. John Corner, Sylvia Harvey and Karen Lury, 'Culture, Quality and Choice: The Re-Regulation of TV 1989–91', in Stuart Hood (ed.), *Behind the Screens: The Structure of British Television in the Nineties* (London: Lawrence and Wishart, 1994), p. 7.

52. Previously referred to in Chapter 3 in relation to *The Forsyte Saga*.

53. Charlotte Brunsdon, 'Problems with Quality', *Screen* vol. 31 no. 1, Spring 1990, p. 86.

54. John Reith, quoted in Andrew Goodwin and Garry Whannel (eds), *Understanding Television* (London: Routledge, 1990), p. 142.

Chapter 6

1. Ironically, the Broadcasting Act became law in November 1990, the same month in which Thatcher was deposed and the same month in which British Satellite Broadcasting merged with Sky Television to form British Sky Broadcasting (BSkyB).

2. Tony Garnett, 'Contexts', in Jonathan Bignell, Stephen Lacey and Madeleine Macmurraugh-Kavanagh (eds), *British Television Drama: Past, Present and Future* (Basingstoke: Palgrave, 2000), p. 22.

3. Robin Nelson, *TV Drama in Transition: Forms, Values and Cultural Change* (Basingstoke: Macmillan, 1997).

4. Source: *BFI Film and Television Handbook 1995* (London: BFI, 1994), p. 57.

5. Nelson, *TV Drama in Transition*, p. 75.

6. Ibid., p. 78.

7. Dennis Potter, *Seeing the Blossom: Two Interviews and a Lecture* (London: Faber & Faber, 1994), p. 38.

8. Ibid., p. 53.

9. Ibid., p. 16.

10. See Robert Giddings and Keith Selby, *The Classic Serial on Television and Radio* (Basingstoke: Palgrave, 2001) and Sarah Cardwell, *Adaptation Revisited: Television and the Classic Novel* (Manchester: Manchester University Press, 2002).

11. John Caughie, *Television Drama: Realism, Modernism and British Culture* (Oxford: Oxford University Press, 2000), p. 216.

12. Ibid., p. 211.

13. Robin Nelson, 'Costume Drama (Jane Austen Adaptations)', in Glen Creeber (ed.), *The Television Genre Book* (London: BFI, 2001), p. 40.

14. Caughie, *Television Drama*, pp. 26–7.

15. Nelson, *TV Drama in Transition*, p. 147.

16. Ibid., p. 146.

17. Ibid., p. 147.

18. For an account of the production history of *Our Friends in the North*, see Mark Lawson, 'Friendly Fire', *Guardian*, 1 January 1996, pp. 2–3; also Jeremy Ridgman, 'Patriarchal Politics: *Our Friends in the North* and the Crisis of Masculinity', in Bruce Carson and

Margaret Llewellyn-Jones (eds), *Frames and Fictions on Television: The Politics of Identity within Drama* (Exeter: Intellect, 2000), p. 79.

19. Michael Jackson, quoted in the *Observer*, 31 December 1995.

20. Peter Flannery, quoted in Sean Day-Lewis, *Talk of Drama: Views of the Television Dramatist Now and Then* (Luton: University of Luton Press, 1998), p. 184.

21. Jimmy McGovern, quoted in the *Guardian*, 4 December 1996.

22. Stuart Jeffries, 'A Walk through the Storm', *Guardian*, 6 December 1996.

23. Nelson, *TV Drama in Transition*, p. 24.

24. Ibid., p. 34.

25. Ibid.

26. Robin Nelson's segmentation of the *Casualty* episode, 'No Place to Hide' (BBC One, 16 October 1993), is included as an appendix in *TV Drama in Transition*, pp. 250–3.

27. Ibid., p. 38.

28. Ibid., p. 42.

29. Ibid., p. 39.

30. Grant Tinker, quoted in Jane Feuer, Paul Kerr and Tise Vahimagi (eds), *MTM 'Quality Television'* (London: BFI, 1984), p. 80.

31. For more on this 'new wave', see Lez Cooke, 'A "New Wave" in British Television Drama', *Media International Australia* no. 115, 2005, pp. 23–32 (reprinted in *Scriptwriter* no. 30, September 2006).

32. Tony Garnett, interviewed by the author, 29 February 2000.

33. Ibid.

34. These ASLs are based on calculations taken from the following episodes: *This Life* (BBC Two, 18 March 1996), *Casualty* (BBC One, 26 February 1994), *Coronation Street* (Granada, 28 January 2002) and *Heartbeat* (Yorkshire, 17 October 1993).

35. Tony Garnett, interviewed by the author, 29 February 2000.

36. Ibid.

37. Ibid.

38. Nicola Shindler, quoted in Tina Ogle, 'It's Glam up North', *Guardian*, 16 January 2000, p. 6.

39. Paul Abbott, quoted in John Naughton, 'Start the Clock', *Radio Times*, 31 March 2001, p. 26.

40. Paul Abbott, quoted in Ogle, 'It's Glam up North', p. 7.

41. Paul Abbott, quoted in Justine Holman, 'Doing the Business', *TV Times*, 31 March 2001, p. 23.

42. Anon, 'Beautiful Lighting and Vibrant Colours underpin Gritty Urban Drama', *In Camera*, April 2001, p. 22.

43. Peter Greenhalgh, quoted in ibid.

44. Nicola Shindler, quoted in Ogle, 'It's Glam up North', p. 7.

45. Ibid.

46. Paul Abbott, quoted in David Gritten, 'Lesson from America', *Radio Times*, 23 February–1 March 2002, p. 35.

47. For a fuller discussion of *Clocking Off*, see Lez Cooke, 'The New Social Realism of *Clocking Off*', in Jonathan Bignell and Stephen Lacey (eds), *Popular Television Drama: Critical Perspectives* (Manchester: Manchester University Press, 2005); also Beth Johnson, *Paul Abbott* (Manchester: Manchester University Press, 2013), ch. 3.

48. Stephen Poliakoff, quoted in Amy Holdsworth, '"Slow Television" and Stephen Poliakoff's *Shooting the Past*', *Journal of British Cinema and Television* vol. 3 no. 1, 2006, p. 129.

49. Stephen Poliakoff, quoted in Nicholas Wroe, 'A Life in Drama: Stephen Poliakoff', *Guardian*, 28 November 2009, www.theguardian.com/culture/2009/nov/28/stephen-poliakoff-interview-nicholas-wroe (accessed 8 October 2013).

50. It is surely no coincidence that the production company Bennett formed with producer Mark Shivas to produce *Talking Heads 2* and *Telling Tales* was called Slow Motion Productions.

51. Michael Brooke, 'Alan Bennett', *BFI Screenonline*, www.screenonline.org.uk/people/id/504794/ (accessed 10 October 2013).

52. Kara McKechnie, *Alan Bennett* (Manchester: Manchester University Press, 2007), p. 8.

53. Glen Creeber, 'Cigarettes and Alcohol: Investigating Gender, Genre, and Gratification in *Prime Suspect*', *Television and New Media* vol. 2 no. 2, May 2001, p. 160.

54. For more on *Prime Suspect*, see Deborah Jermyn, *Prime Suspect* (London: BFI, 2010).

55. Robin Nelson, 'Performing (Wo)Manoeuvres: The Progress of Gendering in TV Drama', in Carson and Llewellyn-Jones, *Frames and Fictions on Television*, p. 66.

56. Janine Gibson, 'Gay Programme Upsets Viewers', *Guardian*, 22 June 1999.

57. Quoted in Peter Billingham, *Sensing the City through Television: Unknown Identities in Fictional Drama* (Bristol: Intellect, 2000), p. 124.

58. Michael Collins, 'Sing If You're Glad to Be Gay (and Cute)', *Observer*, 30 January 2000, pp. 6–7. For more on *Queer as Folk*, see Glyn Davis, *Queer as Folk* (London: BFI, 2007).

59. Steven Barnett and Emily Seymour, *'A Shrinking Iceberg Travelling South …': Changing Trends in British Television: A Case Study of Drama and Current Affairs* (London: Campaign for Quality Television, 1999).

60. Ibid., p. 69.

61. Ibid., pp. 51–2.

62. Ibid., p. 53.

63. John McGrath, interviewed by the author, 27 April 2000.

64. Barnett and Seymour, *'A Shrinking Iceberg Travelling South …'* , p. 56.

65. David Liddiment, 'Impaired Vision', *Guardian*, 25 August 2001, p. 22.

66. Mark Thompson, 'What's Wrong with Our TV?', *Guardian*, 24 August 2002, p. 18.

67. Ibid.

68. Robert J. Thompson, *Television's Second Golden Age: From Hill Street Blues to ER* (Syracuse: Syracuse University Press, 1996).

69. Robert J. Thompson, 'Preface' in Janet McCabe and Kim Akass (eds), *Quality TV: Contemporary American Television and Beyond* (London: I.B.Tauris, 2007).

Chapter 7

1. ITV was re-branded ITV1 in August 2001, following the introduction of ITV2 and in anticipation of the launch of ITV3 and ITV4. On 14 January 2013 the channel returned to its old name, ITV.

2. 'ITV Commissions a Fifth Series of Downton Abbey', www.itv.com/presscentre/press-releases/itv-commissions-fifth-series-downton-abbey#.Uu5drD1_uSp, 10 November 2013 (accessed 10 June 2014).

3. After getting audiences of around 2.4 million for series one, a second series of *Peaky Blinders* was commissioned in October 2013: 'Peaky Blinders Commissioned for Second Series in 2014', www.bbc.co.uk/news/uk-england-birmingham-24684419, 26 October 2013 (accessed 14 November 2013).

4. Estella Tincknell, 'Dowagers, Debs, Nuns and Babies: The Politics of Nostalgia and the Older Woman in the British Sunday Night Television Serial', *Journal of British Cinema and Television* vol. 10 no. 4, p. 780.

5. For more on *Bleak House*, see Christine Geraghty, *Bleak House* (London: BFI, 2012).

6. More recently, Davies has written *A Poet in New York* (BBC Two, 18 May 2014), a feature-length drama about Dylan Thomas, and two feature-length episodes of *Quirke* (BBC One, May–June 2014), an Irish crime drama based on novels by John Banville (writing under the pseudonym of Benjamin Black). At the time of writing (June 2014), Davies is working on a six-part adaptation of Tolstoy's *War and Peace*, due to be screened on BBC One in 2015: www.bbc.co.uk/mediacentre/latestnews/2013/war-and-peace, 18 February 2013 (accessed 10 June 2014).

7. It was common practice for Channel 4 to screen dramas first on E4 or More4, a few days before showing them on Channel 4, in order to encourage viewers to watch the new digital channels.

8. This does not include the live episodes of *The Bill*, *Coronation Street* and *EastEnders*, marking significant anniversaries of those series.

9. The first series of *Spooks* had an average audience of 7.49 million, with the opening episode gaining an unprecedented 9.6 million viewers. Howard Brenton wrote thirteen episodes altogether (one with David Wolstencroft), before leaving after the fourth series in 2005.

10. In the first episode of series two it is revealed that the bomb failed to detonate.

11. The scene generated over 250 complaints from viewers.

12. Paul Cobley, '"It's a fine line between safety and terror": Crime and Anxiety Re-drawn in *Spooks*', *Film International* vol. 7 no. 2, 2009, p. 44.

13. Three of the London bombers were the sons of Pakistani immigrants.

14. Stephen Harper, '"Terrible things happen": Peter Bowker's *Occupation* and the Representation of the Iraq War in British Television Drama', *Journal of British Cinema and Television* vol. 10 no. 1, 2013, p. 219.

15. Ibid., p. 221.

16. *White Girl* won a BAFTA for Best Single Drama in 2009.

17. Quoted in Sarita Malik, 'Locating the "Radical" in *Shoot the Messenger*', *Journal of British Cinema and Television* vol. 10 no. 1, 2013, pp. 189–90.

18. Ibid., p. 203.

19. *Inspector George Gently* was originally just called *George Gently* for the 2007 pilot and the first series in 2008.

20. For more on Jimmy McGovern, see Steve Blandford, *Jimmy McGovern* (Manchester: Manchester University Press, 2013).

21. For more on Paul Abbott, see Beth Johnson, *Paul Abbott* (Manchester: Manchester University Press, 2013).

22. See Robin Nelson, *Stephen Poliakoff on Stage and Screen* (London: Methuen, 2011).

23. Ibid., p. 42.

24. Ibid., p. 49.

25. 1973 was the year in which David Bowie's song, 'Life on Mars', which gave the series its title, was released as a single.

26. James Chapman, 'Not "another bloody cop show": *Life on Mars* and British Television Drama', *Film International* vol. 7 no. 2, 2009.

27. The replacements for Bolam and Armstrong in 2012/13 – Denis Lawson and Nicholas Lyndhurst – would also be well-known to an older audience.

28. See John Ellis, 'BBC Goes Steampunk: *Ripper Street, Peaky Blinders* and the Memorialisation of History', cstonline.tv/bbc-goes-steampunk, 15 November 2013 (accessed 27 January 2014).

29. See Rebecca Williams, '"The past isn't dead … it's deadly": Horror, History and Locale in *Whitechapel*', *Journal of British Cinema and Television* vol. 11 no. 1, 2014, p. 83.

30. For a detailed analysis of a scene from *Teachers*, see Lez Cooke, *Style in British Television Drama* (Basingstoke: Palgrave Macmillan, 2013), pp. 125–38.

31. Susan Berridge, '"Doing it for the kids"? The Discursive Construction of the Teenager and Teenage Sexuality in *Skins*', *Journal of British Cinema and Television* vol. 10 no. 4, 2013.

32. Ibid., p. 791.

33. Ibid., p. 793.

34. See Lorna Jowett and Stacey Abbott, *TV Horror: Investigating the Dark Side of the Small Screen* (London: I.B.Tauris, 2013).

35. Charlie Brooker, 'Charlie Brooker: The Dark Side of our Gadget Addiction', *Guardian*, 1 December 2011, www.theguardian.com/technology/2011/dec/01/charlie-brooker-dark-side-gadget-addiction-black-mirror (accessed 29 January 2014).

36. Following the appointment of a new channel controller, *The Fades* was not recommissioned for a second series, a decision taken prior to the series receiving the BAFTA award for Best Drama Series in 2012.

37. *Top Boy* (Channel 4, 2011–) also featured a cast of black teenagers, but as they were mostly working for local drugs dealer Dushane (Ashley Walters) the representation was less positive.

38. Ben Dowell, 'From *The Fades* to *Misfits* – Is Youth Drama Leading the Way?', www.theguardian.com/tv-and-radio/tvandradioblog/2011/sep/22/the-fades-teen-drama, 22 September 2011 (accessed 30 January 2014).

39. The extent to which digital technology has transformed *Doctor Who*, in production and post-production, is evident from this technical note on the new series in *The Kaleidoscope BBC Television Drama Research Guide*: 'The 2005 series is shot on 625i50 Digital Betacam, using the Sony DVW790 series cameras through a HD lens and a ProMist filter. This is then copied onto Betacam SP and used to load the AVID where the show is edited. Once the show is "picture-locked", an edit decision list is exported from the Avid and sent to the Mill where the original DigiBeta tapes are conformed via a Snell and Wilcox Alchemist Platinum (to give the film effect). These tapes then have the effects added, are graded and then become the master tape for the show', Simon Coward, Richard

Down and Chris Perry, *The Kaleidoscope BBC Television Drama Research Guide 1936–2011*, first digital edition (Dudley: Kaleidoscope, 2011), p. 660.

40. A selection of the many recent books on *Doctor Who* includes: David Butler (ed.), *Time and Relative Dissertations in Space: Critical Perspectives on Doctor Who* (Manchester: Manchester University Press, 2007); James Chapman, *Inside the Tardis: The Worlds of Doctor Who – A Cultural History*, 2nd edn (London: I.B.Tauris, 2013); Matt Hills, *Triumph of a Time Lord: Regenerating Doctor Who in the Twenty-First Century* (London: I.B.Tauris, 2010); David Mellor, Matt Hills and Benjamin Earl (eds), *New Dimensions of Doctor Who: Adventures in Space, Time and Television* (London: I.B.Tauris, 2013); Andrew O'Day, *Doctor Who – The Eleventh Hour: A Critical Celebration of the Matt Smith and Steven Moffat Era* (London: I.B.Tauris, 2013).

41. Glen Creeber, *Small Screen Aesthetics: From TV to the Internet* (London: BFI, 2013), pp. 106–7.

42. BBC press release, 'Doctor Who TARDISODES – Travel with the Time Lord', 30 March 2006, www.bbc.co.uk/pressoffice/pressreleases/stories/2006/03_march/30/who.shtml (accessed 17 February 2014).

43. Matthew Reynolds, '"Doctor Who: Adventure Games" to Return', *Digital Spy*, 20 September 2010, www.digitalspy.co.uk/gaming/s7/doctor-who/news/a277773/doctor-who-adventure-games-to-return.html (accessed 17 February 2014).

44. Meg Carter, 'Teenage Kicks', *Guardian*, 24 September 2007, www.theguardian.com/media/2007/sep/24/mondaymediasection.television2 (accessed 17 February 2014).

45. Jon Dovey, 'Time Slice: Web Drama and the Attention Economy', in Paul Grainge (ed.), *Ephemeral Media: Transitory Screen Culture from Television to YouTube* (London: BFI, 2011), p. 144. While *lonelygirl15* has been cited as the first web drama, Glen Creeber writes about a similar 'hoax', a video blog (or vlog) called *Emokid21* which appeared in spring 2006 (several months before *lonelygirl15* was first posted), named after a vlogger who was supposedly from Cleveland, USA. An online romance developed when 'Emogirl21' responded to his vlog and an internet audience began following their romance. But, after a few weeks, 'Emokid21' was revealed to be an English university student studying at Aberystwyth University in Wales and 'Emogirl21' a friend of his who participated in the hoax. See Creeber, *Small Screen Aesthetics*, pp. 130–1.

46. See Elizabeth Jane Evans, '"Carnaby Street, 10 am": *KateModern* and the Ephemeral Dynamics of Online Drama', in Grainge, *Ephemeral Media*, pp. 160–9.

47. *LG15* totalled 547 episodes and *KateModern* 312 episodes (or webisodes).

48. *Sofia's Diary*, en.wikipedia.org/wiki/Sofia%27s_Diary#DVD_release (accessed 18 February 2014).

49. BBC press release, 'BBC Launches Multi-platform Soap for Teens, The Cut', 14 May 2009.

50. www.crisisinthecreditsystem.org.uk/index.html (accessed 17 February 2014).

Bibliography

Articles

Baker, Stephen, 'Shameless and the Question of England: Genre, Class and Nation', Journal of British Cinema and Television vol. 6 no. 3, 2009.

Berridge, Susan, '"Doing it for the kids"? The Discursive Construction of the Teenager and Teenage Sexuality in Skins', Journal of British Cinema and Television vol. 10 no. 4, 2013.

Brunsdon, Charlotte, 'Structure of Anxiety: Recent British Television Crime Fiction', Screen vol. 39 no. 3, 1998.

Cardwell, Sarah, 'Patterns, Layers and Values: Poliakoff's The Lost Prince', Journal of British Cinema and Television vol. 3 no. 1, 2006.

Chapman, James, 'Not "another bloody cop show": Life on Mars and British Television Drama', Film International vol. 7 no. 2, 2009.

Cobley, Paul, '"It's a fine line between safety and terror": Crime and Anxiety Re-drawn in Spooks', Film International vol. 7 no. 2, 2009.

Cook, John R., '"Between Grierson and Barnum": Sydney Newman and the Development of the Single Television Play at the BBC, 1963–7', Journal of British Cinema and Television vol. 1 no. 2, 2004.

Cooke, Lez, 'Three Ring Circus: The Ur-text of Modernist Television Drama', Screen vol. 50 no. 4, Winter 2009.

Gardner, Carl, and Wyver, John, 'The Single Play: From Reithian Reverence to Cost-Accounting and Censorship', Edinburgh International Television Festival 1980, Official Programme published by Broadcast, reprinted in Screen vol. 24 no. 4–5, July/October 1983.

Geraghty, Christine, 'Aesthetics and Quality in Popular Television Drama', International Journal of Cultural Studies vol. 6 no. 1, 2003.

Geraghty, Christine, 'Exhausted and Exhausting: Television Studies and British Soap Opera', Critical Studies in Television vol. 5 no. 1, Spring 2010.

Gielgud, Val, 'Policy and Problems of Broadcast Drama', BBC Quarterly vol. 2 no. 1, 1947.

Goode, Ian, 'The Quality of Intimacy: Revelation and Disguise in the Dramatic Monologue', *Journal of British Cinema and Television* vol. 3 no. 1, 2006.

Harper, Stephen, '"Terrible things happen": Peter Bowker's *Occupation* and the Representation of the Iraq War in British Television Drama', *Journal of British Cinema and Television* vol. 10 no. 1, 2013.

Holdsworth, Amy, '"Slow Television" and Stephen Poliakoff's *Shooting the Past*', *Journal of British Cinema and Television* vol. 3 no. 1, 2006.

Holmes, Su, '(Re)visiting *The Grove Family* – "Neighbours to the Nation" (1954–7): Television History and Approaches to Genre', *New Review of Film & TV Studies* vol. 4 no. 3, December 2006.

Kennedy Martin, Troy, 'Nats Go Home: First Statement of a New Drama for Television', *Encore* vol. 11 no. 2, March–April 1964.

Kennedy Martin, Troy, 'Up the Junction and After', *Contrast* vol. 4 no. 4/5, Winter 1965/Spring 1966.

Kennedy Martin, Troy, 'Sharpening the Edge of TV Drama', *The Listener*, 28 August 1986.

Kerr, Paul, 'Classic Serials – To be Continued', *Screen* vol. 23 no. 1, May/June 1982.

Lewis, Peter, 'Z Cars', *Contrast* vol. 1 no. 2, Summer 1962.

Liarou, Eleni, 'British Television's Lost New Wave Moment: Single Drama and Race', *Journal of British Cinema and Television* vol. 9 no. 4, 2012.

Lovell, Alan, 'Television Playwright: David Mercer', *Contrast* vol. 2 no. 4, Summer 1963.

Macmurraugh-Kavanagh, Madeleine, '"Drama" into "News": Strategies of Intervention in "The Wednesday Play"', *Screen* vol. 38 no. 3, Autumn 1997.

Macmurraugh-Kavanagh, Madeleine, 'The BBC Wednesday Play 1964–1970: Researching and Interpreting a Formative Moment in British Television Drama', *Media Education Journal* no. 23, Winter 1997/8.

Macmurraugh-Kavanagh, Madeleine, 'Boys on Top: Gender and Authorship on the BBC Wednesday Play, 1964–70', *Media, Culture & Society* vol. 21 no. 3, May 1999.

Malik, Sarita, 'Locating the "Radical" in *Shoot the Messenger*', *Journal of British Cinema and Television* vol. 10 no. 1, 2013.

McElroy, Ruth, 'Post-imperial Drama: History, Memory and Narrative in Peter Kosminsky's *The Promise*', *Journal of British Cinema and Television* vol. 10 no. 1, 2013.

Mills, Brett, 'Invisible Television: The Programmes No One Talks About Even Though Lots of People Watch Them', *Critical Studies in Television* vol. 5 no. 1, Spring 2010.

Mundy, John, 'Singing Detected: *Blackpool* and the Strange Case of the Missing Television Musical Dramas', *Journal of British Cinema and Television* vol. 3 no. 1, 2006.

Nelson, Robin, 'Locating Poliakoff: An Auteur in Contemporary TV Drama', *Journal of British Cinema and Television* vol. 3 no. 1, 2006.

Paget, Derek, 'Making Mischief: Peter Kosminsky, Stephen Frears and British Television Docudrama', *Journal of British Cinema and Television* vol. 10 no. 1, 2013.

Panos, Leah, 'Trevor Griffiths' "Absolute Beginners": Socialist Humanism and the Television Studio', *Journal of British Cinema and Television* vol. 10 no. 1, 2013.

Panos, Leah, 'Stylised Worlds: Colour Separation Overlay in BBC Television Plays of the 1970s', *Critical Studies in Television* vol. 8 no. 3, Autumn 2013.

Petley, Julian, 'The Quatermass Conclusion', *Primetime* no. 9, Winter 1984/5.

Piper, Helen, 'Vintage Entertainment: Nostalgia, the Archive and the Disappearing Pleasures of Collective Television Viewing', *Journal of British Cinema and Television* vol. 8 no. 3, 2011.

Purser, Philip, 'Landscape of TV Drama', *Contrast* vol. 1 no. 1, Autumn 1961.

Purser, Philip, 'Head of Drama', *Contrast* vol. 2 no. 1, Autumn 1962.

Ridgman, Jeremy, 'Duty of Care: Crime Drama and the Medical Encounter', *Critical Studies in Television* vol. 7 no. 1, Spring 2012.

Rolinson, Dave, '"The Surprise of a Large Town": Regional Landscape in Alan Plater's *Land of Green Ginger*', *Journal of British Cinema and Television* vol. 4 no. 2, 2007.

Saville, Philip, 'Director and Writer', *Contrast* vol. 2 no. 2, Winter 1962.

Smart, Billy, 'Cosmic Effects on the Intimate Screen: J. B. Priestley, Ralph Richardson and *Johnson Over Jordan* (1965)', *Critical Studies in Television* vol. 7 no. 1, Spring 2012.

Smart, Billy, '*The Life of Galileo* and Brechtian Television Drama', *Journal of British Cinema and Television* vol. 10 no. 1, 2013.

Tincknell, Estella, 'Dowagers, Debs, Nuns and Babies: The Politics of Nostalgia and the Older Woman in the British Sunday Night Television Serial', *Journal of British Cinema and Television* vol. 10 no. 4, 2013.

Walters, James, 'Inflections of Character Role-play in *Shameless*', *Journal of British Cinema and Television* vol. 3 no. 1, 2006.

Wheatley, Helen, 'Putting the Mystery Back into *Armchair Theatre*', *Journal of British Cinema and Television* vol. 1 no. 2, 2004.

Wickham, Phil, '*New Tricks* and the Invisible Audience', *Critical Studies in Television* vol. 5 no. 1, Spring 2010.

Williams, Rebecca, 'Cannibals in the Brecon Beacons: *Torchwood*, Place and Television Horror', *Critical Studies in Television* vol. 6 no. 2, Autumn 2011.

Williams, Rebecca, '"The past isn't dead ... it's deadly": Horror, History and Locale in *Whitechapel*', *Journal of British Cinema and Television* vol. 11 no. 1, 2014.

Willis, Andy, 'Jim Allen: Radical Drama Beyond *Days of Hope*', *Journal of British Cinema and Television* vol. 5 no. 2, 2008.

Wilson, Sherryl, 'Dramatising Health Care in the Age of Thatcher', *Critical Studies in Television* vol. 7 no. 1, Spring 2012.

Wolff, Janet, 'Bill Brand, Trevor Griffiths, and the Debate about Political Theatre', *Red Letters* no. 8, 1978.

Wyver, John, 'Dallas Bower: A Producer for Television's Early Years, 1936–9', *Journal of British Cinema and Television* vol. 9 no. 1, 2012.

Book chapters

Barr, Charles, '"They Think It's All Over": The Dramatic Legacy of Live Television', in John Hill and Martin McLoone (eds), *Big Picture, Small Screen: The Relations between Film and Television* (Luton: University of Luton Press/John Libbey, 1997).

Bignell, Jonathan, 'Citing the Classics: Constructing British Television Drama History in Publishing and Pedagogy', in Helen Wheatley (ed.), *Re-viewing Television History: Critical Issues in Television Historiography* (London: I.B.Tauris, 2007).

Cardwell, Sarah, 'The Representation of Youth and the Twenty-Something Serial', in Michael Hammond and Lucy Mazdon (eds), *The Contemporary Television Series* (Edinburgh: Edinburgh University Press, 2005).

Caughie, John, 'Before the Golden Age: Early Television Drama', in John Corner (ed.), *Popular Television in Britain: Studies in Cultural History* (London: BFI, 1991).

Cook, John R., 'Adapting Telefantasy: The *Doctor Who and the Daleks* films', in I. Q. Hunter (ed.), *British Science Fiction Cinema* (London: Routledge, 1999).

Cooke, Lez, 'The New Social Realism of *Clocking Off*', in Jonathan Bignell and Stephen Lacey (eds), *Popular Television Drama: Critical Perspectives* (Manchester: Manchester University Press, 2005).

Cooke, Lez, 'An Experiment in Television Drama: John McGrath's *The Adventures of Frank*', in Laura Mulvey and James Sexton (eds), *Experimental British Television* (Manchester: Manchester University Press, 2007).

Dovey, Jon, 'Time Slice: Web Drama and the Attention Economy', in Paul Grainge (ed.), *Ephemeral Media: Transitory Screen Culture from Television to YouTube* (London: BFI, 2011).

Ellis, John, 'Is it Possible to Construct a Canon of Television Programmes? Immanent Reading Versus Textual-historicism', in Helen Wheatley (ed.), *Re-viewing Television History: Critical Issues in Television Historiography* (London: I.B.Tauris, 2007).

Evans, Elizabeth Jane, '"Carnaby Street, 10 am" *KateModern* and the Ephemeral Dynamics of Online Drama', in Paul Grainge (ed.), *Ephemeral Media: Transitory Screen Culture from Television to YouTube* (London: BFI, 2011).

Evans, Elizabeth Jane, 'The Evolving Media Ecosystem: An Interview with Victoria Jaye, BBC', in Paul Grainge (ed.), *Ephemeral Media: Transitory Screen Culture from Television to YouTube* (London: BFI, 2011).

Harris, Kate, 'Evolutionary Stages: Theatre and Television, 1946–56', in Dominic Shellard (ed.), *The Golden Generation: New Light on Post-War British Theatre* (London: British Library, 2008).

Hill, John, '"Creative in its own right": The Langham Group and the Search for a New Television Drama', in Laura Mulvey and James Sexton (eds), *Experimental British Television* (Manchester: Manchester University Press, 2007).

Jacobs, Jason, 'No Respect: Shot and Scene in Early Television Drama', in Jeremy Ridgman (ed.), *Boxed Sets: Television Representations of Theatre* (Luton: University of Luton Press, 1998).

Kerr, Paul, 'F for Fake? Friction over Faction', in Andrew Goodwin and Garry Whannel (eds), *Understanding Television* (London: Routledge, 1990).

Leman, Joy, 'Wise Scientists and Female Androids: Class and Gender in Science Fiction', in John Corner (ed.), *Popular Television in Britain: Studies in Cultural History* (London: BFI, 1991).

Macmurraugh-Kavanagh, Madeleine, 'Too Secret for Words: Coded Dissent in Female-Authored Wednesday Plays', in Jonathan Bignell, Stephen Lacey and Madeleine Macmurraugh-Kavanagh (eds), *British Television Drama: Past, Present and Future* (Basingstoke: Palgrave, 2000).

Messenger Davies, Maire, 'Salvaging Television's Past: What Guarantees Survival?', in Helen Wheatley (ed.), *Re-viewing Television History: Critical Issues in Television Historiography* (London: I.B.Tauris, 2007).

Nelson, Robin, 'The Television Adaptation of *The Cheviot, the Stag and the Black, Black Oil*', in David Bradby and Susanna Capon (eds), *Freedom's Pioneer* (Exeter: University of Exeter Press, 2005).

O'Sullivan, Tim, 'Television Memories and Cultures of Viewing 1950–65', in John Corner (ed.), *Popular Television in Britain: Studies in Cultural History* (London: BFI, 1991).

O'Sullivan, Tim, 'Researching the Viewing Culture: Television and the Home, 1946–1960', in Helen Wheatley (ed.), *Re-viewing Television History: Critical Issues in Television Historiography* (London: I.B.Tauris, 2007).

Sandon, Emma, 'Nostalgia as Resistance: The Case of the Alexandra Palace Television Society and the BBC', in Helen Wheatley (ed.), *Re-viewing Television History: Critical Issues in Television Historiography* (London: I.B.Tauris, 2007).

Smart, Billy, 'Brechtian Television: Theatricality and Adaptation of the Stage Play', in Andre Loiselle and Jeremy Maron (eds), *Stages of Reality: Theatricality in Cinema* (Toronto: University of Toronto Press, 2012).

Wheatley, Helen, 'Rooms within Rooms: *Upstairs, Downstairs* and the Studio Costume Drama of the 1970s', in Catherine Johnson and Rob Turnock (eds), *ITV Cultures: Independent Television Over Fifty Years* (Maidenhead: Open University Press, 2005).

Wheatley, Helen, '"And now for your Sunday night experimental drama ...": Experimentation and *Armchair Theatre*', in Laura Mulvey and James Sexton (eds), *Experimental British Television* (Manchester: Manchester University Press, 2007).

Books

ABC Television, *The Armchair Theatre* (London: Weidenfeld & Nicolson, 1959).

Aldridge, Mark, *The Birth of British Television: A History* (Basingstoke: Palgrave Macmillan, 2012).

Allen, Robert C. (ed.), *To Be Continued ... Soap Operas Around the World* (London: Routledge, 1995).

Alvarado, Manuel and Buscombe, Edward, *Hazell: The Making of a TV Series* (London: BFI, 1978).

Alvarado, Manuel and Stewart, John, *Made For Television: Euston Films Limited* (London: BFI, 1985).

Ansorge, Peter, *From Liverpool to Los Angeles* (London: Faber & Faber, 1997).

Baird, John Logie, *Television and Me* (Edinburgh: Mercat Press, 2004).

Barry, Michael, *From the Palace to the Grove* (London: Royal Television Society, 1992).

Bennett, Tony, Boyd-Bowman, Susan, Mercer, Colin and Woollacott, Janet (eds), *Popular Television and Film* (London: BFI, 1981).

Bennett, Tony, Mercer, Colin and Woollacott, Janet (eds), *Popular Culture and Social Relations* (Milton Keynes: Open University, 1986).

Bignell, Jonathan, Lacey, Stephen and Macmurraugh-Kavanagh, Madeleine (eds), *British Television Drama: Past, Present and Future* (Basingstoke: Palgrave, 2000).

Bignell, Jonathan, and Lacey, Stephen (eds) *Popular Television Drama: Critical Perspectives* (Manchester: Manchester University Press, 2005).

Billingham, Peter, *Sensing the City through Television: Urban Identities in Fictional Drama* (Bristol: Intellect, 2000).

Black, Peter, *The Mirror in the Corner: People's Television* (London: Hutchinson, 1972).

Blandford, Steve, *Jimmy McGovern* (Manchester: Manchester University Press, 2013).

Born, Georgina, *Uncertain Vision: Birt, Dyke and the Reinvention of the BBC* (London: Vintage, 2004).

Bourne, Stephen, *Black in the British Frame: The Black Experience in British Film and Television* (London: Continuum, 2001).

Brandt, George (ed.), *British Television Drama* (Cambridge: Cambridge University Press, 1981).

Brandt, George (ed.), *British Television Drama in the 1980s* (Cambridge: Cambridge University Press, 1993).

Briggs, Asa, *The History of Broadcasting in the United Kingdom, Volume II: The Golden Age of Wireless* (Oxford: Oxford University Press, 1995).

Briggs, Asa, *The History of Broadcasting in the United Kingdom, Volume IV: Sound and Vision* (Oxford: Oxford University Press, 1995).

Briggs, Asa, *The History of Broadcasting in the United Kingdom, Volume V: Competition* (Oxford: Oxford University Press, 1995).

Brunsdon, Charlotte, *Screen Tastes: Soap Opera to Satellite Dishes* (London: Routledge, 1997).

Brunsdon, Charlotte, *The Feminist, the Housewife and the Soap Opera* (Oxford: Oxford University Press, 2000).

Brunsdon, Charlotte, *Law and Order* (London: BFI, 2010).

Bryant, Steve, *The Television Heritage* (London: BFI, 1989).

Bussell, Jan, *The Art of Television* (London: Faber & Faber, 1952).

Butler, David (ed.), *Time and Relative Dissertations in Space: Critical Perspectives on Doctor Who* (Manchester: Manchester University Press, 2007).

Buxton, David, *From The Avengers to Miami Vice: Form and Ideology in Television Series* (Manchester: Manchester University Press, 1990).

Cardwell, Sarah, *Adaptation Revisited: Television and the Classic Novel* (Manchester: Manchester University Press, 2002).

Cardwell, Sarah, *Andrew Davies* (Manchester: Manchester University Press, 2005).

Carney, Ray and Quart, Leonard, *The Films of Mike Leigh: Embracing the World* (Cambridge: Cambridge University Press, 2000).

Carpenter, Humphrey, *Dennis Potter: A Biography* (London: Faber & Faber, 1998).

Carraze, Alain and Oswald, Helene, *The Prisoner* (London: Virgin, 1995).

Carson, Bruce and Llewellyn-Jones, Margaret (eds), *Frames and Fictions on Television: The Politics of Identity within Drama* (Exeter: Intellect, 2000).

Caughie, John, *Television Drama: Realism, Modernism and British Culture* (Oxford: Oxford University Press, 2000).

Caughie, John, *Edge of Darkness* (London: BFI, 2007).

Chapman, James, *Saints and Avengers: British Adventure Series of the 1960s* (London: I.B. Tauris, 2002).

Chapman, James, *Inside the Tardis: The Worlds of Doctor Who – A Cultural History*, 2nd edn (London: I.B. Tauris, 2013).

Cook, John R., *Dennis Potter: A Life on Screen* (Manchester: Manchester University Press, 1995); rev. edn 1998.

Cooke, Lez, *Troy Kennedy Martin* (Manchester: Manchester University Press, 2007).

Cooke, Lez, *A Sense of Place: Regional British Television Drama, 1956–82* (Manchester: Manchester University Press, 2012).

Cooke, Lez, *Style in British Television Drama* (Basingstoke: Palgrave Macmillan, 2013).

Corner, John (ed.), *Popular Television in Britain: Studies in Cultural History* (London: BFI, 1991).

Coveney, Michael, *The World According to Mike Leigh* (London: HarperCollins, 1996).

Creeber, Glen, *Dennis Potter: Between Two Worlds* (Basingstoke: Macmillan, 1998).

Creeber, Glen (ed.), *The Television Genre Book* (London: BFI, 2001).

Creeber, Glen, *Serial Television* (London: BFI, 2004).

Creeber, Glen, *The Singing Detective* (London: BFI, 2007).

Creeber, Glen, *Small Screen Aesthetics: From TV to the Internet* (London: BFI, 2013).

Crissell, Andrew, *An Introductory History of British Broadcasting* (London: Routledge, 1997); rev. edn 2002.

Currie, Tony, *A Concise History of British Television 1930–2000* (Tiverton: Kelly, 2000).

Davies, Steven Paul, *The Prisoner Handbook* (London: Boxtree, 2002).

Davis, Glyn, *Queer as Folk* (London: BFI, 2007).

Day-Lewis, Sean, *Talk of Drama: Views of the Television Dramatist Now and Then* (Luton: University of Luton Press, 1998).

Docherty, Mark J. and McGown, Alistair, *The Hill and Beyond: Children's Television Drama – An Encyclopedia* (London, BFI, 2003).

Duguid, Mark, *Cracker* (London: BFI, 2009).

Dunleavy, Trisha, *Television Drama: Form, Agency, Innovation* (Basingstoke: Palgrave Macmillan, 2009).

Dunn, Kate, *Do Not Adjust Your Set: The Early Days of Live Television* (London: John Murray, 2003).

Dyer, Richard, Geraghty, Christine, Jordan, Marion, Lovell, Terry, Paterson, Richard and Stewart, John, *Coronation Street* (London: BFI, 1981).

Eaton, Michael, *Our Friends in the North* (London: BFI, 2005).

Ellis, John, *Seeing Things: Television in the Age of Uncertainty* (London: I.B.Tauris, 2000).

Fairclough, Robert and Kenwood, Mike, *Sweeney! The Official Companion* (London: Reynolds and Hearn, 2002).

Feuer, Jane, Kerr, Paul and Vahimagi, Tise (eds), *MTM 'Quality Television'* (London: BFI, 1984).

Fiddy, Dick, *Missing Believed Wiped* (London: BFI, 2001).

Finch, John, with Cox, Michael, and Giles, Marjorie (eds), *Granada Television: The First Generation* (Manchester: Manchester University Press, 2003).

Fitzwalter, Ray, *The Dream That Died: The Rise and Fall of ITV* (Leicester: Matador, 2008).

Franklin, Bob (ed.), *British Television Policy: A Reader* (London: Routledge, 2001).

Friedman, Lester (ed.), *British Cinema and Thatcherism* (London: UCL Press, 1993).

Fuller, Graham (ed.), *Potter on Potter* (London: Faber & Faber, 1993).

Fuller, Graham (ed.), *Loach on Loach* (London: Faber & Faber, 1998).

Geraghty, Christine, *Women and Soap Opera: A Study of Prime Time Soaps* (Cambridge: Polity, 1991).

Geraghty, Christine, *Bleak House* (London: BFI, 2012).

Geraghty, Christine and Lusted, David (eds), *The Television Studies Book* (London: Arnold, 1998).

Giddings, Robert and Selby, Keith, *The Classic Serial on Television and Radio* (Basingstoke: Palgrave, 2001).

Giddings, Robert and Sheen, Erica (eds), *The Classic Novel: From Page to Screen* (Manchester: Manchester University Press, 2000).

Gilbert, W. Stephen, *Fight and Kick and Bite: The Life and Work of Dennis Potter* (London: Hodder & Stoughton, 1995).

Goodwin, Andrew and Whannel, Garry (eds), *Understanding Television* (London: Routledge, 1990).

Goodwin, Andrew, Kerr, Paul and McDonald, Ian (eds), *BFI Dossier 19: Drama-Documentary* (London: BFI, 1983).

Goodwin, Peter, *Television under the Tories: Broadcasting Policy 1979–1997* (London: BFI, 1998).

Grainge, Paul (ed.), *Ephemeral Media: Transitory Screen Culture from Television to YouTube* (London: BFI, 2011).

Gregory, Chris, *Be Seeing You … Decoding the Prisoner* (Luton: University of Luton Press, 1997).

Hall, Stuart, Chrichter, Charles, Jefferson, Tony, Clarke, John and Roberts, Brian, *Policing the Crisis: Mugging, the State, and Law and Order* (London: Macmillan, 1978).

Hallam, Julia, *Lynda La Plante* (Manchester: Manchester University Press, 2005).

Harris, Geraldine, *Beyond Representation: Television Drama and the Politics and Aesthetics of Identity* (Manchester: Manchester University Press, 2006).

Hayward, Anthony and Rennert, Amy, *Prime Suspect* (London: Carlton, 1996).

Henderson, Lesley, *Social Issues in Television Fiction* (Edinburgh: Edinburgh University Press, 2007).

Hill, John, *Ken Loach: The Politics of Film and Television* (London: BFI, 2011).

Hill, John and McLoone, Martin (eds), *Big Picture, Small Screen: The Relations Between Film and Television* (Luton: University of Luton Press/John Libbey, 1997).

Hills, Matt, *Triumph of a Time Lord: Regenerating Doctor Who in the Twenty-First Century* (London: I.B.Tauris, 2010).

Hobson, Dorothy, *Crossroads: The Drama of a Soap Opera* (London: Methuen, 1982).

Holland, Patricia, *The Television Handbook* (London: Routledge, 1997).

Hood, Stuart (ed.), *Behind the Screens: The Structure of British Television in the Nineties* (London: Lawrence and Wishart, 1994).

Hood, Stuart and Tabary-Peterssen, Thalia, *On Television* (London: Pluto, 1997).

Hopkins, John, *Talking to a Stranger* (Harmondsworth: Penguin, 1967).

Howett, Dicky, *Television Innovations: 50 Technological Developments* (Tiverton: Kelly, 2006).

Hunter, I. Q. (ed.), *British Science Fiction Cinema* (London: Routledge, 1999).

Jacobs, Jason, *The Intimate Screen: Early British Television Drama* (Oxford: Oxford University Press, 2000).

Jermyn, Deborah, *Prime Suspect* (London: BFI, 2010).

Johnson, Beth, *Paul Abbott* (Manchester: Manchester University Press, 2013).

Johnson, Catherine and Turnock, Rob, *ITV Cultures: Independent Television Over Fifty Years* (Maidenhead: Open University Press, 2005).

Jowett, Lorna and Abbott, Stacey, *TV Horror: Investigating the Dark Side of the Small Screen* (London: I.B.Tauris, 2013).

Kelly, Richard (ed.), *Alan Clarke* (London: Faber & Faber, 1998).

Kennedy Martin, Troy, *Edge of Darkness* (London: Faber & Faber, 1990).

Kidd-Hewitt, David and Osborne, Richard (eds), *Crime and the Media: The Post-Modern Spectacle* (London: Pluto, 1995).

Lacey, Stephen, *British Realist Theatre: The New Wave in its Context 1956–1965* (London: Routledge, 1995).

Lacey, Stephen, *Tony Garnett* (Manchester: Manchester University Press, 2007).

Lacey, Stephen, *Cathy Come Home* (London: BFI, 2010).

Laing, Stuart, *Representations of Working-Class Life 1957–1964* (London: Macmillan, 1986).

Lazell, David, *What's on the Box?* (Cheltenham: Evergreen, 1991).

Leigh, Jacob, *The Cinema of Ken Loach: Art in the Service of the People* (London: Wallflower, 2002).

Madden, Paul (ed.), *British Television Drama* (London: BFI, 1976).

McArthur, Colin, *Television and History* (London: BFI, 1978).

McCabe, Janet and Akass, Kim (eds), *Quality TV: Contemporary American Television and Beyond* (London: I.B.Tauris, 2007).

McGrath, John, *The Cheviot, the Stag and the Black, Black Oil* (London: Methuen, 1981).

McGrath, John, *A Good Night Out* (London: Nick Hern, 1996).

McGregor, Tom, *This Life: The Companion Guide* (London: Penguin/BBC, 1997).

McKechnie, Kara, *Alan Bennett* (Manchester: Manchester University Press, 2007).

Medhurst, Jamie, *A History of Independent Television in Wales* (Cardiff: University of Wales Press, 2010).

Mellor, David, Hills, Matt and Earl, Benjamin (eds), *New Dimensions of Doctor Who: Adventures in Space, Time and Television* (London: I.B.Tauris, 2013).

Miller, Toby, *The Avengers* (London: BFI, 1997).

Millington, Bob and Nelson, Robin, *Boys from the Blackstuff: The Making of TV Drama* (London: Comedia, 1986).

Molesworth, Richard, *Wiped! Doctor Who's Missing Episodes* (Prestatyn: Telos, 2010).

Moseley, Sydney A. and Barton Chapple, H. J., *Television To-day and To-morrow*, 2nd edn (London: Sir Isaac Pitman & Sons, 1934).

Neame, Christopher, *A Take on British TV Drama: Stories from the Golden Years* (Oxford: Scarecrow, 2004).

Nelson, Robin, *TV Drama in Transition: Forms, Values and Cultural Change* (Basingstoke: Macmillan, 1997).

Nelson, Robin, *State of Play: Contemporary 'High-end' TV Drama* (Manchester: Manchester University Press, 2007).

Nelson, Robin, *Stephen Poliakoff on Stage and Screen* (London: Methuen, 2011).

Newman, Kim, *Doctor Who* (London: BFI, 2005).

Norman, Bruce, *Here's Looking at You: The Story of British Television, 1908–1939* (London: BBC/RTS, 1984).

O'Day, Andrew, *Doctor Who – The Eleventh Hour: A Critical Celebration of the Matt Smith and Steven Moffat Era* (London: I.B.Tauris, 2013).

Page, Adrian (ed.), *The Death of the Playwright?* (Basingstoke: Macmillan, 1992).

Page, Adrian, *Cracking Morse Code: Semiotics and Television Drama* (Luton: University of Luton Press, 2000).

Paget, Derek, *No Other Way to Tell It: Dramadoc/Docudrama on Television* (Manchester: Manchester University Press, 1998); rev. edn, 2011.

Paterson, Richard (ed.), *BFI Dossier Number 20: Boys from the Blackstuff* (London: BFI, 1982).

Pettinger, John W., *From Dawn Till Dusk: A History of Independent Television in the Midlands* (Studley: Brewin, 2007).

Pike, Frank (ed.), *Ah! Mischief: The Writer and Television* (London: Faber & Faber, 1982).

Pilling, Jayne and Canham, Kingsley (eds), *The Screen on the Tube: Filmed TV Drama* (Norwich: Cinema City, 1983).

Pines, Jim, *Black and White in Colour: Black People in British Television Since 1936* (London: BFI, 1992).

Points, Jeremy, *Teaching TV Drama* (London: BFI, 2007).

Poole, Mike and Wyver, John, *Powerplays: Trevor Griffiths in Television* (London: BFI, 1984).

Potter, Dennis, *Seeing the Blossom: Two Interviews and a Lecture* (London: Faber & Faber, 1994).

Prior, Allan, *Script to Screen* (St Albans: Ver, 1996).

Purser, Philip, *Done Viewing: A Personal Account of the Best Years of Our Television* (London: Quartet, 1992).

Rakoff, Ian, *Inside the Prisoner: Radical Television and Film in the 1960s* (London: Batsford, 1998).

Ridgman, Jeremy (ed.), *Boxed Sets: Television Representations of Theatre* (Luton: Arts Council of England/John Libbey Media/University of Luton, 1998).

Rogers, Dave, *The Ultimate Avengers* (London: Boxtree, 1995).

Rolinson, Dave, *Alan Clarke* (Manchester: Manchester University Press, 2005).

Rowbotham, Sheila and Beynon, Huw (eds), *Looking at Class: Film, Television and the Working Class in Britain* (London: Rivers Oram Press, 2001).

Salt, Barry, *Film Style and Technology: History and Analysis* (London: Starword, 1983).

Sanderson, Mark, *The Making of Inspector Morse* (Basingstoke: Macmillan, 1991).

Self, David, *Television Drama: An Introduction* (Basingstoke: Macmillan, 1984).

Sendell, Bernard, *Independent Television in Britain Volume 1: Origins and Foundation, 1946–62* (London: Macmillan, 1982).

Shubik, Irene, *Play for Today: The Evolution of Television Drama* (London: Davis-Poynter, 1975); rev. edn, Manchester University Press, 2000.

Stead, Peter, *Dennis Potter* (Bridgend: Seren, 1993).

Steemers, Jeanette, *Selling Television: British Television in the Global Marketplace* (London: BFI, 2004).

Strinati, Dominic and Wagg, Stephen (eds), *Come On Down? Popular Media Culture in Post-War Britain* (London: Routledge, 1992).

Sutton, Shaun, *The Largest Theatre in the World: Thirty Years of Television Drama* (London: BBC, 1982).

Swinson, Arthur, *Writing for Television* (London: Adam & Charles Black, 1955).

Swinson, Arthur, *Writing for Television Today* (London: Adam & Charles Black, 1963).

Sydney-Smith, Susan, *Beyond Dixon of Dock Green: Early British Police Series* (London: I.B.Tauris, 2002).

Taylor, Don, *Days of Vision – Working With David Mercer: Television Drama Then and Now* (London: Methuen, 1990).

Taylor, John Russell, *Anatomy of a Television Play: An Inquiry into the Production of Two ABC Armchair Theatre Plays* (London: Weidenfeld & Nicolson, 1962).

Thompson, Robert J., *Television's Second Golden Age: From Hill Street Blues to ER* (Syracuse: Syracuse University Press, 1996).

Thornham, Sue, and Purvis, Tony, *Television Drama: Theories and Identities* (Basingstoke: Palgrave Macmillan, 2005).

Thumim, Janet, *Small Screens, Big Ideas: Television in the 1950s* (London: I.B.Tauris, 2002).

Tulloch, John, *Television Drama: Agency, Audiences and Myth* (London: Routledge, 1990).

Tulloch, John, *Trevor Griffiths* (Manchester: Manchester University Press, 2006).

Tulloch, John, and Alvarado, Manuel, *Doctor Who: The Unfolding Text* (London: Macmillan, 1983).

Tulloch, John, and Jenkins, Henry, *Science Fiction Audiences: Watching Doctor Who and Star Trek* (London: Routledge, 1995).

Vice, Sue, *Jack Rosenthal* (Manchester: Manchester University Press, 2009).

Wheatley, Helen, *Gothic Television* (Manchester: Manchester University Press, 2006).

Wheatley, Helen (ed.), *Re-viewing Television History: Critical Issues in Television Historiography* (London: I.B.Tauris, 2007).

White, Leonard, *Armchair Theatre: The Lost Years* (Tiverton: Kelly, 2003).

Williams, Raymond, *Culture and Society 1780–1950* (London: Penguin, 1966); first published 1958.

Catalogues and reference books

Baker, Simon and Terris, Olwen (eds), *A for Andromeda to Zoo Time: The TV Holdings of the National Film and Television Archive 1936–1979* (London: BFI, 1994).

Baskin, Ellen, *Serials on British Television 1950–1994* (Aldershot: Scolar Press, 1996).

Cornell, Paul, Day, Martin and Topping, Keith, *The Guinness Book of Classic British TV 2nd Edition* (London: Guinness, 1993).

Coward, Simon, Down, Richard and Perry, Christopher (eds), *The Kaleidoscope British Independent Television Drama Research Guide 1955–2010*, first digital edition (Dudley: Kaleidoscope, 2010).

Coward, Simon, Down, Richard and Perry, Chris (eds), *The Kaleidoscope BBC Television Drama Research Guide 1936–2011*, first digital edition (Dudley: Kaleidoscope, 2011).

Dyja, Eddie (ed.), *BFI Film and Television Handbook 2000* (London: BFI, 1999).

Evans, Jeff, *The Guinness Television Encyclopedia* (London: Guinness, 1995).

Fulton, Roger, *The Encyclopedia of TV Science Fiction* (London: Boxtree, 1990).

Gambaccini, Paul and Taylor, Rod, *Television's Greatest Hits: Every Hit Television Programme since 1960* (London: Network Books, 1993).

Madden, Paul (ed.), *Keeping Television Alive: The Television Work of the National Film Archive* (London: BFI, 1981).

Vahimagi, Tise, *British Television: An Illustrated Guide, 2nd Edition* (Oxford: Oxford University Press, 1996).

Reports

Barnett, Steven and Seymour, Emily, 'A Shrinking Iceberg Travelling South …': Changing Trends in British Television: A Case Study of Drama and Current Affairs (London: Campaign for Quality Television, 1999).

Index

Page numbers in *italic* denote illustrations; those in **bold** indicate detailed analysis. *n* = endnote.

List of Illustrations

While considerable effort has been made to correctly identify copyright holders this has not been possible in all cases. We apologise for any apparent negligence and any omissions or corrections brought to our attention will be remedied in any future editions.

The Grove Family, BBC; *Fabian of Scotland Yard*, BBC; *Nineteen Eighty-Four*, BBC; *The Adventures of Robin Hood*, Incorporated Television Company/Sapphire Films/Yeoman Films Ltd; *Emergency – Ward 10*, Associated Television; *Coronation Street*, Granada Television; *Lena, O My Lena*, ABC Weekend Television; *Dixon of Dock Green*, BBC; *Z Cars*, BBC; *Doctor Who*, BBC; *Diary of a Young Man*, BBC; *Up the Junction*, BBC; *Talking to a Stranger*, BBC; *The Forsyte Saga*, BBC; *The Avengers*, ABC Weekend Television/Associated British Corporation/Associated British Picture Corporation; *The Prisoner*, Everyman Films/Incorporated Television Company; *Days of Hope*, BBC; *The Cheviot, the Stag and the Black, Black Oil*, BBC; *The Sweeney*, Euston Films; *Rock Follies*, Thames Television; *Pennies from Heaven*, BBC; *Boys from the Blackstuff*, BBC; *Edge of Darkness*, BBC; *Widows*, Euston Films; *Brookside*, Mersey Television; *EastEnders*, BBC; *Brideshead Revisited*, Granada Television; *Heartbeat*, Yorkshire Television; *Pride and Prejudice*, BBC/Arts Entertainment Network; *Our Friends in the North*, BBC; *This Life*, BBC/World Productions; *Clocking Off*, Red Production Company/BBC; *SilentWitness*, BBC; *Queer as Folk*, Red Productions; *Spooks*, Kudos Film and Television/BBC; *Skins*, Company Pictures/E4/Stormdog Films; *Misfits*, Clerkenwell Films/© Channel 4 Television.